D A T E   D U E

Three (3) week loans are subject
to recall after one week

For Righteousness' Sake

For Righteousness' Sake

Contemporary Moral Philosophies

A. Roy Eckardt

Indiana University Press   *Bloomington & Indianapolis*

Library of Congress Cataloging-in-Publication Data

Eckardt, A. Roy (Arthur Roy), 1918–
  For righteousness' sake.

  Includes index.
  1. Christian ethics. I. Title.
BJ1251.E25 1987   241   85-45891
ISBN 0-253-32241-3

1 2 3 4 5 91 90 89 88 87

To the memory of my mother and my father
ANNA F. ECKARDT
(1892–1962)
FREDERICK W. ECKARDT
(1889–1966)

To the memory of the pastor of my early years
ARCH TREMAYNE
(1886–1969)

And to the memory of my teacher
H. RICHARD NIEBUHR
(1894–1962)

The Holy God proves himself holy by righteousness.

—Isaiah 5:16

In Israel all religion is history.

—Martin Buber, *Hasidism*

Nothing is so whole as a broken heart.

—Rabbi Nachman of Bratislav

Contents

Preface

This essay in moral philosophy concerns itself with resources for real-life decision-making. The work is largely descriptive and analytic but it also evaluates. In the last-mentioned respect, I try to identify the place to which I have come after some fifty years' reflection upon moral questions.

My debt is great to H. Richard Niebuhr, who was the first to teach me what it means to do Christian moral philosophy.

For their many kindnesses, I express gratitude to President David Patterson and his staff of the Oxford Centre for Hebrew Studies at Oxford University, where as a visiting scholar I was enabled to conduct part of the research for this book and to do much of the writing. I am also most grateful to Dr. Muriel Berman and Dr. Philip I. Berman for their steady friendship and concrete support. When I started this inquiry, my friend and colleague Carey B. Joynt told me to go back to the biblical prophets. His counsel helped mold the whole work. Had my wife Alice Eliza Lyons Eckardt not aided me in my efforts, my thanksgiving for her would remain the same. In addition, I offer a special word of appreciation to myself, not only for serving as my research assistant but for a very good job of typing. The task of transcribing the handwritten text was not easy, since at times the materials were almost indecipherable.

I take most scriptural citations from the Revised Standard Version; exceptions are usually noted.

Had my mother only been given the opportunity, some of the thoughts and words that follow could have been hers. As Alice Walker wrote: "Perhaps in more than Phillis Wheatley's biological life is her mother's signature made clear."

I. Orientation

1

Beginnings

WILL a more comprehensive structure and foundation than we have had in Christian moral philosophy provide deeper and more effective resources for decision-making? Here is the debatable question of the present study. I shall reckon with that question against the background of the well-known fivefold schema of H. Richard Niebuhr's classic *Christ and Culture*.

I understand "Christian moral philosophy" dialectically: to mean on the one hand a Christian apprehension of the moral life rather than some other apprehension (though never invidiously); yet on the other hand not alone a Christian apprehension but also a philosophic one. A major drawback in the phrasing "Christian ethics" is its implied downplaying of intellectuality.[1]

This study in Christian moral philosophy entails a fourfold meeting and relation: (a) I treat a number of figures, literatures, and movements from the Western tradition. (b) The purpose of such analysis and assessment is not historical endeavor as such but, as mentioned above, to gain help and perspective in real-life decision-making. Truistically, there is no such thing as autonomous or self-contained history. There are only events, acts, and ideas as reacted to and interpreted. Furthermore, page-for-page the weight of my materials falls within recent and contemporary experience, reflection, and praxis. (c) I offer an originative conceptual framework as an aid in grappling with the subject matter. Without such a structure, we should be left with morality by "itself"; *with* the structure, we have moral *philosophy*. (d) My own points of view and evaluative stance are involved, largely in the later pages though not only there. Yet I trust that these personal elements will not detract from a willing recognition of a plurality of moral outlooks. (Of course, assent to such a plurality itself reflects a personal commitment.)

I

The moral-philosophic and theological views I cover are treated for their specific bearing upon the anguishing contemporary question of the relation

3

between faith and history, and this in the context of an even more anguishing question of today: the divine righteousness. These two questions knock at everyone's door, not only the intellectual's door. And they plead that moral decisions be made. Some of the issues I discuss may appear to be "theological" rather than "moral." That could even be said of the overall problem of faith and history. However, this essay centers upon the problem: In what sense may decisions for or against various views of the faith/history relation be themselves treated as moral decisions and as raw materials for our own moral decisions? Furthermore, no question could be a more moral one than that of the reputed divine righteousness, particularly when it is related, as it finally must be, to the question of human righteousness. However, I should be the last to argue that moral issues can be dealt with apart from theological issues and claims.

I call attention to the title of the essay: *For Righteousness' Sake* (Isa. 42:21; Matt. 5:10; I Pet. 3:14). In a theological-moral frame of reference, "righteousness" as a concept is fraught with ambiguity, and as a reality it is fraught with incertitude. There is "the righteousness of God" in the sense of an unconditional righteousness that stands over against us. And there is the righteousness that is glimpsed within human experience as such. We shall be reminded as we go along of how these two meanings are ever impinging upon each other.

A preliminary word is also in order upon the key concepts "faith" and "history." To have faith is to be dedicated to, and to trust in, a center of value that makes possible, actualizes, and sustains all values. To link faith to value is to make the human natural and social worlds integral to religion.[2] Insofar as we identify our center of value as God—although it is so that faith often wishes to consort with a multiplicity of gods—we may be led to affirm that God acts and will act within history, even within our own history. In such a case faith extends to waiting upon the events of God. Walter Rauschenbusch speaks of faith in an objective way as "expectancy and confidence in the coming salvation of God."[3] But in addition, to refer to Friedrich Gogarten's form of expression, faith permits human beings to take responsibility for their world.[4] Together, the eventuality of acts of God within history and the ideal of human responsibility already connect history and faith dialectically.

The concept of "history" refers to the province of our human world, more discretely to "the course of human events," the happenings of time and place together with their interrelationships, continuities, and human meanings. As Uriel Tal writes, "the meaning of man's existential experience and not only the object of man's experience as such . . . constitutes historical reality."[5] History, encompassing the past, is by no means restricted to the past: it is as much future as past. However, as Frederick E. Crowe observes, to grapple with history means, of necessity, a limitation to *selected* events.[6]

A special hope for this book is implied by the question posed at the beginning of the chapter: Will greater moral-philosophic comprehensiveness contribute to wiser and more responsible moral decisions? The goal of comprehensiveness applies strictly to my conceptual structure, and surely not to the empirical, historical, literary, and biographical data utilized. These latter are highly limited and selective. Thus, ecological ethics is not considered. Its potential treatment would be illustrative rather than substantive, since it can be dealt with under one or more of the several "normative images" I shall introduce. The comprehensiveness of the book makes for a certain superficiality at places, with special reference to forays into subjects wherein I can claim no more than amateur status.

One consequence of my work may be to supplement and partially to correct the influential typology of H. Richard Niebuhr in *Christ and Culture*, wherein Niebuhr seeks to supplement and in part to correct Ernst Troeltsch's *The Social Teaching of the Christian Churches*.[7] The continuities and discontinuities between Professor Niebuhr's typology and my own schema are explained just below.

This study has implications for some of the major issues that constantly challenge ethics and moral philosophy within and beyond the churches, theological schools, and universities. Examples include: truth in relation to goodness; fate and freedom; morality and Scripture; the authority of the Bible; commandment and grace; Law, Covenant, and gospel; eschatology and ethics; sacred times and sacred places; the meaning of Christian secularity; sin and salvation; death and resurrection; the new social gospel; and what it may mean to speak of God in the time after the *Shoah* (Holocaust).

II

The schema I develop takes its origin in, but then goes beyond, H. Richard Niebuhr's fivefold typology of Christ and culture. Several points will help bring out the resemblances and differences between the two schemas.

(a) Apart from a few brief and necessary allusions, my exemplifications of figures and movements differ from those utilized at length by Niebuhr. This serves to avoid duplication.

(b) My overall dialectic of "faith and history" is cognate to the dialectic Niebuhr expresses as "Christ and culture." "Faith" obviously entails a broader conceptualization than "Christ," although of course "faith in Christ" is fundamental to the Christian tradition.

(c) Niebuhr, following Bronislaw Malinowski, conceives of "culture" as the human superimposition upon nature of "language, habits, ideas, beliefs, customs, social organization, inherited artifacts, technical processes, and values." The cultural domain—frequently referred to by New Testament writers with aid from the concept "world"—is always social, is a peculiarly human achievement, and involves a world that seeks to realize and conserve values, dominantly those values construed as good for humanity, but yet of a highly manifold sort.[8] Perhaps it is a moot question whether "culture" or "history" more adequately conveys the distinctiveness of humankind. From my point of view, humanity's historical quality, encompassing as it does an indeterminate spatio-temporal cosmos, outstrips culture (as well as all other activities and unique meanings of the human being). Further, on the matter of Niebuhr's inclusion of values and valuation as being central within culture, the concept "history" sometimes appears relatively more avaluational or transvaluational. It recognizes the world of value all right, but it extends it-self as well to disvalues and to areas not ordinarily comprehended or treated axiologically. (When construed as a field of study, "history" is in this one respect rather closer to "science" than to "culture," or, alternately, to "being" than to "value.") Finally, it is not possible—at least not within a bib-lical frame of reference—to speak of human history, as of human culture, as wholly "evil" or "godless." The confession of God as Creator and Ruler bars that conclusion.

(d) In setting forth major historic efforts to relate Christ and culture, H. Richard Niebuhr takes in hand the familiar social-scientific tool of "type" and "typology." He readily acknowledges that individuals and movements are too complex ever to be subjected strictly or exhaustively to the inevita-bly hypothetical and even artificial descriptions that collect around one or another type. Life is always bigger than even the wisest attempts to concep-tualize and explicate it. However, Niebuhr finds in typological method the virtue "of calling to attention the continuity and significance" of great motifs that have appeared and reappeared in Christian history, and of orienting Christians today as they wrestle with the issue of Christ and culture.[9] Similar reservations and functions may be applied to my own schema. However, the word "type" has come to have, I feel, too rigid a connotation. Herbert Butter-field seeks to express what he characterizes as "essential processes in his-tory" by turning to the concept "myth."[10] I considered employing this latter word but decided that the objective ambiguities it has developed in recent years tend to compromise its usefulness. I suggest a still different conceptu-alization. In keeping with the more or less elastic and dynamic elements in the views we are to study and assess, together with their valuational aspects, I propose the term *normative image*. Setting down the two schemas side by side, we have the dual listing of Figure 1.

A mere change in terminology from "type" to "normative image" will hardly remove simplistic dangers from different categorizations. Because we are dealing with the thinking/praxis of actual human beings, it is inevitable that our normative images will overlap in greater or lesser measure and thereby obtrude across theoretical lines. Praxis is more than practice alone; it is that critical relation "between theory and practice whereby each is dia-lectically influenced and transformed by the other."[11]

I believe that the points of view of Jesus of Nazareth and of the Jewish rabbinic/talmudic tradition are sufficiently distinctive to be identified as supplying discrete images and discrete moral norms (although, as we shall

Figure 1

H. Richard Niebuhr Typology	Normative Images
Christ against Culture	Faith against the World
	The Kingdom/Righteousness of God (Jesus of Nazareth)
	Concretions of Righteousness and Goodness (Glimpses of the Rabbinic Tradition)
The Christ of Culture	Faith for the World
Christ above Culture	Faith above History
Christ and Culture in Paradox	History and Faith in Tension
Christ the Transformer of Culture	Faith Transforming History
	History Transforming Faith

see, there are continuities between both of these images and others, particularly with the image "faith for the world").

(e) The typological method of H. Richard Niebuhr is pluralist. While he is himself an advocate of one type, "Christ transforming culture," he denies that there is only one valid Christian ethic or only one Christian moral principle.[12] The same is the case with my own cadre of normative images. I assume that each and every image is possessed of a certain authenticity and/or historical force, and is therefore to be taken seriously. Of course, this does not preclude criticism by one image of another or of all others. Niebuhr points out that if a typologist's schema is "well constructed and so empirically relevant he will belong to one of the types himself." The fact remains that one purpose of typology is to help the individual "understand his own type as one of many and so to achieve some measure of disinterestedness."[13]

(f) Niebuhr states: "It is one thing to distinguish sociological types of Christian ethics, but another to claim that the kind of sociological organization which prevails in a group determines the ethical character."[14] The same goes for my somewhat more religio-theological schema. The kind of theological orientation that prevails within a particular normative image does not determine the moral character of the group or the person involved—though, needless to say, such orientation may have a bearing upon this moral character. As Niebuhr puts it, "correlations, not determinations, can be dealt with by typology. . . . The typologist needs to remember that he is not constructing a value-scale."[15]

(g) An overall assessment of Professor Niebuhr's typology lies implicit in our entire exposition. For the present, I may venture the suggestion that the absence of any type at no less than three places on the left side of Figure 1 conveys a lot more than the simple statement that the schema on the right side is a later one. The blank spaces are at least partially indicative of the fact that the Christian church has traveled quite far from its biblical and Jewish rootage. For the limitations of the typology of Niebuhr as a representative twentieth-century theologian are paralleled within a considerable amount of Christian thinking, still today. (It could be objected that the identity of Jesus as a strictly Jewish person and of the rabbinic/talmudic tradition as entirely Jewish act to exclude these images from coverage within "Christ and culture." Yet is this not a restatement of the problem? How did such phenomena ever come to be excluded from the Christian corpus? And is the exclusion defensible?)

(h) There is no way to deal with moral-philosophic and moral-theological materials without presuppositions and commitments that somehow affect the presentation. Accordingly, a writer in this field is obliged to identify the perspective from which she or he writes. Of the various normative images we shall encounter, the one with most appeal to me at present is "history transforming faith"—not in refutation of other views, but as one viable choice within the pluralist moral scene of today. Superficially, "history transforming faith" may appear to carry forward "the Christ of culture." I shall endeavor to show the discontinuities while allowing for the continuities.

According to agathological (and teleological) theory in ethics, the wellspring of morality is the anticipation and belief that "the good" will be identifiably realized within time and place. On that view, an expectation of some form of success lies close to the heart of the moral enterprise. Few moral persons are prepared wholly to cast aside visions of positive accomplishment. However, we do well to remember that agathological hope is but one possible motivation within moral behavior. Available as well are the inspirations of a deontological ethic and of an ethic of response/responsibility. Deontological understanding asks, What is our duty, what are we obligated to do, what is the first law of our lives? An ethic of response/responsibility asks, What is going on in the world, and what, accordingly, appear to be the most fitting actions for us to take? As H. Richard Niebuhr summarizes these foundational alternatives: teleology (or agathology) is concerned with "the highest good to which it subordinates the right; consistent deontology is concerned with the right, no matter what may happen to our goods"; while for an ethic of responsibility "the *fitting* action, the one that fits into a total interaction as response and as anticipation of further response [from God and/or man], is alone conducive to the good and alone is right."[16] A biblically-based moral philosophy or theological ethic seeks to hearken to the intentions of God for today's human history, as at the same time it has recourse to the divine grace and, ultimately, to the divine forgiveness. While such a view will never frown upon "achievement" or "effectiveness," yet it is not fatefully or ultimately dependent upon hopes or dreams of success. It concentrates upon the life of response and the obedience that befits such a life, thus combining the second and third theories of ethics. (Within a historical dispensation that must remain far from ideal, right responses to the God who not only creates and sustains but also judges and redeems can never wholly dispense with the factor of obedience.[17]) An *ethic of obedient response* asks: What is happening in the world? What can be expected to happen? And what is fittingly required of us? Thus may this ethic be inoculated against cynicism, the ever-menacing lot of disillusioned idealists.

One facet of this study will be a suggestion of relations between different normative images and the major theoretical foundations of ethics, and more particularly between "history transforming faith" and an ethic of obedient response.

III

This beginning chapter is continued with two interrelated sets of comments: upon the problem of sexist language, and upon the possibility of humor within moral-philosophic and religious writing. (A glimpse of the interrelatedness of the two areas is caught in the truth that someone who insists upon exclusively male language in "God-talk"—or, for that matter, exclusively female language—will probably not recognize something comical in such insistence.)

Dorothee Sölle maintains that our God-language has become a prison. She argues that when we speak of God, the substituting of "she" for "he" helps make clear "that it is wrong to think of God as father" within a dominantly sexist exclusivity. "We do not propose a dominant feminist exclusivity, but within a patriarchal culture one must use a reverse symbolism for people to understand at all what kind of problem we have here, and so that people can identify themselves differently."[18]

It is indeed the sins of the *fathers* that have been visited upon the children unto many generations. However, even those of us who think of God in androgynous terms and/or are resolved to fight the evil to which Sölle refers may yet doubt whether her solution will actually break the bars of the prison we have built for ourselves. For one thing, where adverse judgments against God are, for one or another reason, held to be morally demanded today— we shall be reckoning with some of these later in the book—the feminization of God-language may only help subtly to perpetuate the age-long derogation of things female. Further, for us today to move to "clean up" the sexist language employed by figures of the past—or of the present—not only does descriptive/historical violence to their (objectionable) viewpoint but also serves to impute a guiltlessness to them that they do not merit. English is among the languages that contain inherent and insurmountable obstacles to needed reform. For instance, any application of the grammatical singular intensive to God makes God either impersonal ("God itself") or male ("God himself") or female ("God herself"). No fourth choice is available. Again, in literary endeavor a proposed linguistic alternation between God as male and God as female (while perhaps not as objectionable as a contrivance like "he/she") may be conducive to confusion. However, I think there are ambiences—perhaps ours is one—where that alternating device can be tried. Another possible way of living with what may well be an essentially insoluble problem is to handle historical materials in a developing and critical manner that may foster a raising of consciousness. (For example, we have ready at hand a small word of potentially large use: "*sic.*") Thus, if it is so that Isaiah, Jesus, Paul, and the rest will simply have to be left in their "male chauvinist" condition, that fate may not be inevitable for some people of the 1980s and beyond. I intend to experiment with this method.

The inclusion of a few notes of humor in this study may appeal to some and annoy others. I suggest that humor, once we can manage to use it constructively (I am not assured that I can), is a moral-theological duty. Krister Stendahl declares that theology is too serious a business to allow its practitioners to escape without humor, which, together with irony, forms a safeguard against idolatry.[19] Theological humor is called for by the truth that the theologizing of humans may well appear ludicrous in the sight of God. But humor may be commissioned as well through the very opposite eventuality: via certain incongruities that surround God and the divine-human relationship, and that we mortals are peculiarly enabled to detect. In Woody Allen's film *Love and Death* Boris Grushenko has the idea that the worst thing we can say about God is that he [sic] is an underachiever. From this point of view, God may be counseled to try harder. Yet what if trying harder only compounds certain mischiefs? And suppose that we are at last impelled to conclude that God is, *kiveyakhol*, more a klutz than anything else. Heinz Moshe Graupe identifies the Hebrew term *kiveyakhol* as an appropriate one in rabbinic literature for conveying religious content "that almost seems blasphemous."[20] The term is variously translated as "so to speak," "as if it were possible," and "as one might be allowed to say." The eventuality of the divine klutzyness or incompetence will shock many, sounding grotesquely sacrilegious to them. However, such people may have opened themselves to a stern question: How do you propose to reconcile the fear of sacrilege with the witness to a transcending human dignity? (Near the end of the book, I shall have more to say on the outrageous eventuality of God as klutz.)

Ideally speaking, religious thinking and life fully recognize the disjuncture between the transcendent attributes of God and our fallible human understandings. Accordingly, in the avowal of any given or possible divine attribute or decision the proviso *kiveyakhol* may be registered. This disjunctive awareness is, I believe, something of an antidote to the idolatries of theology. It also comprises a primordial theological ground of Jewish

humor. Yet in the paragraph above I have stretched the practice to include a characteristic not normally and perhaps not legitimately associated with God.

IV

As an aid to readers, I include an overview of the essay as a whole.

Chapter two, the second orienting chapter, considers the biblical foundations of righteousness and justice. Central here is the tremulous question of
justice vis-à-vis mercy, a question that directs us to the pathos of God.
Chapters three through ten analyze our eight "normative images" or types,
all of which involve efforts, explicit or implicit, to come to terms with or to
unfold the divine righteousness.

Chapter three is representative of the opposition of faith to the historical
world. Exemplifications included are the Dead Sea community of the Essenes and Paul of Tarsus, the latter especially for his spiritual stand against
the world of Judaism.

Chapter four expounds the message and contribution of Jesus of Nazareth.
In Jesus is found a dialectic of, on the one hand, a catastrophic but liberative, coming political-moral reign of God and, on the other hand, a renewed
and singular advocacy of the prophetic-Pharisee (and Essene) tradition and
Torah. Paul was a (Jewish) Christian; Jesus was a Jew.

Chapter five expresses another dialectical viewpoint, beyond that of Jesus
(although in much continuity with it): the effort within the vast talmudic and
rabbinic tradition to provide historical concretions of justice for the sake of
life (*haim*), yet in the spiritual frame of reference of a transcending Torah and
the divine eternity.

Chapter six gives voice to the assimilation of faith to history, in contradistinction to "faith against the world." This outlook is exemplified through the
modern Jewish thinker Hermann Cohen; John Locke, cheerful proponent of
Christian reasonableness; and Walter Rauschenbusch and the Social Gospel.

Several persuasions are next represented and assessed that mediate dialectically between "faith against the world" and "faith for the world." In all
these neither faith nor history is lost to the other. All median views are, as H.
Richard Niebuhr observes, "tormented by problems of rebirth." The first of
these persuasions is "faith above history" (*chapter seven*), which strives for an
architectonic synthesis of spiritual and extra-spiritual reality. The supernatural order is held to rest upon but also to complete the natural order. This
normative image finds illustration in Thomas Aquinas and Catholic political
theory; the ethos of the Shakers and of the Hutterians; and the historicist-
moral mysticism of the Jewish Kabbalah.

Chapter eight exhibits the most heavily dialectical outlook of all the images:
faith and history are seen to live in unending tension. No peace is forthcoming between the legitimate demands of faith and the legitimate demands of

the secular order. The chapter concentrates upon Reinhold Niebuhr and Christian politico-ethical realism.

Chapter nine offers the first of two transformationist convictions, "faith transforming history." Here is a revolutionist norm that stands in judgment upon all and sundry cultural-historical achievements and claims, as at the same time it fights paradoxically for the conversion of the world to meet that very norm. For exemplification I report on certain movements within today's Islam (with some attention to the Iranian Revolution) and I give prevailing attention to contemporary Latin American liberation thinking (Gustavo Gutiérrez, Juan Luis Segundo, Hugo Assmann, and company).

Chapter ten introduces the normative image of "history transforming faith," followed in *chapters eleven through thirteen* by relatively intensive consideration of questions and challenges that must be addressed to that point of view. I call adherents of this final image "eighth people" or "people of eight." The fundamental summons they bring is the transfiguration of the religious community and of religious thought before the presence of historical event and political praxis. In these chapters Dietrich Bonhoeffer, Emil L. Fackenheim, Irving Greenberg, David Hartman, Choan-Seng Song, David Tracy, and Elie Wiesel are among those in places of influence.

Other than in oblique ways, this study does not enter far into philosophic justifications and refutations of faith; neither does it provide a full or systematic theological foundation of its own analysis.[21] It is true that philosophical-theological exposition such as the present work tends largely and perhaps unavoidably to be intellectualistic and impersonal. Yet expositions of this kind ought to make room for existential concerns and expression if they are not to betray their human and humane calling. In describing the help and influence of Paul Tillich upon himself, Lawton Posey has said that "any preaching I do which does not come out of agony, out of my own experience, and from my own life *as lived*, is academic in the worst sense of the word."[22] If "preaching" is here replaced by "writing," the quoted words are a fair expression of my own attitude.

Perhaps we are a little prepared now for our journey.

2

Human History and the Divine Righteousness

ARE there ways to identify or at least to live with the primordial reality or source to which the normative images before us may constitute responses? To grapple with this question is to seek and hopefully to receive orientation for the encounter with all the images. Beyond this philosophical and theological problem, we have to reckon with the historical ground and the apperceptive mass[1] that also make possible each one of these normative images. This necessitates a threefold assumption: that the original historical-religious traditions remain more or less rediscoverable; that subsequent and contemporary interpreters of the traditions will have rendered them in more or less meaningful ways; and that our own readings both of the traditions and of their interpreters are more or less sensible and responsible. In sum, the overall challenge is: Do our eyes see and do our ears hear what other eyes and ears have seen and heard? In many respects we today have a surer knowledge of our originative or historical traditions than earlier generations had. And yet, those generations were existentially closer, in many ways, to those traditions.

I

Judaism and Christianity share the conviction that the purposes of God are linked in positive ways to the human scene and the human condition. But since the will of God is identified as absolute, and hence poses absolute requirements, the normative substratum and the theological nexus out of which Jewish and Christian moral reflection and life have evolved are expressible in the wording: *history under command and judgment*. The several interpretations we are to review and assess in subsequent chapters constitute developments from, fulfillments of, variations upon, and in some instances partial negations of, an originative persuasion that human history stands open to commands and judgments of transcendent, apodictic (absolute) quality—a persuasion we may denominate "the message of the divine righteousness." That message has its origins in biblical Israel and biblical Judaism. Accordingly, a salient and arguably indispensable basis for setting forth differing and successive views upon the relation of faith and history is biblical historicalness, i.e., the ways Scripture expounds and is dedicated to temporal, geographical, and geopolitical cruciality. From that standpoint, only within some kind of historical theater, only through the unfolding of some form of story, can human meaning and wholeness be actualized.

But what does it mean to attest that in and through divine absoluteness, human significance and wholeness may be attained? This question dogs us throughout the study.

A caution is necessary. Biblical historicalness is multi-voiced; the Bible is hardly above pluralism. James A. Sanders writes of the "growing consciousness among serious students of the Bible that biblical pluralism simply will not go away but begs to be formally recognized as a blessing equal to any other the Bible has to offer." Sanders argues that within biblical studies the subdiscipline of canonical criticism provides a means for formalizing biblical pluralism into a system for understanding the Bible. An implication here is that "there is no one right view of Scripture. On the contrary, canonical pluralism assures" that no construct "can be built on Scripture which is not judged, and, we hope, redeemed, by something else in it." Canonically, Scripture "may be seen as an ongoing prophetic voice that can keep us from absolutizing any one biblical viewpoint."

Two added implications, according to Sanders, are the need for honesty and the need for humor. "To fail to recognize pluralism in the Bible is to be dishonest. One of the reasons fundamentalism is abhorrent to many Christians is its dogmatic dishonesty. Nothing called Christian should require dishonesty at the very heart of what it professes." Could it be that the conflict between irreconcilable passages in the "Word of God" is her prevenient laughter at biblical literalists? To Professor Sanders, the need for humor means "taking God a little more seriously each time we read Scripture and ourselves a little less so." The biblical perspective "is to celebrate what God can do with almost any fouled-up situation we can devise, for none could be worse than those the canon describes in its utter realism about ancient struggles."

But both honesty and humor are double-edged swords. I have just hinted at the other side of the dialectic: the attestation to pluralism only throws into sharp relief the biblical transcendence of pluralism. Sanders represents the single absolute beyond all the relativities:

> The greatest challenge the Bible has for us all is the challenge to monotheize—to affirm the integrity of God both ontologically and ethically. . . . Christian antisemitism stems largely from a failure to monotheize.
>
> But the promise of these canonical traditions is that if we make the effort to monotheize, nothing in all creation can claim us: there are no idols; on

the contrary, polytheism is reduced to pluralism, which, submitted to the judgments of God, can be a blessing. But monotheism is not easy: the dark side of Yahweh becomes repugnant to liberals and conservatives alike, and we lose even our tremulous hold on reality.[2]

The impulse to monotheize, so Sanders proposes elsewhere, is the very thing that distinguishes true prophecy from false prophecy.[3] For all its pluralism, Scripture achieves a unity through its summons to faith in the singular God and the honoring of the divine righteousness.

The issue of whether the Bible is the work of human beings or of God, or of both parties, is endlessly debated. Full attention to the debate would take us beyond our province. Our working presupposition for this book's purposes is that Scripture is to be linked to the meeting of God and certain human figures who are often inspired by God and sometimes by themselves. This judgment does not really settle any arguments; it probably exacerbates them. In any case, we here assume the presence in the Bible of human and divine elements alike, but with two essential qualifications respecting the divine elements: these elements are conveyed through the languages, and accordingly within the limitations, of humanity; and they are addressed in the first instance to the particular Sitz im Leben of human beings. Basil Mitchell writes: "There is an evident incoherence in the notion that God, as conceived in the Judaeo-Christian tradition, should create men [sic] in his [sic] own image with the intention that they should come to know and love him [sic], and yet should in no way communicate with them. But it is more radically incoherent to suppose that God should indeed 'communicate' with men [sic], but in a language wholly discontinuous with that which they ordinarily speak."[4] (Four times in a row, "sic" is already tiresome.) As Sanders observes, "the Bible comes to us out of the liturgical and instructional lives of the ancient believing communities which produced and shaped it. . . . Canon and community must be thought of as belonging together both in antiquity and today. . . . The question of the authority of canon resides in the ongoing dialogue between the believing community and its canon."[5] Gabriel Josipovici offers collateral advice: "To accept speech, and time, and history, means to accept that no finality is ever possible, that there is no moment when speech ends and we enter a world beyond responsibility and doubt. To accept speech, therefore, means to accept the possibilities of promises, and of covenants, but also of lies and of deceit."[6]

Thus, there is never a last word. At best, there is only the word before the last word.

II

With words that are far from being named last, let us arrange the scenario.

The inner identity of truth and goodness that pervades the Hebrew Bible moves there into union with knowledge, righteousness, mercy, and love. The word "good" (*tov*) is itself often used almost synonymously with, or is linked with, "right," as in the mandate, "you shall do what is right and good in the sight of the Lord" (Deut. 6:18). "Truth" is a reality "sent forth" from God (Ps. 57:3). Essentially, it means dependableness, the doing of that which is required. It is something that "shows," along with kindness (II Sam. 2:6). This explains why the Hebrew words that translate "truth" (*emeth, emunah*) are many times rendered as "faithfulness." The prophet Hosea describes the marriage that Yahweh arranges with Israel. (Because of its holiness, "the Ineffable Name" of God is not ordinarily pronounced by religious Jews. Instead it is read as "Adonai.") After declaring "I will betroth you to me for ever— this "in righteousness and in justice, in steadfast love, and in mercy"—Hosea continues: "I will even betroth you to me in faithfulness; and you shall know the Lord" (Hos. 2:19–20). Truth, faithfulness, and the knowledge of God are here brought into unity (cf. Deut. 32:4). The verb form *aman* means "stand firm" or "trust," and from its root comes the adjective *amen*, meaning "true" in the sense of "sure" or "reliable." From the primary idea of a quality inherent in God, truth evolves into a quality of his behavior. God

> will judge the world with righteousness,
> and the people with his truth. (Ps. 96:13b)

In the biblical poetic style called "synonymous parallelism," the second line repeats the thought of the first. Accordingly, God's righteousness and God's truth are here made identical. Again, truth is collocated with mercy or "steadfast love" (Gen. 32:10). The paths of God are "mercy and truth" (Ps. 25:10). The realities of mercy and truth are often paired (Ps. 61:7; 85:10; 86:15; 98:3; 108:4; Prov. 20:28). Finally and climactically, truth is demanded of humankind in the form of obedience to the will of God as made known in the Torah: "thou art near, O Lord, and all thy commandments are truth" (Ps. 119:151). The Law of the righteous God is the truth (v. 142).[7]

The single word *yada* means "to know" (in the sense of learning, perceiving, understanding, etc.) but it also means to experience good and bad (including sexual union; cf. Gen. 4:1). In biblical Hebrew *yada* often involves an act of concern, dedication, and sympathy for a person. In Abraham J. Heschel's wording, *yada* compasses "inner appropriation, feeling, a reception into the soul." From the standpoint of the Hebrew Bible, knowledge is never a matter of abstract principles or of the comprehension of a noumenal world. Reality is "what happens," and knowledge is, accordingly, the apprehending of events. In the same way, the knowledge of God means, not contemplation of an eternal Being or Principle, but recognition of, and obedience to, the One who acts purposefully in this world (cf. Deut. 11:2ff; Isa. 41:20).[8] "He has showed you, O man, what is good; and what does the Lord require of you but to do justice, and to love mercy, and to walk humbly with your God?" (Mic. 6:8).

Hosea, with the other prophets, was obsessed by righteousness. How, then, could his central complaint be that his people did not know God?[9] The answer reaches a kind of ecstasy of moral logic: to know God is to do righteousness (as to do righteousness is to know God). A shattering question thereby obtrudes: Could it be that there is *no way* to know God—even properly to worship her in prayer, fasting, or other cultic acts—apart from doing righteousness? According to the prophet Amos, "to seek Yahweh and live" is to "hate evil, and love good." It is, in sum, to "establish justice" (Amos 5:4, 6, 14–15). "Let justice roll on like a river, and righteousness like an ever-flowing stream!" (Amos 5:24, NEB). The fast that Yahweh requires is "to loose the fetters of injustice" (Isa. 58:6, NEB). Heschel indicates the difficulty in establishing the precise difference between the biblical terms *mishpat* (justice, signifying both right and duty) and *tsedakah* (righteousness). "It seems that justice is a mode of action, righteousness a quality of the person." Significantly, the noun taken from *shafat* (to judge) is *shofet*, which eventually meant a judge or arbitrator, while the noun taken from *tsadak* (to be just) is *tsaddik*, a righteous man.[10]

The indissolubility of all the foregoing praxises—truth, goodness, knowledge, righteousness, justice, mercy, love, faithfulness, obedience—is epitomized by Jeremiah: "Thus says the Lord: 'Let not the wise man glory in his wisdom, neither let the mighty man glory in his might, let not the rich man glory in his riches; but let him who glories glory in this, that he understands and knows me, that I am the Lord who exercise lovingkindness, justice, and righteousness in the earth; for in these things I delight, says the Lord'" (Jer. 9:23–24).

III

Let us take up with the history, in a way that leads into a preliminary encounter with the plaguing question of judgment vis-à-vis mercy and deliverance.

Down in Egypt the people of Abraham, Isaac, and Jacob had been put into one hell of a situation. They were being afflicted beyond endurance. So God resolved, *kiveyakhol*, to intervene in their fortunes. Possibly even the Egyptian name of the Hebrews' human savior pointed to the infant's destiny: the etymology "I draw him out of the water" (Exod. 2:10) ought to have required the form *mashui* ("one that has been drawn out") instead of *moshe* ("one that draws out"). It was the child himself who one day was "to 'draw out' his people from the Sea of Reeds and bondage."[11]

The pitiable, erstwhile slaves of the Pharaoh made it out of Egypt all right—only to become involved (so the biblical tale continues) in a most awesome confrontation:

> And God spoke all these words, saying,
> "I am the Lord your God, who brought you out of the land of Egypt, out of the house of bondage.

"You shall have no other gods besides me.

"You shall not make yourself a graven image, or any likeness of anything that is in heaven above, or that is in the earth beneath, or that is in the water under the earth; you shall not bow down to them or serve them; for I the Lord your God am a jealous God, visiting the iniquity of the fathers upon the children to the third and fourth generation of those who hate me, but showing steadfast love to thousands of those who love me and keep my commandments.

"You shall not take the name of the Lord your God in vain; for the Lord will not hold him guiltless who takes his name in vain...." (Exod. 20:1–7)

Various efforts have been made to reconstruct the Ten Commandments ("Ten Words") in their original form.[12] Here is Walter Harrelson's reconstruction:

1. There shall not be to thee (or: Thou shalt not have) other gods.
2. Thou shalt not make for thyself an idol.
3. Thou shalt not lift up the name of Yahweh for mischief.
4. Thou shalt not despise (or treat with contempt) the sabbath day.
5. Thou shalt not curse thy father or thy mother.
6. Thou shalt not kill (or take the life of) thy neighbor.
7. Thou shalt not commit adultery with the wife of thy neighbor.
8. Thou shalt not steal anything that is thy neighbor's.
9. Thou shalt not answer thy neighbor as a false witness.
10. Thou shalt not covet the household of thy neighbor.[13]

The Jewish community has always numbered as the first commandment (or "word") the phrasing, "I am the Lord your God, who brought you out of the land of Egypt, out of the house of bondage." Although Harrelson lists a different commandment as belonging first, he nevertheless agrees that the Jewish usage "gives great force to the theological point" that "God's mercy precedes his laying down of the covenant requirements." In other words, "the Decalogue arises in a context of divine grace."[14]

James Parkes contends that nothing has contributed more to misunderstanding between the Jewish and Christian communities than the Septuagint translation of "Torah" by the much narrower term *nomos*, which is further narrowed by the translation "law."[15] Since many Jewish scholars today employ the term "Law," I have decided to retain it.

For all the multi-voicedness of the Torah (Word, Teaching), certain absolutes are put forth therein. The terms of the Covenant (*brith*) stipulate that the people of God are permitted no deity but God. ("Covenant" in capitalized, singular form is intended to symbolize the overall, abiding link between God and the people of God that was in some sense celebrated or acknowledged at Sinai. There is in fact a plurality of covenants in Scripture together with many covenantal renewals. In the expressed form we now have it in Scripture, the Covenant is a product of the sixth-century Exile in Babylon.[16]) Yahweh alone is to be worshiped and served (Josh. 24:14–24; cf. Matt. 4:10). Absolute (apodictic) norms and obligations are set before human beings. The absolute quality of such requirements as the prophetic demands for righteousness and justice suffuses the entire Hebrew Bible and penetrates the New Testament as well. (As Harrelson indicates, the claim that apodictic commands were without parallel outside Israel is now known to be incorrect. And yet, nowhere in the ancient Near East do we find anything like the *collection* of commandments that is found in the Decalogue.[17]) Of course, in specific cases and under special conditions the selfsame apodicticity that obtains in connection with unconditioned demands is not found. Thus, the law in the Pentateuch respecting Hebrew slaves refers to various contingencies that may or may not enter the picture (Exod. 21:2–6), whereas the commandment, "Whoever curses his father or his mother shall be put to death" (Exod. 21:17), is devoid of conditions or contingencies.[18] However, even with respect to the latter command, execution as a dire consequence can be avoided by simply refraining from cursing one's parents. The command to honor God is an entirely different matter; here; non-action can offer no escape from judgment. Such a command calls, in and of itself, for *positive* affect and behavior.

As we review the list of original commandments a peculiar consideration is to be noted. Granted humankind's proclivity to idolatry (adherence and obedience to false gods)—which includes and is climaxed in the universal and fateful tendency to self-idolatry—a crucial, substantive difference is present as between the first commandment and all the others. To borrow phrasing from Reinhold Niebuhr, the initial commandment entails an "impossible possibility." Here the divine absoluteness is truly shattering: the righteousness of God is manifest in all its fearsomeness. For what mortal has ever succeeded in totally honoring God? By contrast, the other commands are all "possible possibilities" for humankind. They are obeyable. (This assertion assumes that the second commandment refers to the fashioning of tangible or material idols. Where idolatry is construed in a spiritual-moral sense, our comment concerning the distinctiveness of the first commandment applies to this one as well.) However, the distinction involved here must not be pushed too far, for it in no way removes the apodictic quality of any and all injunctions that embody the divine righteousness. As Professor Harrelson points out, God provides no explanations but "simply commands."[19] (The path from apodicticity to a deontological ethic is direct. So too is the path to an ethic of response and responsibility.) In order to represent the inner bond between Moses—who was prophet as well as lawgiver—and the other biblical spokespersons for the righteousness of God, we may suggest the wording *Torah-cum-Prophecy*. Which came first (historically speaking), Torah or Prophecy, is an old question. Modern scholarship contends that while the Pentateuch in its final form was prepared quite late, it is grounded in ancient oral traditions that preceded the classical prophets.

And the prophets repeatedly appeal to the ancient traditions. They "always take it for granted that Israel has long known what is expected in the covenant with Yahweh."[20] Thus, Amos condemns Judah for rejecting "the Torah of the Lord" and failing to keep his statutes (Amos 2:4a).

"The voice of prophecy, heard in the latter part of the eighth century B.C., was like the roar of a lion that pierced the marketplaces and solemn assemblies, awakening people to a sober sense of historical reality and raising consciousness to a higher level." The prophets' message was not a deduction from a coherent fund of truths self-evident to reason. . . . [The] words they spoke in concrete situations were laden with the 'incarnate' power of the word of God, that is, a word that was directed into actual situations of human life . . . , the particularities of human history."[21] The prophetic role may be epitomized in this way: "the prophet in Israel was the one who spoke God's word for the immediate future."[22] The prophetic thinkers were fairly driven by the praxis and purposes of God: her promises, her acts, her demands, her kingdom.

Let us reproduce additional scriptural affirmations of God's righteousness. (Many celebrations of the divine righteousness appear in parts of Scripture not technically or canonically called "prophetic.") The sources are of two sorts: declarations of the absolute will, intention, and person of God apart from specific reference to humankind and human behavior; and (the far more prevalent type) expressions of the demands and character of God in some form of relation or response to human action or the human condition. Sometimes, however, the two sides alternate, in a kind of theological antiphony:

> The law of the Lord is perfect,
>   reviving the soul;
> the testimony of the Lord is sure,
>   making wise the simple;
> the precepts of the Lord are right,
>   rejoicing the heart;
> the commandment of the Lord is pure,
>   enlightening the eyes;
> the fear of the Lord is clean,
>   enduring for ever;
> the ordinances of the Lord are true,
>   and righteous altogether. (Ps. 19:7–9)

The righteousness of God is bonded to the divine holiness: "Who is able to stand before the Lord, this holy God?. . ." (I Sam. 6:20a). "How unsearchable are his judgments and how inscrutable his ways!" (Rom. 11:33b). The knowledge of God's dreadful closeness and power, while expressible, yet seems to elude final comprehension (Ps. 139:1–10). "For the word of God is living and active, sharper than any two-edged sword, piercing to the division of soul and spirit, of joints and marrow, and discerning the thoughts and intentions of the heart. And before him no creature is hidden, but all are open and laid bare to the eyes of him with whom we have to do" (Heb. 4:12–13).

No clearer avowals are forthcoming of the divine righteousness vis-à-vis the human calling than in words attributed to Jesus. He counsels his disciples to "seek first" God's "kingdom and his righteousness. . ." (Matt. 6:33a). He insists that they must be perfect, as their heavenly Father is perfect (Matt. 5:48). And in reply to a scribe's question of which is the first commandment, Jesus answers, "The first is, 'Hear, O Israel: The Lord our God, the Lord is one; and you shall love the Lord your God with all your heart, and with all your soul, and with all your mind, and with all your strength.' The second is this, 'You shall love your neighbor as yourself.' There is no commandment greater than these" (Mark 12:28–31). (That the very first words of Jesus' response should comprise the Sh'ma—"Hear, O Israel"—strikingly accords with God's self-identification to Israel via the Jewish community's first commandment or "word" of the Decalogue, the latter as noted above.)

In relation or response to evil human dispositions and behavior, the righteousness of God is said in Scripture to manifest itself in the form of wrath. The Psalms are replete with this response:

> If his [David's] children forsake my law
>   and do not walk according to my ordinances,
> if they violate my statutes
>   and do not keep my commandments,
> then I will punish their transgression with the rod
>   and their iniquity with scourges. . . . (Ps. 89:30–32)

A moral complication in the Psalms is the directing of the divine wrath, not against Israel, but against Israel's enemies. In this context the laughter of God resounds, and it is a laughter of scorn:

> Why do the nations conspire,
>   and the peoples plot in vain?
> The kings of the earth set themselves,
>   and the rulers take counsel together,
>   against the Lord and his anointed, saying,
> "Let us burst their bonds asunder,
>   and cast their cords from us."
> He who sits in the heavens laughs;
>   the Lord has them in derision. (Ps. 2:1–4)

However, God's choice of Israel does not mean obliviousness to the fate of other peoples or lack of care for them. "The God of Israel is the God of all nations, and all men's history is His concern."[23]

> "Are you not like the Ethiopians to me,
>   O people of Israel?" says the Lord.

"Did I not bring up Israel from the land of Egypt,
and the Philistines from Caphtor
and the Syrians from Kir?" (Amos 9:7)

To the prophets Hosea and Amos the punishment of God will fall peculiarly upon her people Israel. The people have wholly forgotten God and everything she has done to save them:

It was I who knew you in the wilderness,
   in the land of drought;
but when they had fed to the full,
   they were filled, and their heart was lifted up;
therefore they forgot me. . . .
I will destroy you, O Israel;
   who can help you? (Hos. 13:5–6, 9)

You are not my people and I am not your God. (Hos. 1:9b)

You only have I known
   of all the families of the earth;
therefore I will punish you
   for all your iniquities. (Amos 3:2)

The coming "day of Yahweh" will not be one of "light" (viz., of victory and wellbeing) but one of "darkness" (Amos 5:18). And to Isaiah, as to Hosea and Amos, the judgment of God is targeted upon God's own people:

Ah, sinful nation,
   a people laden with iniquity,
offspring of evildoers,
   sons who deal corruptly:
They have forsaken the Lord,
   they have despoiled the Holy One of Israel,
   they are utterly estranged. . . .
Therefore the anger of the Lord was kindled against
   his people. . . . (Isa. 1:4; 5:25a)

Bernhard W. Anderson sums up the perceptions of the eighth century prophets: "God's future is not our human future. On the contrary, the imminence of his coming out of the future introduces into the present such an eschatological shock that present plans, behavior, and style of life are called into question." The prophet's task was to administer this shock so that Israel might recover its identity and vocation "and so that possibly, in the incalculable grace of God, there might be a transition from death to life."[24]
A century and a half later we yet find Jeremiah, "prophet to the nations" (Jer. 1:5), constrained to issue further edicts of denunciation. He too has to tell his own people to remember their past. He reminds them of the com-

mand that God gave them when he brought them out of the land of Egypt: "Obey my voice, and I will be your God, and you shall be my people; and walk in all the way that I command you, that it may be well with you." Yet none of this happened: "they did not obey or incline their ear, but walked in their own counsels and the stubbornness of their evil hearts, and went backward and not forward. From the day that your fathers came out of the land of Egypt to this day, I have persistently sent all my servants the prophets to them, day after day; yet they did not listen to me, or incline their ear, but stiffened their neck. They did worse than their fathers" (Jer. 7:23–26).

The theme of God's anger and accompanying punishment is carried over fully into the New Testament. Here is part of the description of the Last Judgment attributed to Jesus:

> Then [the King] will say to those at his left hand, "Depart from me, you cursed, into the eternal fire prepared for the devil and his angels; for I was hungry and you gave me no food, I was thirsty and you gave me no drink, I was a stranger and you did not welcome me, naked and you did not clothe me, sick and in prison and you did not visit me." Then they . . . will answer, "Lord, when did we see thee hungry or a stranger or naked or sick or in prison, and did not minister to thee?" Then he will answer them, "Truly, I say to you, as you did it not to one of the least of these, you did it not to me." And they will go away into eternal punishment, but the righteous into eternal life. (Matt. 25:41–46)

The apostle Paul discerns the wrath of God as "revealed from heaven against all ungodliness and wickedness of men who by their wickedness suppress the truth" (Rom. 1:18). The writer of II Peter characterizes God as knowing how "to keep the unrighteous under punishment until the day of judgment" (II Pet. 2:9b). The seer John has visions: "Then the kings of the earth and the great men and the generals and the rich and the strong, and every one, slave and free, hid in the caves and among the rocks of the mountains, calling to the mountains and rocks, 'Fall on us and hide us from the face of him who is seated on the throne, and from the wrath of the Lamb; for the great day of their wrath has come, and who can stand before it?'" (Rev. 6:15–17). John further envisions one called "The Word of God": "From his mouth issues a sharp sword with which to smite the nations, and he will rule them with a rod of iron; he will tread the wine press of the fury of God the Almighty. On his robe and on his thigh he has a name inscribed, King of kings and Lord of lords" (Rev. 19:13, 15–16).

IV

Many of the biblical passages before us raise terrible questions: How is poor humanity to endure the absoluteness, and hence the severity, of the divine righteousness? "It is a fearful thing to fall into the hands of the living

God" (Heb. 10:31). Is not human life utterly abashed? How, if at all, is the transcending will of God to be reconciled to, or implemented within, the immanent structures of human existence, "the finitude of the finite" (Paul Tillich)? If the foregoing witness of the Hebrew Bible and the New Testament is any guide, God does not seem exactly to be grandmotherly. She can *laugh* all right, but, as we have noted, even her laughter is marked by derisiveness (Ps. 2:4). The human problem here is that God asks for more than "works"; he asks "for action, but above all for love, awe, and fear. We are called upon to 'wash' our hearts (Jer. 4:14), to remove 'the foreskin' of the heart (Jer. 4:4), to return with the whole heart (Jer. 3:10). 'You will seek Me and find Me, when you seek Me with all your heart' (Jer. 29:13). The new covenant which the Lord will make with the house of Israel will be written upon their hearts (Jer. 31:31–34).''[25] The "Preacher" adjudges that in the end and after "all has been heard," the counsel endures, "Fear God, and keep his commandments" (Eccles. 12:13). But the Psalmist intrudes that "no man living is righteous" before God (Ps. 143:2b). We have been concentrating upon the divine righteousness. How is *shalom* (peace, welfare) ever possible between the unrighteousness of humankind and the righteousness of God? *Shalom* can only be realized when human beings, "motivated by the demands and blessings of life in community," are bound to each other and to God through a prevailing justice.[26]

In ensuing chapters we shall review some major historic ways of living with (or in some cases failing to face) the above questions. For the present, and with precursory consolation, we may remind ourselves of two things: first, biblical anthropology posits a continuity between the absolute righteousness of God and the possibilities of righteousness within humankind; and second, within Torah-cum-Prophecy itself (to go back to an earlier intimation) the absoluteness of the divine word does not remain unqualified. Brief exemplification of these two considerations may be introduced.

(1) The judgment that "no man living is righteous" is in some measure offset, under the aegis of biblical pluralism, by rather more happy testimonies. We are assured that humanity is created in the image of God (Gen. 1:27), that

> thou hast made him little less than God,
> and dost crown him with glory and honor. (Ps. 8:5)

Accordingly, Israel is able to choose between obeying and disobeying God (Deut. 11:26-28; cf. Zech. 6:15). Israel has never lost the capability to implement the divine intention. Indeed, the disgrace and distress that Israel has undergone may even be unjustified:

> All this has come upon us,
>   though we have not forgotten thee,

> or been false to thy covenant....
> Why dost thou hide thy face?
> Why dost thou forget our affliction and oppression? (Ps. 44:17, 24)

There *are* righteous men:

> The wicked is overthrown through his evil-doing,
>   but the righteous finds refuge through his integrity. (Prov. 14:32)

For all their concentration upon human sinfulness, even the prophets do not disallow the potentiality and the reality of human goodness:

> If you are willing and obedient,
>   you shall eat the good of the land.... (Isa. 1:19)

Second Isaiah foresees the historical righteousness of Israel:

> by his knowledge shall the righteous one, my servant,
>   make many to be accounted righteous;
>   and he shall bear their iniquities. (Isa. 53:11b)

And Ezekiel joins the celebration: "When the son has done what is lawful and right, and has been careful to observe all my statutes, he shall surely live" (18:19b).

In sum, not only *can* Israel be faithful to God, sometimes Israel *is* faithful to God.

(2) At some of the very places where the transcendent righteousness of God is proclaimed, a special form of scriptural pluralism steps in—never, to be sure, in the sense of polytheizing, but always as an affirmation of *something additional* about the life and being of the one God. The ultimate depth out of which such a counter-affirmation is made possible is the pathos of God, which manifests an incredible capacity for change, indeed for repentance.

> "O Lord God, forgive, I beseech thee!
>   How can Jacob stand?
>   He is so small!"
> The Lord repented concerning this;
>   "It shall not be," said the Lord. (Amos 7:2–3)

"The preoccupation with justice, the passion with which the prophets condemn injustice, is rooted in their sympathy with divine pathos. The chief characteristic of prophetic thought is the primacy of God's involvement in history. History is the domain with which the prophets' minds are occupied."[27]

Let us return to the Psalter, with its assurance of a God who is able to create "a new and right spirit" within us (Ps. 51:10). The profound impression that was made upon the Israelites by God's deed of deliverance from Egypt was never to be forgotten. The chant of Ps. 136 is perhaps the best-known response to that event. The antiphonal wording, "for his steadfast love endures forever," appears no less than twenty-six times as a response to such individual lines of praise as, he "brought Israel out from among them," and, "with a strong hand and an outstretched arm" (Ps. 136:11–12).[28] But the uncanny thing is that the delivering God, the One who for the sake of her own righteousness must judge and condemn, also forgives.

> If thou, O Lord, shouldst mark iniquities,
>   Lord, who could stand?
> But there is forgiveness with thee,
>   that thou mayest be feared. (Ps. 130:3-4)

And if forgiveness is to the end of the fear of God, we are assured elsewhere that "the fear [reverence] of the Lord is the beginning of wisdom" (Ps. 111:10a). In a parallel passage in Job that celebrates Wisdom, a notable equation is provided (under the rubric of synonymous parallelism):

> "And he said to man,
> 'Behold, the fear of the Lord, that is wisdom;
>   and to depart from evil is understanding.'" (Job 28:28)

The fear of God proves to be identified, not with abject trembling or humiliation, but rather with triumph over evil—the wise goodness that can bring true blessedness. It is today more and more agreed that the prophets, beginning with Amos, were greatly influenced by the wisdom movement in Israel, which had its origins as far back as Solomon.[29] The wording "walk humbly with your God" (Mic. 6:8) is altered in the New English Bible to "walk wisely with your God." Within this context, Professor Anderson offers a significant exposition in connection with the poem upon the Day of Yahweh in Isaiah 2:6–21, which, as Anderson is perfectly willing to acknowledge, is a powerful expression of "the prophetic proclamation that Yahweh is King absolutely and that, in his holy presence, all human values and cultural pride are ultimately bankrupt."[30] However, Anderson then alludes to an independent suggestion that the following words from a little later in Isaiah should be inserted after 2:9 in the poem:

> Humanity is brought low, humankind is abased;
>   haughty eyes are humbled.
> But Yahweh of hosts is exalted in justice,
>   the Holy God proves himself holy by righteousness. (Isa. 5:15–16)

Were it *de rigueur* to italicize biblical passages, the last eight words above would be most eligible, for they epitomize an entire theology for a time of anguish. In those few words is found one epigraph for this book as a whole. And let us remember the impliedly inverse order of the line: no righteousness, no holiness.

Here is Anderson's exegesis:

> There is no textual basis for transposing these verses, but they help us to understand the theme of "the dread of Yahweh" in the poem (2:10, 21). The encounter with the Holy God on his Day will be dreadful only because, in contrast to the proud and the mighty on earth, he demands and executes justice. Here Isaiah gives his own exposition of a major theme of Israel's psalms, one that celebrates Yahweh's coming to inaugurate his kingdom on earth as it is in heaven. All of nature is summoned to sing for joy, before Yahweh, who comes "to judge the earth" (Ps. 96:11–13). . . . Thus for Isaiah, as for the other prophets, the experience of the holy is not an encounter with mysterious, numinous power wholly beyond the mundane sphere where human beings struggle to find meaning and fulfillment in society. Isaiah stands firmly in the Mosaic tradition which testified to the in-breaking of divine holiness into the world with redemptive concern and ethical demand. . . . The holiness of Yahweh, then, is manifest as saving power directed toward the realization of justice/righteousness. Therefore, those who "boast" should boast that they "know" (acknowledge) Yahweh who "executes righteousness and justice in the earth" (Jer. 9:23–24).[31]

Righteousness and justice are nothing abstract or heavenly. They are not the private property of God. They are to be executed *in the earth*, which means in behalf of human dignity and welfare. The divine commands are not issued in order to satisfy or flaunt God's ego, much less in order to satisfy or flaunt themselves, but rather they are proclaimed to the end of human and cosmic salvation. In the prophet's cryptic phrasing, "Zion will be redeemed by justice" (Isa. 1:27a). "Righteousness is not just a value; it is God's part of human life, *God's stake in human history*." It is from out of the divine compassion that God's concern for justice grows.[32]

Any seeming scriptural derogation of the domain of human history is actually a path to the ideal fulfillment of history. An emphasis of Walter Harrelson is relevant here: God's leveling of the covenant demands upon Israel is itself an act of grace and love. "God loves Israel so much that he both delivers her from bondage in Egypt and places upon her the requirements of the covenant law." From this vantage point, we comprehend the Decalogue, not as a terrible burden inflicted upon people by an arbitrary judge, but instead as "Israel's great charter of freedom."[33] Hans Werner Wolff alludes to the sabbath as exemplary: "The sabbath commandment shows in an especially instructive way that the basic commandments are a great gift to Israel to help and benefit her. Far from being demands, the Commandments are exactly the opposite: they free Israel from demands."[34]

Perhaps we can put it in yet another way: In the very moments when the One who reigns over unmeasured galaxies bespeaks the utmost gravity imaginable, he betrays something of, *kiveyakhol,* a sense of humor (the kind that sheds tears, and will shed them unendingly). He draws back from his own awesomeness. Why? Just for the sake of love, of faithfulness, of truth, of goodness, of righteousness. The divine anger is shackled by God's sorrow, his compassion; God's wrath is conquered by his anguish,[35] his anger is washed away by his holy weeping:

> You shall say to them this word:
> "Let my eyes run down with tears night and day,
>   and let them not cease,
> for the virgin daughter of my people
>   is smitten with a great wound,
> with a very grievous blow. . . ." (Jer. 14:17)

The lineage here is an ancient one, reaching as far back as Abraham's query to God: "Shall not the Judge of all the earth do right?" Abraham was insisting that it would be immoral for God, as for anyone else, to slay the righteous indiscriminately with the wicked (Gen. 18:25). (The city of Sodom was destroyed anyway, although we are told that Lot got out because "the Lord remembered Abraham" [Gen. 19:29]. Here is an instance of *salvation by remembrance,* which is crucial to covenantal thinking.) God herself is here brought before—or, better, opens herself to be brought before—the bar of a human judgment (itself made possible, of course, by an ultimate divine justice). This tradition is carried forward and developed elsewhere in the Pentateuch, the Psalms, and the prophets:

> . . .Moses besought the Lord his God, and said, "O Lord, why does thy wrath burn hot against thy people, whom thou hast brought forth out of the land of Egypt with great power and with a mighty hand? Why should the Egyptians say, 'With evil intent did he bring them forth, to slay them in the mountains, and to consume them from the face of the earth'? Turn from thy fierce wrath, and repent of this evil against thy people. Remember Abraham, Isaac, and Israel, thy servants, to whom thou didst swear by thine own self, and didst say to them, 'I will multiply your descendants as the stars of heaven, and all this land that I have promised I will give to your descendants, and they shall inherit it for ever.'" And the Lord repented of the evil which he thought to do to his people. (Exod. 32:11–14)

> . . . I will not remove from [David] my steadfast love,
>   or be false to my faithfulness.
> I will not violate my covenant,
>   or alter the word that went forth from my lips.
> Once for all I have sworn by my holiness;
>   I will not lie to David.

His line shall endure for ever,
  his throne as long as the sun before me.
Like the moon it shall be established for ever;
  it shall stand firm while the skies endure. (Ps. 89:33–37)

When Israel was a child, I loved him,
  and out of Egypt I called my son. . . .
It was I who taught Ephraim to walk,
  I took them up in my arms;
  but they did not know that I healed them.
I led them with cords of compassion,
  with the bands of love,
and I became to them as one
  who eases the yoke on their jaws,
  and I bent down to them and fed them. . . .
How can I give you up, O Ephraim!
  How can I hand you over, O Israel!
How can I make you like Admah!
  How can I treat you like Zeboiim!
My heart recoils within me,
  my compassion grows warm and tender.
I will not execute my fierce anger,
  I will not again destroy Ephraim;
for I am God and not man,
  the Holy One in your midst,
  and I will not come to destroy. (Hos. 11:1, 3–4, 8–9)

We have come part circle from our original reference earlier in this chapter to the divine holiness as *fons et origo* of God's apodictic righteousness. Holiness now is for the sake of justice and love. The grace of God countervails the rigor of God's demands. We have cited Bernhard W. Anderson: "God's future is not our future." The other side of the coin of Torah-cum-Prophecy is that God's future *is* our future. Consequent queries include these: Is there not an obligation to question the holiness of God should it seem to become a threat to authentic righteousness? Is it not eminently wise to honor Wisdom? Is there anyone who is willing, deep underneath, to forswear justice? If the answer to the first two queries is Yes, and to the third is No, and if the logic we have suggested is sound, a singular conclusion may be reached: Augustine of Hippo was right when he said, "Thou madest us for Thyself, and our heart is restless, until it repose in Thee."[36] For is there not a kind of bondedness to God that can become perfect freedom?[37]

Now it is time to examine our several normative images for their representation of, and bearing upon, "the message of the divine righteousness."

II. Unfoldings of the Divine Righteousness

Eight Normative Images

3

Faith against the World

THE presence within the biblical writings of certain attestations to the saving concerns of God (mercy, love, forgiveness) suggests an independent theological sanction for raising the question: Is the absoluteness of the divine commands in fact unqualified? The previous chapter's final section indeed qualifies, though it does not negate, the affirmation that history is "under command and judgment." An important consequence is that the different efforts we shall review that grapple with the issue of faith and history have, on the basis of parts of Scripture, already gained a certain prevenient support. On this ground, it is legitimate to think of our several normative images as linked to the overall biblical apprehension of God and the divine purposes. In this sense, these images constitute *unfoldings of the divine righteousness*. They manifest varying measures of continuity with Torah-cum-Prophecy. They carry forward that tradition. Yet they also alter the tradition. They are creatively discontinuous with it, some more than others.

I

The first normative image parallels H. Richard Niebuhr's type "Christ against culture," or what he often refers to as the "radical" alternative and sometimes as "exclusive Christianity." "Faith against the world" entails the least possible conscious assent to any accommodating of the divine righteousness to human interests and goals. Stress falls instead upon discontinuities between history and faith. If anything, history is assimilated to faith. The dedication of representatives of this view to the absolutes of God brings studied opposition to worldly standards and needs. What human beings wish for themselves in their selfishness and sin is negated in principle. Human experience and traditions as guides to what is good or right are suspect—unless by some miracle the praxis that is there advocated and followed succeeds in spite of itself in glorifying the righteousness of God. In brief, any independent value within time and space is disallowed.

This normative image is nonetheless an instance of the unfolding of the divine righteousness. True, its opposition to "the world" must come into a large measure of conflict with an overall biblical devotedness to the structures and values of history in the latter's ideal possibilities. Nevertheless, various aspects of the biblical witness themselves make the viewpoint possible. Thus, H. Richard Niebuhr is able to use the First Letter of John to illustrate "Christ against culture." (He includes as well Tertullian and Leo Tolstoy under that heading.)[1] In longing for the truth of God, adherents of this outlook will not permit—I introduce John Line's conceptualization—a truth that is "in order to goodness,"[2] at least not in any universal-historical sense. Yet in another sense their allegiance to the divine righteousness appears to be thoroughgoing, since they refuse to qualify that righteousness in any way. If all this suggests a measure of incoherence, the original responsibility may not be so much theirs as that of biblical pluralism.

As between Judaism and Christianity, "faith against the world" has had a more influential place within the Christian corpus, not least because of the influence upon the church of extra-biblical and extra-Jewish spiritualizing tendencies together with the requirement in the course of the history of Europe that a "Christian civilization" retain its distinctive visage. Over the centuries since Christianity began, the concept of "church versus world" has thus differed in range and substance from that of "Jewish community versus the world." The disparity was complicated and compounded by the fact that for Jews, "the world" came largely to mean a Christian world. However, anti-worldly spiritualization is not an absolute monopoly of the church vis-à-vis the Jewish community. Our first normative image is not lacking in exemplification within the more independent story of the Jewish people. And by way of neutralizing the (just-mentioned) historical happenstance within the Jewish-Christian relation, we may turn for Jewish illustration of the initial image to the time before the coming of the Christian Empire.

A cautionary note: It is essential to bear in mind through our entire study that the rejection of "the world" (or of "culture" or "history") can extend to the rejection of a markedly religious world as well as of a secular one.

II

My initial example is prompted by Eugene B. Borowitz's discussion of "Torah against culture," wherein he mentions the Essenes, the Therapeutae, and the various Dead Sea groups.[3] The Essenes, who appeared in the second century B.C.E. and endured until the end of the first century C.E., were organized as quasi-monastic communities that had withdrawn from the historical-political scene. Here was an esoteric group living on the fringes of Jewish society. It thus constituted "a sect proper" (Geza Vermes) in contrast to the Sadducees, Pharisees, and Zealots. As with true sectarians everywhere, membership was on the basis of volitional, adult commitment.[4] Not a large body, the Essenes probably never numbered more than four thousand. For the most part women were excluded (unlike Therapeutae practice). Holding all possessions in common, the Essenes lived austere, rigorously organized lives. They regarded luxury and pleasure as despicable. Central to their existence was the detailed, life-long study of Torah. The sect showed very great reverence to its priests (of the Aaronic line), but it evidently loathed the official Temple priesthood in Jerusalem. The Essenes considered corrupt the religious observances of the Second Temple and in the cities. Rejecting animal sacrifice, they sanctioned offerings of flour, oil, and incense. The Essenes vowed total fidelity to the Law of Moses. They were in this respect much less flexible and much less humane than the Pharisees. They emphasized the norm of personal piety and separation from the "defilements" of the world. Justice was to be shown to all men. (Essenes were opposed to slavery.)

Essene ritual purity was typified in communal baptism, communal meals, and dietary laws. The sect regarded itself as the only "true Israel," the true sons of light in contrast to the sons of darkness (Jews as well as Gentiles). However, a great deal in Essene hymns and prayers is reflective of deep spiritual humility and an admission of the unworthiness of the elect, together with expressions of total dependence upon God's grace as the only way to persevere in holiness and to obey the divine Law. For the Essenes, the community as a whole represented the sacrifice offered to God in atonement for Israel's sins. It is true that asceticism of the form practiced by these men (as by the Qumran sect in general) is not entirely absent from rabbinic literature.

Some scholars argue against the claim that Essene belief and praxis were in opposition to established Judaism, while others stress Essene separation from the normative Judaism of the time, including Temple services. The Qumran (Dead Sea) sect was an extremist offshoot of the Jewish apocalyptic outlook. Its fundamental persuasion was that the end of days is at hand, the agenda of history having been ordained by God. "Assuredly, all the times appointed by God will come in due course, even as He has determined in His inscrutable wisdom" (Pesher Habakkuk 2:4, trans. T. H. Gaster). Until the coming of the end, humankind is partially under "the dominion of Belial," but preceding the end God will set apart (or has already set apart) an elect community that is destined to be saved and will form the core of a new society. With the advent of the end, all evil will cease, the wicked will be consumed, and Israel, the people of God, will be liberated from the yoke of the nations. Israel as a community of the future is to be a fighting society, executing God's plan to establish the reign of this righteousness in the end of days. The Essenes entertained highly activist and militarist messianic expectations.[5] They

> not only considered themselves to be the "remnant" of their time, but the "remnant" of all time, the "final" remnant. In the "age of wrath," while God was making ready to annihilate the wicked, their founders had repented.

They had become the "Converts of Israel". . . . As a reward for their conversion, the Teacher of Righteousness had been sent to establish for them a "new Covenant," which was to be the sole valid form of the eternal alliance between God and Israel. Consequently, their paramount aim was to pledge themselves to observe its precepts with absolute faithfulness. Convinced that they belonged to a Community which alone interpreted the Holy Scriptures correctly, they devoted their exile in the wilderness to the study of the Bible. Their intention was to do according to all that had been "revealed from age to age, and as the Prophets had revealed by His Holy Spirit" . . .

Thus, the Covenant theology of the Jewish tradition was foundational to Essene (and Qumran) belief.[6]

Furthermore, our own phrasing "Torah-cum-Prophecy" is granted a certain historical verification, or at least exemplification, through the views of the Qumran-Essene sectaries, for whom fidelity to the Covenant required not alone obedience to the Law, to everything that God had "commanded by the hand of Moses," but in addition adherence to the teaching of "all his servants, the Prophets." This special attention to the prophets implies two things:

firstly, that the Essenes subscribed to the principle incorporated into the opening paragraph of the Sayings of the Fathers that the Prophets served as an essential link in the transmission of the Law from Moses to the rabbis.

Moses received the Torah from (God on) Sinai and passed it on to Joshua; Joshua to the Elders (= Judges); the Elders to the Prophets; and the Prophets passed it on to the members of the Great Assembly (= the leaders of Israel in the post-exilic age). (mAboth 1:1)

The second inference to be drawn is that the sect believed the Prophets to be not only teachers of morality, but also guides in the domain of the final eschatological realities.[7]

However, as was the case with the Law, the prophetic books cried out for correct interpretation. The right path to be followed during the cataclysms of the final days was being disclosed, so the Essenes believed, through the inspired teaching of the community, on the basis of which the sectaries could see themselves "living in the true City of God, the city of the Covenant built on the Law and the Prophets. . . ."[8]

III

We turn now to the Christian side, and consider Paul of Tarsus as representative of "faith against the world."

Responsibility for the markedly differing interpretations and assessments of Paul devolves in considerable degree upon the apostle himself.* Thus at times Paul upholds the social distinctions of the Roman Empire as evidently normative for Christians; at other times he resorts to peculiarly Christian norms in repudiation of secular structures. One interpreter finds the explanation for this and other inconsistencies in the fact that

> there are two Pauls. One is the radical, antinomian, libertarian Paul who calls for a total freedom from all forms of oppression and domination in the world, with divine love and Christian *koinonia* [sharing] replacing the strife of the world. The other Paul is the arch-conservative and reactionary. This is the Paul who preaches total subservience to God, which is interpreted then as a total subservience to the powers of evil: slave masters, men, and Caesar. Without exception woman is to obey her husband, women are to be silent in the church, the slave is to obey the master, homosexuals are cast out of the community, and only the WCTU is left worthy of heaven. The radical Paul preaches an absolute justification by grace through faith alone; the reactionary Paul compiles a list of good deeds for people to imitate.[9]

I am not assured that we have to divide Paul wholly in two. To refer to one major affirmation just cited as coming from "the radical Paul," an important development in today's Pauline scholarship is the serious questioning of "absolute justification by grace through faith" as being all-decisive within the apostle's thinking, or at least as in and of itself the heart of the conflict between Paul and his mother-faith of Judaism. In this connection, it is essential that Paul be read in and for himself, and not as a Lutheran of the sixteenth century—or even as an Augustinian of the fifth century.

With reservations, H. Richard Niebuhr places Paul under the rubric of "Christ and culture in paradox," yet acknowledges as well that the type "Christ the transformer of culture" was prepared for by Paul only to be "overshadowed in the end by his thoughts about flesh and death and the restraint of evil." However, Niebuhr concedes that Paul, like Luther, is too complex a figure to permit ready identification with a stylized pattern.[10]

The mere fact that Paul did not flee the world but worked within and through the brute structures and trials of ordinary life already makes his version of faith appear less hostile to worldly, cultural things than was the outlook of the Dead Sea community. However, while Paul does not typify the same sectarian spirit we have noted in conjunction with the Essenes, it can yet be argued that he exemplifies the image of "faith against the world," and in ways not wholly discontinuous with the Essene outlook.[11]

---

*The question of how to assess Paul turns in part upon decisions respecting the authenticity of the letters attributed to him. It is generally acknowledged that Romans, I and II Corinthians, Galatians, Philippians, I Thessalonians, and Philemon are from his hand. Doubts obtain concerning II Thessalonians, Colossians, and Ephesians.

As with such a Jewish sect as the Essenes, the issue of how to describe Paul's relation to "the world" is dependent upon which world or worlds we are talking about. The relative authorization for placing Paul within the category of "faith against the world" lies in the multiplicity and richness of the several worlds against which he came to stand: (1) the present spatio-temporal dispensation as such; (2) Greco-Roman culture; and (3) the tradition and historical foci and nexus of Judaism (not to mention certain parties within the primitive Christian community itself[12]). The fact that Paul reveals continuities with the second and third of these worlds may modify our categorization of him but it does not controvert it. After brief attention to the first two categories, we shall concentrate upon the Pauline attitude to the world of Judaism.

(1) The apostle Paul marshalls the sureties of the Christian gospel against the objective world of sin and woe, of false wisdom and false strength, a world that, to him and to other first Christians (as to many Jews), was passing away. Expressed more generally, Paul's theology is throughout conditioned by his eschatology.[13]

In his foremost epistle, written to "all God's beloved in Rome," Paul sounds what had always been a keynote of his Christian outlook: "The creation itself will be set free from its bondage to decay and obtain the glorious liberty of the children of God." "Do not be conformed to this world [*aion*, age] but be transformed by the renewal of your mind, that you may prove what is the will of God, what is good and acceptable and perfect" (Rom. 1:7; 8:21; 12:2). The apostle here carries forward prophetic-apocalyptic counsel he earlier gave through the Christians of Corinth, in Philippi, and in Thessalonica:

> Even if our gospel is veiled, it is veiled only to those who are perishing. In their case the god of this world has blinded the minds of the unbelievers, to keep them from seeing the light of the gospel of the glory of Christ, who is the likeness of God. . . . For this slight momentary affliction is preparing for us an eternal weight of glory beyond all comparison, because we look not to the things that are seen but to the things that are unseen; for the things that are seen are transient, but the things that are unseen are eternal. . . . Therefore, if any one is in Christ, he is a new creation; the old has passed away, behold, the new has come. (II Cor. 4:3–4, 17–18; 5:17)

> Do all things without grumbling or questioning, that you may be blameless and innocent, children of God without blemish in the midst of a crooked and perverse generation, among whom you shine as lights in the world, holding fast the word of life. . . . (Phil. 2:14–16a)

> When people say, "There is peace and security," then sudden destruction will come upon them as travail comes upon a woman with child, and there will be no escape. But you are not in darkness, brethren, for that day to surprise you like a thief. For you are sons of light and sons of the day; we are not of the night or of darkness. (I Thess. 5:3–5; see also I Thess. 4:13–17)

Although the Book of Acts provides only secondary reportage on the apostle, the words of the risen Jesus, whom Paul envisioned, are consistent with the foregoing passages. Paul is to be sent to the Gentiles "to open their eyes, that they may turn from darkness to light and from the power of Satan to God, that they may receive forgiveness of sins and a place among those who are sanctified by faith in me" (Acts 26:17–18).

(2) Paul places what is for him the redeeming truth of the gospel against the ways and standards of Greek and Roman culture.

As observed above, the apostle is not always at odds with his cultural world. Most notable, or notorious, is Paul's theological-political advice to the believers of Rome: "Let every person be subject to the governing authorities. For there is no authority except from God, and those that exist have been instituted by God. Therefore he who resists the authorities resists what God has appointed, and those who resist will incur judgment" (Rom. 13:1–2). In his exposition of the type "Christ the transformer of culture," H. Richard Niebuhr describes the apposite link between Christian affirmation and the cultural world: "The Word that became flesh and dwelt among us, the Son who does the work of the Father in the world of creation, has entered into a human culture that has never been without his ordering action." At the same time, we are not wholly free of the nagging remembrance that "the authorities" would never have been needed had something not gone awry. "Creation" and a "fall" from created goodness somehow come together.[14]

Paul's persuasion of the gospel versus the cultural world enters into clearer view, paradoxically enough, via his sexism and the external institutions of marriage and the family. E. P. Sanders finds quite reasonable the conclusion that the apostle's effort to keep women silent in church (I Cor. 14:34)—along with Paul's assumption that slavery would continue as an institution until the eschaton (I Cor. 7:21)—simply reveals him as a man of his time, and that such notions may be treated in the same way as Paul's declaration that nature requires males to wear their hair short (I Cor. 11:14).[15] However, the Pauline outlook here can be received in quite alternative fashion. Precisely because his faith ranged him "against the world," Paul could shrug his shoulders at certain cultural norms. Such practices were part of the aeon that would soon pass—when the creation itself was set free from bondage. We have a case of the convergence of apocalyptic radicalism and ostensible social conservatism. The truth is that while the apostle did not deem sexual relations or marriage as in any way sinful (I Cor. 7:28), he did look upon the institution of marriage as a concession to human passion and a block to temptations to immorality. What really matters is that "the appointed time has grown very short; from now on, let those who have wives live as though they had none. . . . For the form of this world is passing away" (I Cor. 7:2, 28, 29, 31).

If Paul's apocalyptic stance often seems to underwrite the social status quo, the moral paradox is compounded but then transformed in and through

the incarnating of God's righteousness within day-to-day human relationships.

> Bless those who persecute you; bless and do not curse them. Rejoice with
> those who rejoice, weep with those who weep. Live in harmony with one
> another; do not be haughty, but associate with the lowly; never be con-
> ceited. Repay no one evil for evil, but take thought for what is noble in the
> sight of all. If possible, so far as it depends upon you, live peaceably with
> all. Beloved, never avenge yourselves, but leave it to the wrath of God; for it
> is written, "Vengeance is mine, I will repay, says the Lord." No, "If your en-
> emy is hungry, feed him; if he is thirsty, give him drink; for by so doing you
> will heap burning coals upon his head." Do not be overcome by evil, but
> overcome evil with good. . . .
>   Owe no one anything, except to love one another; for he who loves his
> neighbor has fulfilled the law. (Rom. 12:14–21; 13:8)

> Love is patient and kind; love is not jealous or boastful; it is not arrogant
> or rude. Love does not insist on its own way; it is not irritable or resentful; it
> does not rejoice at wrong, but rejoices in the right. Love bears all things,
> believes all things, hopes all things, endures all things.
>   Love never ends; as for prophecies, they will pass away; as for tongues,
> they will cease; as for knowledge, it will pass away. For our knowledge is
> imperfect and our prophecy is imperfect; but when the perfect comes, the
> imperfect will pass away. When I was a child, I spoke like a child, I thought
> like a child, I reasoned like a child; when I became a man, I gave up childish
> ways. For now we see in a mirror dimly, but then face to face. Now I know in
> part; then I shall understand fully, even as I have been fully understood. So
> faith, hope, love abide, these three; but the greatest of these is love. (I Cor.
> 13:4–13)

(3) As between Pauline conviction and the world of Judaism, there is a
parting of the ways. However, this cannot be expressed in just the fashion
that has prevailed within the Christian tradition. Particularly misleading and
erroneous is the dichotomy of justification by faith/justification by works.

A useful way to come to grips with the problem of Paul's relation to Torah
Judaism is to review several renditions: (a) the celebration of Torah (Clark M.
Williamson); (b) the condemnation of Torah (David Flusser); and (c) the dialectic between the "participation in Christ" emphasis of E. P. Sanders and
the pro-Judaic stress of Krister Stendahl. That all four of these interpreters
more or less licitly ground themselves within Paul's writings underscores the
complexities in coping with his point of view.

(a) Paul believes that God graciously and forgivingly imputes his own
righteousness to undeserving humanity (cf. Rom. 4:1–12). This fact qualifies
(though it does not upset) the situating of Paul under the image of "faith
against the world." At the same time, the belief attests to the apostle's firm
place within the Jewish historical-scriptural tradition. The Judaism of Paul's

time was not a religion of salvation by works, and it had never been such. Paul would know from his childhood and as a good Pharisee (Phil. 3:5) that, in Clark M. Williamson's phrasing, "Judaism has no works that do not rely on God's grace." The Torah was itself the manifestation of "God's covenanting grace calling Israel to response and responsibility.... For Paul, as for rabbinic Judaism, justification was by grace."[16] The apostle's judgment that "no human being will be justified" in God's sight "by works of the law" (Rom. 3:20a; Gal. 2:16; Phil. 3:9) is good, straight Jewish teaching. (It is always possible to read Paul here in an opposite way, as polemicizing against Judaism.[17]) Yet at the same time, for Paul as for rabbinic Judaism, there is the insistence, often overlooked, that "judgment was also in the light of works."[18] "All who have sinned without the law will also perish without the law, and all who have sinned under the law will be judged by the law. For it is not the hearers of the law who are righteous before God, but the doers of the law who will be justified" (Rom. 2:12–13). In Williamson's summarization (following E. P. Sanders), "as with rabbinic Judaism, justification is by grace," while judgment is "on the basis of deeds." As Sanders concludes, "In all of this, Paul's view is typically Jewish."[19] Correspondingly, the apostle can testify of himself that "as to righteousness under the law," he is "blameless" (Phil. 3:6). Thus was Paul remaining a faithful exponent of the Law and of the capability of fulfilling it: "I agree that the law is good" (Rom. 7:16b). As Stendahl has it, the anthropological references in Romans 7 are the "means for a very special argument about the holiness and goodness of the Law." In a word, Paul exalts the role of the Torah for Israel.[20]

Were the conviction of God's transforming grace in combination with God's righteous judgment the only salient one within the apostle Paul's viewpoint, we should have to associate him with a normative image other than "faith against the world" of Judaism. But a number of other factors are commanding, as we shall see.

(b) David Flusser is categorical in depicting Paul as anti-Law. The apostle "strongly opposed the observance of all Jewish practices in his gentile Christian communities." It even "began to be said in Jerusalem that Paul was teaching 'the Jews who are among the gentiles to forsake Moses, telling them not to circumcise their children or observe the customs' (Acts 21:21)." Behind all this was the apostle's antipathy to the Law:

> Although Paul's assertion that "no human being will be justified by the works of the Law" (Rom. 3:20) can be understood in a broader theological and philosophical sense, what he was chiefly opposing was the Law of the Jews. Paul's concept that Christ's death abolished the Mosaic Law cannot be explained as a new development of the eschatological idea which sometimes occurs in later rabbinic sources, namely that in the world to come the commandments will no longer be valid; of this idea there is no trace in his teachings.

> Paul's attitude toward the Jewish Law is extreme and cannot be explained
> as stemming only from his theology of the Cross. For him the old Mosaic
> covenant was "a dispensation of death, carved in letters on stone . . . a dis-
> pensation of condemnation . . . [which] . . . fadeth away," in comparison with
> the new covenant, which is the "dispensation of the Spirit" (II Cor. 3:6–11).
> "For the law brings wrath, but where there is no law there is no transgres-
> sion" (Rom. 4:15), and "all who rely on works of the law are under a curse"
> (Gal. 3:10–14). . . .
>   It seems clear from all his assertions that Paul's conversion meant for him
> liberation from the yoke of the Jewish law.[21]

That Professor Flusser's summation is oversimple is suggested through
the brief exposition above under (a). But that Flusser's interpretation can be
considerably vindicated, if not in quite so severe a way, will become evident
as we assay at some length the Sanders/Stendahl dialectic.

(c) E. P. Sanders denies that the teaching of justification by faith is at the
center of the apostle's point of view. W. D. Davies and Krister Stendahl,
among others, agree with this denial.[22] As Albert Schweitzer put it many
years ago, a theme cannot be a central one if it does not explain anything
else. Sanders, following Schweitzer, observes that "righteousness by faith
can be derived from and understood on the basis of other aspects of Paul's
thought such as possession of the Spirit and living in the Spirit, but not vice
versa." More positively, Sanders enumerates two primary convictions as governing Paul's Christian life: (i) Jesus Christ is Lord, i.e., through participation
in Christ, God provides salvation for all who believe, and Christ will soon return to bring everything to an end; (ii) Paul was called by God in Christ to be
the apostle to the Gentiles. These two convictions go hand in hand: "Paul's
role as apostle to the Gentiles is connected to the conviction that salvation
is for all who believe, whether Jew or Gentile, and also to the nearness of the
end of the age. In view of the approaching end, he was under compulsion, as
apostle to the Gentiles, to preach the gospel as quickly as possible to the
whole world. It is on the basis of these two *convictions* that we can explain
Paul's *theology.* . . ."[23]

Krister Stendahl's interpretation of Paul's doctrine of justification by faith
is that it arises from "his reflection on the relation between Jews and Gentiles," and not from any personal difficulties with the Law nor from "the
problem of how *man* is to be saved, or how man's deeds are to be accounted, or how the free will of individuals is to be asserted or checked."
(Cf. Stendahl's reading of Rom. 1:16–17; 3:28–29.) Justification by faith as a
doctrine "was hammered out by Paul for the very specific and limited purpose of defending the rights of Gentile converts to be full and genuine heirs
to the promises of God to Israel." The apostle's ministry "is based on the
specific conviction that the Gentiles will become part of the people of God
without having to pass through the law. This is Paul's secret revelation and
knowledge." The Messianic Age has, after all, begun. Accordingly, the teach-

ing of justification "must be subsumed in the wider context of Paul's mission to the Gentiles, part of God's total plan for his creation.... Paul's thoughts about justification were triggered by the issues of divisions and identities in a pluralistic and torn world, not primarily by the inner tensions of individual souls and consciences. His searching eyes focused on the unity and the God-willed diversity of humankind, yes, of the whole creation." Paul would have nothing of any subjection of the divine righteousness to human wishes. Yet, with specific relation to the early Christian community,

> when one spoke of the manifestation of God's righteousness, God's *tsedaqah*, it was a word of salvation. As in the Song of Deborah in earliest times, it meant salvation, rescue, victory, triumph. Here we have the chief reason for Paul's emphasis on the terms, justification and righteousness. This emphasis presupposes a faith in which the church knows itself as belonging to God, knows its enemies to be God's enemies. There is a certain arrogance to this but it is at the heart of covenant faith. And in such a setting, that term righteousness/justification (*tsedaqah, dikaiosune*) once again took on its whole glorious meaning.[24]

The passage immediately above presses home the question: If it is the church that now truly belongs to God—to be sure, as no more than a graft into the olive tree of his people (Rom. 11:17)—what is to be the fate of Israel? If Stendahl is correct that Paul came to the doctrine of justification by faith for the purpose of defending the rights of the Gentiles to become heirs of God's promises to Israel, where are left the original people of God? On Stendahl's reading of Paul, the Jewish people are left, it would seem, where they have always been: with God. (Sometimes Stendahl is compelled by the brute content of the Pauline materials to write in ways that question his own position. Thus, in analyzing Gal. 3 he has no choice but to say, "Paul concludes that all are one in Christ Jesus and that there can be no divisions between Jew or Greek, slave or free, male or female; all are heirs to the promise of Abraham [3:28–29]." If the Jew in truth joins the Greek as being "one in Christ," the Sanders interpretation of Paul [as we shall identify it] is conveyed. All in all, Stendahl's problem is that he is forced to recognize as a basic issue for Paul what happens to the Law once the Messiah comes, while at the same time he [Stendahl] is continuing to plead that Paul's fundamental concern is the Gentiles as against the requirement of a Christian mission to the Jews. Perhaps Stendahl's clearest self-indictment appears in these two sentences: "Rom. 1–3 sets out to show that all—both Jews and Gentiles—have sinned and fallen short of the glory of God [3:19, cf. v. 23]. Rom. 3:21–8:39 demonstrates how and in what sense this tragic fact is changed by the arrival of the Messiah."[25]) Stendahl can insist, against Günther Bornkamm, that in Romans, especially chapters 9–11, Paul is not carrying out "a polemic against the Jews, but is rather giving an apology for his mission in which he reflects on the mystery of God's dealings with Israel."[26] To the point as well is Sanders's own observation that "there is no body of Jewish literature which expects the abolition of the law with the advent of the Messiah. . . ."[27]

It is most instructive, with respect to the interpretation of Paul's attitude toward the world of Judaism, to ponder how Krister Stendahl and E. P. Sanders, agreeing as they do upon so much, can yet tender opposite conclusions. Stendahl writes: "Paul's message was related not to some conversion from the hopeless work righteousness of Judaism into a happy justified status as a Christian. Rather, the center of gravity in Paul's theological work is related to the fact that he knew himself to be called to be the Apostle to the Gentiles, an Apostle of the one God who is Creator of both Jews and Gentiles (cf. Rom. 3:30)."[28] These two sentences could just as well have been written by Sanders. The two exegetes together stress the cruciality of Paul's vocation as apostle to the Gentiles; they reject not alone justification by faith but also the plight of humankind as keys to Paul's point of view; and they are in accord that (quoting Stendahl) "the central issue claiming Paul's attention [in Romans 9–11] is that of the inclusion both of Gentiles and Jews."[29] Yet they remain apart on the question of the apostle's position vis-à-vis Judaism and the Jewish people. How can this be? And who, if either one, is right?

Stendahl maintains that in Romans 11, Paul provides for the salvation of "all Israel" quite apart from any confession of Jesus Christ as Lord. "Paul does not say that when the time of God's kingdom, the consummation, comes Israel will accept Jesus as the Messiah. He says only that the time will come when 'all Israel will be saved' (11:26). It is stunning to note that Paul writes this whole section of Romans (10:17–11:36) without using the name of Jesus Christ. This includes the final doxology (11:33–36), the only such doxology in his writings without any christological element."[30]

The response from Sanders concentrates upon the soteriological question: "Paul says repeatedly that the *only* way to be justified or righteous is *by faith in Jesus Christ.*" The decisive fact is that the apostle "deliberately and explicitly applies" this "both to Jews and Gentiles (e.g., Rom. 4:11f., 16f.; 3:21–26; Gal. 2:15f.)."[31] If "justification" and "righteousness" are in fact soteriological terms for Paul, it follows that the apostle is questioning, by implication, the salvational power and role of Judaism now that Jesus Christ has come. Sanders agrees with Stendahl that the problem originates in Paul's "grappling with the problem of how to defend the place of the Gentiles in the Kingdom," but Sanders contends that "a place in the Kingdom" definitely implies soteriology:

> Whenever Paul uses the verb "justify" or "be justified" it has "transfer" significance. One is justified from being sexually immoral and idolatrous to being cleansed and pure (I Cor. 6:9–11); one is "justified" (= freed) from the power of sin (Rom. 6:7, where the translations obscure the terminology). Transferring from sins or from Sin is what we must call a soteriological con-

ception, although Paul himself reserves the word "saved" and its cognates
for the end-time salvation. But operatively, when Paul is discussing being
justified, or becoming a son of Abraham or a son of God, or inheriting the
promises to Abraham, or receiving the Spirit, or participating in the blessings to Abraham—all of which he terminologically connects with faith in
Christ Jesus—he is in fact discussing soteriology: not end-time soteriology,
to be sure, but how to become a member of the body of Christ, which alone
provides end-time salvation.

Sanders believes it to be

> beyond objection to say that for Paul "faith" is not a general attitude, but
> always means "faith in Jesus Christ." If this is granted, Rom.10:17–11:36 is
> not so nonchristological as Stendahl's observation about the appearance of
> the name "Jesus Christ" would at first lead one to think. At the crucial place
> of discussing, by means of the metaphor of the olive tree, the inclusion of
> Gentiles and the exclusion of Jews, Paul bases inclusion and exclusion on
> faith and unfaith: "It was because of unfaith that they (the Jews) were bro-
> ken off, while you stand fast (only) by faith" (11:20). The point is that the
> Gentiles should not be proud (11:20b). Further, Paul proceeds to threaten
> the Roman Christians that if they lapse into unfaith . . . , they will be cut off
> (11:22). It is only by faith that anybody is "in." Paul then applies this to the
> Jews: "And even the other (Jews), if they do not persist in their unfaith, will
> be grafted in . . ." (11:23). The "if" clause must be taken seriously . . . . the
> Jews as such will not be saved apart from faith in Christ.[32]

As Romans 11 moves to completion, is the condition of faith in Christ
somehow dropped or is it simply understood without being mentioned?
Several reasons for the latter view are adduced by Sanders. Perhaps the
most telling is based upon verses 28–32, which read:

> As regards the gospel they are enemies of God, for your sake; but as re-
> gards election they are beloved for the sake of their forefathers. For the
> gifts and the call of God are irrevocable. Just as you were once disobedient
> to God but now have received mercy because of their disobedience, so
> they have now been disobedient in order that by the mercy shown to you
> they also may receive mercy. For God has consigned all men to disobedi-
> ence, that he may have mercy upon all.

Here is the exposition of these verses by Sanders:

> Paul contrasts Israel with the predominantly Gentile readers. Israel is loved
> (and has been loved) for the sake of the forefathers, although now they are
> enemies of God. The Gentiles were once disobedient (= enemies) but are
> now included in God's mercy. Then Paul concludes: "For God has consigned
> all men to disobedience, that he may have mercy on all" (11:32). But on
> what grounds have the Gentiles gained access to God's mercy? Not by their
> merit, but only through faith in Christ (cf. 11:20). The condition of mercy for

"all men" ("faith") is not stated in 11:32, but the only reasonable reading is that the previously stated condition still applies for Gentiles, and should follow that it also applies to Jews. The sole condition which Paul ever states is "faith in Christ" . . . and 11:32 seems to prove that the condition still stands. 11:32, among other things, repeats Paul's standard view that Gentiles and Jews stand on the same footing. . . . and the same condition applies to all. . . . Paul never intends to say that anyone can be saved apart from Jesus Christ.[33]

In the following proposition E. P. Sanders brings together, in their consequences for the Law, the two main issues we have discussed: "*It is the Gentile question and the exclusivism of Paul's soteriology which dethrone the law, not a misunderstanding of it or a view predetermined by his background.*"[34] In his latest work on Paul, Sanders concludes that the apostle's break with Judaism is manifest in his denial of the "two pillars common to all forms of Judaism," viz., the traditional Jewish doctrine of election, and faithfulness to the Mosaic Law. Paul insists that faith in Christ is necessary to membership in the people of God.[35]

Sanders clearly has the better of the argument.

Through the interpretation of Sanders we are enabled to understand how Paul's mission to the Gentiles can be objectively described as no more than a kind of division of labor, it having been agreed that other apostles would work to convert Jews. In Galatians, Paul himself explicitly affirms the compact according to which James, Peter, and John should go to "the circumcised," and "we should go to the Gentiles" (2:7–9). There had been, of course, a sharp division between Paul and other apostles on the issue of whether newly converted Gentiles were required to observe the Law.

IV

The fundamental moral and theological mark of Paul remains his rendering of the absolute divine righteousness as a righteousness freely purposed or imputed to ordinary mortals through the power of God's forgiving grace in Jesus Christ. Here he at once carries forward and goes beyond Judaism. As evident from our consideration of Torah-cum-Prophecy in chapter two, an existential blunting of the fearsome judgment of God long preceded Paul. Yet by taking God's long-suffering and forgiveness and, with essential aid from the death and Resurrection of Jesus, implanting these qualities within human history, the apostle could claim concrete exemplification and incarnation of that earlier Jewish teaching. But the nagging question must yet be met of whether there is any way to resolve the evident contradiction between (i) the denial that justification by faith is the center of Paul's thought, and (ii) the reputedly universal need and opportunity for faith in Christ as comprising that center. The paradoxical effort of E. P. Sanders to deal with this problem involves showing how, in Paul, faithful participation in Christ, instead of comprising some kind of "answer" to an anterior problem of justification, takes prevenient priority over that problem just as it does over all other exigencies of life. The apostle, rather than proceeding from the human predicament to its resolution, goes in the very opposite direction: "for Paul, the conviction of a universal solution preceded the conviction of a universal plight."[36] In summing up the matter, William Baird finds especially suggestive the conviction in Sanders

> that Paul's theology should not be viewed first from the perspective of man's plight (contra Bultmann), but that Paul's understanding of the plight of humanity results from his acceptance of Christ. [The same orientation applies, remarkably enough, to Krister Stendahl's viewpoint—A.R.E.] Sanders concludes that Paul is both similar and different from Judaism. The striking feature of the comparison, however, is that where he is usually thought to be different—on the idea of grace and works—Paul is in fundamental agreement with the rabbis. Paul's difference from Judaism, on the other hand, is found in his concept of participation in Christ. "In short, *this is what Paul finds wrong in Judaism: it is not Christianity.*" ([Sanders, Paul,] p. 552)[37]

All of this entirely accords with the fact that before his acceptance of the Christian faith, Paul neither showed the slightest dissatisfaction with Judaism nor found the Law to be in any way a burden. He was content and at peace.[38] But subsequently, the apostle's priorities came to parallel the special apprehension among the prophets that God's righteousness is the window upon a comprehension of the plight of humanity.

A deciding consideration cannot be that of mere agreement or disagreement with the apostle but instead what it is that Paul believes and says. As a matter of fact, Sanders holds that Paul is quite wrong in his position on the Jewish people and Judaism.[39] Within recent years, Romans 9–11 has often been cited by Christian apologists in Europe and North America as scriptural support for the conviction that Israel remains God's people and for opposition to the effort to convert Jews to Christianity. This procedure does not wash because it is grounded in faulty exegesis. (As far back as 1967 I was arguing this way.[40] I submit that the subsequent work of E. P. Sanders has helped support the argument.) Whatever the limitations within the work of Sanders, he shows convincingly the error of making Paul a support for Christian acceptance or recognition of Judaism. However, even though the New Testament record forces us to agree with Sanders against the exegesis criticized by him, we have to do our best to understand the situation of many of those Christian interpreters who turn to Romans 9–11 for aid. Usually, these are people who sustain a conservative, sometimes even fundamentalist view of Scripture (this does not hold for Stendahl), and yet are also honestly seeking to affirm the integrity of Judaism and the Jewish reality, including the unbroken character of God's Covenant with original Israel. They believe that they must honor full New Testament authority, and they are trying hard to avoid anti-Jewishness. It is a great pity, therefore, that Paul cannot be made to say what they claim for him. If the struggle against Christian triumphalism and faulty conversionism is to be carried forward, its warrant has to rest elsewhere than upon the shoulders of Paul.

The failure of Paul is that he is not able to show (though he should naturally have yearned to do so) how his honoring of Torah as the instrument of God's gracious relation to his people Israel (as Stendahl and Williamson accentuate) is to be creatively linked and reconciled with participation in Christ as the instrument of God's gracious relation to humankind (as Sanders demonstrates). Again, if, as Sanders and Williamson have it, justification is by God's grace while judgment is according to deeds, this leaves agonizingly open the entire question of the mutual bearing and consequences that the divine grace and human deeds have upon each other—which means the question of the covenantal relationship as a whole. If only the apostle Paul had met, rather than skirted, this all-determining question! His difficulty cannot be expressed as that of "faith versus works"—such a duality would be more or less out of the question in first-century Christian (and Jewish) thinking—but it is instead that of two competing variations within the life of faith itself. Differently put, once we have been convinced by Sanders, Davies, Stendahl, and the rest that "justification by faith" is not the center of Paul's thinking, where then are we to find, if anywhere, the *necessity* of Christianity? Clearly, to reckon that Christianity is a useful, even providential, vehicle for bringing Gentiles into the people of God still fails to establish the Christian faith's universal necessity.

That Paul can be comprehended in diametrically opposite ways (Williamson vs. Flusser; Stendahl vs. Sanders) is ultimately traceable, for its responsibility, to the apostle himself. Each interpreter is traveling in a direction somehow authorized by Paul. The trouble is that the apostle never really settled upon a single direction. This failure of Paul (as of an evangelist like Matthew) was to have terrible consequences in the history of the Christian treatment of Jews—although it must be added, for the sake of the apostle's name, that part of the causal blame here attaches to the dominant misreading of Paul to which reference is earlier made.[41] For all the anti-Judaic bent he came to have, Paul, the Jewish messianist, was never anti-Jewish—granted the assumption (a debatable one) that anti-Judaism and anti-Jewishness are at some points distinguishable. As the foregoing analysis has suggested, Paul remained, instead, rather confused. A little more charitably, he could not seem to make up his mind concerning an all-decisive continuity and an all-decisive discontinuity as between Torah Judaism and faith in Jesus Christ. For example, if in fact Pauline Christian faith stands (as our present usage has it) "against the world" of Judaism, how is that interpretation of Christianity to be made coherent with Paul's essentially disparate conviction that love of neighbor fulfills the Law (Rom. 13:8; Gal. 5:14; cf. Matt. 19:19;

22:35–40; Jas. 2:8)? The latter conviction is straight Torah Judaism (cf. Lev. 19:18); it is out of the question to propose that Paul is here not proclaiming Torah. As H. Richard Niebuhr used to remind us as students, in Romans 12ff. the Law is paradoxically reinstated. Again, how is the apostle's repeated and celebrated advocacy of participation in Christ—"Christ mysticism," we liked to say in the great old days—to be made coherent with Paul's claim that do-ers of the Law will be fully justified before God (Rom. 2:13)? In writing this last, is Paul somehow forgetting that he had penned Galatians 3:11? In view of the apostle's personal history, the two verses would be reconcilable only if, contrary to fact, the one in Romans had been composed before the other.[42] The interjection of E. P. Sanders that Paul seems implicitly to be working with a distinction between commandments directed to relations be-tween man and man, and commandments governing relations between man and God,[43] does not take Paul off the hook, for any such dichotomy is granted no definitive meaning within Judaism.

(Pauline incoherence even rubs off slightly on Sanders himself; he has the apostle making faith in Christ "the only means of entering the people of God,"[44] despite the plain affirmation of Romans 11 and elsewhere that Israel *is* the people of God.)

In effect, Paul was trying (at least below-consciously) to have things two ways. This is particularly ironic because this apostle could sometimes re-ceive the grace to rise above confusion and indecision, as in the unbeliev-able Hymn to Love of I Corinthians 13.

V

As has been stressed, the world with which a given faith may conflict can itself be a religious world. This phenomenon is exemplified in Paul's con-frontation with the established Judaism in which he had been reared. In-deed, "Paul's type of religion is basically different from anything known from Palestinian Judaism."[45] In cases such as this the religious world plays a cul-tural-historical role comparable to secular reality: it acts as a foil. To Paul, an entire history was giving way to another; one world was being succeeded by another. "Christ crucified," whom alone the apostle resolved to know and preach (I Cor. 2:2), must indeed remain "a stumbling block to Jews" (I Cor. 1:23)—this for good Jewish reasons: Jesus' death meant the demise of possi-ble messianic fulfillment through him and his efforts. The all-determining consideration regarding Paul is that the apostle could not and would not permit the matter to rest there.

For Paul, the absolute of God's righteousness—the righteousness that is revealed through faith (Rom. 1:17)—centers in Jesus Christ. In speaking of "the righteousness of God" (Rom. 3:25), the apostle "is declaring that God has taken the initiative in restoring man to his proper relation to God and man."[46] All this is verified in and through what is for Paul the absolute fact of the Resurrection: "if Christ has not been raised, then our preaching is in vain and your faith is in vain. We are even found to be misrepresenting God, because we testified of God that he raised Christ, whom he did not raise. . . . If Christ has not been raised, your faith is futile and you are still in your sins" (I Cor. 15:14–15, 17). That Paul should cleave to the Resurrection of Jesus as strictly an act of God is the seal, not alone upon the conflict between the apostle and a dying aeon mixed together with Greek foolishness, but also upon his conflict with the world of Judaism. This latter means that only when we address ourselves to the question of the Resurrection as a historical event do we come to the heart of the traditional Christian-Jewish *Auseinandersetzung*. For from Paul's point of view, "the Age of the Resurrection of the Dead was in the process of dawning."[47] Herein lay the apostle's singular blow against the faith of his fathers. The one really convincing Christian rejoinder to Paul is accordingly that of Father Gerard S. Sloyan: "Obedient acceptance of God's will means that the Law will have a place in Christian faith forever."[48]

VI

H. Richard Niebuhr declares the radical or exclusivist position to be at once "necessary and inadequate." It does draw essential lines "between Christ and Caesar, between revelation and reason, between God's will and man's." It has contributed to the reformation of church and world, even though this was never its intention. Thus, monasticism was to become a great conserver and transmitter of cultural tradition, strengthening the very institutions from which its own founders had separated themselves. "Every Christian must often feel himself claimed by the Lord to reject the world and its kingdoms with their pluralism and temporalism, their makeshift compromises of many interests, their hypnotic obsession by the love of life and the fear of death." Where this claim is lacking, "Christian faith quickly degenerates into a utilitarian device for the attainment of personal prosperity or public peace. . . . So long as eternity cannot be translated into temporal terms nor time into eternity, so long as Christ and culture cannot be amalgamated, so long is the radical answer inevitable in the church."[49]

The radical position's inadequacy derives from several factors: the claims of Christ are never independent of the countervailing power of culture (language, attitudes, customs, beliefs); Christ's claims have to be applied in cultural terms if they are to be applied at all; the new "race" of Christians "borrowed from the laws and customs of those from whom they had separated what they needed for the common life"; and "the needs of the withdrawn community" ensure "the development of a new culture." In a word, the radical Christian must have recourse to principles that he cannot derive "directly from his conviction of Christ's Lordship." So often, the radical fails to apprehend what he is doing. He fancies, quite incorrectly, that he has succeeded in separating himself from the world.[50]

Finally, the exclusivist advocate is up against a number of theological problems. In his denigrating of reason and exalting of revelation he tends to blunt the distinctions that ought to be made "both with respect to the reasoning that goes on outside the Christian sphere and to the knowledge that is present in it." He himself discovers that the sinfulness of human beings arises as much from nature as from culture. His opponents find in him a certain bent toward legalism that neglects the significance and power of grace. Knottiest of all is the challenge of how to relate Jesus Christ as Lord to the Creator of nature and Governor of history. There is a temptation among radicals ultimately to "divide the world into the material realm governed by a principle opposed to Christ and a spiritual realm guided by the spiritual God." Why it is that radical Christians "should be so subject to the temptation of a spiritualism that leads them away from the principle with which they begin, namely Christ's authority, is difficult to fathom. Perhaps it is indicated that Christ cannot be followed alone, as he cannot be worshipped alone; and that radical Christianity, important as one movement in the church, cannot itself exist without the counterweight of other types of Christianity."[51]

4

The Kingdom/Righteousness of God: Jesus of Nazareth

WITHIN and through our second normative image, Christian history and Christian devotedness converge with singular force.

I

Certain preliminary remarks are in order.

Much argument is invited and much cogitation demanded by the question of where Jesus (Yeshua) of Nazareth, native son of Israel, belongs within the dialectic of divine righteousness/human righteousness, and how thereby he joins the encounter of faith with history. When the writer of Ephesians assures his Gentile readers that they "are no longer aliens in a foreign land" (2:19, NEB), he is empowered to do this only because the event of Jesus has taken place. Indeed, numbers of people have found in Jesus the meeting ground *singularis* of the two dimensions of righteousness. While to many persons in the history of our planet this eventuality is not serious enough even to qualify as comical, to the faithful Christian it opens the way to laughter and to joy, and thence to objective peace (*shalom*). To speak of Jesus as the *sine qua non* of Christian faith is to declare that without him Christianity would never have come to pass, and without him there would be no Christianity now. A cherished theological way to testify to this state of affairs is to affirm that for Christians, Jesus is Lord—in the sense that he is their way, their truth, their life (John 14:6). They believe themselves to be reconciled, through him, to the God of Israel (II Cor. 5:19).

Although in *Christ and Culture* H. Richard Niebuhr does include a portrait of the person and teachings of Jesus, he does not assign Jesus to a particular type in the encounter with culture. This omission evidently accords with his understanding of Jesus Christ as mediatorial: Christ is identified as the one who involves men "in the double movement from world to God and from

52

God to world," and who, accordingly, transcends any particular type.[1] That we should number Jesus among figures who represent or embody a unique, normative image does not have to contradict Professor Niebuhr's viewpoint. It does emphasize the one side of the perennial Christian claim: that incarnation is not confessed apart from the historical Jesus, and that, indeed, the historical Jesus is the one who is meant by incarnation.

Ben Zion Bokser contends that "many Christian scholars have abandoned the quest for the historical Jesus because this leads to Judaism and not to Christianity."[2] That judgment may involve a partial *non sequitur*. The Jesus of "the quest" is, as we shall be noting, devoted to Judaism. But the issue of Christians and their relation to Judaism is a different one. It turns upon at least two further questions: How is Judaism to be comprehended? And how are we to speak of Christians? Are we to refer to them in empirical-phenomenological fashion (including their own self-understanding) or in normative fashion? A decisive consideration is that Christians who are prepared to face up to the normative question can hardly escape the fact that the Jesus whom they follow was himself a follower of Judaism. Here is the element of truth in Bokser's argument. In this connection, we may note a provocative word from Nicholas de Lange: "Whoever lays claim to the name of Israel implicity renounces the status of gentile."[3]

It is well to reflect upon a point similar to the concordance expressed above between history and incarnation: The normative historicalness of biblical faith encompasses the story of Jesus. A certain homage to historicity is suggested through the familiar wording, "the quest of the historical Jesus." Clearly, any contemporary Christian return into historicalness and history will give a place of honor to that quest, however difficult the task and however elusive its consummation. For if it is so that humankind's distinctive quality is its historicalness[4]—identified as the recognition and acceptance of history as the determining condition and opportunity of all human life—the endeavor to characterize and to cope with Jesus of Nazareth in all his historicity thereby gains human and moral sanction. To pursue this latter course offers aid to knowledge, to praxis, and to faith, although to be sure it also points to the limits of knowledge/praxis/faith. For while within the bounds of human historicity there is no necessary objection (in Judaism as beyond it) to identifying Jesus as in some sense the bearer of a revelation of God, such revelation must also reflect God's hiddenness—as is the case with any and all historical revelation.

The norm of historicalness can sometimes function as a control factor. One of its implications is that avowals of faith ought not contradict what we know of actual history. On that reasoning, whatever we may confess or not confess respecting "the Christ of faith" is not permitted to go against what we may find ourselves obliged to say concerning "the Jesus of history." For insofar as the Christian faith insists that history is a special instrument of divine revelation, whatever is to be said of Jesus the historical figure becomes a criterion of what is to be said of "the Christ of faith" (rather than the other way round). There is no wish here to absolutize history; rather the essential need must be recognized to keep together two things: history as a stage of God's work, and the rightful testimonies of faith. We may ponder the existential paradox that while faith is not to be subjugated to history, yet faith cannot elude or disavow history. The overall relation between faith and history is an architectonic one: history stands as the foundation-meaning of human life, and then the life of faith comes to build upon and to soar beyond that foundation. Faith may well rise far above history, but not in ways that subvert the data of history. This architectonic presupposition colors—some would say distorts—the treatment of all the normative images in this volume. The presupposition points up an essential element of continuity between the normative image of "history transforming faith," which I represent, and that of "faith above history," our fifth image.

Finally, if the quest of the historical Jesus carries potential meaning for our own history, the total character of historicity suggests the converse as well: the history that we know, i.e., experience, from the past and the present has meaning for the history of Jesus. One need not have become captive to Rudolf Bultmann's *affaire* with existentialism to agree with Bultmann's early-expressed intent to help us see Jesus as part of the history in which we have our own being.[5]

II

Granted that the pertinent and available documents of the New Testament are, with reference to Jesus, secondary or even tertiary in character, is it possible for us to retrieve his own viewpoint/praxis? There is overwhelming agreement that sayings and acts are reported in the record that are not, in fact, his. And yet, it is widely believed by scholars and others that the early renderings of Jesus' teachings and life can and do throw light upon the real history. The (not exceptional) view to which I subscribe is that through subjecting the New Testament record to thorough critical analysis, and through applying incremental knowledge of first-century Judaism, of Christianity, and of their environments, we may be enabled to establish considerable historical truth. Such truth is realized once critical-historical study achieves continuing contact with the record itself. The essential veracity and consequent usefulness of the record is affirmed, *mutatis mutandis*. Today scholars increasingly acknowledge the marked validity of the interpreted New Testament account of Jesus' message/praxis. We are witnesses to a significant form of dialectical confluence. From the one converging direction, the interests of historicalness are nurtured by historical labor; from the other converging direction, the historical work gains authorization as a constituent part of a historicist, or at least a historical, worldview. In approaching here the teachings and contribution of Jesus, we shall not detail the complicated linguistic, documentary, redactional, and other data and evidence through which scholars seek to determine the authenticity/nonauthenticity of New Testament passages attributed to Jesus or reputed to convey historical truth about him and the primitive church.

Our study of Jesus approaches the problem of his message/mission, first, by placing that subject within the broader and deeper context of questions concerning his person; and, second, by analyzing his teachings and life against the background of the faith/praxis of his fathers. While our emphasis falls upon "the historical Jesus" rather than "the Christ of faith" (insofar as these can be distinguished), yet in awareness of the difficulties in identifying the praxis *of* Jesus in contrast to the several claims made *about* him, we include some reference to the oldest recoverable layers of New Testament confession—this by means of a brief review of titles assigned to Jesus together with some allusion to the question of his own self-identification. Stress is put upon attestations to his person that are pertinent, directly or indirectly, to his teachings/behavior. It is not possible to describe Jesus' ideas adequately if we abstract them from his deeds or from his person. All of the pertinent categories—the message/praxis of Jesus, the vocation of Jesus, and the interpretations of Jesus and responses to him by his followers—impinge upon one another. These three categories are not finally separable, and they are mutually influential.

The major reputed titles of the historical Jesus as found in the Synoptic Gospels (the Gospel of John belongs in a later and largely separate class) are "prophet," "lord," "Messiah," "son of man," and "son of God."[6] A primary venture is to determine the import of these titles within the Galilean milieu of the first century C.E.; "if this can be done, there is a good chance of approaching closer to the thought of Jesus and his first disciples."[7]

(a) Unlike the case with certain other titles, Jesus seems to have accepted characterizations of himself as a prophet. Evidently, for his followers as for him, the terms "prophet" and "miracle-worker" were synonymous.[8]

(b) It is a paradox that whereas Jesus is not often called "prophet" although he apparently approves of that title, he is many times named as "lord" (*kyrios*), despite the truth (according to the Synoptics) that he refuses to proffer "lordly" claims. Various objections raised against the actual historical application to Jesus of the title "lord" are probably untenable. In Jewish Aramaic "(the) lord" is utilized in connection with either God or secular dignitaries or authoritative teachers or persons noted for their spiritual power. More specifically, Mark and Matthew associate Jesus as "lord" with his capacity to perform miracles. The evidence of the Gospel of Mark is that the title was a customary form of address to a miracle-worker, and constituted the peculiar way the disciples would either allude to or speak to their master. Matthew gives voice to the same predominant practice: *kyrios* is for the most part used by that Gospel in accounts of miracles. In addition, Matthew extends "lordship" to other aspects of Jesus' work—viz., teacher and religious leader—aspects that finally predominate with the Gospel of Luke, wherein "lord" in a miraculous frame of reference is less evident than elsewhere. All in all, the appellation of "lord" primarily "links Jesus to his dual role of charismatic Hasid and teacher, and if the stress is greater in the earlier strata of the tradition," this accords with "the fact that his impact as a holy man preceded that of teacher and founder of a religious community."[9]

(c) During the intertestamental age the nature of the general Messianic expectation of Palestinian Jewry had become more or less stable, at least for a time. A son of David, i.e., a king of Davidic lineage, was expected and prayed for, a royal and holy figure who as coming victor over the Gentiles would save and restore Israel and establish God's righteousness and justice. It is observed that the modern claim of disparate forms and guises for the Messiah as a future savior or redeemer fails to differentiate the prevailing, normative Messianic expectation from a congeries of speculations among certain learned and/or esoteric minorities. Such speculations came to include priestly, prophetic, "pre-existent," and "slain" Messiahs. In truth, ancient Jewish prayers and biblical interpretation combine to show unequivocally that if during the intertestamental period "a man claimed, or was proclaimed, to be 'the Messiah,' his listeners would as a matter of course have expected to find before them a person endowed with the combined talents of soldierly prowess, righteousness and holiness."[10]

Some New Testament texts that present Jesus as the Messiah (e.g., the infancy narratives) are, developmentally speaking, quite late. The phrase "Jesus Christ" rarely appears in the Synoptic Gospels. But the centering of Messianic hope upon Jesus is clear in the petition of James and John that Jesus grant them places of honor when he comes to "glory" (Mark 10: 35–40; cf. Matt. 20:20–23). The persistence of such a hope is intimated in the pre-Ascension query of the apostles, "Lord, will you at this time restore the kingdom to Israel?" (Acts 1:6). Even more conclusive is the episode at Caesarea Philippi where, in answer to Jesus' question to his disciples, "Who do you say that I am?" Peter confesses: "You are the Christ" (Mark 8:27–29; Matt. 16:13–16; Luke 9:18–20). From such texts as these "the apostles' faith may be taken as established."[11]

It is striking that Jesus himself should say little on the Messiah; in his surviving teaching the subject is not prominent. We recall his enigmatic insistence, responding to Peter's confession, that the disciples were "to tell no one about him" (Mark 8:30). The only authentic literary context "in which Jesus is treated as a self-proclaimed King Messiah" is the account of his appearance before Pilate together with the sequel to that appearance. Yet the most that Jesus offers, in answer to Pilate's question of whether he is "King of the Jews," is "You have said so" (Mark 15:2; Matt. 27:11; Luke 23:3). (Later on, we shall place this passage within an affirmational context.) All in all, great doubt is expressed that Jesus ever maintained, directly or spontaneously, that he was a promised Messiah.[12] Yet how, then, could he ever have been executed as "King of the Jews"? We must return to the issue of Jesus' Messianic status in all its perplexity.

(d) The phrase *son of man** occurs more than sixty times in the Synoptic Gospels (and fairly often in the Fourth Gospel); yet, paradoxically, the Synoptics give voice to this formulation solely through the lips of Jesus. Seemingly exasperating is the datum that this term, which were it a specific or authentic title ought to have aroused some kind of reaction among its Synoptic hearers, is instead wholly ignored by them. In the record everyone lets it pass, as if it were not being uttered at all.[13] Can we, in consequence, continue to number it among Christological titles?

A negative reply to the above question is suggested. Contrary to much New Testament scholarship, "there is no evidence whatever, either inside or outside the Gospels, to imply, let alone demonstrate, that 'the *son of man*' was used as a title." This finding is occasioned by the discretely Aramaic origin of the *son of man* sayings. It is shown that in Galilean Aramaic (the language of Jesus and his first follwers) *son of man* often appears as a synonym for "man" and also as a substitute for the indefinite pronoun; less often, it serves as a circumlocutional reference to the self prompted by either awe or reserve or humility. The fact that no trace is to be found of its titular use leads to the inference that no case can be made "for an eschatological or Messianic office-holder generally known as 'the *son of man*.' "[14]

If the above negations are correct, we are given an explanation for the absence in the Synoptics of any particular curiosity or notice respecting Jesus' frequent employment of the term.

(e) A more positive temper is encouraged when we take up the signal title *son of God*, which the New Testament bestows upon Jesus many times. As always, we are challenged to distinguish original from later usage. We have to keep before us the church's religious-philosophic-geographic evolvement *from* Palestinian-Jewish thinking/praxis *to* the Gentile-Christian-Hellenistic-Roman world. Within Palestinian-Jewish thinking "son of God could refer, in an ascending order, to any of the children of Israel; or to a good Jew; or to a charismatic holy Jew; or to the king of Israel; or in particular to the royal Messiah; and finally, in a different sense, to an angelic or heavenly being. In other words 'son of God' was always understood metaphorically in Jewish circles. In Jewish sources, its use never implies participation by the person so named in the divine nature."[15]

As with the titles "prophet" and "lord," the early application of *son of God* to Jesus seems to be linked to two factors: his activity as a charismatic miracle-worker and exorcist, and his hasidic consciousness of a special

---

*To the end of exactness, the wordings *son of man* and, later, *son of God* are set in italics.

bond with the heavenly Father. Although our religious conditioning (including especially the lingering power of Hellenism, even in the late twentieth century) makes almost irresistible the assumption that when the evangelists refer to Jesus as *son of God* they must be making him in a real way equal to God—as if he possessed or were claiming *divine* sonship (divinity or Godness)—the actual historical morphology of the New Testament record demands quite an opposite position. This opposite view is required by everything we know of Jesus' own conviction and behavior, his "special filial consciousness."[16] Precisely because, in an especially intimate way, he accepts and worships *God* as his very own Father—would not a *"sic"* sit wrongly here?—his awareness of sonship is thereby intensified. This fact rules out the view that by calling God "his own Father," Jesus makes himself "equal with God" (John 5:18). The fatherhood of God means that Jesus is *unequal* to the Father. In his effort to introduce (alleged) Pharisee opposition to Jesus' "claims," Michael Grant calls upon post-biblical materials.[17] This is inadmissible. Grant's attempted use of the Fourth Gospel at this juncture is also illicit. And so is his endeavor to make historical a Pharisee or scribal opposition to Jesus for "claiming divinity." The Jesus of history does not make the latter claim. Jesus can ask, *sans façon*, "Why do you call me good? No one is good but God alone" (Luke 18:19). All this is in sharp contradistinction to the Hellenistic *son of God*/"divine man" hypothesis that was waiting to be superimposed upon Palestinian-Jewish Gospel belief and terminology.[18]

It appears indisputable that Jesus thinks of himself as *son of God* (contra *"the son of God"** and perhaps even contra "Messiah *son of God*"[19]), and that his followers, caught up in his charisma, accordingly and admiringly respond to him and address him in the same way. (Later on, theological revisionism will assert itself, as in the case of the Fourth Gospel's prologue, "the Word became flesh and dwelt among us, full of grace and truth; we have beheld his glory, glory as of the only Son from the Father" [John 1:14]. This and other affirmations of the "divinity" of Jesus are post-Jesus phenomena. However, even the Fourth Gospel has Jesus denying the charge that he had made himself equal to God.[20])

Geza Vermes provides a summary of the ground we have thus far covered: "The positive and constant testimony of the earliest Gospel tradition, considered against the natural background of first-century Galilean charismatic religion, leads not to a Jesus as unrecognizable within the framework of Judaism as by the standard of his own verifiable words and intentions, but to another figure: Jesus the just man, the *zaddik*, Jesus the helper and healer, Jesus the teacher and leader, venerated by his intimates and less committed admirers alike as prophet, lord and *son of God*."[21]

---

*For the replacement of *son of God* by "the Son," cf. Mark 13:32; Matt. 11:27; and Luke 10:22, in sayings quite uncharacteristic of Jesus.

III

The foregoing section has provided some clues to Jesus' ties to the faith/ praxis of his fathers. Now we must pursue the latter theme with greater intensity, as we ask: Wherein is found the focus of the message of Jesus, and what is the basis for including his teaching/praxis upon our list of normative images?

The first part of this question is relatively easy to answer; the second part demands a complex response. Jesus' basic teachings can be recaptured fairly readily. The complexity arises from a conjunction of three formidable, interconnected problems: the relation between the teachings and Jesus' life-mission-fate in its entirety; the question of the reconciliation/nonreconciliation of the central theme of his message with other aspects of his teaching; and the impact of his teaching/praxis in general upon the kind of historical fruition that ultimately serves to determine whether his image of divine/ human righteousness qualifies as a persuasively normative one.

It is well to bear in mind the question of Jesus' developing purpose or intention. (The New Testament sources do not yield a fully desired portrait of his inner life and personality.) Possible criteria for identifying Jesus' purpose or purposes are found in whatever we may recover of his message/praxis, with full attention, as John Riches emphasizes (in accord with the History of Religions School), to the evolvement of the Judaism of Jesus' time. The theme of Jesus' purpose is basic to Riches, *Jesus and the Transformation of Judaism,* which rekindles the eighteenth-century tradition of Hermann Samuel Reimarus and Gotthold Ephraim Lessing.

The message of the craftsman from Nazareth is epitomized in an utterance recorded from the very start of his public career: "The time is fulfilled, and the kingdom of God is at hand; repent, and believe in the gospel" (Mark 1:14). At the outset Jesus thus recalls the witness of Israel's classical prophets in one integral aspect of their collective teaching: the coming of the kingdom or reign of God. The kingdom of God is almost universally accepted today as the center of the Nazarene's message/praxis.[22] It is in and through his persuasion of God's kingdom that Jesus is drawn into the fundamental question of the nature and power of the divine righteousness.

In the biblical understanding, the concept of the "kingdom of God" does not refer to the realm over which God governs so much as it does to the divine sovereignty itself. This sovereignty is linked up with biblical messianism, the persuasion of the coming of a royal Messiah. Further, the kingdom of God was "to ensue from the victory on earth of heavenly angelic armies over the hosts of Satan. Israel's final glorious triumph was to be the corollary in this world of God's total dominion over the world of the spirits. Such a kingdom was of course not to be built. It was to erupt into the world here below, annihilate it, and set itself up in a new heaven on a new earth." Finally, there is the quite distinctive idea of a pure and sanctified Israel drawing the Gentiles to God, this (especially in post-biblical times) through the vehicle of obedience to God's Torah.[23]

Distinctively, yet with the sectaries of Qumran and also with John the Baptist (Matt. 3:1; Luke 16:16), Jesus is convinced that the kingdom will come upon earth at any moment. That is to say, in a short while the present world (aeon) will end through God's cataclysmic intervention. As Wolfhart Pannenberg writes, Jesus' ultimate concerns are with history and its End, which he expects very soon.[24] The imminence of the kingdom is "the very heart" of Jesus' message. Indeed, God "is shortening the days" (Mark 13:20), as other apocalypticists* also pronounce.[25] The *hasid* from the Galilee assures his hearers: "Truly, I say to you, there are some standing here who will not taste death before they see that the kingdom of God has come with power" (Mark 9:1; cf. Matt. 16:28; Luke 9:27). To Peter, James, John, and Andrew the stern admonition is given: "Take heed, watch; for you do not know when the time will come. . . . And what I say to you I say to all: Watch" (Mark 13:33, 37; cf. Matt. 24:42–44). Commensurately, Jesus teaches all the twelve to pray "like this":

> Our Father who art in heaven,
> Hallowed be thy name.
> Thy kingdom come,
> Thy will be done,
>   On earth as it is in heaven.
> Give us this day our daily bread;
> And forgive us our debts,
>   As we also have forgiven our debtors;
> And lead us not into temptation,
>   But deliver us from evil. (Matt. 6:9–13)

The "Our Father" form of address is taken from the Pharisee liturgy.[26] Jesus' insistence upon the abrogation of worldly hostilities and contentiousness, upon "turning the other cheek," and upon unrestricted love is not motivated by pacifism or gentleness or sympathy (though he is conspicuous for his compassion; cf. Mark 6:34), but instead by the overriding need to prepare for and gain entrance to God's kingdom. The instruction to "turn the other cheek" in Luke 6:29 and Matt. 5:39, like the command to love one's enemies (Matt. 5:44), cannot be treated literalistically, any more than can the text requiring would-be disciples to hate father, mother, wife, children, brothers, and sisters (Luke 14:26). As Vermes points out, the independent Passion account in the Gospel of John has Jesus doing the opposite of turning the other cheek: "If I have spoken wrongly, bear witness to the wrong; but if I have spoken rightly, why do you strike me?" (18:23).[27] The motivation

---

*Probably Jesus is an apocalypticist in just one respect, but it is a crucial one: his assurance that God is (about) to intervene catastrophically and decisively within world and human history.

to get ready to enter God's kingdom appears to be somewhat qualified in Matt. 5:43–45, where love of one's enemies and persecutors is "so that you may be sons of your Father who is in heaven." The latter emphasis parallels the Pharisee teaching that love is to be practiced for its own sake, regardless of reward or compensation.[28] However, preparation for the kingdom through love does not ultimately conflict with love for the sake of sonship. As Jesus says elsewhere, "Whoever seeks to gain his life will lose it, but whoever loses his life will preserve it" (Luke 17:33; cf. Luke 9:24; Matt. 10:39; 16:25; Mark 8:35). Admission to the kingdom, "the one and only aim that is worth pursuing," the pearl of greatest price (Matt. 13:45), is contingent upon total receptivity. "I tell you this: unless you turn round and become like children, you will never enter the Kingdom of Heaven. Let a man humble himself until he is like this child, and he will be the greatest in the Kingdom of Heaven" (Matt. 18:3–4, NEB). Those who would prepare themselves for entrance into the kingdom must do a complete about-face (*metanoia*); they must turn away from "this world" and to God, undergoing a total change of heart, mind, and soul.[29]

With great singularity Jesus is evidently convinced that the kingdom of God is in certain respects already here. This is seen in conjunction with many of his "mighty works" (Matt. 12:20; Mark 6:2; Luke 19:37). (Here is a form of praxis that Jesus himself does not always seem to comprehend [cf. Mark 5:30; Luke 8:46] and about which he shows very strong reserve.) When John the Baptist is reported as asking whether Jesus is "he who is to come," the answer is given: "Go and tell John what you hear and see: the blind receive their sight and the lame walk, lepers are cleansed and the deaf hear, and the dead are raised up, and the poor have good news preached to them" (Matt. 11:2–5). Upon healing a blind and dumb demoniac, Jesus declares: "If it is by the Spirit of God that I cast out demons, then the kingdom of God has come upon you" (Matt. 12:28). And after an occasion of the cleansing of ten lepers, Luke has Jesus assert: "The Kingdom of God is, in fact, amongst you," or, in another rendering, "it is given into your hands" (Luke 17:21). Matthew summarily connects three elements—the Nazarene's work as a teacher of Judaism, his proclamation of the kingdom, and his healings: Jesus goes "about all the cities and villages, teaching in their synagogues and preaching the gospel of the kingdom, and healing every disease and every infirmity" (Matt. 9:35). Along with his attacks upon Satan and his own nature wonders, Jesus' healings are treated as at once "symbols and events in the dawning of the Kingdom of God."[30]

A full treatment of the phenomenon of Jesus' miracles is beyond our purview. But part of an interpretation by Anthony E. Harvey is relevant in the present context. Harvey contends that Jesus' cures of the deaf, the dumb, the blind, and the lame were without precedent within the Nazarene's own culture. It appears not accidental that all these maladies should be named by the prophet Isaiah as conditions to be remedied in a coming new age:

> Then the eyes of the blind shall be opened,
>   and the ears of the deaf unstopped;
> then shall the lame man leap like a hart,
>   and the tongue of the dumb sing for joy.
>   (Isa. 35:5–6)

In Matthew a connection is explicitly made: "And great crowds came to him, bringing with them the lame, the maimed, the blind, the dumb, and many others, and they put them at his feet, and he healed them, so that the throng wondered, when they saw the dumb speaking, the maimed whole, the lame walking, and the blind seeing; and they glorified the God of Israel" (Matt. 15:30–31). Harvey comments that in the jargon of New Testament scholarship, these are eschatological miracles, i.e., in God's good time such intractable and intolerable affronts to human dignity will be removed.[31]

The advent of the kingdom of God is also vividly represented through the parables of Jesus. "With what can we compare the kingdom of God, or what parable shall we use for it? It is like a grain of mustard seed, which, when sown upon the ground, is the smallest of all the seeds on earth; yet when it is sown it grows up and becomes the greatest of all shrubs, and puts forth large branches, so that the birds of the air can make nests in its shade" (Mark 4:30–32; cf. Luke 5:36–39; 13:20–21). Michael Grant ties together the parables, the praxis of miracle, and a sense of crisis and urgency that is "acute and pressing":

> It is imperative for all men and women to define their position, *both* because of what is happening now *and* because of what is going to happen shortly. The teaching of Jesus dwells on both these aspects at length. First, the present dawning: the strong man is disarmed, the forces of evil are in retreat, the physician comes to the sick, the lepers are cleansed, the great debt is wiped out, the lost sheep is brought home, the door of the father's house stands open, the poor and the beggars are summoned to the banquet, a master pays full wages to a man who does not deserve it, a great joy fills all hearts. The hour of fulfillment has come. It has come, or rather it has *begun* to come: its full realization still lies in the future, and this, too, is equally stressed in Jesus' utterances. That is the reason for all this insistence upon alertness: do not be caught asleep; be ready to render your account. The Kingdom is with us, but not all of it is with us yet. Himself on the battlefield, Jesus struck Satan down and "watched how he fell like lightning from the sky." Nevertheless, the *final* battle still remains to be fought.[32]

Grant's semi-popular *Jesus* must be used with great caution. He retains and perpetuates much of the anti-Jewishness of the Gospels and of the long Christian tradition (e.g., in his uncritical treatment of John 8:41–44). Grant is among the many who prejudicially refer to the people of Jesus as "the Jews" or as "Jewish" in the same breath with reference to Jesus himself—as though Jesus were not himself a Jew.

Lastly, one peculiarity of Jesus' teaching/praxis (as today's theology of liberation emphasizes[33]) is his concern, empathy, and intimate association with the poor, the downtrodden,* even the outcast—yet all in the context of the coming of the kingdom of God. "The prophets spoke on behalf of the honest poor, and defended the widows and the fatherless, those oppressed and exploited by the wicked, rich and powerful. Jesus went further. In addition to proclaiming these blessed, he actually took his stand among the pariahs of his world, those despised by the respectable. Sinners were his table-companions and the ostracised tax-collectors and prostitutes his friends."[34] Jesus says:

> Blessed are you poor, for yours is the kingdom of God.
> Blessed are you that hunger now, for you shall be satisfied.
> Blessed are you that weep now, for you shall laugh.
> Blessed are you when men hate you, and when they exclude you
>   and revile you, and cast out your name as evil, on account of the
>   Son of man! Rejoice in that day, and leap for joy, for behold, your
>   reward is great in heaven; for so their fathers did to the prophets.
> But woe to you that are rich, for you have received your consolation.
> Woe to you that are full now, for you shall hunger.
> Woe to you that laugh now, for you shall mourn and weep.
> Woe to you, when all men speak well of you, for so their fathers did to
>   the false prophets. (Luke 6:20–26)

In a word, everything is about to be turned upside down.

Yet, the "cataclysmic eruption of God into history"[35] never takes place. There is a battle all right, but few are they who attend it.

We are caught up in a crisis of apprehension. Here is a historical paradox that taxes belief. On the one hand, when it comes to the imminent arrival of the kingdom of God, the Jesus of the authentic New Testament record is so aggressive, so intolerant, so assured, even oracular. On the other hand, when it comes to his own place (as potential Messiah) in God's future, he is so nonbelligerent, so reticent, so diffident, even psychically withdrawn. How are we to reckon with this incongruity?

IV

In seeking to confront the enigma of Jesus' aggressiveness/reticence, we must try to give voice to the intended/unintended silences of the biblical documents (not to mention the distortions and the authentic materials therein), since, as will be made evident, much of the actual story is hidden inside those silences.

---

*Jesus here carries forward the Pharisee championing of the oppressed.

Part of our problem is that according to the record, Jesus speaks so little about himself. However, there are at least two even greater stumbling blocks. First, the New Testament minimizes implicitly and explicitly the truth that the Eretz Yisrael of the time was a country under foreign occupation. The inhabitants were suffering under the tyranny of Rome, which in fact they greatly resisted. Second, the Gospels were written a full generation and more after Jesus' death, and were inspired with and motivated by apologetic and missionary designs toward the people and leaders of the Roman Empire. In consequence, the ongoing conflict between the Romans and the people of Jesus is underplayed, while contentions between the church and the Jewish community as a whole are overplayed and often simply fabricated. Most seriously, the actual events of Jesus' last days are altered. With their vested interest in fostering good relations with Rome, the New Testament evangelists seek to establish the Jewish "rejection" of Jesus and to set "the Jews" and their leaders against Jesus. The Gospel writers *intend* to blame "the Jews."[36] Any substantive historicity behind the New Testament effort to shift Roman culpability to "the Jews" is discredited by modern scholarship.[37]

Let us introduce a negative finding of Geza Vermes: "There is little evidence in the Gospels of a kingdom of God to be established by force. There was no plan for Jesus to reconquer Jerusalem, or any indication that he intended to challenge the power even of Herod, let alone that of the emperor of Rome." This finding responsibly summarizes the record, phenomenologically speaking. Yet it also epitomizes our problem. The Synoptic tradition is ambiguous on Jesus' attitude to the use of force; his recorded sayings and deeds appear to condone both "pacifism" and "nonpacifism."[38] We do not get very far when we pursue the question of whether the focus of Jesus is upon human violence or human nonviolence. For his primary obsession is with God's active intervention in history. The finding of Vermes is more a description of what was to be the written (= literary) fate of Jesus' story than it is of his history *qua* history. For the relentless question does not let us go: How is it that Jesus of Nazareth comes to meet his death? At the same time we can freely accept the "strict definition of 'Messiah' as a valorous, holy, just and mighty Davidic king of the end of time."[39]

Now perhaps it is the moment to offer a hypothesis: For Jesus, during the months or days when in his own spiritual solitude he is striving to meet the demands of his calling, "kingdom of God" comes to converge upon "King Messiah" and "King Messiah" comes to converge upon "kingdom of God." (In the nature of the historical case, hypotheses concerning the intention of Jesus, as of any figure of the past, are the farthest that we can reach. A given historical hypothesis is to be understood as one way, among other contending ways, of endeavoring to account for certain events that have transpired. When a particular hypothesis appears capable of explaining a gestalt of events, it becomes worthy of application or attention. Very often, several creditable hypotheses will vie with one another and perhaps even manage to live side by side, in relative peace.) In order to develop my own hypothesis, I advance two considerations.

(1) The hypothesis finds especial support in Mark, which still seems to be the earliest Gospel. The point is that in the very face of all his self-doubts, Jesus does come at last to marshall enough assertiveness to marry the initiating of God's kingdom to his own self-acceptance of the Messianic challenge as interpreted by him. This serves to explain why, as the end approaches, the prophet from Nazareth refuses to deny the allegation of Messiahship (Mark 15:2–5; Matt. 27:11–14; Luke 23:3). And it is strictly in his identification as King of the Jews that Jesus will die. He "asks for it." Every one of the Synoptic Gospels testifies to this truth of history (Mark 15:26; Matt. 27:37; Luke 23:38). Even the writer of the Fourth Gospel does not quite have the spiritualizing audacity to omit or falsify the facts (John 19:19). It is unthinkable to presume that Jesus never has to confront in life-and-death terms the question of his own relation to the Messianic office, just as it is out of the question to assume that the kingly role is foisted upon him as some kind of dupe. There must be some explanation of why Jesus does not flee from his Roman persecutors, as he doubtless could have done were he not counting upon divine intervention. At the same time we have to remember the definitive tradition that as long as the people of God remain under oppression, there is no Messianic fulfillment.

All Jesus' certainties (about the kingdom) will be contradicted by events— see below, under (2)—yet all his uncertainties (about the Messiahship) will have two futures that are opposite to each other: the wholly justified nonacceptance by most of his own people of the Messianic claim he finally manages to make, or at least to act out; and the objectively questionable, but historically momentous, revisionist acceptance of that claim by the nascent Christian community. The church will pay a heavy price for the acquisition of its Lord. That price is the radical transmuting of the Messiahship into a thoroughly spiritualized reality. Irony of ironies, the Messiah will be changed into a strictly "religious" figure and indeed into a subject for "religion" to exploit.

The only way that Jesus can become "Messiah" to the church is through not being the expected Messiah of Israel, which means through the unhappy nonrealization of God's kingdom. No kingdom, no Messiah; no Messiah, no kingdom. So, astonishingly, the residual reticence of Jesus as King Messiah is to be granted a measure of exculpation in and through the very non-arrival of the kingdom. The ultimate paradox is that the really unacceptable combination would have been, not Jesus' certainty of the kingdom and his uncertainty as King Messiah, but rather his certainty of the kingdom and his (potential) self-assurance as Messiah. Had the latter combination proved to be the real one, the factual nonrealization of the kingdom would have shown Jesus to be not merely a failed Messiah but also a false one—in everyone's eyes. His diffidence toward the Messianic office goes some way to excuse, so to speak, his pretension respecting the kingdom. But even the latter pretension is heavily qualified by his constant directing of hearts and minds away from himself to fix upon the acts of God.

(2) We nevertheless have to live with the truth that the entire foundation-hope of Jesus proves to be a grand illusion. Correspondingly, the Galilean healer-prophet—this *hasid* whom some called "lord," "Messiah," and even "*son of God*"—is to be eliminated. The failure is his all right, yet, for him, it is God's as well.

To concretize the shared failure of son and Father we must finish out, if briefly, the drama of Jesus' life and death. The temporal end of the Nazarene is not here pursued in the interests of technical historical study but for the purpose of apprehending the quality of his mission/praxis as a potential normative image within Christian moral philosophy. However, in our context the all-determining question respecting Jesus is not what his theological destiny was to be in the eyes and heart of the church, but rather, What is the recoverable truth of his history?

The crucial factor here is at the same time a most rudimentary one: Jesus is other than just one more apocalypticist. For example, although he and Paul equally err in their imminent-eschatological expectations, all the evidence makes Jesus' mistake infinitely more egregious because, in contrast to Paul, he somehow comes to presume, however haltingly, an isochronism between his own person-history and the about-to-be realized eschatology of the kingdom. This state of affairs may be elucidated in two steps, the one philological-historical and the other "political"-historical.

(a) What may we contribute to veracity of language respecting the relation between Jesus' person and the hoped-for intervention of God? A finally perfect balance is obviously impossible to attain.

Michael Grant overweights the scales on the one side. He has Jesus soliciting "*faith in himself*" as the one who is "introducing the divine Kingdom upon earth." Again, says Grant, Jesus believes "that the actual inauguration of God's Kingdom *had been placed in his own hands*." It is "*by his agency*" that the kingdom has "already started happening."[40] But this is substantially to exaggerate the true place of Jesus' person in the coming of the *eschaton—from Jesus' own point of view*. For he is not some *agent provocateur*, or even a *Cristo liberador*, however much his proclamation of an imminent kingdom of God is "indissolubly bound up with the liberation of Israel."[41] The point is that Jesus would never solicit "faith in himself" but only faith in his heavenly Father, the sole instigator of the kingdom and sole liberator of his people. "Fear not, little flock, for it is your Father's good pleasure to give you the kingdom" (Luke 12:32). Would-be members of the kingdom are to pray only to God— "Thy kingdom come"—as in all urgency they ready themselves for the Day: "Let your loins be girded and your lamps burning" (Luke 12:35). The Father alone establishes his own righteousness in the world.

Yet just here we must note how tempting it is to overweight the scales on the other side, thus annulling the uniqueness of Jesus' historical vocation. True, the action that takes place in and between the lines of the Synoptic Gospels extends to the very human predicament of Jesus as he sweats out what he is to do next. However, his behavior is just the kind we should expect from a person who is being specially used of God. To reduce Jesus to one among many representatives or spokespersons of God's reign is to understate the actual relationship. For among unnumbered sons of God this one is singularly chosen (or, humanly put, comes to believe himself chosen), if not to inaugurate the kingdom, then to proclaim that it is coming, to risk everything because of God's promise, and to stake his life upon the kingdom, yet never apart from a hoped-for interposition of the revivified political integrity of his people. This existential condition, the inner aspect of objective-historical truth, takes us into the "political"-historical dimension. But first, we must ask, What philological conclusion is suggested by the above weighing upon the scales?

Among the titles of Jesus, we have noted that *son of God* may reflect the Nazarene's special filial consciousness. Certainly he thinks of himself as *son of God*. Yet this son is distinguished from other sons. (I continue to speak historically.) At several places in the New Testament it is said that a heavenly voice called Jesus "my beloved Son" (Mark 1:11; 9:7; Matt. 3:17; 17:5; Luke 3:22; II Pet. 1:17). Until his final disillusionment—Jesus, upon the cross, no longer calls God "Father" but E*loi*, "my God" (Mark 15:34)—he had probably come to some such self-understanding in relation to God. Evidently he had come to see himself as the decisive *human occasion* of the expected reign of God, the special instrument through whom God is to act eschatologically. Yet since "Jesus turned out to be wrong"[42] and the kingdom never materialized, we are obliged to modify his self-understanding as "beloved" of God; otherwise there is a lack of historical explanation and completeness. Jesus is thwarted in his role as "beloved Son." In other language he is (to be more conclusive concerning an earlier point) a failed Messiah—not a false Messiah (for he never once betrays the Messianic imperative) but a terribly mistaken Messiah.

(b) As in the province of philology, so too the "political"-historical question may be addressed by calling attention to extreme positions. The reason for attaching inverted commas (pardon the Anglophilic minute) to the word "political" is to caution us that any historical exposition of New Testament times must treat first-century political life as the generalized though still amorphous reality it is, and not according to the compartmentalized, sophisticated, and restricted meaning of modern times, by virtue of which the political domain is separated off from economic, religious, social, etc. life. Rightly projected back to the days of Jesus, the political category is to be construed as more or less synonymous with the comprehensive category of collective life and fate. Any modern understanding of the kingdom of God

that sets out a sharp dichotomy between worldly-political-military-material-
ist affairs and otherworldly-nonpolitical-pacifist-spiritual realities would
have been impossible in first-century Palestine. The kingdom of God involves God's reign over all of life. The difficulty of the historian's task is compounded by the proclivity of the Gospels to depoliticize the life of Jesus.[43]
An inability to recognize the presence of depoliticization may help account
for Martin Hengel's failure to comprehend the causes of Jesus' death at the
hands of the Romans. Hengel, following Bultmann, seeks to explain Jesus'
execution as due to the fact that his activity was *misunderstood* "as something
political."[44] "The kingdom of God is a social order and not a hidden one."[45]
But were it interjected that we ought therefore substitute "social" as the
proper concept, the correct response would be that such a replacement for
"political" inadvertently gives the nod to a religious ideology that wrongly
seeks to subtract and thereby obliterate the interests of political power and
liberation from the mission/praxis of Jesus.

Theoretically speaking, two extremes of interpretation offer themselves.
They are alike reductionist. In the one view, Jesus becomes in effect a purely
soldierly figure, a first-century Ché Guevara, a guerrilla fighter, a revolutionary soldier of (his own) fortune, dreaming that he and a potential army that
is supposedly gathering somewhere will alone and of their own resources
dispatch the Roman oppressor and restore justice and freedom "to the people."

Any such "secularistic" argumentation as this is cut off by Jesus' unremitting, eschatological theocentrism. It is out of the question to remove the divinely apocalyptic element from his struggle, with particular reference to his
struggle against Rome. An interesting rhetorical query is attributed to Jesus,
who, upon reportedly being captured by certain opponents, says to a member of his entourage who has just been putting his sword to use: "Do you
think that I cannot appeal to my Father, and he will at once send me more
than twelve legions of angels?" (Matt. 26:53). Such an act would entail more
than purely human power; divine aid is presupposed.

An alternative form of reductionism has been put forth repeatedly within
empirical Christian history. Jesus is made over into a purely "religious"
leader, a wholly nonpolitical character. On this assumption, he simply has no
interest, one way or the other, in the Roman overlordship and the "worldly"
fortunes/misfortunes of his people. His "kingship is not of this world" (John
18:36).

As is the case with "secularistic" reductionism, the authentic New Testament passages and the available historical data combine to refute this second point of view. To transubstantiate Jesus' struggle into something
labeled "pure spirituality" is to betray that struggle. Above all, any such "religious" hypothesis is ruled out by Jesus himself as coming pretender to the
throne of David and as one who came to read the advent of the kingdom of
God through apocalyptic spectacles (thus negating preveniently the idea of

John Riches that the Nazarene must have deleted the "militaristic" associations of the kingdom[46]).

The pathway of Jesus' actual "political" destiny winds between the two types of reductionism. The label "reductionism" itself conveys to us that neither of those views is totally wrong. To say that Jesus is *only* such-and-such goes too far, while to adjudge that he is this and also something more points the way to the truth. Jesus cannot be just a soldierly figure, not because he is not one at all, but instead because his entire commitment is to the realization of the kingdom of God, which is greater than, and is the transformation of, every earthly kingdom. In the same way, he cannot be just a religious figure, not because he is not one at all, but instead because of his magnificent obsession with the coming of the kingdom of God *upon earth*, which means anything but a purely "heavenly" or "spiritual" reality. When we either politicize Jesus or religionize him, we give offense to him. That he is dedicated to a divine kingdom means that he is not a "politician" in today's narrow rendering of that term. Yet in the last resort Jesus *is* a politician, or he ultimately becomes one, that is to say, he is a man who concerns himself with and then gives his life for the total welfare and power of his people, the people he loves. Jesus' counsel "Render to Caesar the things that are Caesar's and to God the things that are God's" (Mark 12:17; cf. Luke 20:25) is interpreted by S.G.F. Brandon to mean, "Let Caesar go back to Rome where he belongs, and leave God's land to the people of God."[47] On this interpretation Jesus forbids the payment of tribute to Rome (as Luke 23:2 bears out). Theologically-politically expressed, in Jesus the righteousness of God unfolds in and through future structures of power.

> The only way to make the career of Jesus comprehensible is to see its organic linkage to the simmering mutiny that gripped Palestine for generations. Jesus' occupation of the Temple, his turning over of the money-changers' tables, his "preaching" in the Temple for days, the charge of King of the Jews, his execution by means of the Roman sentence of crucifixion, reserved for the vilest criminals and for political insurrectionists, were all part and parcel of a political upheaval against the Romans that while insignificant, apparently, compared with the later explosions in 66 and 132, was important enough to make its mark.

That mark was—Christianity, a faith that was to benefit incalculably by the Roman defeat of the Jews in 70 C.E.[48]

For any historical analyst, a measure of "reading between the lines" of the Gospels is unavoidable. And yet, the burden of disproof appears to lie with the skeptic, who has to account for two inseparable and stern historical facts: Jesus' eventual death in the office of "King of the Jews," and the Nazarene's tireless insistence that God's divine/kingly power is about to become regnant.

Jesus was apparently not a member of the Zealots,[49] and it is probably misleading to speak of him in that fashion (even if perhaps half his twelve disciples came from that element). "The Zealots were the militant activist wing of the Pharisee party, sharing all religious viewpoints with their fellow-Pharisees and differing from the majority . . . only on the question of the timing of active resistance against the Romans. . . . [From] first to last, the Resistance against Rome came from the Pharisee party." However, despite their yearning for freedom from Rome, the Zealots had given up belief in the Messiah. As matters were to turn out, this clearly separated Jesus from the Zealots (rather than the issue of rebellion against Rome). Jesus evidently came to take into his own personal calling the conviction, held also by the Zealots, that God would go to his people's aid against the foreign occupier. (Thus, ostensibly superior Roman military strength would not be deemed an obstacle to Jewish success.) At the same time the Zealots did not believe that God would help his people were they simply to await deliverance passively.[50] The truly significant consideration, from the viewpoint of the history of Jesus, is that his apocalypticism and his latter-day Messianic commitment correspond closely to the two elements just mentioned: the required action of God, and the required action of human beings.

John Townsend reminds us of how the oldest extant Christian literature (Paul's letters) sustains the finding that Jesus is disposed of by the Romans as a political rebel. Having proclaimed himself King of the Jews—Townsend continues—Jesus has been seeking to free his people from the foreign occupier of Eretz Yisrael. Further, the picture in the Gospels matches closely what we learn from Paul.[51] Somewhere along the way, Jesus has apparently convinced himself that in the world after the Fall the only answer to the collective suffering of the people of God, a suffering made inexorable by powerlessness, is the weight and authority of historical/physical power. Jesus has evidently become persuaded that the idolatrous principalities and powers of this world must be fought, not just with the sword of the spirit (whatever that may mean; cf. Zech. 4:6), but with real swords, in the hope of corresponding intrusion "by the hand of God."[52]

Accordingly, we may enter as a most salient judgment that Jesus was giving himself to the historicization of the eschatological hope of the liberation of the people of God from the yoke of the nations. And so he effectively identifies himself "with his people's cause against the government of heathen," yet strictly from the standpoint of "an uncompromising emphasis upon the sovereignty of Yahweh." If Jesus is "King of the Jews," it is the Father, and the Father alone, who must bring the kingdom to earth. But the very affirmation of King Messiah is in itself a revolutionary act. It means that the occupation of Israel by a foreign power is, in principle, brought to its end. In this affirmation, as in his apocalypticism, Jesus stands in the line of the sectaries of Qumran—and of the Pharisees as a whole—both of which groups envision a final real-life battle with the Romans, leading to the latter's defeat and the establishing of the divine kingdom on earth.[53] But Jesus is a thoroughgoing presentist. The time for action is now. He is to do his part through the claim (as "beloved Son" of God) to the throne of David. And God is to do his part (as Jesus believes, or fervently hopes) through the judging yet grace-full descent of his reign. Has not the Father made the promises of his coming clear? Demons have already been cast out, and children of God have been healed of their maladies.

The drama moves along relentlessly. All roads lead to Rome: The Galilean *hasid*, "beloved Son" of God in the establishing of the kingdom, and apocalypticist now fully become an activist figure, is to be found guilty as a seditionary[54]—and guilty he is. (According to the uninterpreted Gospel explanation, Jesus is of course innocent of sedition and is executed as the result of a trumped-up charge brought by Jewish leaders. This is not to say that the New Testament materials do not support our own historical accounting. They do, once they are subjected to careful historical analysis.) There is no reconciliation between the absolute claims of the City of God and the idolatrous claims of the city of Man. It will be recalled that when, according to Mark, Jesus is asked which commandment is "the first of all," he responds with the great anti-polytheist S*h'ma* of Judaism, "Hear, O Israel: The Lord our God, the Lord is one; and you shall love the Lord your God with all your heart, and with all your soul, and with all your mind, and with all your strength" (Mark 12:29–30). As Jesus draws near to Jerusalem, the "multitude of the disciples" cries out, "Blessed is the King who comes in the name of the Lord! Peace in heaven and glory to the highest!" (Luke 19:37–38). Down almost to the very end, the Nazarene assures his friends (at the "Last Supper"), "I shall not drink again of the fruit of the vine until that day when I drink it new in the kingdom of God" (Mark 14:25). According to Luke, after the "Last Supper" Jesus issues an order to his disciples to make sure they are armed before going to Gethsemane (22:36). Mark may well have "deemed it politic" to suppress this event. (Why do so many studies of Jesus pass over in silence this revealing passage?) All four Gospels record that in Gethsemane, the arrest of Jesus is met by armed resistance (Mark 14:47; Matt. 26:51; Luke 22:38, 49–50; John 18:10–11).[55] The fateful charges that are entered against the Nazarene are preserved by Luke: "We found this man perverting our nation, and forbidding us to give tribute to Caesar, and saying that he himself is Christ a king" (Luke 23:2). The facts involved, allowing for Gospel distortions respecting culpability for Jesus' death, are stipulated as follows: "Every item in this indictment was true. Jesus *was* 'perverting the nation,' in the sense of turning them away from allegiance to Rome. He *was* 'forbidding to give tribute to Caesar.' He *was* saying that he himself was 'Christ, a King.' The charge was subversion and rebellion, not blasphemy."[56]

Michael Grant's conclusion that Jesus' claim of a special relationship to the divine power would be received by his (reputed) opponents as seeming "to them to infringe blasphemously upon the monotheism which was essential

to the Jewish faith" is not justified.[57] According to Jewish law, only the unau-
thorized uttering of the holy name Yahweh constituted blasphemy. Any
claim to be Messiah, for example, had nothing to do with blasphemy,[58] and
the same would extend to a possible assertion of being God's "beloved
Son."

The Roman penalty in the capital crime of high treason is of course death
by crucifixion. At Golgotha the taunt resounds, "Let the Christ, the King of
Israel, come down from the cross, that we may see and believe" (Mark 15:32;
cf. Luke 23:37). Upon the cross, the Davidic pretender demands to know why
his Father has abandoned him (Mark 15:34; Matt. 27:46). No answer is given,
and none shall be given. If Jesus is not a Zealot, the point so often missed is
that, for him, God *is* (*kiveyakhol*). Yet his Father betrays him.

Whether Jesus will be "saved" via the Resurrection is left for our subsequent attention. It may be sufficient at this juncture to point out that Paul
never identifies Jesus as Messiah during the latter's earthly life. Paul (and
the disciples) evidently became convinced that Jesus is (the) Christ only by
virtue of the Resurrection.

In the very hour when the heavenly legions are supposed to strike, they
prove to have gone off on leave. No avenging hosts of heaven join the fray,
no warrior angels come to the rescue. Unlike his patriarch Moses, Jesus does
not save his people. Instead, he dies "a martyr's death for Israel."[59] The Crucifixion represents, i.e., re-presents, the final weakness of man—but also of
God.[60] Later on, two of the apostles, traveling to Emmaus, will confide to the
resurrected Jesus (whom they do not recognize): "We had been hoping that
he was the man to liberate Israel" (Luke 24:21, NEB). And just before the
Ascension, as previously noted, a larger company will ask the risen Jesus:
"Lord, will you at this time restore the kingdom to Israel?" (Acts 1:6). The
normative Messianic hope continues on, unabated.

We are given three alternatives. First, there is the view of Joseph Klausner:
"Jesus came and thrust aside all the requirements of [Jewish] national life."[61]
This is not correct. Second, Jesus fulfilled the requirements of Jewish national life. This has no basis in fact, but not because he did not try. Third,
Jesus did his best to satisfy the God-wished requirements of his people's
collective and personal life. Yet he did not make it: The Romans destroyed
him.

The integrity of a historicist perspective on the New Testament is fostered
by the full acceptance of Jesus' failure for what it was: a failure. It is highly
significant that John H. Yoder's attempt to make Jesus into a political pacifist
also tries to turn him into a success—this, from (allegedly) the very standpoint of Jesus' clear intention. The Nazarene's "failure," so Yoder puts it, was
purely apparent. But the price for a conclusion such as Yoder's is an exorbi-
tant one indeed: it is nothing less than the abandonment of history. Quixoti-
cally, Yoder is quite ready to accede to a revolutionary consequence:
Today's followers of Jesus are to accept impotence and give up all claims to

"govern history." "God's will for God's man in this world is that he should renounce *legitimate* defense." The use of violence is absolutely forbidden to the Christian; he is called to follow "Jesus' way" of the cross. Naturally, Yoder has Jesus refusing "to be king or to defend himself"—"not that there was anything wrong with kingship or self-defense; *he just could not have met his destined cross that way.*"[62]

Several lessons may be drawn from Yoder's incongruous dialectic of Jesus' failure/"success." (a) We are forcibly reminded of how a seeming commitment to historical activism and responsibility may sometimes end up in an anti-historical position. This is exemplified in the infiltration and subversion of the Christian witness by the ideology of nonviolence. (b) Even a failed endeavor to fight the oppression of one's people is better, from the perspective of moral responsibility, than a successful endeavor to accede to that oppression in an impotent way. Jesus' reputed success, à la Yoder, means in truth the historical abandonment of the people of Israel. Jesus' actual failure at least opposes such a betrayal. (c) A failed effort to have a voice in the directing of history is better, morally speaking, than a successful effort to abandon history. As ever, the moral question is that of whether responsibility is going to be taken for today and tomorrow. (d) Only a nonspiritualizing recognition that Jesus' life-work was a failure can retain the historical truth (and thereby the theological truth) about him and his mission. This was no success story: "God sacrifices his Son."[63]

Who, then, is being more faithful to the Lord of history, the fabricator of Jesus' "success" or the witness to his abject failure?

V

In what way or ways, if any, does Jesus' mission serve to unfold the divine righteousness? Does the teaching of the kingdom of God negate the quiddity of the people of God or does it somehow prove able to sustain it? Is the reign of God essentially discontinuous or essentially continuous with the historical being of Israel? Does the event of Jesus yield a genuinely normative image for utilization in theological ethics and thereby in everyday affairs? Can Jesus' message/praxis contribute to the moral life, the life of responsible decison-making—despite the non-actualization of the kingdom? Two types of response are suggested to these questions, a largely negative type and a positive one.

(1) Jesus participates in all the naïveté of his forbears: God is held to intervene within human history in ways not unlike that of lightning striking the earth.

Let us recall the prophetic tradition respecting entanglements of the people of God with other nations. Certain of the prophets assumed an artless stance of opposing alliances with the nations on the ground that in God, Israel already has its strong support, "a very present help in trouble" (Ps.

46:1b). Who needs the Egyptians, the Assyrians, or the Babylonians? Jesus is an inheritor of this tradition. He would probably agree with Isaiah and Ezra that the chosen of God are well-advised to stay away from capricious (and idolatrous) human friends. While it does not have to follow that Jesus would totally exclude the prudence of an armed entourage of his own,[64] yet the working principle evidently remains that the Lord and his hosts comprise Israel's all-sufficient allies, the only allies the people of God ultimately require. Herein lay a companion-illusion to Jesus' grand illusion that God was about to overturn the world and institute his kingdom. We have a case, in short, of a tacit rendering of God the Father as *deus ex machina* (a recurrent temptation for any historicist faith).

From within these illusions Jesus is yet able to convey a partial truth. (He is not the first prophet to be called to the well-nigh impossible task of relating the absolutes of God to the relativities of time.) Implicitly, Jesus is declaring that human oppression cannot be vanquished by "deeds of loving kindness"; oppression is destroyed only by power from beyond: power that is made historical/physical. Jesus must surely have known that in the fulfillment of his calling, he would require massive aid from the Father himself. The Roman legions would not suddenly be made impotent by exposure to the charms of pacifism. In this respect, Jesus was not naïve. Somehow or other, he was glimpsing the hard truth that prophetic "religiousness" cannot suffice as a foundation of political praxis. The apolitical spiritualism of an Isaiah or a Jeremiah will not do. Activism is the order of the time. Faith in the advent of God's power is to be joined by human deeds.

Jesus' error remains twofold: a misapprehension of the ways in which God must operate within the restraints of a natural and human world; and prematurity of persuasion. The original tragedy of Jesus persists. It is made inevitable by a particularly obdurate collaborationism with God. For, as has been intimated, in his finally assumed place as King Messiah, Jesus sees his own presence as constituent to the arrival of the kingdom. And as special witness to the kingdom's advent, the son is convinced that the Father will intervene in support of the son's action against Rome. Yet neither collaborator carries through (can carry through?) his side of the ostensible covenant. What the seeming conspiracy ends up with is nothing other than a cross outlined against the lowering sky.

As stated, the present response to the questions found at the start of this section is largely a negative one. To sum up, the abortive eschatology of Jesus may itself be brought to terms by means of a negativistic eschatological judgment: If in fact the Egyptians or the Ethiopians are untrustworthy allies to the ends of Israel's historical deliverance and freedom, must not the same be said of God himself? In other words, there is just no way to manipulate or hasten the epiphany of the divine righteousness, not even by virtue of visible acts performed by the "beloved Son." The irony is that Jesus seems otherwise to have been cognizant of this truth: "The kingdom of God is not coming with signs to be observed; nor will they say, 'Lo, here it is!' or 'There!' for behold, the kingdom of God is [suddenly] in the midst of you" (Luke 17:20b–21). "Of that day or that hour no one knows, not even the angels in heaven, nor the Son, but only the Father" (Mark 13:22). The time of the kingdom's coming is God's secret.[65] The divine righteousness retains its sovereignty.

A troublous consequence of all this is the persisting demoralization of historical hope. However, in Jesus a second alternative is offered.

(2) A more positive and felicitous response may be developed to the questions listed at the beginning of this section, a response that looks to the discontinuities and continuities that are adduceable among Jesus, Paul, and (to a lesser extent) the Essenes.

Is anything recoverable, despite the non-arrival of the *eschaton*? I think that the responsible, perhaps even obvious way to reckon with this issue is to inquire whether there are aspects of Jesus' message that are not crushed by, but that persist in some way independent of, his unrealized apocalyptic. Indeed, is it not possible that this very failure may throw into commanding relief a genre of proclamation/praxis that does not fail?

The most striking paradox within Jesus' message/behavior as a whole is that his imminent apocalypticism is never able to crowd out, but may even be said to rest upon, the kerygmatic observance and celebration of an omnipresent, authoritative Torah. I suggest that the latter element goes far to save his message/praxis from futility.

We have alluded to the conviction within some Jewish messianism that with the advent of the Messiah, the authority of the Law comes to an end. As Paul writes, "Christ is the end of the Law" (Rom. 10:4). If, as Richard L. Rubenstein has it, Paul makes Christ the goal toward which the Law points and also the one who abolishes its binding authority,[66] none of this can be said of Jesus' own message. Thus, the radical conflict with the faith of the fathers that marks the one side of Paul is quite unknown to Jesus. (But the conflict between the faith of Jesus and the faith of Paul, a condition that yesterday's scholarship tried to obliterate, is undeniably present.)

Jesus does not separate himself from the normative Judaism of his time or from his people at large. At these points he is distinguished from the Essenes.[67] Yet with the men of Qumran, and in a measure of contrast to Pauline indecisiveness, the Nazarene fully honors the Torah of God.[68] He carries on the tradition of the Pharisees, the creative, self-critical heirs of the Law and disciples of the prophets.[69] "All the arguments placed in Jesus' mouth in his supposed conflicts with the Pharisees are themselves Pharisee."[70] "The scribes and the Pharisees sit on Moses' seat; so practice and observe whatever they tell you ..." (Matt. 23:2). In contrast to the thesis of John Riches, Jesus does not transform Judaism. That does not seem to have been his intention. Jesus appears to be much more concerned to help human beings and to proclaim and obey the will of God than with anything else, including saying something new. Riches argues that Jesus shows a "radical response to the situation of Judaism in first-century Galilee" through a distinctive stress on God's love and forgiveness.[71] That Jesus emphasizes these things is beyond question. But the deciding consideration is that the divine love and mercy are already constituent to the biblical faith Jesus has inherited (as we have seen). Ezekiel's word from God serves as a reminder: "Have I any pleasure in the death of the wicked, says the Lord God, and not rather that he should turn from his way and live?" (18:23). Riches is so committed to distinguishing Jesus from the Judaism of his day[72] that he fails to understand how Jesus' concentration upon the love of God and neighbor, and upon God as Creator and Father, carries forward and revivifies the teachings of the Torah and the prophets and is thus integral to a Judaism that was already there (and was being perpetuated and developed by the Pharisees contemporary to Jesus).[73] Thus does the fundamental thesis of Riches dissipate itself.

Is all this to call into question the singularity or originality of Jesus' contribution? Not at all. What Jesus does that is entirely unique is to gather up the major strands of the Jewish tradition (Torahist, prophetic, wisdom, apocalyptic, Messianic) and finally to fuse these perceptions distinctively into the *kairos* of his own vocation and *kerygma*.[74]

Correspondingly, Jesus insists (as Matthew records him): "Think not that I have come to abolish the law and the prophets; I have come not to abolish them but to fulfill [*plērōsai*, to complete] them. For truly, I say to you, till heaven and earth pass away, not an iota, not a dot, will pass from the law until all is accomplished" (Matt. 5:17–18). A. E. Harvey suggests that "to fulfill" here means to reveal the true meaning of the Law by giving "a personal demonstration of how that meaning might be carried out in daily living."[75] Torah-cum-Prophecy is in one sense the *Interimsethik* of Jesus. But it is much more than that. For there is an unqualified connection between the observance of Torah and the judging praxis of the kingdom of God: "Whoever then relaxes one of the least of these commandments and teaches men so, shall be called least in the kingdom of heaven; but he who does them and teaches them shall be called great in the kingdom of heaven" (Matt. 5:19). For Jesus, Torah is not only normative in the pre-kingdom dispensation; its normativeness reaches into the very domain of the kingdom. Since today's honoring of Torah is determinative for life in the kingdom, the present is, in effect, treated as though the future were already here while the future is treated as though it were present. Thus is there continuity between Jesus and that major strand within Judaism which does not sanction any hiatus between the Law and the Messianic age.[76]

When it comes to the Law, Paul is a Christian (of a sort) while Jesus is a Jew (though hardly of a sort). Any proposal that Jews "could not be saved apart from faith in Christ," or, for that matter, that Gentiles *are* saved in this way, would probably be met by Jesus with puzzlement or laughter or simple denial. From the standpoint of the ever-impinging kingdom of God, as from the perspective of needed moral norms, any Christian abandonment of the Law is wrong while Jesus' retention of the Torah is right. Since, unlike Paul, Jesus does not have to contend against the Law, he can, morally-historically speaking, help foster, and unqualifiedly so, the abiding validity of the Torah within human affairs, not alone in a judgmental–normative sense but also in an applicational one.

In keeping with the heritage of Jewish apocalypticism, and like the Qumran sectaries before him and Paul after him, Jesus' point of view is of course conditioned everywhere by his eschatology. But he knows too, with his forefather David, that the Torah is "sweeter than honey" (cf. Ps. 19:7–10). Nowhere does Jesus doubt the integrity-absoluteness of the divine will. We have taken note of the uncompromising demand that his disciples be perfect as God is perfect, that they seek first the kingdom of God and his righteousness. And we have alluded to the story attributed to Jesus of the fearsome terms of the Last Judgment. Yet the prophet of Nazareth does not stop with the judging character of God's righteousness. (We have seen that earlier prophets do not stop there either.)

> Your Father . . . makes his sun rise on the evil and on the good, and sends rain on the just and on the unjust. (Matt. 5:45)

> Do not be anxious about your life, what you shall eat or what you shall drink, nor about your body, what you shall put on. . . . Look at the birds of the air: they neither sow nor reap nor gather into barns, and yet your heavenly Father feeds them. Are you not of more value than they? . . . And why are you anxious about clothing? Consider the lilies of the field, how they grow; they neither toil nor spin; yet I tell you, even Solomon in all his glory was not arrayed like one of these. But if God so clothes the grass of the field, which today is alive and tomorrow is thrown into the oven, will he not much more clothe you, O men of little faith? (Matt. 6:25–26, 28–30)

God's business is much more diversified than the transactions of judgment; indeed, his first responsibility is to look after his creation, in an accepting and loving way. His "mercy is not simply to the Sons of Light, but to the fallen, to the sick, the sinners. Indeed Jesus seems explicitly to deny that God sets . . . boundaries to his mercy. It may be impossible for a rich man to enter the Kingdom of Heaven, but with God all things are possible!"[77] With the men of Qumran, Jesus embodies an utter dependence upon God's grace and compassion. Indeed, it is in the very midst of his final agony that, according to Luke, the *hasid* from the Galilee asks divine forgiveness upon those who are destroying him: "Father, forgive them; for they know not what they do" (Luke 23:34).

Furthermore, the fact that Jesus' entire worldview is isochronically out of joint says nothing against the coming of the reign of God within five minutes/ five years/five hundred years/five thousand years from now. One day the divine righteousness will be triumphant, upon earth. The kingdom of God will be marked by the historicalness of a transformed world. In this transcendent respect, the Nazarene's miscalculations are something of a mere momentary lapse. The weight of his sayings about the future "does not lie on the time-factor so much as on the God-factor."[78]

For Jesus, as previously noted, the purpose of doing Torah in the interim before the *eschaton* is to prepare for membership in the kingdom of God (cf. Matt. 7:21). Once the kingdom comes to be realized, this teleological disposition may be permitted to fade away, and we shall be as "angels in heaven" (Mark 12:25)—or perhaps like God herself. For it is sometimes told that one way God occupies her time, now that the task of creation is more or less out of the way, is in the study of Torah (that is, when she is not helping to arrange marriages). Presumably, she too operates without ulterior motives.

VI

Finally, there is the issue of socio-political status quo-ism and its antithesis, within the eschatological outlooks of Jesus and Paul. We have made reference to the convergence in Paul of apocalyptic radicalism and implicit social conservatism. However, we noted as well that the apostle never quite shows his back to the demands of the Law. He is convinced of the presence within daily life of God's judging righteousness and its requirement that love and goodness be exalted. Paul is never an antinomian. Thus far he and Jesus walk together. They alike exalt the high ethic of Torah-cum-Prophecy. Yet between them there is also a strong note of discontinuity. Jesus' apocalypticism does not end in the kind of nonchalance toward the social order that characterizes Paul. (The apostle had, after all, experienced the risen Christ, a fact that defined all his thinking and praxis. The viewpoint of the Nazarene is, by contrast, pre-Messianic.) If Paul's apocalyptic expectations ally him with the socio-political status quo, Jesus' eschatological hopes do the opposite. They make him infinitely less accepting of things as they are. The very power of the kingdom as imminent overturns the status quo and sustains a radical ethic (beyond the day-to-day demands of Torah):

> And behold, one came up to [Jesus], saying, "Teacher, what good deed must I do, to have eternal life?" And he said to him, ". . . If you would enter life, keep the commandments." He said to him, "Which?" And Jesus said, "You shall not kill, You shall not commit adultery, You shall not steal, You shall not bear false witness, Honor your father and mother, and You shall love your neighbor as yourself." The young man said to him, "All these I have observed; what do I still lack?" Jesus said to him, "If you would be perfect, go, sell what you possess and give to the poor, and you will have treasure in heaven; and come, follow me." When the young man heard this he went away sorrowful; for he had great possessions.

> And Jesus said to his disciples, "Truly, I say to you, it will be hard for a rich man to enter the kingdom of heaven. Again I tell you, it is easier for a camel to go through the eye of a needle than for a rich man to enter the kingdom of God." (Matt. 19:16–24; see also 25:31–46)

This revolutionary ethic of Jesus goes beyond purely individual transformation. As Gustavo Gutiérrez writes, the universality and totality of Jesus' work "go to the very heart of political behavior, giving it its authentic dimension and depth. Human wretchedness and social injustice reveal 'a state of sin,' a betrayal of brotherhood and communion. By freeing us from sin, Jesus attacks the very roots of an unjust social order. For Jesus, the liberation of the Jewish people was just one aspect of a universal and permanent revolution."[79]

In pledging himself to his people's liberation, Jesus manifests an implicit solidarity with human beings everywhere who yearn for freedom from oppression. For once King Messiah comes, Israel will be enabled to resume its vocation as "a light to the nations" (Isa. 42:6; 49:6; cf. Acts 13:47), and all the oppressed will be "set at liberty" (Luke 4:18; cf. Isa. 61:1). The ethos exemplified in Jesus the Nazarene may not be wholly unique, yet it is an "ethos of universal responsibility." That this ethos could and can appear elsewhere does not change the truth that for Christians it happens here, in this man.[80] I suggest an analogy. The universality of marriage as a good does nothing to negate the goodness—or wonder—of *this* marriage. On the contrary, a particular marriage can be good only because marriage as such is good.

Chronologically and from a doctrinal standpoint, Paul comes after Jesus. But from the vantage point of the historical unfolding of the divine righteousness, Jesus may be said to come after Paul. Jesus is in many respects an intermediate figure between the Judaism he inherited (of which Paul was a not ungrudging part) and the developing corpus of rabbinic Judaism. More broadly stated, the event of Jesus falls between a prophetic apodicticity that frets not over pragmatic perplexities, and a practicality that obligates itself to puzzle over day-to-day, even institutional prescriptions. (We are about to consider the latter form of obligation through reviewing the concretions of the rabbis.) For Jesus, contemporary human history lives and moves under the suasion of God's coming reign. In Jesus the balance of faith and history is subtly altered, to the profit of history. Here is no "faith against the world" in exactly the Essene or the Pauline apprehension, but instead grace digging its way into time, via the Father's love and justice. The paradox is that the severity and the uncompromisingness of Jesus' apocalypticism can contribute to a socio-historical transformation more radical and revolutionary than in Paul (or in Qumran dualism), as at the same time the Nazarene's zeal for Torah is tempering his eschatology in ways that Paul can never provide. If Jesus acts to overturn one world, this is only in order to bring about another one. (Here is where the allegation by some scholars that he is not an apocalypticist cannot be entirely discarded. His eschatology is supremely historicist.*) And if Jesus' version of the kingdom never materialized, there is yet consolation for all: his message/praxis is enabled to enter the lists of competing, normative images in ethics within the only world that we have.

It can be argued, then, that the fact that Jesus was dead wrong about the historical dating or advent of the kingdom of God does not destroy his place as a most creative contributor, wholly from inside Judaism, to the theological ethics of today.

---

*The virtue of John H. Yoder's *The Politics of Jesus*, not despoiled by the book's pacifism, is its insistence that the kingdom of God means, not the transcending of time, but a new historical order.

5

Concretions of Righteousness and Goodness: Glimpses of the Rabbinic Tradition

GERARD S. SLOYAN provides a near-ideal transition to a third normative image in the unfolding of the divine righteousness: "The New Testament writers, being eschatologically oriented, did not have a this-worldly interest quite like that of the Jews of the Bible. But then, neither did Jews of the period generally, until the rabbis turned their attention from the non-historical future to the duties of the present."[1]

As the hours of their days pursue each other, is there something human beings can do to keep the times of God from entirely passing them by? Is it possible for them to reach out, now here, now there, and receive into their lives small fragments of eternity, so that all sense will not forever elude them and their years may win some vestige of a meaning that endures? Questions such as these are addressed within and through that massive block of the Jewish tradition known as rabbinic Judaism. As with all the images or types, this particular one shows resemblances to alternative categories. Yet it has its own singularity.

I

I shall first venture some identification of the rabbinic tradition. ("Rabbi" encompasses teacher, scholar, judge, community leader, trustee of the tradition.)

Scholarly and moral dangers abound in any summary-handling of enormously complicated materials. Jack N. Lightstone warns of the perils in subjecting early rabbinic literature, with its vastness and internal controversies, to the arbitrary interests of "systematic theology."[2] Such rabbinic thought must not be homogenized. The pluralism that marks the biblical literature also marks the Talmud, but in infinitely greater measure. However, I make no attempt to characterize rabbinic morality in all its historicity and com-

81

plexity; I simply offer a short background commentary—with great help from those who are expert in the area, as I am not, and to the end of understanding the thrust of the ethic that has developed within the rabbinic tradition. Lightstone recognizes that the hermeneutic of historical data, not excluding the reponsibility to proffer generalizations, can hardly proceed in abstraction from a scholar's own personal interests, understanding, and categories. Past history is never reckoned with apart from present historicalness.

Let us recall the apodictic quality of the divine Law in its two aspects: the commands have their source in the will of the Absolute (God); and they are categorical imperatives. These imperatives often encompass, to be sure, various reasons for, values in, or good consequences of, their observance. The great adventure of the rabbis has been and continues to be to grasp after heaven itself, not in the sense of a flight into "pure spirituality," but instead to gain counsel and direction for the welfare and the blessing of human beings in the here and now. There is to be a bridge between the Torah of God and humankind. I call the building of this bridge *concretion*: the day-by-day structuring of ways from the domain of transcending truth to this world's human scene, and back again. The eternal Word is to take on, *kiveyakhol*, the flesh of dos and don'ts, so that within the most ordinary of times and places, the children of God may at once give voice and hearken to echoes from eternity. In their own quest after righteousness they may, in fact, do the truths of God. This persuasion both contributes to and results from the rabbinic assurance that history can actually realize the divine providence through realizing a right and just way of life. As the Psalms of David teach, it is "in the midst of the earth" that God works his salvation (Ps. 74:12).

Within rabbinic Judaism the "sages of the Mishnah and Talmud" are the major historic instrumentalities for propounding concretions of the divine righteousness and goodness. (Although the phrase just cited is customary, the Mishnah is in fact the earlier of two main components of the Talmud. The other part, commentary on the Mishnah, is known as the Gemarah. The Talmud has been in existence in some form for roughly 1500–2000 years. Formally defined, it is "the summary of oral law that evolved after centuries of scholarly effort by sages who lived in Palestine and Babylonia until the beginning of the Middle Ages."[3] The Babylonian Talmud generally has priority over the Jerusalem Talmud, with special reference to religious law.) The huge literature of the Talmud or "Oral Law" is the primary source of Jewish law—although it is not itself a law book or law code. And while it exhibits an organic unity, it is anything but free from internal dispute or disagreement.

The Talmud has as its historical-theological precedent the Torah itself, within which the process of concretion is well begun. Already in the Written Law a "dialectical interaction" is fully established between "the divine intrusion into history" and the patterns of human community. Indeed, the very aim of divine revelation is to build a community. "Revelation to a community for the sake of that community" entails continuity and order within "the dynamics of the divine encounter with man in history." The revelation of Sinai "established a community through *mitzvah* and Halakhah, which created a political and legal framework for the relationship of the community with God."[4] The entire encounter of God with his (*sic?*) community thus reflects his grace. It is out of love that God enters into covenant with his people. Israel's side of the Covenant is comprised of the obedience that is constituent to salvation. *Mitzvah* (pl., *mitzvot*) means "commandment," usually today with the connotation of "good deed." *Halakhah* is the accepted Hebrew term for "law"; derivatively, it signifies "way of life." Something can become *halakhah* in several ways but the principal one is majority vote.

The rabbinic tradition carries forward the view, found in Jesus' time, that associates the kingdom of God with intensiveness of obedience to Torah.[5] A cardinal ethical principle implied and partially implemented in Scripture is now to be expressed unqualifiedly (though always by implication and by lessons rather than in so many words). This principle is that any affirmation of the transcendently absolute character of the divine righteousness cannot be allowed to mean the inapplicability of that righteousness to, or its total irrelevance for, daily human relationships. When the prophets demand that the poor be fed, that widows and orphans receive special care, and that injustice be fought, they are asserting that the righteousness of God can and must gain a substantial measure of reality within the mundane affairs of men. The Law itself is rooted, after all, within prophetic revelation. Moses, chief of the lawgivers, is as well the greatest of the prophets. What the biblical prophets yet lack is universality/specificity of application: structure, practicality, concretion.

Rabbinic Judaism is both grounded in and made possible by the endeavors and teachings of the Pharisees, who preserve the entire prophetic tradition (though of course in rather less thundering fashion) and who then transcend (= fulfill) that tradition in concretional ways that pave the road for the Judaism of today. Pharisee concerns come to extend to what would in our times be deemed wholly "secular" affairs (political, social, economic, cultural). All this is fully in keeping with the integral concept of Torah itself. For while Jewish religious law extends to all spheres of life, the Torah-concept is immeasurably wider than that of religious law.[6]

This point concerning the continuity of Torah-Prophecy-Pharisees must not lead us to ignore, but may instead help us to remember, a parallel element of discontinuity between the (non-scholarly) Hebrew Bible and the (scholarly) Pharisees, between the Written Law and the Oral Law, and between, in general, biblical Judaism and post-biblical Judaism.[7] The very fact that we are finding for rabbinic Judaism a distinctive normative image—disparate from, yet in many ways continuous with, that of Jesus of Nazareth—is designed to allow specifically for this element of discontinuity, along with the marked continuity.

For all the differences involved, the heirs of the prophetic (i.e., moral) emphases of the Pharisees have been the rabbis, who are persuaded that the application to all of life of the categorical (apodictic) commands of Torah is representative of the kingdom of God itself. According to the Mishnah, the Israelite "first takes upon himself the yoke of the Kingdom of Heaven and afterwards takes upon himself the yoke of the commandments" (*Berakhot* 2.2). The rabbis teach that for Jews to fail to observe God's Law would return the world to chaos. For Torah serves to sustain the creation itself. (Conversely, according to one attestation within rabbinic teaching "the world and its fullness were only created for the sake of the Torah."[8]) In other phrasing, love needs law "to help create conditions in which love may flourish."[9] Briefly put, the challenge to and from rabbinic Judaism is to erect a concretional structure upon "the sweeping proclamations of the prophets." As Clark Williamson sums up the matter, "Oral Torah is the Pharisees' answer to the Sadducees' attempt to freeze the Torah in its written form. The Pharisees understood that no society can achieve higher levels of justice and mercy without provision for rendering its laws and moral norms contemporary. Old arrangements become impracticable in new circumstances; 'new occasions teach new duties.' According to rabbinic tradition, there are two sources of authority from the outset: the written Torah—Scripture—and the oral Torah."[10]

II

In keeping with the character of the rabbinic tradition, which stresses the primacy of life/praxis, we shall concentrate in the first instance upon specificity and only then engage in some general commentary and evaluation. Following upon an outline of an elementary typology of the commandments of Torah-Talmud, a few exemplifications of rabbinic concretion will be given.

The obligation to find human ways to draw near to the very Torah of God has to reckon with two polar types of practical edict together with an intermediate type. In the one extreme case, a given commandment may be so general or imprecise that it requires aid from the human faculties of definition and particularization. Thus, the command "You shall love your neighbor as yourself" (Lev. 19:18) carries within itself interpretive questions that must be dealt with if the command is to be practically normative and meaningful: What is the meaning of "love"? And who is our "neighbor"? At the opposite extreme, a given prescription may already be so completely specific or precise that it requires theories and acts of rationalization and generalization if it is to remain in any way binding or normative. Thus, the command "You shall not boil a kid in its mother's milk" (Exod. 23:19b) begs, not for specificity (contra the other extreme case), but for fresh understandings of the intent and possible reapplication of such an edict for use amid changing times and altered circumstances. Then we have intermediate-type prescriptions, which are at once specific and general. Take the command "Remember the sabbath day, to keep it holy" (Exod. 20:8). The occasion of the observance is most definitely expressed, but how to understand "remember" and "holy" remains for interpretive clarification.

To distinguish the above types is at once to realize and to move on to the shared need of all commandments for historical concretion. Since in principle all law, secular as well as religious, requires interpretation and application, it follows that biblical law shares hermeneutical problems with human law as such. Indeed, one helpful aid to grasping the nature of Torah-Talmud is to remember that it has close affinities to secular-civil law. It is *law-for-living*. That Jewish law is so largely law for everyday life helps counter the allegation by Christians and others that it is "legalistic." For any law to be effective, it must be as exact as possible. Persons who recognize, at least upon reflection, the need for such exactitude do well to apply the same standard in their attitude to Jewish law. And should someone adjudge that the specifics of non-Jewish, "secular" law are to be adhered to because that kind of law is "important," while the specifics of Jewish law do not have to be followed since such praxis is "unimportant," the influence of a debatable value scheme and perhaps of an ideology* is evident. As a matter of fact, Jewish law often manifests a flexibility exceeding that shown within some other forms of law.

Let us return to the "Ten Words" (Decalogue).

Remember the sabbath day, to keep it holy (Exod. 20:8).

A metaphysical foundation of Shabbat, the sabbath, is offered by Rabbi Abraham J. Heschel through his rendering of the difference between time and space: "Everyone of us occupies a portion of space. The portion of space which my body occupies is taken up by myself in exclusion of anyone else. Yet no one possesses time. This very moment belongs to all living men as it belongs to me. We share time, we own space. Through my ownership of space, I am a rival of all other human beings; through my living in time, I am a contemporary of all other human beings."[11]

The Hebraic injunction to "remember" (*zachor*) entails much more than keeping one's memory in tune. It extends to participation within historical realities that point, in turn, to transhistorical truth and transhistorical norms. What is the reality in which Israel participates, and what, accordingly, are the concretions it is called to form through sabbath observance? Both a primordial-ontological element and a moral element are involved: the *imitatio dei* and the *imitatio justitiae*.

"God blessed the seventh day and hallowed it, because on it God rested from all his work which he had done in creation" (Exod. 2:3). Israel sanctifies Shabbat through its imitation of God; the people are to refrain from creative

---

*Ideology is understood in this book as the recourse to certain ideas and idea-systems in the service of self-interest, more particularly collective self-interest.

work on that day because God so refrained when he made the world. Israel is summoned to recapitulate the divine praxis. The Torah also states: "On the seventh day you shall rest; that your ox and your ass may have rest, and the son of your bondmaid, and the alien, may be refreshed" (Exod. 23:12). This aspect of the command is further defined and elaborated in the Deuteronomic development and parallels. Shabbat rest for the manservant and maidservant is immediately linked with Israel's historical experience—its plight but also its deliverance. "You should remember that you were a slave in the land of Egypt, and the Lord your God brought you out thence with a mighty hand and an outstretched arm; therefore the Lord your God commanded you to keep the sabbath day" (Deut. 5:12–15).

The coherence and the all-inclusiveness here are not short of astonishing: the symbolization and the praxis of Shabbat reach all the way back to the creation of the world; then they encompass Israel's slavery in Egypt and the human struggle against, and redemption from, slavery; and at last they extend by implication, all the way forward to the eschatological liberation of the animals and of humanity, when "refreshment" and "rest" will be all in all. Shabbat is a bridge between God and humankind, not just through the specifics of its observance, but through the vertical-horizontal duality of its rationale.

If the two norms of remembrance and holiness are alike fundamental to the sabbath command, we ought to be able to discern connections between them. By calling upon the typically dialectical approach of Judaism, Irving Greenberg provides a concretional frame of reference:

> Holiness is not pure projection (which would make it a collective neurosis); it is the discovery of a depth dimension that underlies the material world. Nor is holiness purely cosmic. Jewish behavior on Shabbat [is what makes the day] special. On this day, one changes rhythms. It is a *mitzvah* to slow down, to take smaller steps and not run. Through repeated acts of sanctification, the flavor of each minute is enhanced. Prayer, *Kiddush*, candle-lighting, learning, eating, dressing, walking, making love—all operate in special ways on this day. A classic Sabbath prayer captures this dialectic: "*The people who sanctify the seventh day* will all be satisfied and pleasured by Your goodness. You wanted and sanctified the seventh [day]; You called it the most desirable of days, *a remembrance of cosmic creation*" (Prayer Book).[12]

Within rabbinic wisdom covering the right observance of Shabbat, perhaps no counsel is possessed of greater theological-ethical import than that of sexual intercourse for husband and wife during Friday night.[13] In this counsel the gulf comes into full view between normative Judaism and all dualistic faiths that, in effect, profane holiness by tying it to sexual abstinence and celibacy. (We may note that Judaism makes this contribution with the aid of a form of praxis not exactly devoid of comic relief.) Within rabbinic Judaism, holiness directs itself to wholeness, the wholeness of life (*haim*). Thus is it highly significant that the very first of the Torah's 613 commandments should read: "Be fruitful and multiply" (Gen. 1:28).

The point of the sabbath ban upon constructive or intentional work is not a negative one but instead a signalization that on this joyous day all classes of persons are *set free* from labor (as are the animals, lacking as they are, pitiably, in any power to demand their rights). A classic ancient example is the prohibition of commerce (cf. Amos 8:5). Derivative restrictions include those upon travel, moving about (traditionally, not over 2,000 paces), and carrying certain objects (cf. Jer. 17:21).[14] Ordinarily, to work or to engage in business is to stand in the presence of God, in keeping with the truth that "the material base of existence is basic to human dignity." The talmudic comment on the verse "I walk before the Lord in the land of the living" (Ps. 116:9) is, "This refers to walking and working in the marketplace" (*Yoma* 71a). Any insinuation that Shabbat means a denial of the dignity of human labor is the opposite of the truth; sabbath observance simply focuses upon that minority of time when creative work is not done. The entire moral frame of reference of Shabbat is the celebration of human labor: "Six days you shall labor and do all your [intentional, creative] work; but the seventh day is a sabbath to the Lord your God . . ." (Exod. 20:9–10). Work of a productive, non-exploiting kind is a holy calling. "Just as the priest served in the holy Sanctuary built by humans, so does the human being working in the world serve in the holy Sanctuary built by God. The universe *is* the divine sanctuary. In perfecting the world, the human being becomes co-creator with the Divine, 'a partner in the work of Creation' (*Sabbath* 119b)."[15]

Rabbi Greenberg applies talmudic counsel and the rabbinic spirit to the late twentieth-century scene and its socio-moral crisis. He places Shabbat within a comprehensive, eschatological frame of reference, showing the relation between historical-existential concretion and ultimate divine fulfillment. The ground of such guidance is the affirmation of Israel as "the people of the dream," the dream "that the world can and will be perfected and that full human dignity will be realized." Greenberg alludes to the permanent dilemma between accepting the world for its goodness and rejecting the world for its evil:

> The classic Jewish solution to this dilemma is to set up *a rhythm of perfection*. The first movement is to plunge into this world, affirm it fully, build it up and enjoy it. This is basically a conservative position inasmuch as participation usually leads to accomodation to present values. But just when complete absorption looms, Jews create an alternate reality—the Shabbat. The community steps outside the here and now of imperfection and collectively creates a world of perfection. This new world is totally different in its rhythms. Here there is no work to do and no deprivation. There is neither anxiety nor bad news. *Since such a world does not yet exist in space, it is first created in time.* . . .The power of this rhythm of redemption is that it allows the fullest participation in the world as it is. At the same time, it gives a recurrent ful-

fillment to the ultimate dreams of perfection. . . . The motive force of the
search for such a perfection is a special kind of love, called in rabbinic tradition, *chessed*. *Chessed* is a love that accepts what is—yet embraces and evokes
unfulfilled possibilities. . . . Shabbat is the temporary anti-reality of perfection.[16]

However, there is much more to the rationale and role of Shabbat than its
perfectionist promise. Greenberg also associates the sabbath renunciation
of work with the question of "pathologies of power." "The mastery and pro-
ductivity which the Torah celebrates bear within themselves the seeds of
potential evil. The nemesis of power is the abuse of nature; the nemesis of
production is alienation. Both power and production can lead to idolatry and
slavery." Power leads to the absolutization of the holders of power. Before
the fact of these evils, Shabbat exerts countervailing power. It is significant
that the Talmud links nonobservance of the sabbath to idolatry. The sabbath
teaches the acceptance of nature, as against its manipulation. And as Shabbat acts to exempt nature from objectification, it saves human beings from
alienation from the objects of their work as well as from slavery to labor.
"Living the Sabbath affirms that I and my work and the economic system are
all grounded in a higher divine existence. Once I deny the work's absolute
authority (by renouncing it, as on Shabbat; by giving a higher loyalty to a
religious or a rest norm), I find the ethical margin to impose moral values on
the work as well. . . . The prohibition at once pays tribute to work's significance while seeking to check a potential metastasis of the individual's involvement and of its role in his life." Since the solution to the abuse of
power is not the renunciation of power, Shabbat can offer the responsible
and constructive alternative of a rhythm of doing and being, work and abstinence, creationhood and creaturehood, action and renewal, power and
powerlessness. The sabbath is the completion and the celebration of the
partnership of God and humanity.[17]

The symbiosis between the Shabbat and divine/human righteousness is
brought to a climax in the precedence of life and the saving of life before the
fact of the sabbath and its imperatives. The rabbis ruled long ago that sabbath necessities are overridden when it comes to the saving of life. Yet this
did not wholly resolve the matter. For example, through the years the question arose of whether, rather than violate Shabbat, people ought to be willing to die (by refusing to dishonor the day or to defend themselves from
physical assault). Accordingly, the question persisted of how the rabbinic
ruling is to be justified. Irving Greenberg finds rather too mechanical and
prudentially calculating the familiar talmudic aphorism, "Violate one Sabbath [to save a life] so that he (the saved person) can [live to] observe many
Sabbaths." For Greenberg, Rabbi Samuel gave the decisive answer, founded
upon Lev. 18:5: Live by the laws of God; do not die by them (*Yoma* 85b).
Greenberg concludes: "The only commandments one must die for are those

(such as the prohibition to murder) whose violation would destroy the basis of life itself. Shabbat and many other commandments play a unique role in enhancing life, but they are overridden to save life. In truth, when life is at stake it is not a case of 'permitted violation.' It is a *mitzvah*—a fulfillment of the purpose of Shabbat—to save a life through whatever means necessary. . . . The Torah creates a framework to nurture holiness. . . . [It] seeks to imbue all of life with this dimension of holiness."[18]

The aphorism of Jesus of Nazareth, "The sabbath was made for man, not man for the sabbath" (Mark 2:27), is thus in total accord with historic Judaism.

A brief *midrash* (commentary) upon Rabbi Greenberg's analysis of work-and-power is occasioned by the rapidly changing situation within the industrial world as the twentieth century draws near its close. The burgeoning utilization of automational processes (including robotics) in the production of goods seems to be reversing on a permanent basis the ratio of work to leisure. As one authority on unemployment observes, the computer, in contrast to all previous technological developments, "is basically a job-destroying tool."[19] We may be facing an era when "employment" in its accustomed meaning will largely become a redundancy, and as little as one day of work in seven for most people may be regarded as a lot. This state of affairs will not resolve the issue of human power over the natural process, but of a certainty it will radically recast the terms of the problem. The consequences for traditional sabbath observance will be revolutionary.

III

You shall not kill. . . . You shall not steal. You shall not bear false witness against your neighbor. You shall not covet. . . anything that is your neighbor's (Exod. 20:13, 15, 16, 17).

Within Jewish criminal and civil law—as through such prohibitions in daily life as falsehood and coveting—the absolutes of holiness, justice, and human sanctity are concretized in ways parallel to those found in the observance of Shabbat.

A *midrash* asks: "How were the Ten Commandments arranged? Five on the one tablet and five on the other. On the one tablet was written: 'I am the Lord thy God.' And opposite it on the other tablet was written: 'Thou shalt not murder.' This tells that if one sheds blood it is accounted to him as though he diminished the divine image."[20] According to the Talmud, the three most grievous sins, i.e., transgressions to be abjured on pain of death, are idolatry, adultery, and murder. The Mishnah asks: "Why was man created a single person? To teach us that he who destroys one life is to be looked upon as if he destroyed an entire world, and he who saves one life as if he saved an entire world" (*Sanh.* 4.5). To murder, or destroy, one human being is to engage in universal destruction. How is that? When Cain slew his brother he shed as well the blood of all Abel's never-to-be-born children. Thus can the rabbis teach that "one man outweighs all creation." The question, "How do we know that we should expose ourselves to death rather than commit murder," is answered: "Who knows that your blood is redder than his?" (*Pesahim* 25a; *Sanh.* 74a); in other words, your life is of no more value than his, and if the authorities order a man to take life, under a threat of being killed himself, he ought to face that threat rather than commit murder.[21]

In the command, "You shall not kill," the word *razah* is traditionally rendered "murder," since, while the verb actually extends as well to nonculpable homicide, to equate it with an absolute ban on killing would contradict the provision for lawful killing, as in punishment for capital crimes such as blasphemy and adultery (cf. Lev. 24:16; 20:10). However, even in ancient days death sentences were frowned upon on the very ground of the sanctity of human life. Accordingly, should a judge have happened to witness the occurrence of an ostensibly capital crime, he was forbidden to try the case himself, because of the experiential taint upon his impartiality. Similarly, childless men and aged persons were not permitted to sit upon capital cases, on the talmudic foundation that "they have forgotten the sorrow of raising children," and might therefore judge with undue severity, minimizing the personal condition and emotions of the accused.[22] Rabbi Johanan (3rd cent. C.E.) declared as an absolute requirement of judicial procedure: "Capital cases must begin with reasons for acquittal and may not begin with reasons for conviction."[23] On the same ground of human sanctity, self-incrimination was early ruled out. The halakhic principle here is that since human beings have no right to inflict physical harm upon anyone, and since this truth must apply to themselves, therefore self-incrimination is unacceptable as legal evidence. Again, the courts were prohibited from acting upon circumstantial, conjectural, theoretical, or hearsay evidence, even if no other kind were available. Witnesses were allowed to testify only to what they had seen with their own eyes, and false or malicious witnessing was condemned and punished harshly (cf. Exod. 23:1–2; Deut. 19:16–19). Were false witnessing to prevail, the integrity of the court and thereby of justice in a society would dissolve (as would such necessities of everyday affairs as transactions in the marketplace).[24]

There is, further, the all-important question of intention. The Torah prescribes that a man who "willfully attacks another to kill him treacherously" is to die (Exod. 21:14). If a man "hates his neighbor, and lies in wait for him," and attacks and kills him (Deut. 9:11), we have premeditated murder, in which case the *lex talionis* would seem to apply: "as he has done it shall be done to him, fracture for fracture, eye for eye, tooth for tooth . . . . he who kills a man shall be put to death" (Lev. 24:19–21; cf. Exod. 21:24–25). However (there is most often a "however"), a lack of malice aforethought entails the inapplicability of capital punishment. Furthermore (there is most often a "furthermore"), how possible is it to prove intent (premeditation)? In contrast to many penal codes, wherein the actions and preparations of the accused may be called upon to demonstrate premeditation, Jewish law does not sanction such a method of drawing conclusions. Instead, it demands authentic proof of intent. Moreover (there is most often a "moreover"), Jewish law maintains that no one can be condemned to death except if no less than two witnesses attest (a number required in civil law as well) that, not only did they see the deed, but the accused was warned just before committing the crime that such an act was forbidden by law, and that the punishment for violating the law was death. In addition (there is most often an "in addition"), to utter the warning was not enough; "it was necessary to verify that the defendant had taken note of it and accepted it by saying: 'I know and I take it upon myself.' Without these elements there is no possibility of proving malicious intent, and consequently of punishing the criminal."[25]

We appear to be up against a tour de force that is either quite convincing or quite absurd. The influence of a prejudgmental bent against capital punishment seems very much in evidence, particularly when we recall that in Jewish society ignorance of the prohibition of murder would be just about non-existent. The right of self-defense is another matter, although it is true that an individual who killed a pursuer when an alternative means of protection was available could be charged with murder. Again, the right to kill someone about to commit a grave crime was sanctioned.[26]

A fierce social commitment to ascertaining the truth as also to protecting the innocent is most apparent here. The question inevitably arose of how lawlessness was to be controlled when such formidable provisions stood arrayed against severe punishment. As long ago as the Second Temple the sages considered this question. One way out lay in a halakhic provision for special royal courts which, in maintaining public order, were not bound by restrictions devolving upon regular courts. A second way out lay in the right of the courts themselves—sitting not as courts of law but as administrative bodies—to take various steps to protect public order and morality. For instance, they could impose life imprisonment (something not found in the basic Mosaic code) and even the death sentence. Thus was a certain dilemma admitted as unavoidable: protection of defendants according to the law versus a necessity to "purge the evil from the midst" of the nation (Deut. 13:5). One consequence was provision for sentences "not from the words of the Torah and not in order to transgress against the Torah." An example of such prudential praxis is that when a court was assured of a capital defendant's guilt, but knew that he had not been properly forewarned, it would decree life imprisonment. Finally, the courts could utilize the weapon of excommunication (herem), a practice only completely abolished in modern times.[27]

So: in the realm of criminal justice the "howevers" have had ways of creating their own "howevers." (However [sic], there is no capital punishment in today's State of Israel.)

To turn to lesser but more popular sins, Rabbi Akiva (d. 135 C.E.) laments that in the moment a thief steals he must be an atheist, for otherwise he would not violate God's command against theft. Herein is shown once more the inner bond between the divine righteousness and human righteousness. However, in the rabbinic outlook the prohibition of theft has been treated quite differently from the prohibition of killing, as have also criminal acts less serious than killing. As a matter of fact, Jewish law construes theft as a civil offense. (Jewish civil law is highly flexible and continually changing.) A decisive element here is the radical variance in penalty as between criminal acts and civil misdeeds. In the Torah, flogging (cf. Deut. 25:1–3) is the punishment for deliberate infringements of negative ("you shall not") injunctions. Significantly, monetary offenses (defined as theft, robbery, etc.) or "offenses that contain no action"—meaning cases where no physical act is involved—are excluded, in principle, from this form of punishment. Instead, the thief is required to restore the goods stolen, and in some cases is obliged to tender a fine to the owner (at least twice the value of the property). But he receives no other punishment.[28]

What is behind the foregoing distinction? To the outsider the distinction may appear arbitrary or arcane. The quest for an explanation demands understanding of the quality of Jewish theological and anthropological affirmation: Who is God? Who is man (not excluding man as transgressor) and what are his rights? And what is the relation of God and man? No halakhic differentiation is more captivating than that between theft and robbery. Here is a description by Adin Steinsaltz:

> The thief sometimes pays a fine, but the robber who takes openly and by force is merely obliged to restore the object or its equivalent in cash. The talmudic explanation is intriguing: the robber is preferable to the thief since he acts openly, and his attitude toward God, in transgressing against his commandments and committing a robbery, is equal to his attitude toward his fellow man, from whom he steals openly, without fear and shame. The thief, on the other hand, demonstrates that he fears men more than he fears God, since he hides himself from his fellow men but not from the Almighty; he therefore deserves to be fined.[29]

To the above I think we can add two considerations: while property may belong to a person, it is not itself that person and thus it lacks the sanctity of the person, the *imago dei*; and the problem of respecting human sanctity is ultimately the problem of universality (= equality). The reason that *compensation*—the original, standard biblical-rabbinic method for dealing with much human wrongdoing (cf., e.g., Exod. 21:18, 22; Levit. 6:1–5)—can be so convincing and effective a legal and moral means for honoring human sanctity is that it not alone upholds the sanctity of the victim but also that of the victimizer. (While the practice of compensation is found outside ancient Jewish law, the teaching of the *imago dei* is, of course, a uniquely Jewish contribution.)

The foregoing analysis may help us to apprehend the fact, strange on first encounter, that Jewish civil law is usually known as monetary law (*dinei memonot*). For preeminent in all *dinei memonot* is the assumption that "money may be given as a gift. This seemingly extraneous or unimportant point serves as the foundation for the entire code, which is founded on public consent to the establishment of various monetary frameworks. . . . [All] monetary claims are demands for justice" and therefore "are vital to the regulation of normal life."[30] Thus, were it not for the praxis of something like compensation, humankind would still be gouging out an eye for an eye, and amputating a limb for a limb. One irony of the Marxists, who bleat on about "Jewish money" and "Jewish capitalism," is that along with unnumbered others they are the unwitting beneficiaries of Torah-Talmud, with its *imago dei* and its God who "knows the secrets" of all human hearts (Ps. 44:21).*

IV

Rabbinic thinking is well aware of the senses in which moral responsibility excels legal responsibility without necessarily clashing with it. Thus, even though the hatred of one human being for another can hardly be allotted a legal penalty (unless or until it breaks forth in destructive action), nevertheless hatred is regarded as a grave wrong[31] to be overcome only by repentance, love, and forgiveness. However, the relation between moral responsibility and legal responsibility is also one of conflict, and perennially so. A primary reason for this is that legal obligation exhibits a natural thrust toward minimalization, the urge to "get away" with or even to authorize the least possible contribution or penalty. Typically, the "not less than" of our punitive allocations is counterbalanced by a "not more than." Moral obligation knows no such bounds. The human spirit is suffused with infinity: the *imago dei*. In Jewish thinking the differentiation of legal obligation and moral obligation is made possible, not merely by the nature of human nature, but uniquely by theological conviction, expressed or implied. And the Jewish recognition of the conflict between the two modes of obligation is made plain in and through the treatment of specific moral issues, in ways that imply that the conflict will always exist while yet teaching that it can always be meliorated.

The dialectic of legal obligation and moral obligation may be further expressed, but now in a way directly contrary to legal minimalization/moral maximalization. Eugene B. Korn provides several examples of the acknowledgment by Judaism of certain moral concepts that "are logically indepen-

*The question of "coveting" entails certain ambiguities. Decisively, Jewish apodictic law is concerned with much more than external acts.

dent of, and cannot be reduced to, legal imperatives." One of his talmudic illustrations shows how at the level of punitive action, legal maximalization may be balanced off by moral minimalization. The Torah states explicitly that a son who is "stubborn and rebellious" can incur the punishment of death by stoning. But since his parents must testify before a rabbinic court that such a son is also "a glutton and a drunkard" (Deut. 21:18–21), the law stipulates that no matter how great a son's stubbornness and rebelliousness, he cannot be identified in those ways until he has consumed a specified amount of stolen meat and of wine. Hence, it is the eating and drinking that becomes the deciding factor.

> Said Rabbi Shimon, "Because one eats a half *manna* of meat and drinks a half *log* of wine can his parents take him and have him stoned?"
> [Obviously not!] Therefore, [a stubborn and rebellious son] never existed and never will exist.
> Why, then, is the law written? That you may study it and receive reward. (*Sanh.* 71a)

Here is Korn's commentary: Rabbi Shimon is disavowing an explicit *halakhah* of the Torah "because it violates his sense of justice." The rabbi's procedure is not to cite another biblical law that might conflict with and perhaps supersede this one; nor does he infer his conclusion from an interpretation passed down by the legal tradition. His conclusion derives instead from a strictly moral argument:

> The idea of retributive justice requires that the punishment for a crime be proportionate to the severity of the crime. No act of eating or drinking could ever be a severe enough transgression to merit the extreme punishment of stoning. Hence, justice requires that the law of the stubborn and rebellious son can never be applied. [The] conclusion that such a son never has existed and never will exist is not an empirical claim determined by fact. It is a necessary truth determined *a priori* by the legal requirements of the concept of justice: There can never be a stubborn and rebellious son to whom these laws justly apply.[32]

In the context of moral obligation vis-à-vis legal obligation a talmudic phrase stands out: "the laws of Heaven." The preeminence of moral responsibility is illustrated in the avowal by some rabbis that it is a moral obligation to recompense a victim in cases where damage is not the result of deliberate action and hence there is no legal responsibility. For while the damager is "exempt from the laws of man," he is morally "bound by the laws of Heaven." According to one haggadic tradition, the evil that consumed the ancient city of Sodom lay in a combining of malice with a fixation upon the letter of the law. No court could ever force a person to refrain from reneging upon an oral guarantee. But the "laws of Heaven" pronounce: "He who punished the men of Sodom will punish those who do not keep their word." The other side of the coin—a transition from justice in a restricted sense to a wider mercy—appears as we move from Sodom up to Jerusalem. In the Talmud the question is raised of why the holy city's Second Temple should have been destroyed when the people of the time were living blameless lives and studying Torah. (This is by no means the only judgment forthcoming concerning the people's behavior. Quite different judgments include: the rampancy of dishonesty, hatred of other people, and neglect of children.[33] But we miss the point if we imagine that the rabbis are reading the destruction of Jerusalem through the eyes of exclusively historical-moral analysis. They are actually doing moral-philosophic analysis, although always within the frame of reference of Jewish spirituality.) The acute though enigmatic comment is made that "Jerusalem was only destroyed because the law of Torah was delivered there." A *midrash* is then developed: Punishment came to Jerusalem because judgments were being put forward in strict accord with the Law and without leniency, i.e., "they did not go beyond the requirements of the law" (*Baba Metzia* 30b). Thus, while the concept of justice is never allowed to lose its force, other factors must be paid due heed, lest the harshness of the law be unbridled. "Torah as a law of life is predicated on the assumption that there will be concession, compromise, generosity, and that its system will not function without these."[34]

Some ethical paradoxes are distinguished by their multifoldness. The above skirmish between strictures and mercy is joined by two additional factors: the inviolability of the self, and the self-sacrifice of the saint. On the one hand, moral obligation cannot be permitted to subvert individual self-interest. We are met by the legal (and moral) principle that "your own has priority over that of any man." This means that no one can be compelled to suffer loss of time, money, health, etc. through coming to someone else's aid. In conflicts of interest "your own life takes precedence."[35] However, in talmudic thinking the persuasion that moral duty must not disregard self-interest is countered by the winsome assurance that some people can be depended upon to practice a nonobligated saintliness and to go a second mile (cf. Matt. 5:41). This brings us to the teaching of "inside the line of the law" (*li-fnim mi-shurat ha-din*).

We are given the instance of a judge presiding over litigation between a poor man and a rich man. We are impelled to ask: Is there not more than one meaning to the concept of a "just judge"? The Torah clearly states: "You shall not be partial to a poor man in his suit" (Exod. 23:3). In other words, justice must never be subverted, even for the sake of poor people. The just judge is one who acts in accordance with the law, which may mean compelling the poor man to pay his debt. But there is another side to justice, to what is right. For the judge is also counselled to recompense the poor man with funds from his own pocket. (All at once the angels are heard breaking into song!) True, the judge may now wish to confide to himself, "How did I ever get into *this* business? What a klutz I am!" But only a moment later he will remind himself that there is "a kind of inner code, binding on all those who aspire to higher spiritual standards." And so he acts "inside the law." We are brought, with joyfulness, to the talmudic definition of a *hasid*: He is a person who conducts himself "inside the law."[36]

Yet what is to happen in collective situations where the person-to-person encounters of a law court are lacking? An example cited is of a group of Jews threatened with mass annihilation were they to fail to hand over one of their number. The halakhic ruling is that, as against abandoning one member (granted that he or she is not a peculiarly culpable party), the entire group must give itself up.[37] It seems to me that the principle of "inside the law" here reaches its outer limit. For the larger the collectivity, the greater the number of members who are not and do not intend to be *hasidim*. We cannot forget that the very meaning of the praxis that is "inside the law" is its voluntariness together with its comparative rarity. But neither can we forget that while moral obligation needs law to give it direction, the law needs moral obligation if it is to flower in full humaneness.

The talmudic provision for praxis of a supererogational kind is reminiscent of Jesus' special demand upon his disciples, "he who does not take his cross and follow me is not worthy of me" (Matt. 10:38).

V

Our reflections in the previous two sections have already suggested a frame of reference for encountering a further commandment, known by the rabbis as "the great positive principle in the Torah."[38]

You shall love your neighbor as yourself: I am the Lord (Levit. 19:18).

The substance of this command contrasts with the "shall not" injunctions of the Decalogue already reviewed. Here now is the dialectic of law and morality in sharpest form. For what can it mean to *command* love? Does not love presuppose unalloyed spontaneity? And can law remain itself, once it begins to transcend itself?

A point of departure for reckoning with the specific injunction before us is the tantalizing fact that Scripture commands the people of God to love according to two varied modes. "You shall love the Lord your God with all your heart, and with all your soul, and with all your might" (Deut. 6:5). "You shall love your neighbor as yourself: I am the Lord" (Levit. 19:18). Love to God is entirely unqualified by any other consideration, while love to neighbor is qualified, or is pointed toward discreteness, through an implicit reminder to the people of how they are already in love with themselves. Presumably, within the anti-blasphemous ambience of the giving/receiving of Torah, the last thing allowed to the Israelites would be to love themselves *with all their heart, soul, and might*. That would surely mean blasphemy! It is noteworthy that the prohibition of blasphemy is included within the Noachic Laws for humankind (beyond the Israelites). The contemporary Jewish philosopher Lenn Evan Goodman comments that what is demanded here, "as a general principle of the moral law," is "the prohibition of the negation of all that the notion of God stands for and requires insofar as the notion of a Being of absolute perfection has regard for human affairs."[39]

A moment's thought may tell us something additional. We love ourselves in a variety of ways, in keeping with and depending upon many different situations. Is not the love of neighbor to be honored in like fashion? It has been well observed that the difference between legalism and the authentic fulfillment of the Law is that the latter takes situations into account (which is, in general, what talmudic thought/praxis is forever doing).

Let us call further upon Lenn Evan Goodman.[40] (I should argue that while the rabbis are not philosophers in any technical or academic sense—thus they do not dwell upon metaphysical issues or challenges—Jewish moral philosophy yet perpetuates the rabbinic vision [Anschauung]. The bond shared is a certain moral-theological tradition urged along and refined by rationality.) By indirection, Goodman immediately throws light upon one of our puzzles, the commanding of love. He does this by introducing a different but not unrelated puzzle: How can people legitimately act or consent for future generations? The issue is that of the nature and responsibilities of an ongoing historical community. Professor Goodman answers that while the generation of Sinai cannot bind other generations to the Covenant, nevertheless when others come to stand in the same place, and are aided by tradition and their own best lights, they may *will* to apply the Covenant to their own situations. "When this is done, there is no heteronomy [alienness of command]. God does not stand apart and impose morality. 'Thou shalt' does not come first, but first 'I am,' and (not by logic but by the dialectic of moral response) 'Thou shalt' follows, now *identical* with 'I will,' since it arises not from culture or tradition or any external source of legislation but from the inward experience of moral appropriation...."[41] Herein is offered a moral ground for recurrent renewals of covenantal life, together with an implied provision for creating fresh and different terms within the Covenant.

Accordingly, love to neighbor can be nourished by love from and to God. We read in *The Wisdom of the Fathers* (*Pirke Avot*): "Beloved is man for he was created in the Image. Extraordinary is the love made known to him that he was created in the Image, as it is said, *For in the image of God made He man* (Gen. 9:6)" (Avot 3). With respect to the overall opportunity to be moral beings, Rabbi Jonah asks, anent Jeremiah 9:24, "How can a man be wise enough to *understand* the Lord? This is impossible! But we know Him by exercising justice and righteousness, for the Lord is the author of these" (commentary upon Avot 1). Justice and righteousness are the ways; love is the motive. "Be not like slaves who serve their master for the sake of their allowance: Let no man say, 'I shall serve my Creator so that he provide me with my needs.' Whether He provides or not, let one serve his

Creator out of love, simply because *The Lord my God commanded me* (Deut.
4:5)" (Vitry commentary upon Avot 1). "When we carry out His commandments we do so for the sake of the commandment, out of love of the commandment—as is the case when a person loves someone and strives
always to please his beloved. The reward will indeed come of itself"
(Meiri commentary upon Avot 1). Thus, the human response to *mitzvah* (the
divine imperative) is *ahavah*, love. And if the command to love is a natural
response to Perfection, the question does not arise of how love can be
commanded. Then the divine imperative takes hold from within, and
there is "a true moral law involving no heteronomy." But even to honor
the first mode of love, love to God, is to observe the *mitzvot*[42]—and no his-
torical/divine imperative can excel love to neighbor.

Here now is a secret; please do not tell anyone—or not more than a few
close friends: Neighbor-love is even ready to play a few tricks upon the
truth—not a great many, lest the moral order of things be capsized. But
neighbor-love sometimes stretches things a little bit. There follows Rabbi
Natan's commentary upon Hillel's counsel in *The Wisdom of the Fathers*, "Be of
the disciples of Aaron, loving peace and pursuing peace, loving mankind,
and drawing all men to Torah":

> When two men had quarreled with each other, Aaron would go and sit down
> with one of them and say to him: "My son, mark what that fellow is saying!
> He beats his breast and tears his clothing, saying, 'Woe unto me! How shall I
> lift my eyes and look upon my fellow! I am ashamed before him, for I it is
> who treated him foully.' "
>   He would sit with him until he had removed all rancor from his heart, and
> then Aaron would go and sit with the other one and say to him: "My son,
> mark what that fellow is saying. He beats his breast and tears his clothing
> saying, 'Woe unto me! How shall I lift my eyes and look upon my fellow! I
> am ashamed before him, for I it is who treated him foully.' "
>   He would sit with him until he had removed all rancor from his heart. And
> when the two men met each other they embraced and kissed one another.
> (Natan, Version A commentary upon Avot 1)[43]

We have been brought full circle: the object of the Image's love is itself
made in the Image.

Insofar as the universality and coherence of human moral law may be affirmed, that eventuality, so Goodman contends, arises out of the impact of
monotheism. The command is forthcoming that various classes of human relations and actions be uniform. "You shall have one justice (*mishpat*), for the
stranger and the homeborn alike, for I am the Lord your God" (Levit. 24:22).
In this passage, as in the command of love to neighbor, it is clear that the
confession of faith in the just and equitable God forms the very foundation
and inspiration of just and equitable behavior.[44] The principle of theocentric
equity is even more manifest earlier in Leviticus, where no less than three

kinds of avowal are made simultaneously: a reaffirming of the command of neighbor-love, which is to be directed not alone to Israelites; a reminder of the Israelites' own history of strangeness, servitude, and deliverance; and the affirmation of God: "When a stranger sojourns with you in your land, you shall not discriminate against him. The stranger who sojourns with you shall be to you as the native among you, and you shall love him as yourself; for you were strangers in the land of Egypt: I am the Lord your God" (Levit. 19:33–34). The stranger is not an Israelite; neighbor-love is here (I repeat) commanded to non-Jews. And, as Hermann Cohen observes, "the alien was to be protected, although he was not a member of one's family, clan, religious community or people; simply *because he was a human being*. In the alien, therefore, man discovered the idea of humanity."[45]

There are, indeed, no limits to the ways in which the concretions of daily behavior stand directly under the power and scrutiny of the "I am" who is the Savior of Israel. This point can be typified through almost random reference to the Torah. Here, for example, is the matter of fair trade: "You shall do no wrong in judgment, in measures of length or weight or quantity. You shall have just balances, just weights, a just ephah, and a just hin: *I am the Lord your God, who brought you out of the land of Egypt*" (Levit. 19:35–36). (There I go italicizing the Bible.)

Finally, the command of love for the neighbor is brought to a climax of a kind through its connection at the hands of the rabbis with, of all things, the punishment of criminals. From Levit. 19:18, two deductions are directly made: Whenever an element of doubt obtains respecting the guilt of the accused, he is to receive a minimal sentence; and in instances where the death penalty must be decreed, the least painful and least humiliating method is to be used (*Sanh.* 45a, 52a).[46]

As Goodman summarizes the Talmud-Torah celebration of neighbor-love, three kinds of meaning converge: affect, moral imperative, and theological rationale. The transformation is "achieved from an emotional tendency (which might equally be countered by other sentiments such as . . . alienness or fear or demands for vengeance) to a categorical moral demand." This occurs

> only by reference to the Absolute Standard of value, before whom all human individuals are alike. . . . "You were strangers . . ." gives the sentimental motive, but "I am the Lord thy God" gives the reason. . . . Thus it is the monotheistic concept of God which renders possible the universalization of the principle of mutuality not only to the helpless or potentially disadvantaged or oppressed but to all persons as a categorical command that they love one another as they love themselves. . . . For it is only in the light of Objectivity (which is itself a norm projected onto history and science as well as human relations from the monotheistic concept of Divinity) that we can regard our fellows' subjecthood (and hence their deserts) as the moral equivalent of our own.

And the consequent, essential requirement to "go beyond the strict sentence of the Law" means two responsibilities: to plumb the intentions of the Law, and to probe the merits of situations. These are "judicial tasks which the Rabbis in their role as judges and legal judicial scholars (but never quite as legislators)" have been "more than willing to undertake."[47]

VI

Perhaps we may now venture a little more general interpretation and appraisal of the talmudic tradition.

I suggest that a systematic exploration of rabbinic thinking—the analysis before the reader is no more than a short prolegomenon—will entail responses to a paradigm in triangularity (see Figure 2).

The three components here—Torah, life, and reasonableness (the last-mentioned is poles away from narrow rational*ism*)—are equal partners, for through many and long years they have fought for and gained parity of force and legitimacy. "Torah" and "life" are wedded in the first instance by righteousness and its quest. "Life" and "reasonableness" are bound together in the first instance by responsibility, for without obligation there is neither humane life nor a legitimate pursuit of reason. Responsible thought/praxis will endeavor to make sense of life and will order it morally in reasonable ways. And "Torah" and "reasonableness" share in the first instance the transcendent Word, the former as the Word's primary agency, the latter as its means of interpretation and practical representation. But the paradigm of triangu-

Figure 2

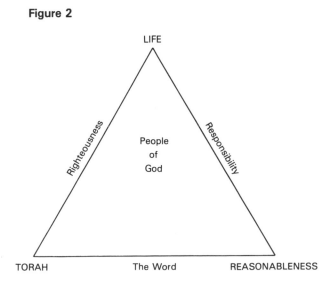

larity apprehended in its totality implies that the three components are to be grasped and explicated within their overall interrelatedness: "Torah," with respect to "life" and "reasonableness"; "life," with respect to "reasonableness" and "Torah"; and "reasonableness," with respect to "Torah" and "life." Let us develop the three dimensions.

(1) The purpose of Torah is to affirm and redeem life through righteousness; the Word of Torah calls for study, dialectics, and judicial decision.

> When your son asks you in time to come, "What is the meaning of the testimonies and the statutes and the ordinances which the Lord our God has commanded you?" then you shall say to your son, "We were Pharaoh's slaves in Egypt; and the Lord brought us out of Egypt with a mighty hand; and the Lord showed signs and wonders, great and grievous, against Egypt and against Pharaoh and all his household, before our eyes; and he brought us out from there, that he might bring us in and give us the land which he swore to give to our fathers. And the Lord commanded us to do all these statutes, to fear the Lord our God, for our good always, that he might preserve us alive, as at this day. And it will be righteousness for us, if we are careful to do all this commandment before the Lord our God, as he has commanded us." (Deut. 6:20–25)

Morris Adler retells a famous rabbinic story, remarking that it illustrates "the jealousy with which the rabbis guarded the inviolability of their thought and the legal process." It seems that one day the colleagues of Rabbi Eliezer the Great refused to accept his argumentation. "If I am right," Eliezer responded, "may this carob tree move a hundred yards away." The tree obeyed but the colleagues said, "A tree is no proof." Eliezer tried again: "May the canal prove it." The canal began to flow backwards but the colleagues said, "We accept no testimony from water." Eliezer then commanded, "May the walls of this House of Study prove it." The walls tottered, as if about to fall, but Rabbi Joshua rebuked them, "When scholars argue over *halakhah*, why do you intervene?" Eliezer tried a fourth time: "If I am right, let the heavens declare it." Immediately a heavenly voice was heard: "Why do you oppose Rabbi Eliezer? His view is right." But Rabbi Joshua intervened and said, "The Torah is not in heaven (Deut. 30:12)." Thereupon Rabbi Jeremiah gave the explanation: "He means that at Sinai the Torah was given to man. We do not consider a heavenly voice to be binding. Does not the Torah tell us, 'You are to decide by a majority' " (cf. Exod. 23:2, read with a measure of license). Then an epilogue is appended, making the story's intent clear. Rabbi Nathan subsequently met the prophet Elijah and inquired what God was doing during the above incident. Elijah answered that God had laughed and confessed, "My children have triumphed over me" (*Baba Metzia* 59b). Adler concludes: "The use of reason by man evidences the divine image in which he was created."[48] Vermes observes: While it is true that after prophetic revelation ceases, rabbinic teaching recognizes a "heavenly voice" (*bath kol*), that "voice" is not granted any authority in issues relating to *halakhah*, for *halakhah* is to be constructed upon tradition and reason.[49] Miracles are likewise forbidden any decision-making vote. In sum, the Torah, no longer residing in Heaven, is "entrusted to the judgment of the majority of sages on earth."[50]

We return to *The Wisdom of the Fathers*: "He who studies the Torah for its own sake merits many things. . . . Men profit from his counsel and wisdom, understanding and strength. . . . [Torah] bestows upon him royalty and dominion and acuteness of judgment" (*Avot* 6). But wisdom is judged by life: "He whose wisdom exceeds his works, to what may he be likened? To a tree whose branches are numerous but whose roots are few. The wind comes along and uproots it and sweeps it down. . . . But he whose works exceed his wisdom, to what may he be likened? To a tree whose branches are few but whose roots are numerous. Then even if all the winds of the world come along and blow against it they cannot stir it from its place" (*Avot* 3).[51]

(2) Hymns to life (*haim*) resound from the rabbinic tradition; the refrains stress and reapply the command of Torah, "This do and live" (Levit. 18:5).

From a talmudic perspective, the precepts of Torah "originated in grace," and they aim to purify humankind. Among the rabbis' commanding principles is that since the Torah's main interest "is to do us good and to protect us from falling into evil," therefore no action could ever be traced to the Torah "which could cause even the slightest injury to the individual or still less to the community." A collateral principle is the intention of the Torah to spare the people unnecessary expense and great cost or strain. The purpose of all the commandments is "the well-being of man" as against burdening him with "a heavy yoke." God cannot have any intention to harm us whom he has made in his image, when it is forbidden to do "the least harm to dumb creatures," and when, according to many talmudic authorities, it is a biblical law "to avoid causing living things suffering."[52] (A basic requirement in the slaughtering of animals, in accordance with *kashrut*, is the non-inflicting of pain.)

However, the concentration of the rabbis upon the sanctity of life does not issue in a self-abnegating pacifism. For one thing, there is nothing in a command like "You shall love your neighbor as yourself" to justify that course. Conditions are not contemplated "in which the loss of one person would be preferable to that of another. On the contrary, from the standpoint of Objectivity there is no net gain if one person's interests are sacrificed for the sake of another's. A *fortiori*, not if the interest in question is life." Of even greater pertinence is the question of feasibility. To turn the other cheek has always seemed a preposterous doctrine to most Jews, with their concern that the Law always be practicable and realizable.[53] From this point of view, pacifism is contrary to human nature as also to the Word. The Law reads "This do and live," not "This do and die."

Steinsaltz adjudges that "the sages did not concern themselves with the pragmatic aspects of problems, since their objective was not the resolution of human questions but study for its own sake." The advice here, oft-re-peated, is a little deceptive. Yes, "when a man is not profound in his learn-ing he cannot properly understand or discern the meaning of fear of Heaven." But: "If a man has not cultivated right behavior, his knowledge of Torah will be useless to him and will not survive." "Learning and proper con-duct are interdependent, the one on the other" (Vitry and Aknin commentar-ies upon Avot 3).[54]

(3) "Come now, let us reason together" (Isa. 1:18). It is primarily along this benign path that the rabbinic tradition seeks to honor its obligation to life, as that obligation is preveniently set forth in Torah. Hence, this third corner of the triangle asks for a visitation somewhat longer than the others.

Not accidentally, each of the rabbis bears the appellation "sage." Yet is it not so that a sage is distinguished from a person "on the street" only in that he has somehow managed or been allowed (a) to discipline his brain exceptionally well, and (b) to learn how to be especially articulate, to per-form out-of-the-ordinary wonders or delights with language? Z. H. Chajes emphasizes the great importance of common sense to the rabbis, as typi-fied in their habit of arguing from one kind of ruling or decision to another analogous kind (the sort of thing that "ordinary" persons spend much of their daily lives doing, if not freely then by constraint). I reproduce a homely illustration of such "common sense": Cattle are to be permitted to pasture in woods without the landlord having the right to raise an objec-tion—but only small herds of cattle in large woods. Large herds in small woods would damage the trees. Within the context of social teachings, it can be argued that reasonableness is a close relative of justice. This is ex-emplified in the area of property rights. In Jewish law, occupancy must be justified by rightful claims, with the labor of the possessor a crucial factor. But there is no such thing as absolute ownership; an individual may be deprived of his property (with compensation) when the welfare of the community demands it. Again, the percentage of legitimate profit accruing from trade in commodities stands in inverse relation to the degree of the community's need for such goods. The more essential the item, the less the profit allowed.[55]

When common sense is related to fairness the consequence can be one of protest against this or that legal ruling. Thus, Eugene Korn today la-ments the injustice of the halakhic institution of mamzerut, which denies children of incestuous or adulterous unions the right to marry Jews, except converts or those also "illegitimate." A conflict is specified by Korn be-tween this institution and retributive and distributive justice, viz., for pu-nitive action to be legitimated, there must be proven guilt; and arbitrary inequality must be eliminated. Korn describes the role of rationality within the moral domain:

The Jew committed to *halakhah* can share with others the same moral concepts. When he speaks of goodness, he means essentially human happiness and fulfillment. He talks of moral rightness, referring to the fair protection of individual interests, and he utilizes the word "justice" to connote reciprocity and the elimination of arbitrary inequalities. As a result of these conceptualizations, his ethical reasoning is governed by certain principles of inference. He need not retreat into a private moral language, for the logic of moral reasoning is identical for both the Jew and the non-Jew. It is a universal king whose sovereignty over clear thinking knows no ethnic or cultural boundaries.

And yet, just when everything seems lovely, just when reasonableness has been given crown and scepter, a surd strides into the court. Korn points out that because the conclusions of morality and of *halakhah* rest upon different logical systems, they may very well prove to be mutually inconsistent. What havoc may this complication wreak upon the norm of rationality! To believe that God commands a certain course of action does not carry within itself the moral justification of such praxis. In the same way, a moral course that is shown to be eminently reasonable cannot be said thereby to bear within itself divine sanction. Wisely, Korn grants that this dilemma is "insoluble and, therefore, eternal." To reserve primary allegiance for *halakhah* while remanding moral obligation to secondary allegiance is to commit oneself to the possibility of doing what one ought not to do. And to reserve primary allegiance to moral reasoning while subjecting *halakhah* to secondary loyalty is to subject *mitzvot* to moral evaluation and thereby to sever oneself "from the historic community of Israel who first proclaimed 'We will do,' and only afterwards stated, 'We will understand.' The theoretical paradox takes its existential toll. In every particular situation where divine commands prescribe action affecting human beings, one can obey only with fear and trembling, hoping that he is not simultaneously trespassing upon a moral prohibition."[56] What keeps us going is the hope and the trust that behind the scenes the God of *halakhah* and the God of moral reason are one and the same Lord. (How could we ever bear two or more hidden gods?) Yet—we shall be asking—how can the hope and the trust continue to be sustained in the epoch of the *Shoah*?

Before we leave the subject of the moral reasonableness of the rabbinic tradition, three additional items may be touched upon briefly: the Talmud, science (*scientia*, knowledge), and the sciences; the paradox of the Talmud as "law"; and the issue of elitism.

As far back as the early thirteenth century C.E. a rabbinic commentator declared that the study of the sciences contributes to the improvement of the soul and a desired fear of the Lord (Aknin commentary upon Avot 5). Some rabbis "branched out into 'worldly' sciences and studies not only the more effectively to interpret and apply the Torah but also because they considered all knowledge a revelation of the greatness of God and a manifestation

of the wonder and beauty with which He filled the universe He had created."
Many rabbis go so far as to make the Torah come before the work of creation, that work being based upon the plan in Torah, the "underlying moral
law upon which the Cosmic Lawgiver reared the structure which as Divine
Architect He had designed. Such a law, while transmitted through one people, could not but be meant for all mankind."[57]

The relation of the Talmud to law in its extra-scientific meaning sometimes appears confusing, at least to the outsider. In view of the length and
depth of the rabbinic tradition, this is perhaps not unexpected. Steinsaltz
writes: "The basic talmudic view is always that the subject under discussion
is not 'law,' in the socio-legal meaning of the term, but the clarification of
facts and actual situations of intrinsic importance." Again, "the Talmud, unlike the Mishnah, is not largely a work of *halakhah*, although it is undoubtedly
the most important and authoritative halakhic source ever composed. In the
last analysis, all *halakhah* rests on the Talmud, and in every case of doubt this
work is consulted. In other words, the primary source for the body of Jewish
law is not itself a legal work." The Talmud's main significance lies "not in its
halakhic conclusions but in the methods of research and analysis by which
the conclusions are drawn. . . . The purpose of the Talmud is *talmud* Torah (literally study of Torah) in the widest sense of the word, that is, acquisition of
wisdom, understanding, and knowledge. . . ."[58]

The Talmud, so the tradition insists, is never completed; this serves to
keep Torah Judaism open to historical experience, contingency, and exigency—thereby, in principle, helping to inoculate the Jewish community
against the biblicism and legalism that have always beset Christian fundamentalism and some forms of Christian pietism. Here is a major reason why
Judaism has not known the same serious conflict between "science" and "religion" that still plagues parts of the Christian community.

Finally, does the talmudic emphasis upon rationality, the scholar, and
scholarship comprise a form of elitism? (The *sexist* elitism is all too overwhelming.) The question is made unavoidable by much of the literature but
nowhere does it become more vivid than in the ancient rabbinic counsel
that should a son find both his father and his teacher in mortal danger, he
must first rescue his teacher. For while the father brings the son into this
world (*sic!*), the teacher brings him into the world-to-come (*Baba Metzia* 33a).
It is so that for hundreds of years the Jewish community has bestowed upon
the scholar a special place of eminence. In Jewish culture, comments Steinsaltz, scholars constitute the aristocracy. However, he continues, the talmudic sages insist that any scholar whose conduct is evil is not to be
respected for his learning, however formidable. He must be condemned and
despised (*Moed Katan* 17a). In *The Wisdom of the Fathers* we read: "Study [To-
rah] which is not combined with work falls into neglect in the end, and becomes the cause of sin" (*Avot* 2). According to the one facet of Jewish
tradition, creative work extends to manual labor as much as to learning.

Thus, while the rabbis of Yavneh believed that the study of Torah was the highest service of God, they said the following concerning farmers: "I am God's creature. My work [learning] is in the town; his work [farming] is in the fields. . . . Perhaps you will say that I do much [that my work is more important] and he does little? We are learned [in matters of the sanctuary and sacrifices]: one may do much or one may do little; it is all one, provided each directs his heart to heaven" (*Berakhot* 17a). The talmudic viewpoint is epitomized by the great Maimonides (1135–1204), who in the Introduction to his *Commentary on Mishnah* declares that it was because of their righteous conduct that the rabbis came to be known as great scholars and righteous men.[59] (Constitutionally, the rabbis would not wish to be dubbed "theologians." But if James Parkes is right that the proper business of theology is "the nature and purpose of the Creator for this particular world,"[60] then the rabbis do little else than apply theology to life.)

VII

Because the talmudic tradition raises the banner of moral reasonableness in the service of life, it opens itself to the question of non-Jews and Torah. For to proclaim such a message is perforce to address not Jews alone but humanity as such (that allegedly rational and moral "animal").

There are two aspects to the question: Israel's reputed obligation to the world; and a possible bond between Torah and humankind as a whole. (At both points our dialectic of faith and history is directly involved, as is the rabbinic tradition in its role as a competing normative image within the theological-ethical marketplace.)

Walter Harrelson, a Christian scholar, addresses himself to the first aspect of the question: "Israel must be faithful to God's Torah because Torah offers the only hope" to any human being "for a rich, full, satisfying life, one with meaning and value that will endure for all time. If Israel fails God by not keeping Torah, then Israel thereby fails herself, her forebears, her descendants, and *also all other human beings* whose health and blessing are bound up with those of Israel."[61] (We must come back to the issue of whether after the *Shoah* such special demands as these can still be made upon Israel.) On the second aspect of the question, the rabbis themselves point to such scriptural verses as "my statutes and my ordinances, by doing which a *man* shall live" (Lev. 18:5), God speaks "with *man*" (Deut. 6:24), and "if *any man* hates his neighbor" (Deut. 19:11), to show that God orders his will in universal ways and more than through Israel. "I call heaven and earth to witness that whether one be a Gentile or an Israelite, man or woman, slave or handmaid, according to their deeds, will the *Shekinah* [divine presence] rest upon them."[62]

Subsequently, and with special reference to the Decalogue, Professor Harrelson brings together the realities of Torah, Israel, and the world:

Israel is bound to Yahweh by actions of Yahweh taken long ago, actions that
are themselves a part of the way of God with the world, with all creatures,
especially with human beings, and most particularly with Israel, the first-
born son.... Keeping Torah is thus no longer a matter of doing the will of
one's God out of fear or gratitude or even love. It is a matter of taking one's
place in a partnership of God and people, the aim of which is righteousness,
peace, wholeness on earth. Therefore the whole of the creation has a stake
in whether or not Israel keeps the commandments. All humankind, and certainly the Christian community ... should do everything possible to help
Israel to be faithful to Torah. But *all* should learn the lesson of bondage to
Torah. For every people and every person, to belong to God is to be in
bondage to him and to his purpose. *All must keep Torah*, even though Israel
and the church must do so in special ways and must help others to see *their*
need to do so.[63]

In partial contrast to Harrelson's universalist rendering of Torah, but not of
necessity in final disagreement with it, I call attention to David Hartman's
disallowance that a commitment to revelation requires some form of absolutism (= false universalization). The succeeding paragraphs will also have
the function of relating the rabbinic emphasis upon reason to the categories
of revelation and creation. These latter categories can have great import for
reasonableness and its place within any general confrontation between faith
and history.

To universalize revelation is to blur the line separating the human from the
divine. Revelation in history is always fragmentary and incomplete. Revelation expresses God's willingness to meet man in his finitude, in his particular historical and social situation, and to speak to him in his own
language.... Revelation ... was not meant to be a source of absolute, eternal and transcendent truth, but is God's speaking to man within the limited
framework of human language and history. Reason and revelation are not
competing sources of knowledge; it is not by virtue of its cognitive content
that revelation is unique.... Revelation is God's speaking to man for the
sake of man and not for the sake of uncovering the mysteries of the divine
mind.[64]

We may take from this that revelation and reason are kindred in spirit. Revelation *qua* revelation contains an important element of "rationality," i.e., it is
adapted as such to humankind's understanding and use. This means that
revelation *qua* revelation has already opened the road to concretion. On the
other hand, rationality is itself "revelational" in one significant way: it receives the raw materials of faith and adapts and applies them to (responsible) reflection and behavior.

Hartman then undertakes to link up the foregoing exposition with the issue of creation and history, thereby carrying forward the question of non-
Jews and Torah broached at the beginning of the present section of this

chapter. Creation "is a metahistorical category." Accordingly, "the creation story in Genesis is not a prolegomenon to history, it is not primeval history, but rather serves as a corrective to possible distortions of history. In particular, it implies that man should recognize the universal sanctity of life, since all life was given through the creative power of God.... The sanctity of life may not be limited by considerations of race, color, nationality, or creed. The principle of creation universalizes the sanctity of life and thereby goes beyond any historical particularization."[65] The creation is here seen to stand in a form of tension with history. It is the primordial reality that makes history possible, and it is the ground against which history, in freedom, asserts itself. Does this not suggest that in a sense, nature is paradoxically testifying to the power of historicalness? For the operations of history can themselves alter the created process. Furthermore, creation allies itself with universal moral rationality in contrast to particularized claims. Hartman alludes to the awareness of the talmudic sages that "norms that are exclusively derived from revelation ('Had they not been written, we *would not* have known them') need not be automatically universalized, whereas norms derived from creation ('Had they not been written, we *would* have known them') apply universally to all human beings.... Faith commitments based on revelation require the universal, *not* in order to universalize a particular revelation, but in order to universalize the ethical consciousness demanded by creation." So there does prove to be one important respect in which faith commitments based on revelation can contribute to universalization, though always with the caveat that moral universalization is quite another matter from the religious universalization that is inevitably imperialistic. "The messianic dream must be of a world in which all human beings realize that they were created in the image of God, that they all owe their existence to God, and that therefore all of life is sacred. Only then can the God of Creation reign in history."[66]

A further contention of Hartman is his correlating of the dimensions of creation and history with, respectively, justice and love. "Justice is universal, love is particular. I can respect the rights of all people everywhere, but I cannot love them all. Love is always of one's neighbor." In love, knowledge and intimacy are presupposed, whereas "justice must in many respects be blind.... Those who seek to universalize [love] make it empty and meaningless.... Those who fail to recognize this feature of the human condition may become not only incapable of love, but blind to their capacity to hate." We can conclude that insofar as the representative bearer of justice is the creation, and the representative bearer of love is history, therefore the dialectic of justice and love is carried along preeminently by the dialectic of creation and history. I think we must allow, however, the respect in which history can sustain and foster justice (as well as it can compound injustice). I refer specifically to history's contribution in the war against absolutistic and idolatrous religious claims. As a matter of fact, while Hartman rightly emphasizes that revelation apprehended as the concretization of the universal means, unhappily, the absolutization of religious claims and the end of religious pluralism, he is also quite aware that historical particularity of a certain stature can associate itself with the struggle against interreligious idolatry and strife. Those "who aspire to a universal community of the faithful are driven toward a universalism of the sword." Against them, we must stress that "revelation and election belong to the domain of history, wherein the individual community serves God in the manner mediated by the memories particular to itself. The radical particularization of history eliminates the necessity for faith communities to regard one another as rivals." We are then freed to experience the blessings of religious pluralism.[67]

VIII

Since the rabbinic tradition itself underwrites an encounter with the world, it may not be wholly inauspicious for one who stands just beyond its gates to give voice to a critical comment or two, but then to allude at the end to the strength and appeal of that tradition.

The talmudic contribution to universal moral reasoning under the only God may itself be called to witness against certain faults within its own history. It is said in the Palestinian Talmud: "When the Israelites do the will of the Holy One, blessed be he, they are called *sons*; but when they do not do his will, they are not called *sons*" (*yKiddushim* 61c).[68] These words were composed, of course, many years ago. The question is whether one of their major presuppositions has ever really been overcome. While the words close the door emphatically to the scholar-snob, they only keep open the door to the massive elitism of the male sex. As with Christianity, Islam, and other world religions, rabbinic Judaism suffers fatefully from a failure to apply to females the very criteria of justice, righteousness, individual dignity, and love that, ironically, it was the first to bring to the world. Insofar as contemporary Judaism perpetuates and even increases the disproportionate power and "chauvinism" of its male constituents, it contradicts itself. (I say this while not unaware of movements within today's Judaism that oppose discrimination against and maltreatment of women. The presence of these movements serves to underscore the point.) This is not the place to take up the matter of women's liberation. Suffice it to say here that injustice toward and exploitation of females is a special blemish upon rabbinic Judaism precisely because that tradition's struggle against idolatry is so masterly and knows no peers: "You shall have no other gods before me." The idolatry that is closest to home—that of the male sex—continues to reign fairly supreme.

A not unrelated factor, though one of less practical moral significance, is the continuation, within a large part of the Jewish tradition, and despite the exercise and influence of reasonableness, of the teaching of pollution. I say "not unrelated" because of the talmudic injunction, still influential, that "sexual relations are prohibited as long as the woman remains impure."[69] That is to say, a menstruating woman is "unclean." (The factor is not insignificant; it raises the whole issue of sacerdotalism.) According to a rabbinic tenet that has not been repudiated, impurity and pollution are found in a corpse ("the supreme cause of impurity") and, in lower degrees, in a leper, a *zav* (anyone with venereal disease), and carcasses of animals and reptiles. It seems to me that this point of view conflicts with other biblical-Jewish teaching of the goodness of creation and the faithful acceptance of the world.

A possible rejoinder to my contention is given by Steinsaltz: "There appear to be two main spheres: life, the most complete expression of which is anything pertaining to sanctity (regarded as the primary source of life); and death and the void, seen as the opposite of life and of sanctity." In general, whatever is living and healthy lacks any impurity; impurity increases only as an object "comes closer to death."[70] I do not believe that this accounting resolves the problem, which has to do, I suggest, with how we are to relate "life" and "creation." It may be argued, for example, that there is a sense in which life in its totality has a certain need for death if it is to maintain its own integrity. (Of course, we are to remember that "purity" and "impurity" in Jewish thinking are not to be confused with physical cleanness or uncleanness.)

A third critical comment is associated with nuances within Jewish anthropology, as these have manifested themselves down through the centuries. The moral-theological courage of the rabbis' work is evident in their assurance that the life of a human society is quite capable of reflecting and manifesting the divine will. But does the rabbinic *Anschauung* ever really oppose the assertion that time will ultimately lead history toward redemption? That assertion is dubious at best. And what is to be done when or if time leads history toward hell? We shall be reviewing, in this book, the attack from within history itself upon all sanguine expectations, particularly from within the history of the twentieth century.

Judaism, as is well known, postulates two impulses within the human spirit: *yetser tov* and *yetser ra*, the impulse toward good and the impulse toward evil. Among the intentions involved here is opposition to essentialist or absolutist anthropologies, as exemplified in such doctrinaire propositions as "humankind is totally depraved" and "humankind is wholly good." The practical question has to do with whether one or the other of the two impulses more often gains the benefit of the doubt. My concern that in Judaism the goodness of humankind seems so many times to come out ahead, and this incorrectly so, may accord with my Christian conditioning. However, any interjection that this judgment is nothing but a matter of such conditioning is subject to the same dismissal as is due any "nothing but" or purely *ad hominem* contention. I rather think that this concern of mine is more experiential than anything else; to wit, the *Shoah* of the Jews of Europe is not exactly an Ode to the Goodness of Man. Happily, in the Jewish tradition the acknowledgment of human sinfulness is never quite lost; e.g., "Were it not for the fear that [government] inspires, every man would swallow his neighbor alive" (Avot 3); and "no man will remain indifferent when his property is threatened."[71] Lastly, the rabbinic stress upon the preciousness of the human being must be celebrated. In the name of that preciousness, a common front against sinful acts is established. We read in tractate Sanhedrin (37b): "Another reason why God created a single human being was to proclaim the greatness of the Holy One, blessed be He. Man stamps many coins with a single die and they are all identical, but the King of Kings, the Holy One, blessed be He, stamped every man with the seal of the primal man yet no one of them is like his neighbor. Therefore each man may say 'for my sake was the world created.' "[72]

Further to the enduring strength and appeal of the normative image under review: In the grand tradition of rabbinic Judaism absolute demands are met with the assumption that somehow they are relative/relevant to human life. Relativeness and relevancy intermingle; otherwise the demands would stay quite abstract, deficient in historical possibility and fruition. At the very least, acts of concretion are a means of seeking reconciliation with the severity of absolute righteousness. From this affirmation, a next and coherent step is to think of concretion as itself a divinely sanctioned method of fostering life lived in the presence of God. The question of whether deeds that are plainly relative can be finally reconciling of demands that are plainly absolute will not stop perplexing us. However, the biblical-Pharisee-rabbinic exaction that goodness be *done* is one positive way of living with this question without its proponents having to become victims of the despair that the question so easily induces. Is it not instructive that Judaism, which has always attested to the transcendent awesomeness of God and to the apodictic quality of the divine Law, should yet keep striving to create effective, practical representations of that Law? The miracle of the power of transcendence and apodicticity is that it helps to prevent the pursuit of concretion from having illusions about itself (and thereby it stands in judgment upon propaganda about the reputed majesty of human goodness). In the tradition of Reb Menahem Mendl of Kotzk, "the elimination of ulterior motives came hard, and to perform a good act with ulterior motives was equivalent to idolatry."[73] Yet a consolation is interposed: Better to perform a good deed with problematic motives than to perform a bad deed with bad motives or even good ones.

It seems out of the question, but proves not to be, that the awesome God, whom to gaze upon may mean to perish, who makes the people tremble and be afraid, and the sound of whose voice may mean death (Exod: 19:21; 20:18–19), also wills that her commandment "is not too hard for you, neither is it far off. . . . the word is very near you; it is in your mouth, and in your heart, so that you can do it" (Deut. 30:11, 14). The protagonists of an uncompromising Absolute are enabled, paradoxically, to produce an extraordinary axiom, but one that insists it is morally cogent: "We do not lay on the people burdens which are beyond their power to support."[74]

The paradox runs very deep. There is a sense in which the "perfect" appears, *kiveyakhol*, to remain unfulfilled so long as it keeps itself wrapped up in a condition of perfection. It becomes fulfilled when it is fragmentarily actualized within and by the "imperfect." Boldly put, history plays the role of helpmate to eternity, relativity acts as the nourishment of absoluteness. The paradox may even run deeper than this; it is, after all, multidimensional: If there is a sense in which the "perfect" courts the "imperfect" by way of being truly perfect, does not the "imperfect" require the "perfect" if it is to be truly imperfect? What am I saying? Here is a possible (imperfect) translation: The ultimate origin of Jewish humor is theological affirmation—perhaps more so than the factor of the unequaled historical suffering of Jews, a more customary explanation. For the life of humor is a child of the monotheizing impulse: not the eldest child but not the youngest either. If God alone is Truth and Goodness, is not everything else set free to be really quite comical? But the paradox is still not exhausted. Perfection through imperfection, and imperfection through perfection, will, when taken together, mean that God herself laughs and can even be laughed over (though never laughed at). Here is a consequent question: Why is there so much "Jewish humor" and so little "Christian humor"? Could the latter deficiency be a consequent of residual polytheism and exclusivism? I have an idea that a hermeneutic of Jewish humor can do much to help us with a hermeneutic of perfection/imperfection.

In the end we may remember Moses back there in the wilderness, doing his anguished best to get the Ruler of all the universes to change his mind—and even succeeding a little (Num. 14:11–25). Do we laugh or do we cry? Or do we cry *and* laugh?

IX

As we close this exposition of and response to the tradition of the rabbis, there may be some use in offering a few elementary observations upon the rabbinic point of view relative to certain other normative images.

Across the centuries of rabbinic reflections and counsel, "faith against the world" is a subdued note. Yet in no measure do the rabbis betray the eschatological heritage and consciousness of their people. The world-to-come (*olam ha-ba*) is greatly stressed in the talmudic record. This is reminiscent of the viewpoint of Rabbi Jesus. "What, in the final analysis, is the Talmud," asks Judah Goldin, "if not the choreography for life in the Messianic Age?"[75]

> This world is like a foyer leading into the world to come—prepare thyself
> in the foyer so that thou mayest enter into the inner chamber. . . .

The ones who are born are to die, and the ones who have died are to be brought to life again, and the ones who are brought to life are to be summoned to judgment—so that one may know, make known, and have the knowledge that He is God, He is the designer, He is the creator, He is the discerner, He is the judge, He the witness, He the plaintiff, and He will summon to judgment: Blessed be He, in Whose presence is neither iniquity, nor forgetfulness, nor respect of persons, nor taking of bribes—for everything is His. Know thou that everything is according to the reckoning. (Avot 4)[76]

The rabbinic teaching of "inside the law," with its provision for "works of supererogation," somewhat parallels the Christian dualism between ordinary lay people and those "religious" who choose to obey the "counsels of perfection," as taught within the normative image of "faith above history." However, the rabbis for the most part oppose any idea of double moral standards within the community. And yet, in consideration of the "religiousness" within many Christian normative images it may be appropriate to remind ourselves that concretions of a moral kind are not the only rabbinic bridge between the commands of Heaven and life upon earth. In Judaism there are strictly religious concretions as well, and these involve everyone. A most sacred example is Yom Kippur (the Day of Atonement), when through an entire day of prayer and fasting all Jews seek reconciliation with God and receive his grace and forgiveness.

While it cannot be maintained that Jewish thinking through the years has unexceptionally taken history with decisive seriousness, forms of historical-ness do permeate the moral and religious tradition of Judaism. There are elements of continuity here with the image of "faith transforming history" and even more of "history transforming faith."

The rabbinic tradition offers some points of contact with the image we are next to consider, "faith for the world." Sociologically speaking, elements of conservatism and optimism within the Jewish outlook—in contrast to the image of "history and faith in tension"—have been made quite apparent by our survey. The readiness of the rabbis to reinterpret old laws and enact new ones for the sake of human happiness and the general welfare is most relevant here. On the other side, the continuing emphasis upon the categorical imperatives of God serves to protect the position from easy accommodation to the world and its questionable standards. For within the august paradoxes of Judaism, none excels the existential finding that the Law sets human beings free. And what system of ethics can compare with a moral dialectic that in one breath thunders out the frightening will of the One who is "high and lifted up" (Isa. 6:1) and in the very next breath takes people to task for not having a good time? "Man will be called to account for all the permitted pleasures which he failed to enjoy."[77] The sages decree that "a man must become intoxicated on Purim until he can no longer distinguish between 'cursed is Haman' and 'blessed is Mordecai.' "[78] And "there is a benediction to be recited upon seeing the ocean for the first time, upon seeing strange animals, upon seeing rare natural phenomena, and even for ostensibly prosaic occasions—upon seeing the first blossoms of spring, on the rain, and even on beautiful women."[79] These subjects are considered at length, primarily in the Talmud's *Berakhot* tractate, devoted as it is to benedictions. Yet where did the (male) author of the above words get the idea that a beautiful woman is "ostensibly prosaic"? Will Herberg used to argue that it is woman who justifies the entire creation. (Query: Does philofeminism have to be a consort of antifeminism?)

What a pity it is that H. Richard Niebuhr and countless other non-Jewish theologians have not appropriated the treasury of talmudic/rabbinic Judaism.

6

Faith for the World

AT several places we have alluded to the this-worldly implications and consequences of a responsible religious faith. Thus, the assurance in Scripture of God's compassion for human life expectably nurtures forms of faith that are concerned with the things of our world. From a general biblical perspective, the unfolding of the righteousness of God is congruent with God's love and care for her creation.

The integrity and the contribution of our next normative image, "faith for the world," turn upon its ability to offer a viable and compelling option to "faith against the world," its polar opposite (chap. 3), as well as, in less severe degree, to the several other images. A pervasive and hardy view, the fourth image requires sustained attention—not least because, for all its influence, it is rejected by a great part of the Christian movement.

I

"Faith for the world" submits as the determining criterion of a truthful faith the power to sustain and advance the values and interests of real societies and persons—not in the sense of kowtowing to these values and interests (though that is its perennial danger), but in the sense of helping to foster human welfare in the world. Representatives of this position are assured that the will of God is advanced through the progress of human society. The unfolding of the divine righteousness is held to take place within human history.

We may suggest the concept *conciliationism*. This stands for the effort to establish the compatibility of faith and the historical world. More extreme instances of the position may be referred to as accommodationism. In the parochial context of Christianity, conciliationists strive to come to terms with time and place, contra radical Christians who are in flight from time and place. A number of conciliationists appear to seek total immersion in history—even though they do not deem themselves historicists.

H. Richard Niebuhr speaks of the Christ-and-culture position sometimes as the "natural law type," sometimes as the "cultural type." Christian spokespersons of this general viewpoint tend to look upon "the revelation of values and imperatives through Christ from the standpoint of the common reason of their culture." They assimilate the church and the injunctions and values of the gospel to culture and to society at large. They "identify cultural good and law with Christian good and law, yet seek also to interpret cultural ends and imperatives in Christian fashion." They regard the imperatives of Jesus as "republications of the law of reason and nature; the values of the Christian life are religious formulations of the values of natural and social existence. . . ." A marked propensity is evident to receive Jesus as "a great hero of human culture history; his life and teachings are regarded as the greatest human achievement; in him, it is believed, the aspirations of men toward their values are brought to a point of culmination; he confirms what is best in the past, and guides the process of civilization to its proper goal." On the one hand, culture is interpreted and evaluated through Christ; on the other hand, Christ is apprehended and proclaimed through culture.[1]

A consequence of all this is a tendency to deal with the Christian gospel in highly selective fashion. "Those elements in it which are most intelligible to culture are taken as primary, and they are understood in the context of the culture." For example, John Stuart Mill thought he discovered "good Anglo-Saxon, bourgeois Utilitarianism in the Sermon on the Mount." Again, the

> philosophers, statesmen, reformers, poets, and novelists who acclaim Christ with [Thomas] Jefferson all repeat the same theme; Jesus Christ is the great enlightener, the great teacher, the one who directs all men in culture to the attainment of wisdom, moral perfection, and peace. Sometimes he is hailed as the great utilitarian, sometimes as the great idealist, sometimes as the man of reason, sometimes as the man of sentiment. But whatever the categories are by means of which he is understood, the things for which he stands are fundamentally the same—a peaceful, co-operative society achieved by moral training. . . . This Christ of religion does not call upon men to leave homes and kindred for his sake; he enters into their homes and all their associations as the gracious presence which adds an aura of infinite meaning to all temporal tasks.

However, the complementary proposition must be added that "those elements in cultural ethics are selected as normative which are most in agreement with the New Testament. Hence this type does not simply sanction prevailing culture. . . ; it emphasizes the 'ideal' in that morality." It accommodates Christ to culture, "while selecting from culture what conforms most readily to Christ." Yet since no ultimate separation is allowed between essential Christianity and the ideal, the strategy of this type is "melioristic rather than separatist or revolutionary." And while the type does not necessarily surrender the idea of another world, the latter is treated as "an extension of the best parts of this aeon." No need is felt to posit "cracks in time."[2]

Back in the early church there were Jewish-Christian groups that "sought to maintain loyalty to Jesus Christ without abandoning any important part of current Jewish tradition" and without giving up the special Jewish Messianic promise. Niebuhr includes the Christian Gnostics (with their interpretation of Christianity as "religion" rather than as "new society"), Abélard, and Albrecht Ritschl as important advocates in church history of the Christ-and-culture type. Ritschl, its "best modern illustration," made the kingdom of God into a comprehensive association of mankind achieved through reciprocal moral action. Jesus became a Christ of culture both "as the guide of men . . . to realize and conserve their values, and as the Christ who is understood by means of nineteenth-century cultural ideas."

The preeminent modern embodiment of the conciliationist ethic within the churches is liberal Christianity in its many sub-types, often collectively identified as "Culture-Protestantism" (*Kulturprotestantismus*). In its teleological form the liberal Christian ethic defines the end of the Christian life as the kingdom of God on earth, construing this reality as a kingdom of ends— within personal understanding, an association of intrinsically valuable individuals; and within social understanding, a realization of "liberty, equality, and fraternity." In its deontological form the liberal ethic opts for "the imperative of love as the essential commandment in the gospel but interprets it perfectionistically; slurring over the end-terms of the gospel imperative— God and neighbor—it tends to regard the virtue of love as the required thing."[3]

II

In our elementary review of the Jewish rabbinic tradition we took note of its characteristic reasonableness. When the rational and religious dimensions of Judaism are opened to extrinsic intellectual and moral influences, there can result forms of religio-cultural accommodationism, rationalism, and conservatism that go far beyond anything the rabbis had in mind. This kind of alternative development may be discerned, though not without qualification, in one of the great modern Jewish thinkers, Hermann Cohen (1842-1918).

Professor Borowitz locates Cohen within the rubric of "Torah of culture" (a Jewish parallel to H. Richard Niebuhr's "Christ of culture").[4] Let us inquire concerning the fittingness of Borowitz's label, through reference to three fundamental issues: the possibility and limits of a rationalist faith, the understanding of Jewishness, and the attitude to Christianity.

Hermann Cohen, a founder of the neo-Kantian school of philosophy in the University of Marburg, reinterprets Judaism by grounding it upon a "religion of reason." In Cohen's words, "true religion . . . is based on the truth of systematic philosophy."[5] More concretely, he identifies the essence of Judaism with the idea of "ethical monotheism" that derives from neo-Kantianism. It is pointed out that the concept of "reason" in Immanuel Kant's *Religion Within the Limits of Reason* means "the particular exercise of man's analytical and synthetic intellectual power characteristic of the best culture of the time."[6] Cohen's neo-Kantian views reflect his deep belief in man's progress as an essentially rational and moral being. He holds that Kant's double stress upon moral autonomy as distinctive of human beings and upon law as the proper form for a rational ethic shows a special and praiseworthy affinity to Judaism.[7] (As shown in the *Critique of Pure Reason*, Kant knew well the massive limitations suffered by human understanding. He opposed all rationalistic metaphysics.)

A tried and true test of the integrity of faith is whether it can survive a witting or unwitting reduction of itself to a schema of philosophic ethics. There is in Hermann Cohen a certain secularizing or theologically domesticationist impulse, as when he links the concept of "one humanity" to an ideal Messianic age, which is for him the goal of ethics and the task that all peoples are to strive to fulfill. The struggle for the kingdom of the Messiah is equated with the struggle for universal human justice. Messianism is treated as "guaranteeing the infinite development of the human race in history."[8] Again, Cohen pleads for the "historical" quality of contemporary Judaism: "Modern Judaism is historical; through historical development it acquires self-consciousness. And, the guide to our religious development is prophetism, the highpoint of which is messianism." Commenting upon the prophecy of Micah, "Then the remnant of Jacob shall be in the midst of many peoples like dew from the Lord" [5:7], Cohen declares: "It is our proud conviction that we are to continue to live as divine dew in the midst of the peoples and to remain fruitful among them and for them. All of the prophets place us in the midst of the peoples and their common perspective is the world mission of the remnant of Israel."[9]

It is true that a "religion of reason" need not entail the subjection of faith to a purely moral, philosophic, or prudential fate. Does not the life of reason direct itself, in its wholeness, to transcendence? Heinz Moshe Graupe remarks that the share of religion within the totality of reason is not dependent upon its inclusion in ethics. Instead, it claims to be recognized "as an independent branch of culture." Again, as David Novak points out, since Cohen is committed to the historical development of Judaism he is free to correlate philosophy and Judaism in a way that each requires the other for fulfilling itself. Perhaps even more important, the concept of the one and only God, with its demands upon humanity, is what gives ethics its very principle of action.[10] Such insistences as these appear in Hermann Cohen's later work. We may add to these provisos the plain truth that the two Kantian emphases upon human moral freedom and upon law as the appropriate form of ethics antecede Kant by hundreds of years, associated as they are with historic Judaism. When speaking of conciliations of faith with history and the world we do not have to mean that faith gets entirely submerged under extrinsic ideas or norms. In Cohen's case, as he nears the end of his life he gives evidence of hungering and thirsting for the faith of his fathers.[11] Yet all in all, his extreme rationalism, in and through the medium of his philosophic idealism, has taken him a good distance from the Torah-reasonableness of the rabbis.

An additional and stronger linkage of Cohen to an accommodationist posture (assimilationism, sociologically speaking) is found in his treatment and understanding of the nature of the Jewish people. He draws a sharp distinction between ethnic "nationality" and the "nation," the latter meaning citizens of a state "by virtue of a pure act of political morality." Speaking in behalf of Liberal Jewry, Cohen declares:

> We do not want to form our own state, or, consequently, to be a separate nation. . . . we are and shall remain a separate religion, we are and shall remain in principle a distinct ethnic group [Stamm], a separate nationality. . . . I favor our political integration into the modern nation-state. . . . We do not understand the messianic future in terms of the image which suggests that the Lord will appoint a table on Mt. Zion for all peoples. Instead, we refer to the many imageless pronouncements in which the unique God is proclaimed "Lord of the entire earth." We thereby view the entire historical world as the future abode of our religion. And it is only this future that we acknowledge as our true homeland.[12]

One may certainly reason that in the presence of the modern rise to dominance of the nation-state, the anti-nationalist Judaism of Hermann Cohen and others can be received as non-conciliationist. Everything depends upon which comparisons and contrasts we are undertaking. In the instance of Liberal Jewry in Europe the effort was being made to accommodate Jewishness to the life and citizenship of Germany and other countries. Cohen insists: "We are free of all discord between our Judaism and our Germanism." He even calls upon non-German Jews to accept Germany as a second spiritual homeland.[13] Is not Germany, after all, the center of ethical idealism, an earnest of true messianism? Jews are "to remain fruitful" among and for the peoples of Germany and Eastern Europe. Yet just here history was to laugh in derision, while irony, in cruelest form, was to gain the victory. For history itself would soon crush under marching boots Cohen's perception that modern Judaism was being historical. To Cohen, as a pair of current analysts observes, the modern nation-state is essentially defined by a "legal system which aspires to a rational conceptualization of justice and by the tendency of the state to unite within its legal framework and national identity disparate peoples."[14] There proved to be one slight trouble here: The "disparate peoples" of Germany and elsewhere were readily united by a legal system whose "rational conceptualization of justice" boasted as its culmination the edict: "If you are a Jew, you are not to live." So much for reason, progress, and morality—the flowers of European culture.

Lastly, Hermann Cohen's conciliationism does not apply to his attitude to Christianity. However, it enters in through the rear door. We have earlier observed that a religious rejection of "the world" may very well extend to rejection of the wider world of religion; by the same token, accommodation to "the world" can involve accommodation by one faith to an alternative or more socially dominant faith. The fact is that Cohen assumes a polemical stance toward Christianity. And yet, the polemic is entirely consistent with his overall outlook.

Among the main troubles with the Christian religion, according to Cohen, are its rational insufficiencies and its moral impotence. In concentrating so much upon "faith," it fails to comprehend the truth that moral obligation has to take the form of law. "In the Kantian frame of reference, rational beings would seek ethics, not faith. They would build their lives on a morality of law. . . . Cohen, who argued that ethics is the essence of Jewish law, had thus demonstrated the rational superiority of Judaism."[15] Sometimes, however, Cohen's Kantian disposition is able to temper his negativism toward non-Jews. He speaks in one place of "the consequence Messianism attains from the idea of immortality." Immortality enables the concept of the soul to elevate "the concept of man above the differences of peoples and even of religions." Yet immediately thereafter Cohen takes the talmudic teaching of the right of the pious of the world to the world-to-come and sets it against a lack of "true humanity" in the notion of Christ as indispensable to salvation. Again, having identified "the fight against the gods" as "the fight of being against seeming, the fight of archetypal being against likenesses that have no archetype," he refers to the church's "iconoclastic turmoil" in conjunction with the problem of Christ as an image that in truth threatens monotheism. Further, "the commandment to love the unique God cannot be made understandable" in Christological terms.[16]

Cohen remains largely unencumbered by the religious tolerationist susceptibilities shared by many Reform Jews. It is instructive to note the contrast between his viewpoint and that of Jacob Emden (1697–1776). Emden, a fearless apostle of Orthodoxy who had no intention of accommodating traditional Judaism to anything or anyone (not excepting Jewish opponents), nevertheless speaks very affirmatively of Christianity (also of Islam) through, in the case of the church, certain sympathetic references to Jesus and to Paul. In a letter to the Council of the Four Lands (the central body for Jewish self-government in Poland) Emden testifies that it is habitual with him to tell of the Nazarene who "brought about a double kindness in the world": He "strengthened the Torah of Moses majestically" and "he did much good for the Gentiles . . . by doing away with idolatry and removing the images from their midst. He obligated them with the Seven Commandments so that they should not be as the beasts of the field. He also bestowed on them ethical ways, and in this respect he was more stringent with them than the Torah of Moses, as is well known. This in itself was most proper, as it is the correct way to acquire ethical practices, as the philosopher (Maimonides) mentioned." Then Rabbi Emden concludes:

> You, members of the Christian faith, how good and pleasant it might be if you will observe that which was commanded to you by your first teachers; how wonderful is your share if you will assist the Jews in the observance of their Torah. You will truly receive reward as if you had fulfilled it yourselves—for the one who helps others to observe is greater than one who observes but does not help others to do so—even though you only observe the Seven Commandments. I have written similarly in my pleasant work Torah Ha-Kena'ot—that the Jew who observes the Torah, but doesn't support it, is considered among the cursed; and the Gentile who does not observe the 613 commandments, but supports it, is considered among the blessed.[17]

So we have a form of Jewish cultural conciliationism that is yet fairly antipathetic to Christianity (Cohen), and a Jewish non-conciliationist view that is yet highly sympathetic to Christianity (Emden).

Eliezer Berkovits pronounces that Hermann Cohen's religious philosophy is not a philosophical reinterpretation of Judaism but its philosophical rejection: "How does a paradigm forgive, how does it redeem?" Berkovits concludes (in a way wholly antithetical to Franz Rosenzweig's reading of Cohen, and in part to David Novak's): "In Cohen's religion of reason God is nothing more than a methodological idea. Even in the [idea of] correlation man remains all by himself with his ideas and thoughts, though they are God-directed as the goal of his relatedness. Man is forever alone; God is only the object of his thinking. Or if we wish to use Buber's terminology, this God is an It."[18] Here is a situation where "idealism" is truly "idea-ism." We may be permitted to wonder: Is not Cohen's conciliationism related to his loss of the living God who judges history, and is not his negative nationhood for Jews related to his loss of the God who sustains the nations? Eliezer Berkovits suggests that, for Cohen, Israel is a negative nation, meaning that its uniqueness simply results from the present inadequacies of others.[19]

In Hermann Cohen a question is framed with imposing force: How is a given faith to relate itself responsibly to history, to culture, and to other faiths while yet retaining its unique identity and witness? Professor Borowitz furnishes a good strong hint of how Cohen's cultural conciliationism and his anti-Christian stance are able to coexist: "That Judaism can apparently accommodate a greater identification with secular culture than Christianity" surely "has something to do with the more positive Jewish teaching about humankind and its capacities."[20]

What happens when Christians come to be at home with the same kind of positive teaching? Thus is opened up the historical eventuality of Christian conciliationism.

III

Following upon a crossing of *La Manche*, but only after a considerable in-version in time, we catch sight of John Locke (1632–1704) at the manor house of Sir Francis and Lady Masham of Oates in Essex. It was here that Locke wrote *The Reasonableness of Christianity*,[21] a monograph that "commended itself to all who not only used their reason but used it in the 'reasonable' manner characteristic of an English culture that found the middle way between all extremes." The monograph, claims H. Richard Niebuhr, shows a well-nigh complete "assimilation of the New Testament to prevailing common sense morality."[22] It appears, however, that Niebuhr's assignment of Locke to "nat-ural law" Christianity (in contrast to a "new law" of "faith against the world") requires some qualification and clarification. To exemplify the difficulty, Locke fervently renders Matthew 5–7 in most antiworldly terms.[23]

The overall and ever-active work of reason extends to varying dimensions of life and reality, and it manifests itself within differing frames of reference. Thus we speak of reason epistemologically, in the sense of a commonly at-tested criterion of truth within historical life, sometimes in comparison or contrast with faith or other reputed ways of knowing. When popularly con-strued or profaned, reason in this primary meaning joins forces with common sense. Common sense is reasonable all right yet it is most usually held to excel rationality in any narrow or exclusive connotation of the latter. For it need not disclaim intuition or emotion. Again, reason may be linked with morality (or some other facet of culture), as when we talk of a rational ethic (or rational aesthetics, rational education, etc.). Or reason may be thought of as constituting or achieving logical and/or empirical coherence, as when we adjudge that a particular structure of thought "makes sense" within its own being and perhaps amidst a particular ambience as well. Then there is the application of the concept of reason to socio-historical life in its generic un-folding. Reason reaches out, rather ideally now, to encompass ongoing human affairs as such. Accordingly, we hear it said that the "life of reason" is the most worthwhile kind of life. Lastly, reason may operate at a level more imperious than cultural-historical life in general. There are forms of tran-scending reason, or rational imagination, wherein reason poses such ques-tions as: Is there anything reasonable in the affirmation that reason is reasonable? Is there any such reality as Reason (Word, Logos)? Reason has here gone to work upon its own self-identity. (This is not meant to be an exhaustive listing.)

We shall note the relation of John Locke to certain of these uses of reason.

As far back as the second century, divergent trends began to develop within the Christian corpus between a retention of the existential-biblical-prophetic primacy of faith as the foundation of life and morality, and the presentation of Christianity "not as an exclusive religious tradition derived largely from Judaism, but as a new philosophical way of life" competing with

Stoics, Platonists, Cynics, and other schools of thought. Justin Martyr stands in the forefront as believing "that the Christian way of life, as well as the Christian belief about Jesus, could be tested at the universal bar of reason." As Robert L. Wilken estimates, we probably owe Christianity's survival in the Roman Empire to this interpretation. Christianity could now offer itself "as a legitimate way of life whose teaching had the power to rescue men from evil and turn them to lives of goodness and virtue." The idea of Christianity as a philosophy "became the standard way Christian apologists presented their faith to critics." These men "altered fundamentally the relation of early Christianity to ancient culture."[24]

In John Locke and the Enlightenment the long rationalist tradition in Christianity is of course renewed. However, there is no doubt that Locke sometimes ties Christianity in its reasonableness to the common sense of lowly souls in contrast to the "wise." Here is how he brings *The Reasonableness of Christianity* to a close:

> Had God intended that none but the learned scribe, the disputer or wise of this world, should be Christians, or be saved; thus religion should have been prepared for them, filled with speculations and niceties, obscure terms, and abstract notions. But men of that expectation, men furnished with such acquisitions, the apostle tells us, I Cor. i, are rather shut out from the simplicity of the gospel, to make way for those poor, ignorant, illiterate, who heard and believed the promises of a deliverer, and believed Jesus to be he; who could conceive a man dead and made alive again, and, believe that he should, at the end of the world, come again, and pass sentence on all men, according to their deeds. That the poor had the gospel preached to them, Christ makes a mark, as well as business, of his mission, Matt. xi.5. And if the poor had the gospel preached to them, it was, without doubt, such a gospel as the poor could understand, plain and intelligible; and so it was, as we have seen, in the preachings of Christ and his apostles.[25]

If conciliationism is present here, it is hardly biased in behalf of "the cultured" or of some higher rationality. In *The Reasonableness of Christianity* we encounter an effort to make the gospel one of good sense for any and every human being in his or her life-situation. The more specific way in which Locke ends his ending suggests a point of departure for approaching his tacit outlook upon "faith and history."

In a rather intriguing anticipation of the Jesus-of-history School and of a deeper historicism, Locke places "the preachings of Christ and his disciples" at the center of the Christian faith. Indeed, he tells his readers that there is no necessity to concern themselves with the New Testament epistles: "'Tis not in the epistles we are to learn what are the fundamental articles of faith, where they are promiscuously, and without distinction mixed with other truths in discourses that were . . . only occasional. We shall find and discern those great and necessary points best in the preaching of Our Saviour and the apostles...." Then we are met with a congeries consisting of God's mercy, the gift of reasonableness, the Torah, human infirmity (Locke is not unaware of human sin and carelessness), and divine deliverance from the frailty of our minds and the "weakness of our constitutions":

> God, out of the infiniteness of his mercy, has dealt with man as a compassionate and tender Father. He gave him reason, and with it a law, that could not be otherwise than what reason should dictate, unless we should think, that a reasonable creature, should have an unreasonable law. But considering the frailty of man, apt to run into corruption and misery, he promised a deliverer, whom in his good time he sent; and then declared to all mankind, that whoever would believe him to be the Saviour promised, and take him now raised from the dead, and constituted the Lord and Judge of all men, to be their King and Ruler, should be saved. This is a plain intelligible proposition; and the all-merciful God seems herein to have consulted the poor of this world, and the bulk of mankind: these are articles that the labouring and illiterate man may comprehend.[26]

For Locke, the fundamental and preeminently reasonable reason why Jesus' preaching is definitive is that it is the preaching of the promised Messiah. This latter affirmation opens up the entire question of Locke's rationalism, or his position on reason and faith.

In *An Essay Concerning Human Understanding* Locke makes his famous distinction among propositions that are (1) According to reason; (2) Above reason; and (3) Contrary to reason. The teachings of Christianity may be (1) and (2) but never (3)—a position that, in George W. Forell's phrase, makes up "the stock in trade of Christian rationalism."[27] "As contradistinguished to faith," *reason* is "the discovery of the certainty or probability of such propositions or truths, which the mind arrives at by deductions made from such ideas which it has got by the use of its natural faculties, viz., by sensation or reflection." *Faith*, on the other hand, "is the assent to any proposition, not thus made out by the deductions of reason, but upon the credit of the proposer, as coming from God in some extraordinary way of communication. This way of discovering truths to men we call *revelation*."[28] However, it is evident that faith is here regarded as reasonable in a wider sense of the latter term, particularly in and through the praxis of "assent." In the *Essay* Locke has earlier spoken of faith as "nothing but a firm assent of the mind; which if it be regulated, as is our duty, cannot be afforded to anything but upon good reason."[29] This brings up the palpable question of what is the ground in reason for making an assent of faith. Can "the proposer" really boast "credit"? Or as Locke himself asks, "How shall anyone distinguish between the delusions of Satan and the inspirations of the Holy Ghost?"[30]

I. T. Ramsey emphasizes that the *Essay Concerning Human Understanding* does not adequately answer such questions. The issue, of course, is that of propositions "above reason." In the *Essay* Locke contends that certain "outward signs" are present to convince people of the divine authorship of relevant revelations.[31] This takes us back to his other work, the full title of which is *The Reasonableness of Christianity as delivered in the Scriptures* (a title to which Hermann Cohen's phrasing *Religion of Reason Out of the Sources of Judaism* shows a striking parallel).

For Locke, the "proposer" of faith is Jesus of Nazareth, and it is on his "credit" that Christians can believe the revealed truths of faith. Their belief is made reasonable by two "outward signs": the fulfilling in Jesus of prophecies of the Messiah, and Jesus' performance of miracles.[32] Our concerns in this volume are ethical more than epistemological—such thinkers as John Locke and Hermann Cohen show how the two categories are inseparable—and hence we cannot pursue the theoretical issues intensively. Brief reference to the first of the two "outward signs" will be appropriate to our purposes.

Professor Ramsey raises the inevitable epistemological question and then offers an interpretation:

> What . . . corresponds to the deductive pattern which . . . links a reasonable assertion with the ideas on which it is based? May not Locke . . . have implied that in bringing alongside the person of Jesus the Messiah label, there strikes us an aptness and appropriateness of the kind which strikes us when, for example, we see at long last the island corresponding to the map we have pondered for years. . . . In other words, though Locke never says so, is it not possible that . . . in thinking of the Messiah as a descriptive label which fitted Jesus, Locke was appealing to some kind of disclosure situation which linked ideas and revealed propositions? Was he appealing to something he called elsewhere "intuition"? . . . May there not be an intuitive link between idea particulars and revealed propositions? May not intuition play the same part for propositions which are above reason as demonstration does in the case of propositions which are according to reason? In this case the broad reasonableness of Christian assent would lie in its intuitive character.[33]

Ramsey goes on to refer to added complexities within the concept of prophecy fulfillment. In the matter of Locke's analysis of miracles or extraordinary wonders, Ramsey suggests a conclusion similar to that respecting prophecy fulfillment. A miracle "must be given the same compelling power as belongs to an intuition."[34] Thus it can be held that with respect to both of the "outward signs," reason is being directed into intuition. For John Locke, the data of time and place that count are experiential (empiricist) in character, which suggests a certain subjective inclination along with all the objectivity. The significance of Ramsey's reading, if valid, is that it allows a place within Locke's reflections for people other than doctrinaire rationalists. Recognizing Locke as a broader empiricist, a kind of Christianizer of the empirical world, we can say that he preserves "the reasonableness as well as the mystery and the distinctiveness of the Christian faith"[35]—this, whether we like or dislike how he does it. Yet in either event we are left with two mammoth problems: What is the specific role of human intuition within the dialectic of faith and history? And granted that reason is surrounded by its own mysteries, what about the mysteries of faith? Are these last reasonable or unreasonable?

If Christianity is held to be distinctive but not reasonable, we have to give up any idea "of integrating the Christian faith with philosophical speculation and culture whether humanist or scientific. The Christian faith will preserve its distinctiveness only at the cost of being utterly irrelevant."[36] The identical kinds of questioning and analysis can be applied to Judaism. Here, then, are decisive challenges to Christianity and Judaism alike, arising out of a relatively mild form of conciliationism.

Perhaps a fitting last word is that in Locke's schema, it is reason in the guise of *coherence* that is seeking to assert itself. This means reason at a more advanced level than any narrow rationalism. True, repentance and "a good life" are joined to faith (= assent) as conditions of salvation. But such conditions give no sign of being beyond the reach of reasonableness. The main thing is that these and all other pieces fit into a harmonious whole, within the divine calculus as within the human one. In directing the "plain and intelligible" truth of the gospel to the world, God has clearly taken the utmost care to ensure its good sense. God knows exactly what he is doing. He thinks of everything. We may celebrate "the admirable contrivance of the divine wisdom, in the whole world of our redemption." "Such care has God taken that no pretended revelation should stand in competition with what is truly divine, that we need but open our eyes to see and be sure which came from him." God is depicted as the most sensible of redeemers—not a shadow of klutzyness here!—and the most fairminded, if holy, of judges. And there is within Christianity itself a corresponding higher logic, a rationality that is able to resolve life-problems. No *credo quia absurdum est* is allowed. The questions that count for everyone—count existentially—are able to reach (allegedly) convincing answers. It is not a matter of what the intelligentsia alone will accept but of what any human being with an open mind and open heart will receive to his or her salvation.[37] Religious faith is a blessedly natural business, attainable in principle by all persons, if only they will pay sufficient, responsible attention. The critic who labels the argument "circular" (i.e., reason authenticates God, and God authenticates reason) is right, of course. But is not this last an instance of the blackened kettle berating the blackened pot? For to break out of Locke's particular circle is only to be captured within another one—e.g., through the claim that truth authenticates itself, or the claim that intuitive awareness is *ipso facto* convincing. Is it not a little more honest to concede that we are all caught here, along with Locke and everyone else? If so, why not simply go on to other challenges and problems? Reason may find itself accumulating a heavy burden of idolatry and other sins, but it does not follow from this that a reasonable course of action is no better than an unreasonable one.

I do not find in John Locke a purely cultural (i.e., cultured) conciliationist. And yet his argument is so transparent, so elementary, so neat, so beyond reproach, so convincing, that he must begin to nettle us—simply because we are, after all, more than reasonable creatures. Even punishment is treated by Locke as brimful with rationality. Even the miracles of Jesus, construed as they are as eminently reasonable in themselves, and inwardly compelling, are held to be performed simply to "convince men" of the truth of the gospel. And a person is said *either* to assent *or* not to assent. If people "live well here, they shall be happy hereafter."[38] We have to ask: Is the human plight quite so extricable as this? Nothing of a *mysterium tremendum* meets us here, nothing of a dark night of the soul, of temptation, of faith under bombardment by doubt, of faith in anguished tension with the world. To pose one final, inevitable query: How can so self-assured, cheerful, and easy a view of faith and the world muster any telling resources for reckoning with vast and stubborn social and individual structures of evil?

IV

The Social Gospel of Christianity addresses and opposes structures of evil systemic to economic, social, and political life, at local, national, and international levels. With respect to the United States, William A. Clebsch helps set the historical stage: "While the Civil War was turning America into an urban and industrial society, Christian prophets arose in all the major denominations to preach that the gospel of repentance, conversion, and salvation applied to the whole society—not alone, as most revivalists urged, to individual persons."[39]

When the phrase "Social Gospel" is heard in the context of images or types of Christian ethics, a natural association is often made with H. Richard Niebuhr's concept of "Christ the transformer of culture" or, in my terminology, "faith transforming history." Yet Niebuhr himself refers to the leading exponent of the Social Gospel in North America in these terms: "Walter Rauschenbusch's social gospel presents the same general interpretation of Christ and the gospel" as does Albrecht Ritschl, "though with greater moral force and less theological depth."[40] Once again, therefore, we are brought to examine the fittingness of one of Niebuhr's identifications.

In A *Theology for the Social Gospel* (1917), the chief and most mature work of Walter Rauschenbusch (1861–1918), one passage immediately suggests substantive links between the Social Gospel and theological historicism. The Social Gospel

> tries to see the progress of the Kingdom of God in the flow of history; not
> only in the doings of the Church, but in the clash of economic forces and
> social classes, in the rise and fall of despotisms and forms of enslavement,
> in the rise of new value judgments and fresh canons of moral taste and sen-

timent, or the elevation or decline of moral standards. Its chief interest is
the Kingdom of God; and the Kingdom of God is history seen in a religious
and teleological way. Therefore the social gospel is always historically
minded. Its spread goes hand in hand with the spread of the historical spirit
and method.[41]

Rauschenbusch argues that the Social Gospel is "the oldest gospel of all.
It is 'built on the foundation of the apostles and prophets.' Its substance is
the Hebrew faith which Jesus himself held. If the prophets ever talked about
the 'plan of redemption,' they meant the social redemption of the nation. . . .
The more our historical investigations are laying bare the roots of Catholic
dogma, the more do we see them running back into alien Greek thought,
and not into the substance of Christ's message nor into the Hebrew faith."
When Rauschenbusch states that the "ethical principles of Jesus" are once
more being taught and preached within and beyond the churches as the alternative to "the greedy ethics of capitalism and militarism," and that the
Social Gospel "is a revival of the earliest doctrines of Christianity, of its radical ethical spirit, and of its revolutionary consciousness," he could be writing
as a liberation theologian of the 1970s–1990s.[42]

In light of the fact that Rauschenbusch's hermeneutic of human sin (and, in
part, of salvation) is representative of the liberal Christian anthropology that
was to come under heavy and sustained attack by other Christian interpreters (contemporary and subsequent to Rauschenbusch), some extra elaboration of his understanding is desirable.

Rauschenbusch never loses sight of the personal dimension and seriousness of sin, nor of the inevitabilities of sin as an individual affliction as well
as a social one, nor of the salvation of the individual as intrinsic to Christianity. What he insists upon is a twofold truth: that our understanding of personal salvation must be deeply affected by the new comprehensions put
forth by the Social Gospel; and that any teaching on sin and redemption that
fails to do justice to social factors and processes, to "the sinfulness of the
social order" (not excluding the domain of religion itself), and to the need
for society's regeneration, has to be "incomplete, unreal, and misleading."[43]

As the reality of sin develops, two elements are held to emerge: the factor
of selfishness, and thence, in higher forms of sin, "a conflict between the selfish Ego and the common good of humanity," or, expressed in religious terms,
"a conflict between the self and God." Three ascending and expanding stages
of sin appear—sensuousness, selfishness, and godlessness—whereby "we sin
against our higher self, against the good of men, and against the universal
good." There is no doubt that, for Rauschenbusch, selfishness is the heart of
sin: "Theology with remarkable unanimity has discerned that sin is essentially
selfishness"; here "is proof of the unquenchable social spirit of Christianity."
However, the "selfish attitude" of which sin consists acts to place man "at the
centre of the universe."[44] There is thus an affinity between Rauschenbusch's

apprehension of sin and later theological understandings of sin as self-idolatry of both an individual and a social kind (e.g., Reinhold Niebuhr). The sinful mind "is the unsocial and anti-social mind." It is "always revealed by contrast to righteousness." "Having lost its vision of organized righteousness, theology necessarily lost its comprehension of organized sin." The trouble with theology is its tendency to make sin "a private transaction between the sinner and God." In truth, "we rarely sin against God alone." It is "when we set our profit and ambition above the welfare of our fellows and above the Kingdom of God" that we rebel against him. By contrast, "when we submit to God, we submit to the supremacy of the common good. Salvation is the voluntary socializing of the soul."[45]

Rauschenbusch is somewhat ambivalent toward the doctrine of "the fall" and "original sin." A "fatal turn toward an individualistic conception of sin was given to theology through the solitariness of Adam." The teaching of "the fall" has a way of blinding us to the evils of ongoing sins and the destructive power of new ones. Our Baptist theologian is concerned lest the notion of complete depravity from out of the past undermine present and future freedom and responsibility. In this regard, "original sin" acts to compound what we after Rauschenbusch have assembled under the taint of "ideology" (as defined in chap. 5 above); the doctrine of "original sin" tends to divert our minds and spirits from the power of the social transmission of sin, "from the authority of the social group in justifying, urging, and idealizing wrong, and from the decisive influence of economic profit in the defense and propagation of evil." Any denial that sin is incarnated in and through social selfishness will only prosper the cause of sin. Yet by the same reasoning Rauschenbusch can be grateful to the proponents of original sin for keeping alive a recognition of the social quality and social assimilation of sin as a universal phenomenon. Indeed, the doctrine of original sin "is one of the few attempts of individualistic theology to get a solidaristic view of its field of work."[46]

The thrust of Rauschenbusch's anthropological polemic is thus social-ethical. It focuses upon the moral need to recognize the social causations and the social solidarities of sin. The consummation of sin appears in "social groups who have turned the patrimony of a nation into the private property of a small class, or have left the peasant labourers cowed, degraded, demoralized, and without rights in the land." It is here that we strike "real rebellion against God on the higher levels of sin." Sin is "the treasonable force" that frustrates and destroys the ideals of social righteousness. The "exponent of gigantic evil on the upper ranges of sin is the love of money and the love of power over men which property connotes." In partial anticipation of Reinhold Niebuhr's thesis of "moral man and immoral society"—according to which individual righteousness and goodness get gathered up and utilized for the sake of dubious and evil collective acts and causes—Rauschenbusch protests that "our theological conception of sin is but fragmentary unless we see all men in their natural groups bound together in a solidarity of all times and all places, bearing the yoke of evil and suffering." He characterizes sin in the individual as "shamefaced and cowardly" except when society "backs and protects it." Once sin is turned into a source of prolific income, "it is no longer a shame-faced vagabond slinking through the dark, but an army with banners, entrenched and defiant. . . . Predatory profit or graft, when once its sources are opened up and developed, constitutes an almost overwhelming temptation to combinations of men. Its pursuit gives them cohesion and unity of mind, capacity to resist common dangers, and an outfit of moral and political principles which will justify their anti-social activities." Theology has given inadequate attention "to the social idealizations of evil, which falsify the ethical standards for the individual by the authority of his group or community, deaden the voice of the Holy Spirit to the conscience of individuals and communities, and perpetuate antiquated wrongs in society. . . . New spiritual factors of the highest importance are disclosed by the realization of the super-personal forces, or composite personalities, in society. When these backslide and become combinations for evil, they add enormously to the power of sin."[47]

Rauschenbusch's argumentation on sin climaxes in the themes, "the super-personal forces of evil" and "the kingdom of evil." Super-personal forces—good and bad—"are the most powerful ethical forces in our communities." Satan and the demons have long since faded out of the modern consciousness, making it very hard any longer to "realize the Kingdom of Evil as a demonic kingdom." Yet it is essential that we achieve "a solidaristic and organic conception of the power and reality of evil in the world," of "the terrible powers of organized covetousness and institutionalized oppression." And the Social Gospel "is the only influence which can renew the idea of the Kingdom of Evil in modern minds, because it alone has an adequate sense of solidarity and a sufficient grasp of the historical and social realities of sin."[48]

In presenting his solidaristic conception of sin, and therefore of salvation, Rauschenbusch acknowledges the special influence of Friedrich Schleiermacher, as to a lesser degree of Albrecht Ritschl. As Schleiermacher writes in *The Christian Faith*, that sinfulness "which precedes all acts of sin" is brought about in each and every individual "through the sinful acts and conditions of others," yet it is also propagated and strengthened by the individual's free actions; accordingly, it is wholly common to all. It is "in each the work of all, and in all the work of each."[49] Fittingly, Rauschenbusch declares that

two doctrines combined,—the hereditary racial unity of sin, and the supernatural power of evil behind all sinful human action,—created a solidaristic consciousness of sin and evil, which I think is necessary for the religious mind. Take away these two doctrines, and both our sense of sin and our sense of the need of redemption will become much more superficial and

will be mainly concerned with the transient acts and vices of individuals. . . .
[An] enlightened conscience cannot help feeling a growing sense of responsibility and guilt for the common sins under which humanity is bound and
to which we all contribute.[50]

V

According to Walter Rauschenbusch, the chief significance the Social Gospel has for the Christian doctrine of sin is that "it revives the vision of the
Kingdom of God."[51] There is a dialectical aspect, or at least a provisionally
dialectical element, in the thinking of Rauschenbusch—despite, or perhaps
even with some aid from, his representation of Culture-Protestantism. I say
"provisionally dialectical element" partly in consideration of H. Richard
Niebuhr's assigning of Rauschenbusch to "cultural Christianity" rather than
to one of Niebuhr's three median or dialectical types. The possibility of discerning a permanent dialectic in Rauschenbusch hinges upon whether we
read him as utopian or as non-utopian (in Reinhold Niebuhr's usage of those
terms in association with perfectionism). Rauschenbusch certainly is aware
of the recalcitrance of sin in human history. Dialectically construed, Rauschenbusch's thinking does set sin and the kingdom of God in a certain present and persisting tension. A complication is that his writings leave the
question of the future considerably open.

The dialectic is comprised, on the one side, of human sin, notably social
sinfulness, and, on the other side, of the kingdom of God:

> Those who do their thinking in the light of the Kingdom of God make less of
> heresy and private sins. They reserve their shudders for men who keep the
> liquor and vice trade alive against public intelligence and law; for interests
> that organize powerful lobbies to defeat tenement or factory legislation, or
> turn factory inspection into sham; for nations that are willing to set the
> world at war in order to win or protect colonial areas of trade or usurious
> profit from loans to weaker peoples; and for private interests which are will-
> ing to push a peaceful nation into war because the stock exchange has a
> panic at the rumour of peace. These seem the unforgivable sins, the great
> demonstration of rebellious selfishness, wherever the social gospel has re-
> vived the faith in the kingdom of God.[52]

This brings us to the major constructive feature of Rauschenbusch's teaching and preaching, his great concentration upon the kingdom of God.*
With Jesus (who, we are admonished, rose above the severe temptations
of mysticism, pessimism, and otherworldly asceticism[53]), Rauschenbusch
centers his attention and his commitment upon "the Kingdom of God which

---

*Today, in keeping with the struggle against sexist language, we should here substitute "reign
of God," a phrase Rauschenbusch employs at least once.

is righteousness"—interpreted, of course, by a Christian socialist and in the perspective of late nineteenth- and early twentieth-century social Christianity. (Rauschenbusch shares fully the traditional Christian misrepresentation of the historical relation between Jesus and Judaism, as well as the ideology that the coming of Jesus meant emancipation from a "nationalistic" Judaism.[54]) The perspective mentioned above is manifest in his speaking of "our determination to establish God's Kingdom on earth," a kingdom that can be instituted "by nothing except righteous life and action." The kingdom of the God who "loves righteousness and hates iniquity" is at once the instrument and the power whereby faith is made real *for the world*—this in moral terms through and through rather than dogmatic ones.[55]

The atrophy of the church's teaching of the kingdom of God has had many serious consequences: a loss of contact "with the synoptic thought of Jesus" and a resultant misunderstanding of him; a betrayal of Jesus' own ethical principles; a weakening of Christianity's moral influence for righteousness and the church's turn to sacerdotalism and ecclesiasticism; an idolatrous notion of the church as "the highest good"; a replacing of the church's conscience by pride, greed, and ambition within the church and an acceptance of unjust social conditions in Christian lands; a substituting of the church's social conservatism for the kingdom's revolutionary force; a loss of religious backing for movements toward democracy and social justice; a belittling of secular life and of Christian service to the community; an unchristian split between the individual's salvation and the social order's redemption; and a lamentable impairment of prophetic inspiration.[56]

Positively speaking, the chief contribution of the Social Gospel to Christian theology is "to give new vitality and importance" to the teaching of the kingdom of God, for without that governing doctrine all conceptions of Christianity "must be not only defective but incorrect." Thus, "a religious experience is not Christian unless it binds us closer to men and commits us more deeply to the Kingdom of God." Nothing has the power to rejuvenate Christian theology save "the consciousness of vast sins and sufferings, and the longing for righteousness and a new life," as these are expressed in the Social Gospel. The prophets of the Old Testament, we must therefore attest, exhibited the very "highest type of God-consciousness." Rauschenbusch offers a number of propositions to show the inner bond between the ethics of the Social Gospel and the kingdom of God. These include the following: The kingdom, as initiated by Jesus Christ and sustained by the Holy Spirit, "is divine in its origin, progress, and consummation" and it will be brought to fulfillment "by the power of God in his own time." Since the kingdom of God is "the supreme purpose of God," we understand the kingdom insofar as we understand God, and we understand God insofar as we understand his kingdom. Along with God himself, the kingdom is both present and future, "eternal in the midst of time." The kingdom of God impels action, which means that theories about its future are probably not valuable or true if they "paralyze or postpone redemptive action on our part." (In ways reminiscent of the main tradition of Judaism, Rauschenbusch stresses divine-human collaboration.) Jesus of Nazareth, by his life and work, initiated the kingdom of God. He emancipated it from "nationalistic limitations" and "made it world-wide and spiritual." The ideal basis for the Social Gospel is Jesus' "affirmation of life." This means—as we keep in mind Jesus' own consciousness—a social order that guarantees the freest and highest development of all personalities, the "progressive reign of love in human affairs," a "free surrender of what is truly our own, life, property, and rights" and also of all opportunities to exploit other people, and "the opportunity of nations to work out their own national peculiarities and ideals." Again, since the kingdom is itself God's supreme end, it must be as well the purpose for which the Christian church exists. The church's mission is to be "the social embodiment of the Christ-spirit in humanity." Every problem of personal salvation must be reconsidered from the perspective of the kingdom. Yet the kingdom of God is not confined to the church or to the Christian province but extends to all of life. Thus does Rauschenbusch ally himself with the cultural type with its openness to extra-Christian truth and achievement. And he contends, in contrast to any affirmation of transcending discontinuities, that the kingdom of God means continuity with the history of this world. For he sees the advent of that kingdom as meaning "the regeneration of the super-personal life of the race." On the other hand, the kingdom involves "the Christian transfiguration of the social order." It "means the progressive transformation of all human affairs by the thought and spirit of Christ."[57] (Note here the conceptual tie to the Niebuhrian type "Christ the transformer of culture.")

The final sentence of A *Theology for the Social Gospel* brings it all together: The Social Gospel is "the voice of prophecy in modern life."[58] The primary element that authenticates the Social Gospel's inclusion within the category of "faith for the world" is its insistence upon the moral-historic cruciality of the social-economic-political, or secular, domain.

VI

George Rupp makes reference to a non-pejorative definition of Culture-Protestantism (based on Emanuel Hirsch) as "an expression of the Christian ethical imperative to inform and shape the whole of life so that it realizes the ultimately religious significance which is its ground and end." Strictly within the bounds of such a definition, the Social Gospel movement within Christian Liberalism could be classed equally under "faith for the world" and "faith transforming history." As Rupp puts it, H. Richard Niebuhr generalizes the cultural type "to include all interpretations that affirm cultural ideals and human institutions *as continuous with* the transcendent reality to which Christianity testifies." Rupp is quite correct that Niebuhr's tacit confinement of the "Christ of culture" motif to a legitimating of the cultural status quo (in

contrast to his fifth or "conversionist" type) has the effect of elevating a pe-
jorative understanding of Culture-Protestantism above its descriptive or
non-polemical meaning.[59] More concretely, to Niebuhr the Social Gospel
never surmounted a "preoccupation with the conservation and extension of
American political and ecclesiastical institutions."[60]

It is just not true that Walter Rauschenbusch ever blessed the social status
quo. However, neither is it the case that his Social Gospel gives even minimal sanction to any radical overturning of socio-political structures. Although
again and again Rauschenbusch employs the terms "revolution" and "Christian revolutionists," he does not do so with any extremist political connotation or intent. We must remember in this regard that the Social Gospel was
not for the most part programmatic. As Robert T. Handy indicates, even at its
strongest it "was more a pulpit and platform movement than it was one devoted to social or political action."[61] Two years before his death in 1918
Rauschenbusch contended that "the best forces of modern life are converging" along the lines of justice and fraternity, and "there is no contradiction
between them and the spirit of Jesus." In 1917 he stated that the realization
of the Christian ideal has to come through development and law, not
through catastrophe.[62] These last propositions give us Christian conciliationism in a nutshell. Overall, the Social Gospel "had a high estimate of the civilization it wished to make more fully Christian."[63]

The measure of plausibility in H. Richard Niebuhr's declared (if somewhat
exaggerated) linkage of cultural Christianity to the social status quo is not
unrelated to a certain apprehensiveness that "faith *for* the world" may not
always be capable of marshalling the spiritual power or independence
needed to keep it from being sold into prostitution by the faiths *of* the
world. To refer to an obvious, egregious, and extreme historical case, why
was it that the proponents of the Faith Movement of German Christians
(*Glaubensbewegung Deutsche Christen*)—not exempting Emanuel Hirsch himself—lacked all moral capital to keep themselves from ecclesiological and
theological approval and collaboration with Nazism? I interpose this question only as a reminder of the costs the world may seek to exact once the
norms and demands of historical life are received, not dialectically, relativis-
tically, and ambivalently, but in unqualified continuity with the norms and
demands of faith. A total embrace of the world opens that world to demon-
ization, just as does a total rejection of the world; these two praxises are
conjoined by a deformation of responsibility and the unhappy, enforced irrelevance of faith to life. An associating of the social idealism of liberal Christianity with the support of Nazism by the Faith Movement of German
Christians is, on the surface, horrifying or downright impossible. A conclusion
respecting the presence or absence of any such affinity turns upon the issue
of whether cultural Christianity wills to emancipate itself from, or instead
manages to retain, the kind of transcendingly apodictic judgment upon
socio-political structures/praxises that can ensure a critical distancing from,

and an independent evaluation of, any and all historical claims. It is sometimes asserted that cultural Christianity, for all its insistence upon moral ideals (or, it may be, even because of these ideals), is peculiarly subject to demonic distortions. Once the Christianizing of historical culture gains allegiance, the next step is exhortations to religiousness for the sake of that culture. Then a succeeding threat soon appears: the culture gives vent to the responding wish to determine what is and is not "Christian." God is finally cast in the role of sacred servant. Yet we still have to agree with George Rupp that no theological position is ever wholly devoid of cultural influence[64]—just as there is no faith that is wholly free from history. (The Faith Movement of German Christians is antithetical to the normative image of "history transforming faith," on at least two foundations: First, in the Germany of the 1930s the causal history that was serving to transfigure religion together with all of the nation's life was wholly "profane"; it came, preponderantly, from outside the Christian domain—although, to be sure, Nazi praxis was by no means wholly discontinuous with Christian doctrine/praxis, with special reference to the treatment of Jews. Second, the German Christian movement was totally and unashamedly anti-dialectical; it had no comprehension at all of the tension between faith and history. It rejected the very possiblity of any such tension.)

No issue in ethics is more delicate or more painful to reckon with than the relation between cultural conditioning and socio-moral responsibility. In principle, responsibility is being responsible when it addresses itself to real problems in real situations. Uppermost in the minds of the Social Gospel people was the exploitation of labor, including children. These people were disturbed by the alienation of workingmen from the churches, although as Winthrop S. Hudson points out, middle-class Protestantism exaggerated the actual state of affairs: the workers were there all right; they "simply did not belong to middle-class churches."[65] With hindsight, we today are much more uncertain than was the Social Gospel of what the phrase "Christian economic order" may be taken to mean. With the same hindsight, we recall that the Social Gospel, primarily concerned as it was with the plight of industrial labor, was virtually silent on the evil treatment of black Americans.[66]

Walter Rauschenbusch never really grasped the ways in which (rightful) love can exercise destructive power within socio-political life. In this same connection, he possessed but fragmentary understanding of the relative moral necessities of self-interest and selfishness within responsible moral achievement. Again, there is a bent toward imperialism and arrogance in the assumption that Christianity holds the keys to the realm of earthly life and culture. In American Christian thought it was left to Reinhold Niebuhr to apprehend such paradoxes and pretensions. In general, the Social Gospel people were really too "Christian," i.e., too nice, ever to overthrow *anything*. To be sure, much in that movement's campaign was eventually won (though hardly through church effort alone or even primarily). Yet the victory was to issue in two curious and ironic states of affairs: (a) "The social gospel's hopes for the kingdom of God on earth became profane achievements in the reform programs legislated under the administrations of the Roosevelts, Wilson, Truman, and L. B. Johnson"; and "as these sacred dreams became worldly realities" some theological heirs of Rauschenbusch could come to treat the achievements "as illusions of progress and delusions of utopia."[67] (What an ungrateful way to welcome in the "kingdom of God"!) Could it be that Jesus had a point after all?: "The kingdom of God is not coming with signs to be observed" (Luke 17:20b). The Jesus of history whom we encountered in chapter four scarcely sustains the effort to conciliate him and his message with cultural or worldly norms, even those of a morally "high" variety. (b) New moral challenges quickly entered the ranks together with fresh and terrible evils. Part of the restless, anxious condition of the human spirit is that even as some of its problems are being blessed by solutions, its solutions are being beset and cursed by problems. For example, who, even as late as 1935, could have dreamed that the magnificent banner of liberal Christianity, "The Fatherhood of God and the Brotherhood of Man," would within less than a generation be revealed in its fate, and properly so, as a chronic case of the disease of sexism?

VII

To return in conclusion to the general image of "faith for the world," H. Richard Niebuhr proposes that behind the cultural type as a whole is the persuasion that the human situation is everywhere marked by a conflict with nature, and primarily human nature. In opposition to this idea Niebuhr sets the thought, which is to him "characteristic of the church as a whole," that the real human conflict is with God and that accordingly, in a Christian context, "Jesus Christ stands at the center of that conflict as victim and mediator." For Jesus, "the will of God is the will of the Creator and Governor of all nature and of all history."[68]

I submit two responses: (a) Niebuhr's contention points up the practical importance to our overall subject of philosophic assumptions and philosophic ventures. Let me illustrate this briefly through reference to certain crucial variables: Nature, history, sinfulness, faith, reason, and Creation all live in moral proximity to one another. No temporal event can take place save in the presence of nature, a nature that behaves either as bystander or participant or both. No nature endures that is not held within the time-frame of some kind of happening and hence some kind of before and after. Where is sin? It is the power that fabricates destructive discontinuities between faith and the world—not in the sense of "good spirit" versus "evil matter," but the very opposite of this: the corruption of a good material world by the exercise of spiritual self-idolatry. Where is reason? It is right there all the time, telling us such things as: Nature and history are very close to each other yet are not the same; sin is the deformation of freedom; etc. Reason is ever-immanent. What, then, is Creation? It is the entire shooting match: all the data, and infinitely more, of the several sentences found under the illustration of (a).

(b) H. Richard Niebuhr does not cover all the significant choices. What if the fundamental human situation is the more catholic one of conflict with ourselves-and/or-God? In such a case we are still finally driven away, with Niebuhr, from culture theology. But a momentous question asserts itself: How can the alternative choices that are granted legitimacy by Niebuhr (possibilities 1, 3, 4, and 5 on his list of types) exhaust all the moral possibilities? After all, each of them is suffusedly "religious." The point is that his failure to make a place for such a category as "history transforming faith" may be related to his delimiting of the human condition to the universal conflict with God.

In the Niebuhr view, not everything in "the Christ of culture" is suspect. Unlike radical Christianity with its attribution of equal darkness to all spheres beyond Christ's Lordship, cultural Christianity is rightly prepared to furnish varying value judgments respecting the movements and facets of society. Rightly too, culture-Protestants preach repentance "to an industrial culture endangered by its peculiar corruptions." And further, the fact that "Christians have found kinship between Christ and the prophets of the Hebrews, the moral philosophers of Greece, the Roman Stoics, Spinoza and Kant, humanitarian reformers and Eastern mystics, may be less indicative of Christian instability than of a certain stability in human wisdom." Yet on the other side of the ledger—to select out a few major considerations—it is clear that the commandments of Jesus Christ "are more radical than the Ritschlian reconciliation of his law with the duties of one's calling allows"; it is certain that Jesus' "conception of his mission can never be forced into the pattern of an emancipator from merely human oppressions"; and it is evident that "no matter how boldly rationalism announces that the theology of law and grace is irrational, it seems to come finally to the humble confession that the kingdom of God is both gift and task and thus simply states once more the old problem."[69]

How, finally, is "faith for the world" to be distinguished from transformationist positions ("faith transforming history," "history transforming faith")? We shall be in a better situation for understanding the relations after we encounter the two latter views in their specificity. As with all normative images or types of Christian ethics, the *Anschauungen* at their outer edges often blend into one another. Accordingly, the different viewpoints taken together form a complex continuum.

Against the cultural persuasion, "faith transforming history" offers an unobstructed theological-ethical vantage point for assessing and, if need be, repudiating cultural-historical achievements and claims (cf. chap. 9 below). Paul Ramsey reminds us that according to Niebuhr's exposition, culture-

Christians are not alone those who identify "loyalty to Christ to too great a degree with upholding monarchy or democracy or capitalism or the American nation.... So also may a Christian Marxist or a Christian feminist if they do not maintain sufficient critical distance from these causes to allow for divine judgment upon and against them.... Loyalty to Christ may be alleged to entail complete support of the social system to come 'beyond the revolution' ... no less than with some existing social system."[70] The essential difference between "faith for the world" and the two transformationist views has to do with the judgment of God. There is a tendency in cultural religion to rest upon a certain achievement, not excluding a most radical or revolutionary one (e.g., Marxist praxis). *Transformationism never rests*; a divine dissatisfaction pushes it on. This is particularly the case with "history transforming faith," because the time process is always open whereas faith often closes itself to change.

Another provisional answer is that when push comes to shove, as it must sooner or later, any potential sacrifice or subjugation of faith to history (i.e., to the values and interests of the social-political-intellectual order) would not be the disastrous thing for conciliationists that it would be for transformationists of either persuasion. Transformationism belongs, as we shall see, under committedly dialectical positions. In neither of the transformationist images is "faith" or "history" lost to the other side. Thoroughgoing changes are to take place within the world, and they are urgent. But submergence is never allowed. There is to be a *new* history, or there is to be a *new* faith. For representatives of "history transforming faith" as of "faith transforming history," neither this world nor another one takes final precedence. By contrast, the advocates of conciliationism, particularly in its accommodationist forms, are not terribly disturbed by attacks upon, or even the seeming eclipse of, faith. For to them the focus of the reign of God remains within this world.* What counts is that human beings be granted justice and achieve fulfillment, right now and in every tomorrow. The fortunes of faith are told to stand second in line, and if too many people in need prove to be queued up for help, faith may have to wait and come back another century. All this fits in with the moral fact that conciliationism tends to be more accepting of non-religious or extra-religious interests and enterprises than is "faith transforming history." (Conciliationists are naturals for "common fronts." Good soldiers for justice ofttimes could not care less about "religion." And they need all the allies they can find.) Transformationist views pay rather more attention to religion—although within transformationism itself there is yet a discrepancy, for "faith transforming history" is much more faith-oriented than is "history transforming faith" wherein all eyes are transfixed by historical events, not excepting very "secular"events. To the trans-

*Just as, for a radical "faith against the world," the focus of the reign of God remains beyond our spatio-temporal order.

formationist, conciliationism keeps playing one note; to the conciliationist, transformationism cannot make up its mind which note to play.

Perhaps a useful working distinction involves two kinds of moral-social domain: one that has already gained a certain reality somewhere and ought to be imitated and reenforced by the church, and one that does not exist anywhere but ought to be brought into being. Conciliationists tend toward the first of these convictions, and accordingly they will settle for improvement rather than revolution. Transformationists of the "faith transforming history" genre are at once more idealist and more radical. The social changes they demand may well involve social revolution; entire structures will have to be replaced, as against the simple if thorough melioration of existing ways.

Yet the normative image that reconciles faith and the world will always be with us, for the plain reason that any faith that conceives the world as the good creation of God and the temporal stage for coming redemption will never turn its back upon historical reality. Accordingly, in any contest between the continuities of faith and history and the discontinuities of faith and history, the former will, for conciliationism, come out ahead. Aside from the demonic culturism of perversions like the Faith Movement of German Christians, it is almost as though the Jesus of the conciliationist camp together with his party across the years are a cross between Minnesota liberal Democrats and California conservative Republicans. But if so, I suppose things could be a lot worse.

7

Faith above History

WITH this chapter we involve ourselves at the outset in the transition to concertedly dialectical viewpoints, and then we examine the first of these views, "faith above history."

I

In considerable contrast to the radical position ("faith against the world") and the conciliationist position ("faith for the world"), we are confronted with a series of refusals to assimilate or sacrifice the one polarity to the other. Neither does any of the final four positions in my own listing merely replicate the distinctive images of Jesus the Jew and of the rabbinic tradition (each of which is dialectical in its own fashion;* see Figure 3). Within the dialectical positions to come, special forms of tension are recognized and special ways of balance are sought.

Advocates of median (= dialectical) views are two-world people, just as spokespersons of the radical and the conciliationist images are one-world people. The latter two groups live apparently under a single set of imperatives "and are directed toward a single end," in contrast to median types that "find an element of discontinuity in their morality." Despite the sharp differences between radical and conciliationist representatives, they are alike "members of only one society and hear the word of God in only one language." In contrast to this, "all the median types are tormented by problems of rebirth."[1]

Dialectical positions agree that divine imperatives and values are received and fostered through both the ventures of faith and the opportunities of history, through both the "religious" or sacral dimension and the

---

*One way to express the dialectic found in the historical Jesus is: kingdom of God and Torah. And to conceptualize the rabbinic dialectic we may speak of normative Torah and concretional Torah.

140

Figure 3

Polar Image	Median (Dialectical) Images	Polar Image
Faith against the World	Jesus and the Kingdom/Righteousness of God	Faith for the World
	Rabbinic Concretions of Righteousness and Goodness	
	Faith above History	
	History and Faith in Tension	
	Faith Transforming History	
	History Transforming Faith	

"secular" or profane realm. At the same time, each of these dialectical images or median types retains an individuating quality: (a) "Faith above history" seeks a hierarchical synthesis of the spiritual and extra-spiritual domains. To revert to a concept emphasized in earlier pages, the reign of God sanctifies the reigns of humankind and it in turn receives support from them. (b) "History and faith in tension," the most heavily and persistently dialectical of all our images, is dualistic in the shattering sense that each and every believer experiences a profoundly dual citizenship that "imposes two distinct moralities though both are exercised under the one God." Attestations to the integrity and value of the historical order have a paradoxical way of driving the advocate in the direction of faith, but so too attestations of the integrity and value of faith have a paradoxical way of driving her or him in the direction of history. (c) "Faith transforming history" knows a fallen and corrupt human world but, protesting as it does that the world of humankind is located somewhere within the world of God, it yet opens the human world to transfiguration, both "through the restraining and renewing presence of God in all things and events"[2] and also through the determinate instrumentality of this or another faith-community. (d) "History transforming faith," committing itself as it does to a given religious community that is never closed to divine grace even though that community be fallen and corrupt, looks for the transfiguration of faith through the works of God and of human beings amid (but also eschatologically beyond) the province of time and place.

The appeal of these dialectical viewpoints ultimately rests, not alone upon their continuities with the two polar images, but upon the extent to which they may be able to diverge creatively from the polar extremes and to meet existential challenges not resolved via those extremes.

H. Richard Niebuhr acknowledges that the two-edged Christian attitude is a baffling one for many "because it mates what seems like contempt for present existence with great concern for existing men, because it is not frightened by the prospect of doom on all men's works, because it is not despairing but confident." Niebuhr identifies the overall rejection of anticultural radicalism and procultural accommodationism as "the great majority movement in Christianity, which we may call the church of the center," an orientation according to which "the fundamental issue does not lie between Christ and the world, important as that issue is, but between God and man." Alternatively put, because the church of the center confesses Jesus Christ as Son of the One who created heaven and earth, that church must approach the question of faith and history, not in either/or fashion, but in both/and terms. Niebuhr continues that since the doctrine of divine creation introduces "into the discussion about Christ and culture the conception of nature on which all culture is founded," it is not possible simply to oppose Christ and the world to each other. And humankind's obedience to God must be embodied in and through this world that God has made. Thus, "culture is itself a divine requirement." However, the church of the center also manifests "a certain harmony of conviction" about the nature of sin.[3] This last furnishes a most telling reason why the cultural or conciliationist position is to be placed under critical judgment.

Now once we allow H. Richard Niebuhr's contention that the ultimate moral question is indeed that between God and man (rather than that between Christ and the world), two all-decisive consequences obtain, despite the curious fact that neither one is followed out by Niebuhr. First, here is a warrant for expanding our dialectic from "Christ and culture" to that of "faith and history," and this latter as against, say, "faith and nature." For humanity is not merely a natural being that happens to have a history; human creatures are instead essentially historical beings who are also within (and beyond) nature. Second, precisely because Niebuhr comprehends the final moral question as that between God and man, the door cannot be kept shut to the question of Judaism and the question of Islam, not to mention other theistic faiths. (Tentatively and in the present context, the special moral question for the Jewish community may be stated as 'Torah and history," and for the Muslim community "Koran and history.") For both Judaism and Islam affirm, with Christianity, God's creation and providence within the historical/natural world. Niebuhr's own theological logic is thus actually driving the moral question out beyond the Christian province. Yet he himself sells no tickets for that kind of journey. He makes only scattered references to Judaism, and none to Islam. He remains at home with "Christ and culture." We have here a major reason why his work demands supplementation, a reason that is supplied, with some irony, by his own exposition.

II

The first of our four assertedly dialectical views is called variously by H. Richard Niebuhr "Christ above culture," the "synthetic" type, and the "architectonic" type. He proposes the visual symbol of a Gothic cathedral. That symbol appears most fitting because the historical representation par excellence of this next image is the great Roman Catholic synthesis reaching back to the Medieval time and perhaps before. Standing center basilica is a singular figure, St. Thomas Aquinas (1227–1274), creator of a most elegant synthesis "between natural law and new law, between this-worldly and otherworldly values, between the claims of culture and those of the gospel." The Thomist teaching of "natural law" is of supreme importance in the development, not alone of Catholic ethics, but of Western secular culture. For example, according to natural-law teaching the possession of private property is authorized because an individual requires goods in order to express his personality.[4] We shall note exceptions to such authorization within the synthetic world itself.

"Faith above history" is but a single conceptualizing expression, though an auspicious one, for a truly galactic intellectual/spiritual structure, which boasts the twofold logical form: A rests upon B, yet apart from A, B remains incomplete. To put the dialectic—I almost said the "galactic dialectic"—in a less formal but still abstract way: *The supernatural order rests upon the foundations of the natural order, yet apart from the supernatural order, the natural order is incomplete.* All of reality and all aspects of human life are assimilable to this proposition. Thus, we can have a grand time substituting various wordings within the italicized principle: Faith rests upon the foundation of history, yet apart from faith, the historical order is incomplete; theology rests upon the foundation of philosophy, yet apart from theology, philosophy is incomplete; etc., etc.

It is wrong to adjudge that there are dual or multiple kinds of truth or knowledge. Ultimately or universally speaking, truth and knowledge are one. However, there are two *sources* of truth: natural knowledge, which is initiated by rational reality through the empirical (sense-based) world; and transnatural knowledge, which has its source in the divine and is finally satisfied only in the beatific vision of God and in eternal life (beyond history). The total corpus of Christian teaching is constituted of levels that are different but not essentially conflictive. The entirety of saving truth is comprised of the natural (philosophic) dimension, involving what St. Thomas calls "the natural light of reason" (which is fully capable of establishing the existence and unity of God); and the supernatural (theological) dimension. While the supernatural order cannot contradict the natural order, the latter requires the supernatural order if it is to be fulfilled. Supernatural knowledge is made possible only through divine revelation; it enables us to affirm such doctrines as the divine creation, the Trinity, the Incarnation, original sin, the sacraments, and life after death. John Locke's distinction between Christian truths according to reason and those above reason is one historical continuation of the Thomistic synthesis, just as in turn the work of Thomas Aquinas is made possible by Aristotle's hierarchical metaphysics.

As simple, contemporaneous people, do we really require a spectacular cathedral? We need only an unpretentious two-storey house, with the lower storey dubbed "historical world" and the upper storey "faith." This allocation of space is not up for haggling (nor even for higgling) because the entire apologia consists in a twofold surety: to get to faith one moves upstairs *from and through* the world; and the storey of faith rests firmly upon, as it is also transcending, the world of culture, history, and reason.

With the foregoing general architectonic structure of things in mind, we may return to our principal interest in moral praxis. St. Thomas's fourfold accounting in the *Summa Theologica* of the necessity for humankind to have a divine law beyond the natural law may be called upon as a departure-point. His exposition takes the form of a commentary upon David's entreaty to God, "Set before me for a law the way of thy justifications" (Ps. 119:33). First, "it is by law that man is directed how to perform his proper acts in view of his last end ... of eternal happiness which exceeds" his purely natural faculty. Second, "the uncertainty of human judgment" leads to "different and contrary" human laws. Therefore, man has "to be directed in his proper acts by a law given by God, for it is certain that such a law cannot err." Third, "man is not competent to judge of interior movements ... but only of exterior acts which are observable; and yet for the perfection of virtue it is necessary for man to conduct himself rightly in both kinds of acts." Human law cannot "sufficiently curb and direct interior acts." And fourth, "human law cannot punish or forbid all evil deeds, since, while aiming at doing away with all evils, it would do away with many good things," thus hindering "the advance of the common good." Therefore, in order that "no evil might remain unforbidden and unpunished," the divine law has come to intervene, "whereby all sins are forbidden."[5]

The itemization that follows may help bring out the intent of St. Thomas's presentation of the need for a divine law. The listing, adapted from H. Richard Niebuhr, presupposes a Christian frame of reference but it is for the most part applicable within an extra-Christian context as well. (a) While divine imperatives are found in both nature and the gospel, discontinuity is also present. Thus, some elements of the divine law are not apprehensible by reason. (b) Discontinuity does not mean antithesis. The values and imperatives of nature, as these come through culture and history, help human beings to receive the values and imperatives of the gospel. (c) Since the imperatives of nature-reason-culture are all realizable by human effort, it is understandable that practical and universal emphasis should center upon them. (d) Of first importance, the values and imperatives of the two domains, nature and gospel, are not equal in significance. The cultural-historical level is *preparatory* to the higher level. It is true that gospel imperatives do not supply adequate directives for cultural life in this world, but this is only to be expected because of their higher, spiritual quality. By contrast, the fact that worldly imperatives do not supply adequate directives for the life of the spirit is due to limitations within the worldly order. (e) Jesus Christ is at once discontinuous and continuous with the life of the historical world. The latter realm can aid in leading human beings to him, but only in preliminary ways. He must enter into life "from above with gifts which human aspiration has not envisioned and which human effort cannot attain."[6]

The image of lower and higher reality penetrates all moral, social, and political life. Human society is a facet of the natural order. Yet therein we may begin to catch sight of a higher sphere. For even within the bounds of society's wholly secular system of ends and purposes we witness how the lower order of reality is striving after better and greater things. In commenting upon biblical prophecy's non-allowance for human frailty, wherein the prophet, along with God, remains "sleepless and grave," Rabbi Heschel asks: "Who could bear living in a state of disgust day and night? The conscience builds its confines, is subject to fatigue, longs for comfort, lulling, soothing."[7] Architectonic representatives are, by contrast, very fortunate; they do not have to know the prophet's anguish. For one thing, they are quite prepared to acknowledge and to make concessions to human weakness. Beyond this, they are assured that certain moral attainments are quite within mortal human power. Human beings are capable, through their own natural, inherent competence, of realizing the classical (natural) virtues of prudence, justice, fortitude, and temperance. In contrast to supernatural gifts, these capabilities were not taken away in the Fall. All this helps to account for Catholicism's rather more sanguine reading of human nature vis-à-vis classical Protestantism. In accord with this relatively greater optimism, traditional Catholic Thomism can exhibit marked confidence in the uses of reason within theology and ethics.[8] Beyond this, human beings may be granted, through God's grace as mediated in the Church, the supernatural virtues of faith, hope, and love.

The foregoing duality of virtues calls attention to the factor of duality of citizenship within the Christian community. In Catholic thought, a primary practical means of adjudicating the overall problem of faith and history is to divide the community into two classes of persons. All people play their own individual roles and make their own contributions. Farmers and craftsmen provide material goods and sustenance; priests provide spiritual sustenance. Most people live within the world and are subject to worldly duties (raising food, procreating, policing the community, waging defensive wars, administering justice, etc.); everything here is quite as it should be. No invidious comparisons are permissible concerning such persons. But then above mundane life is the life of the monastic and priestly part of the community, which is dedicated to Jesus' "counsels of perfection" (cf. Matt. 5:48). These counsels were to come primarily to mean the triad of poverty, chastity, and obedience. The two levels are intimately related, and there are no absolute barriers to a human being's movement from one level to the other. The prayers and merits of "the religious" have great bearing upon the salvation of ordinary believers, while the latter, as they carry on the work of the world, are supporting the Church and indeed making possible the sanctifying and exemplary life of the few.[9]

The architectonic ethic may be granted fuller exemplification through brief scrutiny of the political order, specifically of the state and its legitimacy. Generally speaking the Catholic view of the state, together with most Christian views, countenances neither a cynical/absolutist disallowance of limits upon political authority nor an idealist/false-universalist reduction of the state to something illicit or anachronistic. Within certain Protestant opinion there has been a tendency to associate the state with the Fall, to identify it as a species of divine intervention for dealing with the consequences of sin. Against this, Catholicism stresses that the state is a creative or at least positive manifestation of humankind's social nature. Since the state is part of nature, it shares an exemption from the consequences of original sin.[10] Obviously, in the Thomist view the Church exists at a level that excels the state. Thomism was heir to the pronouncement of Pope Gelasius (494) that the spiritual power is superior to the civil power, "to the degree that the things of the spirit and the life to come are superior to the things of the body and the life terrestrial."[11] Nevertheless, the worldly magistrate's authority is entirely licit, deriving as it does from divine ordination of the secular sphere (cf. Rom. 13:1–7), so long as the ruler does not arrogate higher privileges or powers. "Render to Caesar the [lower] things that are Caesar's, and to God the [higher] things that are God's (Matt. 22:21).

Two sentences by James P. Scull epitomize the fundamentals of Catholic political theory: "The State is a society demanded by man's social nature and its authority comes from God as the author of man's social nature. But the State exists not as an absolute power, but only to achieve the true common good of its citizens."[12] This passage can be readily rephrased to accommodate our two-storey house: The legitimacy and function of the state are integral to the natural order (a concept not wholly dissimilar to the idea within Protestant thinking of "the orders of creation") without which higher, spiritual attainments are not possible. But the state does not itself belong to the supernatural order of grace: it can make no pretension to absoluteness. This latter implies that the integrity of the state is relative in character. Its relativeness is linked to certain forces and events, with special reference to the quality of its behavior within the family of nations. National rights gain their validity in a moral context of recognition and observance of other nations' rights. Pervasively hostile or evil behavior may mean a regime's destruction and its rightful replacement by an entirely new one.

An alternate conceptual form for identifying the state is simply to speak of its preeminently historical genre. This kind of language is sometimes conducive to doubt concerning one or another nation's historical (and juridical) rights. But any such line of attack easily gets into trouble because so much of the planet's territory ultimately belonged to someone else only to be forcibly taken from them (for example, the only truly *Native* Americans). Again, human collectivities have a proclivity to seek to certify national rights by moving upward from the natural order to something approximating the supernatural order. There is often a tacit recourse to dubious ideological interests or mythological yearnings. The Catholic teaching on the state seeks to disallow claims of "national destiny," "special divine gift," and the like as possessing legitimacy in establishing national sovereignty. (Query: How about Vatican City?) On the other hand, once in a given instance state legitimacy may be presumed, a nation's recourse to symbolic confessions or celebrations of its collective meaning or ethos is not perforce mischievous. The architectonic rule remains in force: the proper direction is from B to A, never from A to B.

Catholic political theory is well known for its doctrine of the "just war." All wars are unholy, but when a given series of conditions comes into effect a particular armed conflict may be declared "just." These conditions are: duly constituted authority must sanction the war; all pacific means of resolving the conflict must have been exhausted; the cause must be just (especially in comparison with the evils a war inevitably brings); there must be a wholehearted intention to establish good or rectify evil; there must be a reasonable chance that the just cause will succeed; and the war is to be waged by proper means.[13]

Ever since 1945, when American atomic bombs destroyed Hiroshima and Nagasaki, the question of the contemporary tenability of "just war" theory has been raised again and again. Father Scull states the issue well:

> In this age of thermonuclear war there is much deep soul-searching, study and disagreement in the search for the Christian answer. This very complicated question has not yet found a unanimous or official Catholic solution. John XXIII in his famous *Pacem in Terris* comes out strongly against nuclear war and the nuclear arms race and makes it abundantly clear that the primary image of the Christian message should always be above all else a sincere and earnest quest for peace. But one cannot necessarily use this to justify unilateral disarmament which could in reality turn out to be the greatest threat to peace under present circumstances.[14]

Query on the above: What has recent history been doing to vaunted Reason?

III

With respect to the degree of applicability of the synthetic image beyond the Catholic corpus, it may be fruitful to turn to empirical, limited parallels—not duplications—within extra-Catholic spirituality.

William M. Kephart characterizes several "extraordinary groups," religious collectivities that have appeared on the American scene and that manifest unconventional life-styles.[15] His treatment and understanding are sociological, which brings such standard sociological constructs as *assimilation* and *culture-conflict* to the fore. These two concepts boast, I submit, considerable relevance to our general category of faith above history. (The socio-political utilization of geographic space is a primordial factor in all collective and individual conflict, yet it can also serve to foster concord.) The element of greater or lesser assimilation corresponds with the ways of the world, while that of greater or lesser culture-conflict corresponds with the higher reaches of group standards and demands. Insofar as extraordinary groups succeed in maintaining their collective individuality, institutionalized culture-conflict vis-à-vis the larger society tends to exceed assimilation. We may suggest that a minimal degree of institutionalized assimilation must always be present, because should this not be the case—for example, should members of an extraordinary group refuse to pay all taxes or to meet elementary health standards—the larger community will very likely reject and perhaps even expel the group. Such a fate is reminiscent of "faith against the world." (Many extraordinary groups can be treated under this latter rubric.) At the other end of the scale, should the factor of culture-conflict fade wholly away, the extraordinary group will have lost its original integrity or raison d'être. Should its collective identity manage nevertheless to endure in some form, we then witness a condition reminiscent of "faith for the world."

Let us illustrate from two of the groups analyzed by Kephart.

The Shakers, so called because of their paroxysms of shouting, singing, · shaking, and talking with God, are an importation from eighteenth-century England. Their official name is the United Society of Believers in Christ's Second Appearing. The founder, Ann Lee, had undergone repeated personal suffering and failure in trying to give birth. She interpreted her misfortunes as divine punishment for yielding to sexual desire and came to say of her bed that it was "made of embers." For her, concupiscence was the root of every evil. And since sex and marriage are so closely intertwined, marriage itself must be wrong. The Shakers were soon condemning all "carnal practices" and denouncing the established church for failing to forbid such practices. They demanded of all members total abstinence from sex. A favorite watchword was: "He who conquereth himself is greater than he who conquereth a city."

Jane and James Wardley, who had started Ann Lee on her spiritual way, believed that the Second Advent of Christ was impending, and that it would take the form of a woman. They were certain that Ann Lee was that woman. (Evidently she possessed strong charismatic qualities.) In consequence, she was invested with messiahship, being known thereafter as Mother Ann Lee. In 1774, after much legal persecution and on the receipt of divinely given instructions, she with eight followers set sail with the purpose of establishing the Kingdom of Heaven in the New World. They built an initial settlement near Albany, New York. Despite many disappointments, including periods in jail and attacks by mobs upon Mother Ann and other leaders, converts began to stream in. Save for the Hutterites, the Shakers "were to become the largest, longest-lasting, and probably the most successful of all the communistic groups in America," at one point attaining a membership of more than seventeen thousand spread over many states and involving over a hundred thousand acres of land plus hundreds of buildings.[16]

In addition to what has been called "congenial celibacy" and the rejection of marriage, Shaker societies, with many other utopian communities, practiced a highly ordered life. Strict regulations were imposed calling for confession of sins, manual labor, separation from the world, segregation of the sexes (necessary intersexual association was carried on only in groups), and renunciation of all private property. Shakers refused to vote, take part in public life, or bear arms. They took a negative view of much education and of the arts. Each brother was assigned a sister who looked after such things as mending of clothes; in exchange, a brother would perform menial tasks for the sister. There were "union meetings" between men and women, involving each of six or so sisters conversing individually with brothers enfilade-fashion. The consumption of pork was forbidden throughout Shakerdom. Some Shaker communities were vegetarian. Everyone could eat as much food as they wanted, but every bit of food put on one's plate was to be consumed. Conversation was prohibited at mealtime. Membership in the community was wholly voluntary and highly egalitarian, and resignations were freely honored. Mother Ann's counsel was, "Put your hands to work and your hearts to God." "You must not lose one minute of time, for you have none to spare." "The devil tempts others, but an idle person tempts the devil." Manual work was exalted on grounds of both moral commitment and spiritual responsibility. For all their antipathy to "the world," these people were anything but anti-technological. True spirituality is the sanctification of everything material. Another of their maxims was the extraordinary saying, "That is best which works best." The list of significant Shaker inventions is impressive: the circular saw, brimstone match, screw propeller, cut nail, clothes pin, flat broom, pea sheller, threshing machine, revolving oven, and machines for turning broom handles, cutting leather, and printing labels. Virtually none of these inventions was ever patented, on the ground that such a practice would be monopolistic. "The same inner commitment that prompted the Believers to work hard was also responsible for the exceptional quality of their labor. Whether the product was a chair, a table, or a broom, the buyer could be assured of top workmanship. . . .It was not simply work but *quality* work that constituted the Shaker trademark." Interestingly, "whereas Shaker religion has left no real mark on the world, Shaker furniture has become appreciated as a distinctive art form."[17]

Theoretically, the Shaker policy of absolute abstinence from sex could be labeled the ultimate sexual delusion. What with humanity's total dependence upon the procreative world to furnish voices within bodies apart from which no one could ever castigate procreation, the arrangement appears more than a little devious. But such reasoning would not impress or daunt Mother Ann and her adherents. Although they did not think of human nature as completely sinful, they were certain that sin entered the world through Adam and Eve's sex act in disobedience of God (even though, in point of fact, the biblical story nowhere makes forbidden sex the cause, or even a cause, of sin). Accordingly, the only way to salvation is to conquer physical desire. On the matter of the end of the human race (a rather sure consequence were the Shaker evangel to prevail universally), the Believers countered that the millennium was close at hand. Hence, there is no real need or reason for humankind to continue. In the new order, sensuality will be replaced by spirituality. While the Shakers refrained from categorizing marriage among the peoples of the world as sinful, yet, in close exemplification of the image of "faith above history," they did believe that non-Shakers comprised a lesser order of people, spiritually speaking.

To bring together the Shaker teaching upon sex with that upon God entails certain incongruities. While rejecting the Trinity, the Believers were anticipating some of today's theology by holding that God is androgynous, a fact they found reflected through all nature. The male-female duality in God is exemplified in the appearance of the spirit, first in Jesus and then in Mother Ann. As Kephart points out, this androgynous concept permeated the Shaker organization in secular as well as religious respects.[18]

In a single, bizarrely paradoxical sense the Believers will soon have won the day: at this writing, the membership of the surviving elect is down to less than a dozen very senior women and a few men.[19] (The one fatal catch is that so many non-Shakers keep on hanging around.) As a matter of fact, when in recent years there was occasion to accept a few new converts, male and female, the Society rejected the opportunity. One complication was the fear that potential initiates had one eye, and maybe both eyes, upon the group's very substantial capital endowment. Current Shaker policy of rejecting applicants for membership will shortly guarantee the group's extinction.[20] This is sad.

Interesting comparisons and contrasts with the Shakers are found in a radical Protestant group, the Hutterian Brethren, who despite unrelenting and extreme persecution are the most successful of the rural communistic and pacifist religious communities in North America. A part of the Anabaptist movement, the Hutterites began in 1528. They were enabled to survive largely through the leadership of Jacob Hutter and Peter Rideman. Staunch proponents of believers' baptism, of the separation of church and state, of religious freedom, and of the supremacy of conscience, the Hutterian Brethren have been among the fastest growing of all sect-type groups. In the

United States over the century following 1875 this highly industrious and de-
vout people multiplied from a few hundred members to 25,000. Such growth
appears related to a steadfast and successful rejection of the assimilation
process together with a traditional willingness to pull up stakes and emi-
grate whenever serious hostility and adversity threaten.

An added factor in the Hutterites' perpetuation, and an element crucial to
understanding them, is that they do not practice or condone birth control in
any form. Their birth rate usually far exceeds that in the outside world. (The
impish thought is irresistible: A Shaker and a Hutterite of opposite sex suddenly discover themselves occupants of the one bed.) Because of their burgeoning population—families customarily have more than ten children—the
problem of sufficient land is a serious one for the Hutterites, and a major
cause of friction with the larger society. Today most of these people are in
Canada, to which they moved due to persecution in the United States during
World War I. Family ties are very important, although loyalty to the overall
community provides a strong check upon family independence. Several families live in each of the residence halls, which are grouped around a communal dining hall. At mealtimes men and women are segregated and silence is
observed. As with the Amish, there are no separate church buildings.[21]

Hutterian social organization involves a limited hierarchical arrangement
reminiscent of the Moravian *Bruderhof* and markedly traditional. Each of the
various colonies maintains a small administrative council comprised of the
clergyman, business manager, farm supervisor, the German teacher, and one
or two elected members-at-large. The minister is the chief leader of the
Bruderhof in a secular as well as a spiritual sense. Yet, significantly, the Hutterian ethos works against placing strong personalities within leadership positions, while preference is given to older people.[22]

Like the Shakers, though much later (the 1920s), the Brethren opted for
technological benefits and advance. In contrast to the Old Order Amish, they
use electricity for certain purposes and they drive automobiles. They utilize
trucks, tractors, sophisticated farm machinery, and modern appliances. They
endeavor to make a distinction between inventions that "help life" and inventions that "run life" and tend thereby to destroy it. The sum and substance of their way of coping with the issue of assimilation/culture-conflict
involves allowance for change only if it is nondisruptive of traditional praxis
and belief. The outside world exerts its influence in various ways: the exchange of goods and services, contacts with government officials, and the
need for and utilization of health services. Yet the Brethren's biblical and
cultural conservatism combines with an agrarian ethos essentially apart from
the world to militate against substantial assimilation or change. Generally
speaking, the path that God laid out for them more than 450 years ago is the
one they still traverse. They wear substantially the same style clothing they
wore then. Most of it is homemade. Smoking, gambling, dancing, card playing, and commercial amusements are all taboo, as are musical instruments,

radio, record players, and television. Such drinking as is done is very moderate, and drunkenness and alcoholism are unknown.[23]

The Hutterites have been highly successful economically. Their farms are among the most thriving and the most efficient in the world. Several aspects of their religion provide the foundation of their economic life: personal and group piety, the essentiality of manual labor, agriculture, and communism. Their day combines prayer and hard work. The work schedule for the able-bodied is long and highly regulated, yet, as with the Shakers, it is deemed an affirmative expression of the way of life. The Hutterians are assured that God intended them to till the soil. Each *Bruderhof* is organized as an agricultural commune. The apostolic practice of having "all things in common" (Acts 2:44; 4:32) further allies the Brethren with the Shakers while it distinguishes them from the Amish and the Mennonites (the other two group heirs of the Anabaptists). Hutterian children early learn that property is to be used, never owned. Private property is a barrier to human solidarity and peace. The children learn as well that the surrounding world with its luxuries and its baubles is to be rejected as an evil temptation. In the Hutterite commune individuals earn no salary and receive no income. Yet as one member of the Society of Brothers testifies, "Nobody is redundant. Everybody has something to do, so you don't have a feeling that when you're older, you're not needed anymore."[24]

Before the facts of sin, orneriness, and the structural elements of human conflict, how is it that the Hutterian Brethren are able, relatively speaking, to get along well? Peter Rideman wrote: "God worketh only in surrendered men." Involved here is the central Hutterian moral concept of *Gelassenheit* (lit., calmness or patience but also translated as "brotherly love" and the "renunciation of self"). This idea/praxis—not dissimilar to the Russian concept of *sobornost* (all-togetherness)—goes very far to explain Hutterian social cooperation. Professor Kephart explains:

> To live and work closely with the same people day in and day out, sharing everything, requires a never-ending concentration of effort. This is facilitated by *Gelassenheit*. For example, although some jobs are obviously more important than others, the Brethren do not think of them in this light. Within the *Bruderhof*, positions have no high or low status, which would imply inequality. Indeed, one of the basic goals of Hutterian society is the *elimination* of social-status differentials. While they have not entirely succeeded, the Brethen have certainly minimized the prestige factor.
>
> . . . The Brethren tend to settle all differences through quiet conversation, group discussion, and consensus. Leaders do not really try to persuade followers; instead, they try to get all members to participate and share in the decision-making process. The end result, in most instances, is truly a group decision. However, if an individual member disagrees with the final verdict, he is nevertheless expected to bow to the group will—for the group will is God's will, or *Gelassenheit*.

This same concept/praxis provides continuity between this world's social organization and solidarity and the life to come: "The Brethren believe not only that man is born in sin, but that sinfulness persists. It is only by repentance and submission to God's will that salvation—in the next world—can be attained. Existence upon earth is thus looked upon as a temporary journey, with eternal life being attained only after death. Self-surrender (*Gelassenheit*), rather than self-development, is the key to this attainment."[25]

That the Hutterites more or less exemplify the image of "faith above the world" is reinforced by their comparison of the *Bruderhof* to Noah's Ark. They like to say: "You are either in the ark, or you are not in the ark." The implication of this attitude, found often among sectarian groupings, is that those outside the ark will either not inherit eternal life or had better act quickly and radically to prevent missing out on that inheritance. The notion that only the Hutterian Brethren are truly following in God's footsteps together with the group's insatiable need for more and more land are two of the major sources of conflict between Hutterites and non-Hutterites.[26] And these two factors are mutually and seriously reinforcing. However, any conclusion that what we are met with is a simple architectonic structure, with the Hutterites standing as a single and expanding entity above a benighted world, would be misleading and over-simple. For it is entirely within the bounds of that community alone that the structure is, objectively speaking, split across the middle. The rupture takes a not unfamiliar form: males above females.

Although *Bruderhof* council members have no special privileges and are very much responsible to the community, it is noteworthy that (contra the Shakers) they are all males and their election is by the male congregation alone. Women have no vote, and the likelihood of their ever being enfranchised or wanting to be approximates zero. All group decisions are made and all business is carried on by the males. Women are not permitted to drive vehicles. There is pronounced division of labor: men occupy all the leadership positions and do the agricultural and craft work; women are assigned cooking, kitchen maintenance, gardening, clothes making, and child care. All of this is understood as part of the natural order of things, in the same category as parent over child and the old over the young.[27] Peter Rideman's word remains final: "We say, first, that since woman was taken from man—and not man from woman—man hath lordship but woman weakness, humility, and submission. Therefore, she should be under the yoke of man and obedient to him. . . . The man, on the other hand, should have compassion on the woman . . . and in love and kindness go before her and care for her; and faithfully share with her all that he hath been given by God."[28] Thus there is a form of sexual noblesse oblige. Warn as they will of the moral and spiritual evils and temptations of acceding to the ways of external society, with respect to male-female relations the Hutterites are the epitome of conformism with the traditional patriarchal world outside. (The Shakers have been just the opposite.) As Kephart sums up the situation: "Female emancipation has no place in the Hutterian scheme of things. Anachronistic or not, the Hutterite world is a man's world. It always has been and probably always will be."[29]

This hierarchical scheme at the point of sex adds nuance to Sydney E. Ahlstrom's general conclusion: The "quiet tenacity" of the Hutterian Brethren through the centuries is among the marvels of church history.[30]

IV

Mysticism is found within unnumbered communities of faith around the world. Where as is often the case mystical claims and praxis seek to dissociate themselves from, or to rise above, obligations of social morality they either fall beyond the compass of this study or exemplify "faith against the world" (cf., e.g., Sufism in Islam[31]). However, there are wide differences in the understanding of the nature of mysticism. Elements of interior, ineffable, and blissful or ecstatic experience appear fundamental to all mysticism.[32] We may venture the paradoxical phrase "historicist mysticism" to convey a mystical outlook that retains components of temporal and moral responsibility (in contrast to amoral emphases upon timelessness and pure transcendence preeminent within many mystical views). Accordingly, the legitimacy of the inclusion of mysticism within the image of "faith above history" is contingent upon the presence of three interrelated conditions: forms of knowledge and insight that are identified as "higher" or ecstatic; a tacit assumption that the reaches of the mystical experience are not normally attained by everyone (mysticism's singularity and pulsating character tend to inhibit universality and to create a kind of spiritual aristocracy); and withal the factor of discrete moral behavior and special moral responsibility.

Let us return to Judaism. The fact that Jews live in "the world" as at the same time many of them believe themselves in some way accountable to a transcendent Torah suggests a certain antecedently synthetic or architectonic aspect to the life of Jewry as a whole. Yet there is not the same insistent duality of the profane and sacred spheres that is found in the Roman Catholic synthesis. The Jewish religious tradition is not known primarily for mysticism, neither is it ordinarily enamored of hierarchies. In the words of Samson Raphael Hirsch, "every son [sic] of Israel" is a priest, "setting the example of justice and love . . . spreading true humanity among the nations."[33] Further, Jewish thought has characteristically shown a wariness of mystical speculations upon the deity. Nevertheless, the tradition does boast a significant mystical strain (not excluding the Talmud itself). In large part that mysticism is of a kind that preserves the moral and practical emphases of Judaism. The architectonic assurance of continuities between nature and supernature is in some measure underwritten by Jewish mysticism as well as by Judaism's relative optimism respecting human nature. Again, certain limited dualities are allowed in the Jewish tradition—witness, for example, the prominent elevation of study above ignorance. There is the rabbinic warning that "only one who is over forty, whose belly is full (with talmudic knowledge), and who is married should be admitted to mystical exercises and speculations."[34]

In medieval Jewry certain esoteric and mystical teachings were put forth that became known as the Kabbalah (lit., tradition received or handed down). The "system" that resulted is enormously complex and sometimes unintelligible (at least to the uninitiated). How can we ever describe it in brief compass and intelligible form?[35] We must restrict ourselves to aspects that bear upon the present study, i.e., to the two-sided question of morality and evil. (The second side is a principal incentive behind all Kabbalistic speculation.)[36]

The Kabbalah entails, in Gershom Scholem's expression, "a paradoxical congruence between intuition and tradition." As the movement developed, the effort was forthcoming to make of the traditional Torah and the life that accords with it a more profoundly inner experience. In general, however, the Kabbalists were quite cautious of speaking of an unqualified mystical union between the soul and God. According to the Kabbalah, the principal realm for the ascent of the soul to ecstatic rapture is prayer. "From the day the world was created until the end of time, no one prayer resembles another." Here is spiritual historicism in pristine form. According to Lurianic Kabbalism—so named after Isaac Luria (1514–1572), who remains the movement's preeminent figure—the personal and active side of prayer is to be stressed. To the question of the Talmud, "From whence can it be known that God Himself prays?" the answer is given (in Scholem's summation) that through mystical prayer man is "drawn upward or absorbed into the hidden, dynamic life of the Godhead, so that in the act of his praying God prayed too."[37]

There has ever been a conflict between those who desired to keep the Kabbalah a closed monopoly and those who yearn to spread its influence among the people. But in either case those who practice Kabbalah are marked for a special or vital role in the world.[38]

The chief literary expression of the (Spanish) Kabbalah is the Zohar ("Book of Radiance"), a work composed probably by Moses de Leon near the end of the thirteenth century. Of pivotal importance is the Shekhinah, God's presence or self-manifestation, the Queen or the feminine principle within the world of the divine. What we have encountered independently as an architectonic apprehension of reality is now developed into a sophisticated schema of theological-mystical understanding—more precisely, into a claim of interrelationships and interpenetrations between events "here below" and those "on high." The Zohar declares: "From an activity below there is stimulated a corresponding activity on high." The lower can influence the higher, just as the higher can influence the lower. Yet a tragic factor is present: Because of the fall of primordial Adam (Adam Kadmon), the entire cosmos is ruptured. In consequence darkness and evil have succeeded in interposing themselves. More catastrophically, the divine itself is in multiple rupture: the *Shekhinah* is tragically broken up into a state of exile from *Ein Sof*, divine Infinity as such, "Most Hidden of the Hidden" (which is sharply distinguished from the revealed divine Creator).[39]

Once upon a time the *Shekhinah* radiated throughout the world. She was present in ancient Israel and she has been continually associated with the Jewish nation despite the latter's calamities and disobedience. But now the Presence is hidden; she comes only sporadically and fragmentarily. What, then, is the Jewish calling? Pious Jews must do everything possible to "mend the broken vessels" and to reunite *Shekhinah* and *Ein Sof*; such reintegration (*tikkun*) and reunification will restore harmony to the entire universe and it will bring to pass the kingdom of God. Crucial here for Jews are adherence to Torah, keeping the commandments, and prayer. Isaac Luria envisions that in the day of Messiah universal harmony will be restored.[40]

Equally central is the doctrine of the *Sefirot*, the divine "emanations," the foundation of this doctrine being "the emergence of God from the depths of Himself into creation," following upon original acts of contraction, concealment, and limitation. Just because the human soul contains some of the *Sefirot*, it follows that "the individual who experiences within himself a sense of . . . reunion and harmony can have cosmic effects. Therefore the faithful are bidden to work through the contemplative life toward the final consummation and the reestablishment of the interrupted harmony of the universe." Or, in Scholem's phrasing, man's role is to complete the process of creation "by being the agent through whom all the powers of creation are fully activated and made manifest"—this in contrast to negative implications in the Christian doctrine of original sin.[41]

We are met with an extraordinary persuasion: At least some human beings are summoned to act *within history* to contribute to the very redemption of God, which means as well helping to liberate God from exile. Could it be that with the end of the Jewish exile, the divine exile will also be broken? Before this book reaches its end the eventuality of the human redemption of God will further direct itself at us.

In the matter of this study's concerns with moral and political responsibility upon the stage of history, the Kabbalah may seem aeons and universes away. But it is not: What could be more political—yet what could be more of a temptation—than a human opportunity to transfigure the praxis of God herself, the divine Helmsperson? This would be political effectiveness with a vengeance. The followers of Frank Buchman thought they could change the whole world merely by converting the individuals who run things: Hitler, Stalin, et al. Think of the consequences of "converting" the Individual who is *really* running the show! This line of reasoning suggests the amenability of the Kabbalah to the normative image of "faith transforming history." Here the Kabbalists broach a most fundamental moral question: What duty could be more sacred than the human calling to redeem God? In any event, the

Kabbalah as a whole has been "one of the most powerful forces ever to affect the inner development of Judaism, both horizontally and in depth."[42]

The historical-religious relation between Kabbalism and modern Hasidism is a severely controversial one, as seen in the fact that Martin Buber and
Gershom Scholem, two of the most noted figures in twentieth-century Judaism, offer diametrically opposite interpretations of the matter. Regrettably,
we cannot consider Hasidism in any systematic way.

V

Gershom Scholem's hermeneutic of *zaddik* vis-à-vis *hasid* will help round off
our illustrative sketch of the bearing of Jewish thinking and praxis upon the
image of "faith above history." Although it is true that the concepts of *zaddik*
and *hasid* both encompass ideals, Scholem shows the respect in which, relative to one another, the figure of the *zaddik* occupies the ground floor, and
that of the *hasid* the upper floor, of our two-storey house. For in Jewish history and tradition the *zaddik*, sententiously described, is "the ideal of the
normal Jew. . . . the ideal *ba'al-bayit*, the family man and citizen of the community. . . . Of course, he will be called upon to resist temptation, to prove
his worth and to overcome great difficulties, but nothing essentially extraordinary is asked of him." The implied point is that while not everyone
attains such uprightness, everyone *could* do so if they would just put themselves to it. When, by contrast, "the great authorities of Judaism" refer to the
hasid (fem., *hasidah*; pl., *hasidim*) and to the quality of *hasidut* they mean the
exceptional Jew who goes beyond all requirements of duty. When the Psalmist declares that God is a *hasid* in all his works (Ps. 145:17), he is far from saying that God is merely being "pious"! He is thinking of "the exuberant and
spontaneous nature" of God's grace. The *hasid* is like that. A famous passage
in *The Wisdom of the Fathers* lists four moral genres of human being. The average man says: Mine is mine and yours is yours. The ignorant man says: Mine
is yours and yours is mine. The wicked man says: Yours is mine and mine is
mine. Only the *hasid* says: Mine is yours and yours is yours (*Avot* 5). The *hasid*,
writes Scholem, "is the enthusiast, whose radicalism and utter emotional
commitment are not to be deterred by bourgeois considerations." There is
"an element of holy anarchism in his nature" together with a readiness to
suffer for his deeds. And contrary to one well-known saying in the Mishnah, a
person can be a *hasid* quite independent of and even innocent of learning.
For while, in principle, people can be educated to become *zaddikim*, that is
out of the question with respect to *hasidim*.[43]

However, this second-storey ensconcement for the *hasid* has to be qualified. To Scholem, the elements of self-denial and even of asceticism among
the *hasidim* help explain a phenomenon of great importance in Jewish history.
Despite the high evaluation and even veneration of the *hasid*, noticeable reservations toward him, even a measure of distrust, are present. This wariness

is reflected in the fact that over a span of hundreds of years, there was never an organization of *hasidim*. Instead, such people were integrated in, or tolerated within, the larger community—this, in marked contrast to Christian monasticism and sectarian separatism. Scholem alludes to "an essentially sober streak to Judaism," which, by bringing together within a single framework the organic functions of three parties, the scholar (*talmid hakham*, lit,. "pupil of a sage"), the *zaddik*, and the *hasid*, strives to avoid spiritual stratification.[44]

The above qualifying factor is further complicated yet is also reckoned with through a fascinating historical metamorphosis. We may assume that only where all varieties of people were enabled to gather "around a central guru . . . of truly hasidic type could Hasidism maintain itself." Yet were it the case that the leaders of Hasidism had created an institutional body made up exclusively of *hasidim*, their movement would probably have succumbed at the hands of old-fashioned (antagonistic) rabbinism. Strikingly, the nomenclature itself was subjected to limited universalization:

> Never would it have occurred to earlier generations, either in literature or in life, to give the title of *hasidim* to people who admired *hasidim*. But this is precisely what has happened here. People who admired the living embodiments of hasidic ideals called themselves *hasidim*, a rather paradoxical, if not to say scandalous, usage of the word—and the true *hasidim*, those who live up to the ideal, now came to be called *tsaddikim*. This novel turn of terminology is surely highly confusing. A *tsaddik* in the hasidic sense has nothing to do with what the term means in the traditional usage which I have tried to explain but rather connotes the "super-*hasid*."[45]

At the last, Professor Scholem alludes to a segment of popular Jewish tradition with very old roots. The original figure of the *hasid* reaches a climax in the concept of the so-called hidden or concealed *zaddik*. There is the intriguing determination that scattered somewhere in time/place a certain limited company of human beings is present whose moral and spiritual stature enables the world somehow to continue on, rather than falling into destruction. According to the legend (as repeated by André Schwarz-Bart, whose blessed obsession is with the final one of these figures[46]), "the world reposes upon thirty-six Just Men [*sic*], the Lamed-Vov, indistinguishable from simple mortals; often they are unaware of their station. But if just one of them were lacking, the sufferings of mankind would poison even the souls of the newborn, and humanity would suffocate with a single cry. For the Lamed-Vov are the hearts of the world multiplied, and into them, as into one receptacle, pour all our griefs." Schwarz-Bart records certain hasidic legends within the overall legend: "When an unknown Just rises to Heaven, he is so frozen [due to the sufferings he has beheld] that God must warm him for a thousand years between his fingers before his soul can open itself to Paradise. And it is known that some remain forever inconsolable at human woe, so that God Himself cannot warm them. So from time to time the Creator, blessed be His Name, sets forward the clock of the Last Judgment by one minute."[47] (How could such legends as these be no more than legends? Do not our hearts give willing and assured assent to them?)

Gershom Scholem concludes:

> There are two types of *tsaddikim*, those who are hidden and keep to themselves and those who manifest themselves to their fellow-men and are working, as it were, under the public eye. The former is called a *nistar*, that is, "a concealed one," and the latter *mefursam*, that is, "famous." The hidden *tsaddikim* are of the higher order, because they are not tempered by the vanity almost inseparable from a public career. Indeed, some of them take it upon themselves to build up an image in sharp contradiction to their true and hidden nature. They may not even be aware of their own nature and go about performing their good deeds in secret without knowing that they are of the elect. [As God is hidden, so too they are hidden. Is God aware of being among the elect?—A.R.E.] They are hidden not only from mankind but from themselves. . . . Legend has it that one of the thirty-six is the Messiah and would reveal himself as such, if only his generation were worthy of redemption. You can never know who these highest bearers of moral standards are. One of them, and this is the final moral to which this idea points, may be your neighbor.[48]

Such a person—one's own wife? one's own husband? one's own child? one's own friend? one's own enemy? (love alone is privy to this kind of secret)—may be among those few who keep the world from perishing. Of course, we could easily observe with a shrug of the shoulders that the "turn of terminology" as between *zaddik* and *hasid* is just another case of historical-linguistic confusion. Alternatively, we could submit a *midrash* upon Scholem's exposition: This entire tale of "mistaken identity"—does it not fall within the secret, camouflaging strategies of the true Lamed-Vov?

VI

In the more or less gladsome world of synthesis, the divine righteousness can freely travel up and down the stairway of the two-storey house. The ability of the synthetic *Anschauung* to wear well appears related to the enormous range of its application to human affairs, and in ways that exceed the sacred sphere as such. In the synthesist's understanding, the world of culture "is both divine and human in its origin, both holy and sinful, a realm of both necessity and freedom, and one to which both reason and revelation apply." Within the circle of Christianity, the synthesist asserts (more than any Christian grouping) that Creator and Savior are one, and that salvation is never a menace to the created order. While maintaining the distinctiveness of their faith and praxis, and the absoluteness of gospel commands, Christians may yet cooperate with other human beings in conducting the work of the world.[49]

Nevertheless, there are problems: (a) The non-dualist—within a Christian frame of reference—will object that Jesus' "counsels of perfection" must, on the face of them, apply to everyone within the spiritual community if they are to apply at all. (b) How can poor mortals ever be absolutely sure that second-storey life is to be prayerful and first-storey life practical, rather than the other way around? (c) A strong tendency is present within the architectonic viewpoint to be essentially conservative, i.e., to accept and justify the contemporary order of things. Medieval Christendom "with its vision of the divine stability of all the members of the *corpus christianum*"[50] was actually working to stop history. Not only was this presumptuous; ultimately, it proved impossible. To H. Richard Niebuhr, "the static syntheses" of "Christ above culture" too frequently fall victim to "institutionalized religion and cultural conservatism."[51] "Faith above history," most particularly in its originative Christian version, is perhaps the least dynamic of all our normative images. Its only real rival in this ethically crucial respect is "faith against the world." (d) Relatedly, we face the twin dangers of either being shipwrecked upon the Scylla of absolutization or being engulfed in the Charybdis of societal accommodationism. The endeavor to bring "God's work and man's, the temporal and the eternal, law and grace, into one system of thought and practice tends, perhaps inevitably, to the absolutizing of what is relative." On the other side, "no synthesist answer so far given in Christian history has avoided the equation of a cultural view of God's law in creation with that law itself." Yet should the synthesist come to recognize the gulf between the law of God and the law of culture, he is then conceding that his apprehension of the synthesis is "only provisional and uncertain"; thus may he be opening the way to a conversionist outlook (Niebuhr's fifth type). In sum: "as a purely symbolic action, as a humble, acknowledgedly fallible attempt, as the human side of an action that cannot be completed without the deed of the God who also initiated it, synthesis is one thing; as an authoritative statement about the way things fit together in the kingdom of God, it is another. But if it is the former it is not really synthesis." (e) As a most major objection, synthesists "do not in fact face up to the radical evil present in all human work."[52]

With difficulties such as these before us, let us inquire what it is that "history and faith in tension" may have to offer.

8

History and Faith in Tension

AS earlier mentioned, our sixth form of argumentation is the most heavily and persistently dialectical of all normative images. Accordingly, I suggest as a capsule expression: *the hyperdialectical outlook*. Transcendence and historicity gain equal persistence. H. Richard Niebuhr denominates this view variously as "Christ and culture in paradox," as a position fraught with dualism, and as the "oscillatory type." Just as the symbol of a Gothic cathedral serves pictorially to represent the architectonic outlook, so here Niebuhr proposes the symbol of an ever-moving pendulum. "Each movement in the direction of one pole is modified by a pull in the opposite direction lest it proceed too far."[1]

I

How are we to apprehend this oscillatory process? One clue to its existential quality is H. Richard Niebuhr's observation that persons of dualist persuasion believe themselves subject throughout life to "the tension that accompanies obedience to two authorities who do not agree yet must both be obeyed."[2] This intimates a certain element of *tragedy*, as that phenomenon is manifest in classic Greek understanding. These people find that life is permeated, inevitably, by conflict.

A listing of several interrelated and not entirely separable characteristics will convey more precisely the hyperdialectical outlook in its Christian version.[3]

(1) Dualists seek to honor the gospel ethic in all its radicalness and universality. Hence, they refuse to refashion that ethic to make it appear reasonable to the "natural" mind, or to make it apply only to the future or to a spiritual aristocracy or to a spiritual level of existence. Dualists agree with synthesists that the Christian community as a whole is subject to double citizenship. However, they are disquieted, as are adherents of several other types, by the way in which synthesists divide the members

of that community (chap. 7). For the real split runs through the soul of each and every Christian. This can only mean anguish and tension—in contrast to the more-or-less happy division of labor provided by architectonic optimism. Again, conciliationism (chap. 6) respecting the cultural/historical world only obscures the corrupted human order's need and cry for redemption. Yet the radical's answer of "faith against the world" (chap. 3) is also ruled out. True, the dualist joins the radical Christian in finding human culture godless and sick unto death. But unlike the radical, the oscillationist "knows that he belongs to that culture and cannot get out of it, that God indeed sustains him in it and by it; for if God in His grace did not sustain the world in its sin it would not exist for a moment." And yet, we cannot expunge the fateful discrepancy "between the righteousness of God and the righteousness of self." For

> *before the holiness of God* as disclosed in the grace of Jesus Christ there is no distinction between the wisdom of the philosopher and the folly of the simpleton, between the crime of the murderer and his chastisement by the magistrate, between the profaning of sanctuaries by blasphemers and their hallowing by priests, between the carnal sins and the spiritual aspirations of men. The dualist does not say that there are no differences between these things, but that before the holiness of God there are no significant differences; as one might say that comparisons between the highest skyscraper and the meanest hovels are meaningless in the presence of Betelgeuse.

(2) The demands of nature and of culture alike constitute divine commands. There is no licit escape from such commands of God as these: procreation, self-preservation, the maintenance of order in a sinful world, and the coercive protection of the just from oppression by the unjust. Oscillationists endeavor to keep together, as well as to distinguish between, loyalty to Christ and responsibility for culture.

(3) The values and imperatives of culture are not translatable into gospel demands. This is the obverse of the avowal that the values and imperatives of the gospel are not translatable into the values and imperatives of culture. In refusing to accommodate the claims of Christ to those of the world, hyperdialecticians argue not alone with conciliationists but also with synthesists. And yet, against the radical opponents of culture, oscillationists are convinced "that obedience to God requires obedience to the institutions of society and loyalty to its members as well as obedience to a Christ who sits in judgment on that society." Thus are human beings subject to two different moralities, for they are citizens "of two worlds that are not only discontinuous with each other but largely opposed. In the *polarity* and *tension* of Christ and culture life must be lived precariously and sinfully in the hope of a justification which lies beyond history."

(4) Amid the effort to fulfill the demands of God in nature and culture, humankind is convicted of sin by the demands of God in the gospel; yet when

people seek simply to fulfill the demands of the gospel, abandoning nature and culture, they are again convicted of sin, particularly the practical sin of irresponsibility. Thus does the very conviction of sin operate to modify each movement of the pendulum, thereby serving paradoxically to prevent sin from taking command of life.

(5) The same God who stands in judgment upon sin also brings forgiveness, assurance, and hope. The individual who seeks to control God through both reason and praxis, who engages in attacks upon God, is yet utterly dependent upon the One "without whose loyalty he could not even rebel." For a "great act of reconciliation and forgiveness . . . has occurred in the divine-human battle—the act we call Jesus Christ." The miracle of God's grace forgives men apart from any merit of theirs, "gives them repentance, hope, and assurance of salvation from the dark powers that rule in their lives, especially death, and makes them companions of the one they willed to kill." Thus does grace abound, and it is "all on God's side."

(6) The human situation and the human-divine encounter can only be conveyed through paradox, of language as of praxis. This means the continuing advocacy of "both-and" in contrast to "either-or." For in the encounter with God dualists are standing on humanity's side, and in the encounter with humankind they are seeking to interpret the Word of God. "The true dualist lives in tension between magnetic poles." Thus in their speech as in their conduct dualists are caught up in both Christ and culture, both reason and revelation, both law and grace, both creation and the need of redemption, both iniquity and God's forgiving attribution of righteousness, both belief and doubt, both the revelation in Christ and the hiding of God, both knowledge and the need to walk by faith. Two paradoxes especially stand out: (a) According to the paradox of law and grace, the law of God in the hands of human beings becomes an instrument of godlessness and self-love; in the hands of God, the law drives the sinner to the divine mercy and is then reinstated, having been written upon the heart. Believer and unbeliever alike pass their days under law and judgment, since cultural life is possible only through God's restraint of human sin. However, the believer lives in another realm as well: the spiritual order of grace. Law has no real place here because God has broken the power of sin. The oscillationist "seems to be saying that the law of life is not law but grace; that grace is not grace but law, an infinite demand made on man; that love is an impossible possibility and hope of salvation an improbable assurance. These are the abstractions: the reality is the continuing dialogue and struggle of man with God, with . . . divine victories that look like defeats," and "human defeats that turn into victories." (b) The second special paradox is of divine wrath and divine mercy, which remain intermingled unto the end. What seemed to be wrath is yet seen to be love, yet this love "appears as wrath against the despisers and violators of love." In facing the problems of culture, the oscillationist cannot forget that the dark and evil sides of life "are weapons in the hands of a

wrathful God of mercy, as well as assertions of human wrath and man's god-lessness."[4]

(7) Niebuhr alludes to varying conceptual efforts to explicate, or to live with, the overall predicament: man as *homo duplex* (spirit and body, transcendent person and empirical individual, essence and existence, man in God and man in society, man in revolt against himself); God as *deus duplex* (grace and mercy in Jesus Christ, wrath and darkness in the world); and *mundus duplex* (the world as created and fallen, good and corrupted).

(8) The long and the short of it is that for the dualist there is no peace. Or if *shalom* is somehow glimpsed, it remains far off, it is a fragile thing, it passes human understanding (cf. Phil. 4:7). The oscillationist is more than a responsible or responsive soul, and more than an anguished soul; he or she is a responsible/responsive soul in anguish. For such a person, not alone peace but also righteousness exist only in faith and hope, only by a kind of anticipation. In the end, a moral life that is passed clinging to the restless pendulum not only receives its power from outside itself but also its meaningfulness from beyond itself.

II

In the judgment of H. Richard Niebuhr, major figures in the dualist camp include Paul of Tarsus (with reservations), Martin Luther, Ernst Troeltsch (with reservations), and Emil Brunner. Since Luther and the Reformation, the most formidable protagonist of an authentically hyperdialectical position, as well as the most widely influential native American theologian and philosopher of politics, is Reinhold Niebuhr (1892–1971), H. Richard's brother.

The quintessence of the oscillatory view is its conviction of the unrelenting doublesidedness of life and, accordingly, of the abiding *discordance* of the human state within the confines of history. In her biography of Reinhold Niebuhr, June Bingham notes well that "both-and," as against "either-or," is "progressively how the truth about the incongruity of the human situation and the irony of history have appeared to him. Indeed, if one could fairly make an oversimplification of Niebuhr's thought, it would be that he is forever at war with oversimplification."[5] For him, the essential incongruity of human existence stems from man's strange residency at the juncture of nature and spirit.[6]

Within a hyperdialectical frame of reference an infinite company of dualities arrays itself before us: particularity and universality, finitude and infinitude, freedom and necessity, love and justice, divine wrath and divine mercy, sin and forgiveness, despair and hope, anxiety and peace, progress and retrogression, the real and the ideal, faith and history, theology and politics, etc., etc. With "the incongruity of human existence" as crucible, and with dominant concerns of Reinhold Niebuhr as directional signs, we shall explore some of these "both-ands." However, it is necessary to include first a few preparatory and clarifying words—I am not telling the truth; there will be more than a few words—on the controversial issue of whether Reinhold Niebuhr came to alter his position, an issue that serves also to call attention to a fault within his conceptual apparatus.

Reinhold Niebuhr ends the chief essay of *Man's Nature and His Communities*, a definitive though brief book from his later years (1965)—he refers to it as a summary of his lifework—with a reaffirmation of "the incongruity of human existence." The context of this declaration is an analysis of the ironic (and accordingly not hopeless) situation of the superpowers, the United States and the USSR, whereby their concern for their own survival is simply powerless to keep away the wider moral challenge that is inescapably brought to them by the norms and the power of a more universal community. National interest and mutual interest have converged. Then Niebuhr offers the other side of the dialectic via his closing paragraph: "This final ironic culmination of the dreams of the ages for the fulfillment of a universal community, consonant with the obvious universality of the human spirit, reveals the whole scope of the relation of human nature, with its finite and indeterminate dimensions of human freedom, to the organization of human communities. They are always more limited than the projects of human imagination. They reveal that, while man may be universal as free spirit, he is always parochial and tribal in the achievement of organized community. Thus we are witnessing a final revelation of the incongruity of human existence."[7]

Few if any declarations could be more hyperdialectical (or more "Christian realist") than the above passages, pointing as they do to both the heights and the depths of the collective human situation. The lateness of the volume is to be carefully noted, particularly in light of Ronald H. Stone's contention, in an authoritative study, that we must approach Niebuhr's thought in terms of his subject's historical development. Stone enumerates four periods in Niebuhr the political philosopher: liberal, socialist, Christian realist, and pragmatic-liberal. I shall return to the matter of Niebuhr as pragmatist. I may simply point out at this juncture that his overall hyperdialectical position is exemplified in, and continues throughout, the various phases. As Stone himself grants, the tension of the ideal and the real is constitutive of Niebuhr's political thought all through his career. And as Stone is further required to admit, in his "pragmatic-liberal period" Niebuhr's "insights into man and his communities were not radically different from the Christian realist period," even if, to be sure, they were expressed in different language.[8] With our concern for normative images in Christian ethics rather than with detailed biography, the issue may perhaps be left open of whether an individual's advocacy of a particular image applies more in one period of his or her life than in another. However, in the case of Reinhold Niebuhr it is clear that Christian realism comprises his central, mature contribution, a point of view that, if moderated in his later days, was never abandoned. (By 1965, he preferred the appellation "moderate realist.")

Professor Stone acknowledges that Christian realism was never repudiated by Reinhold Niebuhr but maintains that aspects of it were dropped and significant alterations occurred in Niebuhr's thought after the Second Great War; viz., he showed increased respect for pragmatism and political liberalism. It is noteworthy that Stone should refer to *Man's Nature and His Communities* as bringing together the various strands of revision in his subject's thinking,[9] for in truth that volume reflects Niebuhr's retention of a hyperdialectical point of view. I think that Stone somewhat exaggerates changes in Niebuhr's position.

Christian realism is here understood as a double recognition: of the reality of persistent evil and of the reality of persistent goodness within the world of humankind. In alternate terminology, for his understanding of man and the human situation, as well as for much of his religious affirmation, Niebuhr consistently seeks to wed the Reformation and the Renaissance.[10] In this respect, he is a synthesist (though not in the latter's architectonic connotation). In an all-decisive sense, Christian realism thus constitutes a subtype within the hyperdialectical *Anschauung*. By fully allowing for integral "goodness" as well as for integral "evil" within the meaning of "realism," we avoid the basic mistake, apparent in many unsophisticated reactions to Reinhold Niebuhr, of dubbing him a "pessimist" or "cynic" who makes no allowance for "optimism" or "hope." The above definition of "realism" thus describes Niebuhr's actual position.

However, Reinhold Niebuhr does have a bent toward conceptual imprecision, and this applies to his use of the terms "realist" and "realism." In *Man's Nature and His Communities* he sets "realism" over against "idealism."[11] This produces an unfortunate ambiguity, because the preeminent or normative meaning of "realism" (argued for in that book as a whole and throughout his writings) remains its both-and quality with respect to optimism/pessimism or hope/despair.[12] The impact of the ambiguity helps to explain how Ronald Stone can refer to Niebuhr's asserted tension between the ideal and the real, and at the same time identify the continuing Niebuhrian position as (more or less) realist. When Stone alludes to Niebuhr's criticisms of realists in *Man's Nature*, he fails to make reference to the radical difference between these "realists" and the dialectical or Niebuhrian realists (those who stress potentialities for both good and evil, and moral as well as immoral or amoral factors in collective life). Thus, Stone perpetuates Niebuhr's own categorial unclarity.[13]

An important collateral factor here is that "realist political theory" (as put forward by, for example, Hans J. Morgenthau), which is identified with *Realpolitik* or *raison d'état*, is most often construed as the antagonist of various forms of political idealism. In *Man's Nature* Reinhold Niebuhr subtitles his major essay "A Critical Survey of Idealist and Realist Political Theories." The fact that Niebuhr is not an adherent of (simplistic) realist political theory (*Realpolitik*)—thus he will have nothing of the Morgenthau assumption that no political action can ever be "just"[14]—compounds the semantic and substantive difficulty.* But in truth neither is he a "political idealist," i.e., an exponent of the (simplistic) notion that, in contrast to the stratagems of *Realpolitik*, man's rational, creative capacities are able to replace social conflict and ambition with ideal justice and peace. Right near the beginning of his essay Niebuhr can depict his own position as follows (though without freeing himself from ambiguity): "The most consistent theories, whether realist or idealist, of political behavior fail to observe the intricate relation between the creative and the disruptive tendencies of human freedom."[15] Once Reinhold Niebuhr's advocacy of Christian moral-political realism is cleansed of his own tendency to conceptual imprecision, that advocacy is seen to be integrally both-and: it finds its being upon the middle ground between self-styled "realism" ("pessimism," "cynicism," "disruptiveness," etc.) and self-styled "idealism" ("optimism," "utopianism," "creativity," etc.). In a word, this is what makes the viewpoint, objectively speaking, realist. Realism is the sworn foe of simplism.

III

*Man: the grandeur and the misery.*** The foregoing introduction to Reinhold Niebuhr has already drawn us into the anthropological question. That question is at the center of his thinking.[16]

Although the issue of the meaning of "human" could not be more complex, many illustrative reminders of that complexity are fairly uncomplicated. (The dialectic goes into operation just as soon as we address it; comfortingly, complexity is twinned by simplicity.) An elementary phenomenon in point is the unique syntactic-linguistic capacity of humankind to place unnumbered, competing adjectives in front of "man," ranging all the way, along one track of reasoning, from "little" to "ultimate." (Yet while the point is elementary, something astonishing is already interposed: Who is this strange being that goes about pinning labels upon itself?) The phrase "ultimate man," as originally used by Reinhold Niebuhr, signifies a human pretension to divinity or its equivalent. Yet just as readily, though grudgingly and even resentfully, man can pronounce that he is "nothing" or even "less than nothing." How could there be such a creature, who in one moment fancies he is equal to God and in another moment determines that he is worthless? Man seems "to be" that equivocal being who is constitutionally unable—or unwilling?—to travel in one solitary direction respecting the

---

*Reinhold Niebuhr is nevertheless in great agreement with Hans Morgenthau, as shown, for example, in his insistence that man's self-regarding impulse is stronger than the self-denying or social impulse.

**Unexceptionally, Reinhold Niebuhr's anthropological language utilizes "man," "he," "him," etc. Yet since so much of his assessment of "man's" behavior and motives is denunciatory, the usage sometimes has the curious psychological effect of being anything but sexist.

meaning of what and who he is, a problem that does not appear to beset either God or the animals.

The answer to the enigma of human uniqueness, or better (since we really have no final, i.e., rational, "answer") the way to keep wrestling with that enigma, lies in concentrating upon a primordial reality or faculty that Niebuhr speaks of as *radical freedom* or indeterminate freedom. The radicalness of freedom means that "when man rises above the necessities and limits of nature, he is not inevitably bound in his actions to the norms and universalities of 'reason.' "[17] As Niebuhr pronounces in the Gifford Lectures, which bear the title *The Nature and Destiny of Man*, the essence of man is "free self-determination." And in an essay first appearing in 1951 and called "Coherence, Incoherence, and Christian Faith" Niebuhr contends that the nature of freedom precludes the achievement of any single or coherent scheme of meaning that will account for the various structures of human life.[18] (By 1965 he will have declared that "only a great multitude of diverse, and sometimes contradictory, traditions can serve to illumine the meaning and mystery of human existence."[19]) The amphibious state of man as at once a creature of nature and a being of spirit, but yet an unqualified unity of these two aspects, means that the conflicting anthropological doctrines known as naturalism and idealism are equally judged and found wanting. They convey half-truths and are alike to be rejected as bringing threats to authentic, anguishing human individuality/peculiarity.[20]

Secularism and Christian Liberalism together failed to comprehend the heights and the depths made possible by primordial freedom (= stark possibility) and hence could appreciate neither the grandeur nor the misery and depravity of the human spirit. Being unable to grasp the truth that sin is linked ineluctably to radical freedom—man's sin in fact consists in "the wrong use of his freedom and its consequent destruction"—Liberalism wrongly thought that it could shackle human conflict through "rational," "educational," "natural," and other resources. The quality of freedom and its creative and destructive consequences arise out of the universal ground of freedom. This is why any final explanation or final disposition of specific forms of human behavior via recourse to specific causes (educational patterns, property, political institutions, restrictions upon the sexual impulse, etc.) is precluded.[21] Liberalism could not bring itself to come to terms with the sinful littleness of man. In Stone's exposition, Niebuhr, like Kierkegaard, finds "that no explanation but the affirmation that sin posits itself is sufficient to account for man's inevitable free choice of false centers of his existence. The sense of responsibility for one's sin is authentic because the sin is freely chosen." The view that "sin posits itself" is akin to Friedrich Schleiermacher's finding (referred to in our discussion of Walter Rauschenbusch) that sinfulness "precedes all acts of sin." Yet in some contrast to Schleiermacher's assumption that this general state of sinfulness is caused in the first instance by "the sinful acts and conditions of others," Reinhold Niebuhr traces the chronic state of sin to a general predisposition deep within the human spirit as such. With Heidegger, Niebuhr focuses upon *anxiety* as at once the condition of human achievement and the precondition of our sin—the former because anxiety is at once the prerequisite and the inspiration of creative acts, the latter because of the accompanying temptation to make idols out of the very same attainments and to gather the universe onto ourselves instead of trusting in God as redeemer. Idolatry is the primal sin. The root of sin, as Stone explains, is "unbelief or lack of trust. Given unbelief, man's anxiety drives him either to claim unconditioned significance for himself or to try to escape the possibilities of freedom by immersing himself in some natural vitality." The human will-to-power, which Niebuhr calls "sin in its quintessential form," does not have some specific, ephemeral cause that is eliminatable; it is instead a generalized, perennial expression of the pathetic attempt to banish the basic insecurity of existence. (Here is why Reinhold Niebuhr is so critical of political views that try to ignore the will-to-power.) Niebuhr readily concedes that it is paradoxical to avow "both the inevitability of sin in man's freedom and his responsibility," yet the paradox is to be retained once we bear in mind that alternative views are unable to account for actual human behavior in personal, social, and political life.[22] The depth of the paradox of the human will penetrates as well to the will-to-powerlessness, or the retreat into moral irresponsibility, yet also to the demonic practice of hiding self-regard behind a mask of self-righteousness and a cloak of virtue.[23]

The biblical-Jewish-Christian conception of man "saves from pretension, complacency and naïveté on the one hand, and despair and flight from the human struggle on the other."[24] In abidingly realist fashion, Man's Nature and His Communities attacks both "the excessive utopianism of modern culture and the counterreaction of nihilistic cynicism." The realist dialectic of man as self-seeking and self-giving is maintained. (Reluctantly, Reinhold Niebuhr concluded that in the modern secular world "original sin" could no longer serve as a meaningful apologetic symbol; he substituted "self-seeking."[25]) As Niebuhr expresses it, "consistent self-seeking is self-defeating; but self-giving is impossible to the self without resources furnished by the community, in the first instance, the family." The impulses of self-seeking and self-giving are held to penetrate all personal and community relationships. Never wholly freed from its coveting of security, the self is nevertheless able to relate creatively to others if it can once embody the needed security. Yet security remains a gift, just as does the capacity to relate to others. Thus does Niebuhr continue "his battle against claims for the perfection of either the individual or society."[26]

Professor Stone comments that while "the motif of tragedy was of continued importance to Reinhold Niebuhr," in his philosophy of history he gradually replaced "tragedy" with "irony." This was indicative of "a new openness to human accomplishment and a less dogmatic approach to history in the post-World War II era." But it must be pointed out that in *The Irony of American History*, wherein Niebuhr fully develops the meaning of irony, that concept is presented in a way wholly consistent with our interpretation of the hyperdialectical viewpoint and the latter's focus upon incongruity: "Irony consists of apparently fortuitous incongruities in life which are discovered, upon closer examination, to be not merely fortuitous."[27] Ronald Stone points out that in at least four books Reinhold Niebuhr argues that history is not tragic. Yet in these same volumes Niebuhr continues to attack American sentimentality and utopianism.[28]

Expatiating upon the substitution of the concept of "irony," Stone writes that on Niebuhr's changed outlook, "men did not have choices only between evil alternatives, for they could with sufficient understanding of their own predicament act creatively."[29] I think that (beyond a mellowing brought with age) Reinhold Niebuhr's later, relatively more sanguine observations about humankind and human history simply point to the moving of the pendulum to the one side of the dialectic. Certainly this did not mean a cessation of the non-sanguine counterthrust. The decisive count against Stone here is that Niebuhr had *never claimed* that human history means "choices only between evil alternatives." On the contrary, evil alternatives contain good aspects, just as good alternatives contain evil aspects. Here, in fact, is the whole point of Christian realism. Niebuhr maintained this dialectical position until the end. (On occasion, Reinhold Niebuhr permitted empirical-historical exceptions within his principled viewpoint; e.g., "it is not invariably necessary to do evil in order that we may do good."[30])

IV

Ethics and politics: possibilities, impossibilities, the dynamics of interest, and the power of power. The understanding of man we have just reviewed, the doctrine of Christian realism, was forged by Reinhold Niebuhr, not as an academic pursuit, but in living partnership with his personal battles against political, economic, and social tyranny. The implications for social and political ethics are far-reaching. Human perversity will assert itself in every social configuration,[31] yet so too will the human impulse to love and justice. The bond between personhood and the social sphere is sealed by the truth that the law of the self is the law of love. Niebuhr's dialectical position here is reaffirmed at the conclusion of *Man's Nature and His Communities*: "[The] law of love is indeed the basis of all moral life, . . . it cannot be obeyed by a simple act of the will because the power of self-concern is too great, and . . . the forces which draw the self from its undue self-concern are usually forces of 'common grace' in the sense that they represent all forms of social security or responsibility or pressure which prompt the self to bethink itself of its social essence and to realize itself by not trying too desperately for self-realization."[32] In and through his favorite phrase, the "law of love" (cf. Rom. 13:8), Niebuhr recapitulates the entire moral norm of Judaism. (Significantly, his insistence, to the end, upon "common grace" transcended all parochial and doctrinaire religiousness.)

On the one hand, Jesus' absolute (apodictic) law of love serves as an ultimate, ideal standard of approximation that judges between greater goods and lesser evils. On the other hand, the ethic of Jesus illuminates the sin in all human relations, thereby mitigating self-righteousness and fostering the contrition requisite to a decent level of justice.[33]

Niebuhr's insistence upon the ideal of love is constant through the years. In conjunction with it he early formulated the phrase, "the relevance of an impossible ethical ideal."[34] He also referred to love as an "impossible possibility," but came to abandon that term as lending itself to misunderstanding. Love is *the* abiding absolute of the Christian moral life. And the works of love remain "the center of gravity" of Niebuhr's thought. Gabriel Fackre enumerates five ways in which Niebuhr discerns the relevance of love: (a) Love testifies to the fundamental structure of the universe. (b) The love absolute is "a lure toward higher approximations of neighborly concern and a judge upon lower ones." The pull of the ideal comes from "out ahead." In declaring for the dignity of every human being, love pleads for a world of individual fulfillment, of equal justice, of political freedom, of social order. (c) Love witnesses to the paradox that "the spirit of selflessness is the only condition upon which mutuality itself can survive" (in contrast, for example, to prudence). (d) There are traces of grace and goodness in the human self and in society which foster continuities with, and even provide inspiration for, self-giving love. (e) The perfect sacrificial love displayed in Jesus' life and death is a rock upon which "the obtuseness of man" is finally shattered. "Before the cross the penitence is born that calls into question the imperious self, and faith in the divine forgiveness is nourished."[35]

The hyperdialectical quality of Reinhold Niebuhr's ethic may be somewhat obscured by the above overarching stress upon love. The oscillatory character and thrust of his social and political ethic are preserved, I suggest, through at least four closely related affirmations. These include three both-ands: *eros* and *agape* as the fundamental forms of love; love and justice; "moral man and immoral society"; and, fourth (not a both-and), the dynamics of interest and the power of power.

(a) Mutual love (*eros*) and sacrificial love (*agape*) are familiar building blocks of Christian moral reflection. Reinhold Niebuhr believed that Anders Nygren's contrast between the two was "too absolute," and he himself "never insisted on a sharp distinction" between them. In any case, Professor Fackre properly speaks of mutual love as a necessary "first de-escalation" that makes absolute love accessible to realizable actions. The difference between the two kinds of love remains, but even prudential self-interest has ways of furthering the ideal harmony of life with life.[36]

(b) "The key to understanding Niebuhr's ethic is the dialectical relationship between love and justice."[37] Normatively construed, justice is at a level inferior to love (*agape*). It presupposes the conflict of life with life. It is closer to *eros* in that it contributes to mutuality and the satisfaction of self-interest. Love cannot replace justice in the world, because human beings require rules in order to maintain their community life. Justice is the social expression and the instrument of love, as love is the final norm of justice, capable of raising justice to new heights.[38] Any ethic of love that "dispenses with the structures and commitments of justice is ultimately irrelevant to the collective life of man."[39] Nevertheless, the praxis of rendering to every person their due echoes the "as yourself" of the love command and thus links itself to the New Testament absolute.[40]

(c) Reinhold Niebuhr's original idea in 1932 of "moral man and immoral society" is reaffirmed by him in 1960 for its central thesis that the secular and religious liberal movement "seemed to be unconscious of the basic difference between the morality of individuals and the morality of collectives," and again in 1965 as having made the "obvious" point that the "collective self-regard of class, race, and nation is more stubborn and persistent than the egoism of individuals." On the last-mentioned occasion he evidently approves a friend's suggestion that in light of his own more consistent realism respecting both individual and societal behavior, a better title might have been *The Not So Moral Man in His Less Moral Communities*. At the same time he states that any attempt to make the spiritual and private world virtuous and pure, and the physical and political realm perennially self-seeking, obfuscates both "the residual self-regard in the personal and interpersonal realm" and "the residual sense of justice in the collective and political realm." However, much of the moral challenge at the level of collectivities involves the disentangling of legitimate self-interest from unacceptable self-interest. A most crucial aspect of Niebuhr's original moral man/immoral society argumentation is his finding that the dubious and even despicable praxis of collectivities is so often claimed as virtuous since reputedly it is being carried out to the end of the welfare of the individual constituents and accordingly amounts to morally responsible and legitimate action. A complication is that the latter allegation may not be entirely false. Hence, the element of virtue cannot be easily ruled out. Nevertheless, ideology and hypocrisy rear their ugly, destructive heads. Individuals do not usually make comparable claims, or when they do the ludicrousness is quickly evident. (The family is not untainted by such claims.) The fact that the hypocrisy could not obtain apart from a measure of moral and rational plausibility and justification, even extending as far as the service of universal moral values, serves to compound and solidify the pretension. Yet the other side of the dialectic is not to be lost: The "hypocrisy of nations, as of individuals, may be an index to a residual creative capacity of their freedom, neither equal to nor effaced by their stronger impulse of self-regard." While hypocrisy is certainly no virtue, yet "its elimination by canceling out the higher loyalty offers no moral gain. Nazi nationalism was not more virtuous because it was bru- tally cynical in making national aggrandizement the only end of its hierarchy of values."[41]

What I have called "the dynamics of interest and the power of power" is taken up below.

For Reinhold Niebuhr, the prime issue in political philosophy is the rela- tion between ideal communities and norms and the stern actualities of life. In an early work, *An Interpretation of Christian Ethics*, he charges that Christian Orthodoxy has too easily dismissed the law of love in and for politics, while the liberal church has too easily affirmed that law's applicability.[42] He stuck to this polemic, though as time went by he cast it in less belligerent terms. A cynical-pessimist interpretation (as typified by Protestant Orthodoxy) loses humankind in the depths of depravity; an idealist-perfectionist view (as typ- ified by Protestant Liberalism) blesses humankind with infinitely attainable goodness. For Niebuhr, each of these views is equally right (as a half-truth) and equally wrong. The fatal problem with both is that they are "either-or" positions. The truth about man is that he is at once an idolatrous sinner and the one who, made in the image of God, can ascend to the heights of moral creativity and responsibility. Correspondingly, says Niebuhr in a relatively late work, the entire political order is suffused with moral ambiguity.[43]

V

A *responsible political ethic*. Such an ethic must embody negative or critical el- ements and positive or constructive elements. Let us develop these two sides.

Negatively speaking, this kind of ethic will avoid the sentimentalities and perfectionisms that are exemplified in such a policy as Christian political pacifism and in such a philosophy as Marxism. Reinhold Niebuhr readily ac- knowledges that the apolitical form of pacifism, sometimes called vocational pacifism, attains a certain spiritual virtue or witness to love and the kingdom of God. In addition, he allows that the small enclaves of Christian pacifist groups (cf. the Mennonites and Hutterians) serve as a judgment of con- science upon human violence and self-aggrandizement. Pacifism can thus marshall a certain appropriateness "as a nonpolitical expression of Christian perfectionism." Again, Niebuhr is paradoxically very much aware that under certain conditions non-violent resistance to evil can be morally and politi- cally efficacious. Thus, at one point he calls Martin Luther King, Jr.'s program of the 1960s "a real contribution to our civil, moral and political life." (Corre- spondingly, to the end of his days King testified that Reinhold Niebuhr was a dominant influence upon his thought.) Niebuhr strongly criticizes "the ro- mantic illusions of the radicals in regard to the redemptive effects of vio- lence. He urged that it be used sparingly and only where necessary. He promoted the development of instruments of nonviolent social change wherever the tactics of nonviolent resistance were relevant."[44]

On the other hand, Niebuhr opposes with a vengeance the Christian political (pragmatic, prudential) forms of pacifism. In the course of replying to a series of essays interpreting and criticizing his work, he marks off the ground of his opposition to this dangerously influential praxis: The New Testament ethic cannot be "reduced to the limits of a prudential ethic, according to which we are counseled to forgive our foe because he will then cease to be our foe; and are promised that if suffering love becomes sufficiently general it will cease to be 'suffering' and change society into a harmony of life in which no one need suffer." As Niebuhr was fond of reminding all who would listen, Jesus never once enjoined non-violent resistance to evil. Apodictically, he demanded *no* resistance (see Matt. 5:39–45). In other words, Jesus stood a million miles away from Mahatma Gandhi. Doctrinaire pacifists are all mixed up eschatologically. They do not understand that the redemption in Jesus Christ is a revelation of God's mercy and not of power to resolve the contradictions of history. Human life is fraught with incongruity and conflict. St. Augustine is right: the peace of the world is gained only through strife; the world's peace is very much like an armistice between opposing legions. These pacifists live in a dream world, but worse, they expect others to do the same. The result is a potentially universal nightmare. Knowing nothing of the reality and demonry of human sin, or of the tragic character of life, they compound both the sin and the tragedy through their political and moral irresponsibility and futility. Reinhold Niebuhr maintains that a proper Christian attitude to moral evil is anger, a response that is made responsible and fulfilled through corrective action (but finally redeemed only through mutual penitence and forgiveness). Here he sounds rather like St. Paul (Eph. 4:26–27; cf. Rom. 12:19) and reflects part of the biblical apprehension of God. The outcome of the praxis of pacifists is not alone their own crucifixion (which is for them no problem, or ought not be), but the crucifixion of "those innocents and values" that could have been protected were non-pacific means followed. The magnification "of the exploitative instinct in large collectivities rendered the pacifist counsel even more dangerous as a political guideline. The Nazi phenomenon was a dramatic case in point. Not only the annihilation of the Jew but the crumbling of the Western charter of freedom and justice would result from the totalitarian juggernaut, if the way of nonviolence were to be chosen."[45]

Political pacifism is, in short, both Christianly heretical and morally insufferable. Accordingly, the Christian church is forbidden to be pacifist.[46] (It ought to be needless to say that this latter does not make the Christian church *qua* church into something coercionist.)

Christian pacifism and secular Marxism are linked by their false idealisms, utopianisms, and perfectionisms, a blindness to the depth and persistence of humankind's self-regarding impulses—although Marxism's provisional

realism and cynicism did enable it to recognize that those who control society will not surrender their power through reason or preachment. As a matter
of fact, it was under a Marxist-inspired critique of political liberalism that
Reinhold Niebuhr's own early pacifism collapsed in the late 1920s and early
1930s. Behind the change in viewpoint lay his developing awareness of the
inner connection between the potential to engage in and sustain violence,
and violence as such. There is overt coerciveness and there is covert or implicit coerciveness, and we have no way to dissociate them. Even though
Niebuhr was becoming increasingly critical of Marxist anthropology, he essentially agreed with Marxism's analysis of economic structures, including
the view that communal ownership of property was prerequisite to social
justice. Persuasions that he adopted from Marxism included: capitalism's
self-destruction through its internal contradictions, and the unique place of
the disinherited as destroyers of the capitalist system. Furthermore,
Niebuhr's political ethic developed in part out of the connections he discerned between Karl Marx's understanding of human alienation and
Niebuhr's own political realism, while his doctrine of sin was in continuity
with, and was buttressed by, the Marxist insight into ideology.[47] All in all,
Niebuhr well comprehended Marxism's massive inheritance from the bibli-
cal-prophetic, Jewish-Christian tradition.

Contrariwise and of direct bearing upon Reinhold Niebuhr's rejection of
Marxism, two experiential sureties came to the fore. First, Marxism's obsession with the economic dimension of life is inordinate. It maintains the falsehood of locating the source of all evil within property as such. Property must
be approached dialectically: its excessive possession and utilization mean
injustice; yet property is a protector against oppression and also a means of
human blessing. Again, by assuming that once the means of production are
assimilated to community responsibility, political power will also gravitate
to the community, Marx did not allow for the fateful eventuality of an oligar-
chy of a ruling party (cf. the Soviet Union).[48] Second, "a free society" is fully
capable of remedying the evils the Marxists were fighting. As Niebuhr writes
in Man's Nature and His Communities, the bourgeoisie, who for Marx were "the
ultimate devils in the drama of history," did not in fact "prove to be the devils of history; but neither were they saints. A century was needed before a
free society could refute their bourgeois ideology. In the process, it also refuted the Marxist apocalypse and perfected the political and economic instruments of justice in the political and economic sphere, and thereby
proved that economic power was not the only form of social power and that
property ownership was not the only form of economic power. In short, Western open and technical cultures refuted the political religion specifically
designed for them and became immune to the Marxist virus of rebellion."[49]
However, the main count in Reinhold Niebuhr's indictment of Marxism is its
utopianism, with the twin offspring of fanaticism and despair. His central criticism is thus essentially the same as that against liberalism; "both creeds

were blinded by utopian illusions to the need for resolute political action for achievable moral ends. Marxist realism had exposed the illusions of liberalism, and Augustinian realism exposed Marxist illusions."[50] Reinhold Niebuhr's relation to Augustine is not unmixed. He saw his own theology and political philosophy as following in the Augustinian realist tradition. His philosophy of history draws heavily upon Augustine, and much of the argumentation in his *magnum opus, The Nature and Destiny of Man*, rests on Augustine's *City of God.* Yet in *Man's Nature and His Communities* Niebuhr labels "fantastic" the Bishop of Hippo's distinctions between *civitas terrena* and *civitas dei*, and he calls Augustine to task (along with Luther) for not recognizing persistent self-love among the "redeemed," and virtue and social responsibility among the "unredeemed."[51]

To move now to the more positive elements within a responsible political ethic, such an ethic will turn to advantage all available "indeterminate possibilities" for moral advance and justice. "The essence of immorality is the evasion or denial of moral responsibility." Moral responsibility in politics must rely upon political wisdom. Against all cynicism we must insist that moral claims are relevant to politics at all its levels. No nation or other collective entity ever wholly transcends its self-interest. However, it is perfectly possible that such self-interest may come to correspond at certain points with the self-interest of other collectivities, thus contributing to justice and to peace, and thence to moral universality. The art of responsible politics demands discriminate moral judgments and the avoidance of all moral absolutisms. A Christian political ethic will capitalize upon "the insights of both moralists and political realists."[52]

The more concrete aspects of Reinhold Niebuhr's constructive political ethic embrace the dynamics of interest and the power of power, including the balancing of power. His ethic is directly related to politics by means of the understanding of justice, not merely as an ideal but as a harmony reenforced by the balance of power. "To pursue justice means to engage in politics. . . . Justice without power is a vague ideal; power without justice is either chaos or tyranny."[53]

Since in modern history national interest most certainly takes precedence, experientially speaking, over higher loyalties, it is vital to work with the "residual creative freedom in collective man." This cannot mean "subordinating the lower to the higher or wider interest"; it means instead—contra a too-consistent cynicism—the providential eventuality "that even a residual loyalty to values, transcending national existence, may change radically the nation's conception of the breadth and quality of its 'national interest.' " Niebuhr uses the American Civil War to bring home the lesson that a nation "is neither able nor willing to enforce universal human rights until its own self-interest, that is, the interest of the whole nation, is involved." (Cf. Abraham Lincoln's first commitment: "to save the Union.") The very same axiom was subsequently to apply in the developing of even partial justice for American blacks. In a memorable passage Niebuhr alludes to the 1954 Supreme Court decision outlawing school segregation as serving to transmute this minority's desperation "into that wonderful combination of hope and despair, which has been the motive power of all rebellions against injustice."[54]

Power, evidently understood as "the capacity to realize one's purposes, either through authority or force,"[55] must itself be apprehended dialectically. On the one hand, it derives from human pride and the false attempt to achieve security by dominating others. But on the other hand, power may be treated as a required expression of social organization and cohesion as well as a preventative of social chaos and anarchy.[56] In a sinful world, inordinate power must be fought, controlled, moderated. The only way to do all this is through the instruments of countervailing power. And power apart from violence or the threat of violence remains powerless. A nation or lesser collectivity that does not, within limits, honor its own self-interest becomes prey to the will-to-power of others, in this respect, the praxis of collective self-interest receives the (relative) sanction of Christian doctrine—its anthropology but also its teaching concerning the created order and even the way to redemption. The particularities of life are never to be negated.

The principle of the balance of power is anything but a cure-all—it is itself "pregnant with the possibility of anarchy"[57]—yet it can aid tolerable order and justice. At the domestic level, the balance of power is enforced by dominant groups. At the international level, it involves the "accommodation of interests of nations relative to their power." Inevitably, therefore, it is the major nations that are charged with the maintenance of decent degrees of international order.[58] The greater the power, the greater the responsibility. And yet, "nothing is more dangerous to a powerful nation than the temptation to obscure the limits of its power."[59]

Reinhold Niebuhr's strictures against secular and Christian Liberalism for falling into utopian idealism do not alter his commitment to a political liberalism shorn of illusion and pragmatically oriented. He came to admit that his earlier understanding of political liberalism as perforce assuming an impossible optimism was mistaken. He had always celebrated the liberal stress upon human freedom and the conditions for making freedom secure, and he was never to doubt the compatibility of Christian realism with liberalism. By his life as by his thought, Niebuhr fully supported the liberal quest to find "meaning" within the tasks and processes of history. What he always denied was any effort to claim ultimate meaning for history.[60]

The best warrant against the temptations and hypocrisies of power is its equilibration and democratization, which entail systems of checks and balances within structures of tolerable social order and a pluralist social framework, together with just allocations of society's resources and opportunities. All structures of power require built-in safeguards against their own corruption and tyranny. Extreme order threatens freedom, but order within limits is a prerequisite as well as a consequence of human community. Niebuhr sees

Christian anthropology and democracy as mutually implicative. "A Christian
view of human nature is more adequate for the development of a democratic society than either the optimism with which democracy has become
historically associated or the moral cynicism which inclines human communities to tyrannical political strategies." Perhaps Niebuhr's most famous aphorism is: "Man's capacity for justice makes democracy possible; but man's
inclination to injustice makes democracy necessary."[61] The moral and political philosophy of democracy most closely harmonizes with the hyperdialectical apprehension of the grandeur and misery of man. The reason the
idolatries of democracy are so much less evil than those of tyranny and fascism is that in democracy the door remains open to social change and melioration without violent destructiveness.

VI

God: wrathful judge, merciful lover. Reinhold Niebuhr is primarily the philosopher of man and the philosopher of politics, yet his anthropology and his
social ethics are alike undergirded by his theological-Christological reflection and his personal faith.

On the embodiment of the dialectic of the divine judgment and mercy we
may bring forward two closely related Niebuhrian emphases: a more general
Christological-moral emphasis, and a stress upon God's forgiveness and
peace in their specific bearing upon the politico-moral realm.

The logic of Niebuhr's teaching of God's judgment rests upon several discerned connections: Obligation, as laid upon man by God, presumes freedom. Man as a free spirit is inclined to abuse his freedom. Yet he remains
responsible for his acts and their consequences. He is genuinely blameworthy for his sins. Being inevitably involved in the primal sin of playing God,
"he is bound to meet God first of all as a judge, who humbles his pride and
brings his vain imagination to naught." Human sin as man's rebellion against
God is taken so seriously by the Bible that an interpretation of history results "in which judgment upon sin becomes the first category of interpretation." According to biblical conviction, history is "a revelation of the wrath of
God upon the sinful pride of man." Judgment presupposes the original sublimity of the human stature and the fall from that height into assorted
depths of depravity. God as judge is the just One. But all this poses certain
anguishing questions: Is there any way that humankind, estranged from the
source of its being, can be reconciled with God? Is God merciful as well as
just? And if he is merciful, how is that mercy related to his justice?[62] Here is
testimony from *The Nature and Destiny of Man:*

> The ... question is whether there is a resource in the heart of the Divine
> which can overcome the tragic character of history and which can cure as
> well as punish the sinful pride in which man inevitably involves himself....

From the standpoint of Christian faith the life and death of Christ become the revelation of God's character with particular reference to the unsolved problem of the relation of His judgment to His mercy, of His wrath to His forgiveness. Christian faith sees in the Cross of Christ the assurance that judgment is not the final word of God to man; but it does not regard the mercy of God as a forgiveness which wipes out the distinctions of good and evil in history and makes judgment meaningless. All the difficult Christian theological dogmas of Atonement and justification are efforts to explicate the ultimate mystery of divine wrath and mercy in its relation to man. The good news of the gospel is that God takes the sinfulness of man into Himself; and overcomes in His own heart what cannot be overcome in human life, since human life remains within the vicious circle of sinful self-glorification on every level of moral advance. . . . [Without] this divine initiative and this divine sacrifice there could be no reconciliation. . . .

The dialectic of divine justice and divine mercy is here placed upon a strictly historical foundation: the Crucifixion of Jesus Christ. In that act of reconciliation, "the judgment of God upon the pride of man is not abrogated"—any such abrogation would mean an impugning of justice and a flouting of the honor of God—and yet "the final word is not one of judgment but of mercy and forgiveness."[63]

The above witness is directed to the human plight as such. Divine-human reconciliation is essential, after all, even for a Simeon Stylites. There is also the effort by Reinhold Niebuhr to relate God's forgiveness and peace more discriminately and specifically to the politico-moral domain. For the political world is particularly subject to temptation as also to sin, to conflict as also to nasty compromises. If there is no way finally to reconcile the praxis of responsible and effective power in historical life with untainted goodness, the question of our resultant separation from the God of absolute righteousness and goodness becomes especially poignant, even conducive to despair.

In a sermonic essay upon the text, "the peace of God which passes all understanding" (Phil. 4:7), Reinhold Niebuhr proposes that "the only possible peace within and between human communities is the peace of forgiveness." Such a proposal is outrageous to moralists since they think that it condones evil and indulges the evildoer. They do not understand "how much the judgment of the righteous upon the evildoer is below the ultimate and divine judgment." Forgiveness "is possible only to those who have some recognition of common guilt. The pain of contrition is the root of the peace of forgiveness," a peace made possible only to those who "know themselves under a judgment which in its final dimension" makes no distinction between the righteous and the unrighteous. Then there is God's forgiveness itself, which means "the readiness of guiltlessness to bear the sin of the guilty." The praxis of forgiveness, human and divine, culminates in "the peace of being forgiven," the only possible peace for a humankind "involved in the contradictions of existence." This is not a peace which prematurely arrests the creative urges of life for the sake of a tranquillity, or which denies the responsibilities of the self toward others for fear of becoming soiled in fulfilling our duty. It *is a peace in which an uneasy conscience is curiously compounded with an easy conscience.* This peace rests upon the faith that God is great enough and good enough to resolve the contradiction in which human life stands; and that His mercy is the final resource of His power, by which He overcomes the rebellion of man against his creator. . . .

The peace of Christian faith passes understanding because it is God's peace, transferred to us. It is the peace of having and yet not having the perfection of Christ; of having it only by grace and yet having it the more surely for not pretending that we have it as a right. This peace will offend both rationalists and moralists till the end of history, because it does not conform to the simple canons of either rationality or morality. But it alone does justice to the infinite complexities and contradictions of human existence. . . . In that peace we understand that man's life in history is fragmentary and frustrated precisely because it is boundless and unlimited.[64]

To be accepted by God within and despite sin—is this not what the Christian Reformation teaches in its doctrine of "justification by faith"? In the end, all community and political life rests upon the forgiveness of God.

The foregoing analysis has established the hyperdialectic of Christian realism within three dimensions: man as Image of God and corrupted adorer of self; the possibilities and impossibilities of moral behavior and political power; and God's righteous judgment and saving mercy. Then a further dimension may be projected overall, in the form of a query that is steadily implicit in all Niebuhr's work and that directs us, I think, to the very heart of his contribution: Which is worse, idolatry or irresponsibility? His own choice is clear: "Every form of human striving is bound to be idolatrous in the ultimate court"; ideally, "the Christian faith enables men, not to escape idolatry absolutely, but to accept responsibilities, knowing that those responsibilities will involve us in idolatries from which no form of human perfection will redeem us. . . . The insistence on divine mercy as the final answer to the human predicament does not absolve us of responsibility but frees us for performing tasks in a world which never confronts us with clear choices of good and evil."[65] This helps explain how an adage of Martin Luther's, "Sin bravely, if also you have brave faith," could be a favorite of Niebuhr.

VII

Dennis P. McCann has serious reservations about the relationship, or lack of relationship, between Reinhold Niebuhr's anthropological and religious insights/affirmations and the need for critical social and political theory. Although "the metaphors of 'selfhood' are psychologically illuminating, they may be less adequate as a framework for social theory." While "Christian realism does provide a plausible theory of human nature, its theoretical understanding of history remains relatively sketchy." Is Niebuhrian realism's anthropology of any singular practical use as a mode of political analysis? For example, Niebuhr's suspicions respecting the sins and utopian illusions of the churches may have unwittingly undermined the requirement of essential institutional and organizational strategies for maintaining his own insistence upon a balance of power. Since it is so "that Niebuhr's theological anthropology dominates his theology of history" (a theology of history that presupposes "the priority of ideas over social structures in understanding historical change"), "it is not surprising that his theological framework for social ethics" should speak "more directly to the concerns of individuals than groups."[66] McCann here sounds a potentially ironic note, since Niebuhr was devoutly wishing to carry forward the Social Gospel's liberation of the church from individualistic pietism, a perennial handicap of the Christian community in some contrast to Judaism.

There have been many adverse reactions to Reinhold Niebuhr since his death, from charges of his tacit support of establishment conservatism to claims that his relevance and contribution have dissipated. Gabriel Fackre summarizes (not necessarily with approval) much of this evaluation: "Critics assert that [Niebuhrian] realism is so preoccupied with balancing power blocks and practicing the art of the possible that commitment to the radical social change necessary for our times is never generated. It lacks a passion for openness to the future, for doing the undoable, thinking the unthinkable, seeing the unseen. Now is the time for mind-blowing, future orientation, revolutionary hope, not captivity to empirical givens, mesmerism with the ambiguities of the present, compromising reformism. It is the age of dreaming of life's possibilities, not sober realism about its impossibilities."[67]

By way of response to the above paragraph I enter, first of all, a reminder prompted by the ending of the quotation. When Niebuhrian realism is being represented fairly, it is seen to stress the "indeterminate possibilities" of moral and social advance just as much as the "impossibilities." Here is Reinhold Niebuhr in the Gifford Lectures of as far back as 1939: "There is no individual or interior social situation, no cultural or scientific task, and no social or political problem in which men do not face new possibilities of the good and the obligation to realize them. . . . There is no limit to either sanctification in individual life, or social perfection in collective life, or to the discovery of truth in cultural life; except of course the one limit, that there will be some corruption, as well as deficiency, of virtue and truth on the new level of achievement."[68] It would appear that the critics in question tend to give ear only to the negative side of Reinhold Niebuhr's dialectical message, the side aware that it is in the last days that the anti-Christ appears[69] and aware as well that before the fact of human diabolism and sin, the divine righteousness is forced to fight every step of its way. These critics forget that Niebuhr was also a theologian of hope. (For him, illusory hope does not qualify as hope.) Ronald Stone states what ought to be obvious: "The movement from the way things are to the way they ought to be implies hope and action."[70] Niebuhr battled unceasingly for a more just world. He was a man of many visions—visions within the historical domain, not merely eschatological visions.[71] A tolerably just society is one where a maximal degree of liberty and equality is realized upon a foundation of order. As Gabriel Fackre comments, it was wholly within Niebuhr's framework that Martin Luther King, Jr., could dream his dream of black children and white children one day walking the streets together in peace. Again, Niebuhr envisioned that the maneuvers and counter-maneuvers of the major nation-states can be adjudicated "by a wise statecraft." Such a statecraft "will be moved both by the ideal of a tolerable mutuality and by a realism which takes into account collective egoisms and the attendant righteous pretensions of all the contenders for world power." Fackre is quite prepared to attest that, at its deepest level, Christian vision *is* Christian realism.[72]

On the matter of conservatism, it is a logical-moral error to fail to distinguish between Niebuhr's empiricist observations concerning the general organic processes that produce social cohesion and the particular processes that are dominant in the here and now. No social process is ever given absolute sanction by him. "The corrupting tendencies of ascending power" are particularly kept in mind. And he is as open as anybody to the eventuality of the replacement of given organic processes by new ones. Stone's comprehensive intervention is apposite: "Scripture, reason, and nature do not provide universally valid concepts of justice for all time. Man in his freedom changes his communities and himself. The double love commandment presupposes this freedom, but particular formulations of principles of justice reveal the particular historical contingencies of the formulators and must be revised in each new era."[73]

I have alluded to Niebuhr's radical judgment that even when compared to idolatry, moral irresponsibility is a greater evil. He often insists that we are to extricate ourselves from the horns of dilemmas and take the best available action.[74] To plunge in to political reformation, to do the revolutionary thing, the unexpected thing, is to *apply* Reinhold Niebuhr, not to replace him. In *Man's Nature and His Communities* he states his conviction that a realist conception of human nature should be "the servant of an ethic of progressive justice and should not be made into a bastion of conservatism, particularly a conservatism which defends unjust privileges." He continues: "I might define this conviction as the guiding principle throughout my mature life of the relation of religious responsibility to political affairs."[75] Ronald Stone shows that the label "conservative," in the denotation of someone who perpetuates privilege and the status quo, is simply inaccurate here. Niebuhr's participation in Americans for Democratic Action and his support of many liberal social programs rule out any such appellation.[76] Of course, absolutist revolutionists—those who would replace the present social order with a totally opposite one—cannot abide Niebuhr, but then they most often cannot abide anyone save themselves.

Much of the criticism of Reinhold Niebuhr does not appear to take into account that he was fundamentally the ethical orientationalist or methodologist rather than a purveyor of final programs or ideologies. This suggests that to advocate a particular or new political scheme, reform, or solution in a way that puts Niebuhr on trial may well be question-begging, in the measure that the objection does not speak to his very contention that there simply are no ultimately satisfactory politico-moral strategies, "solutions," or finally consistent ideologies. We hardly deal responsibly with people who question whether there are answers if we insist that they supply answers.[77] Furthermore, Niebuhr meets the demand for absolutist passion and the allegation of irrelevance with a challenge: Which party is actually being constructive? As John C. Bennett makes clear, to avoid the fanaticism that accompanies absolutist solutions "is no mere negation, because it is the condition for the releasing of the constructive and cooperative elements in the human situation."[78]

In his concentration upon history as the immanent/transcendent structure for the possibilities and limits of human praxis, Reinhold Niebuhr has contributed a great deal to contemporary historicist consciousness. While the more intensive pragmatism and political liberalism of his later years do not negate the hyperdialectical character of his position, they do point to his developing affinity with transformationism of both a faith-grounded type and a history-grounded type (cf. below, chaps. 9ff.). Much of Niebuhr's moral counsel belongs within the rubric of "middle axioms," proposals that are "more concrete than a universal ethical principle and less specific than a program."[79] Such proposals may be applied to changing situations, but, as soon as practicality or expediency demands it, these proposals may have to be replaced. As we have seen, all moral judgments and schemes are, for Niebuhr, relative to, and conditioned by, historical states of affairs and discrete historical challenges. Here is the great truth in Ronald Stone's interpretation of Niebuhr's position as reaching its zenith in pragmatism.[80] And here is a major reason why the claim that Niebuhr is now irrelevant or dated is so heavily misplaced. The best refutation of the criticism is found within the structure of Niebuhr's own ethic.

I do submit that whatever aid, comfort, and truth are marshalled in Reinhold Niebuhr's advocacy of radical freedom as the ultimate ground/denouement of moral-theological reflection/praxis, such an approach cannot evade the most serious problem of the divine responsibility (= culpability?) for the entire noumenon of freedom (see below, chap. 13).

VIII

To return to our chief expository guide: H. Richard Niebuhr admires the dualists for a consummate honesty that accords with what Christians actually know about themselves, their struggles, and their churches, and also for excelling other groups in a recognition of "the dynamic character of God, man, grace, and sin." Again, the oscillatory ethic means an ethic of freedom "in the sense of creative action in response to action upon man."[81] On the other side, H. Richard Niebuhr is concerned lest an unrelieved dualism too readily fragment life "into an unalloyed mix of tragedy and joy, of demand and gift."[82] And he finds some force in the two charges that dualism tends to bolster an antinomian spirit, at least among "the wayward and the weak"; and that it enhances cultural conservatism.[83]

I am persuaded that none of us can entirely evade the impulsion of "history and faith in tension." The reason has to do with the effectuation, by this sixth image, of a convergence of phenomenological-existential insight and evaluative claim. As creatures who are blessed/cursed by a paradoxical, simultaneous habitation within two discrepant realms (the world of nature and the world of spirit), we have no real choice but to know the tidal pull of both these forces. In this sense, the hyperdialectical viewpoint appears not so much as one more argument as it does an unsparing, empirical report upon the overall human condition. As Abraham J. Heschel, himself a dialectical realist, says of Reinhold Niebuhr, "he reminds us what we are."[84]

Accordingly, dualist reasoning has a certain power to bring an objective-descriptive perspective upon all normative images: "Faith against the world" and "faith for the world" are thus seen, not as final resting places, but as inchoately dialectical way stations upon an unceasing journey between two primordial dimensions of life. Again, the normative images made possible by Yeshua of Nazareth and by the rabbis of Jewish tradition are apprehended as additional efforts to struggle, rather more dialectically than in images one and four, with the self-same enigma of transcendence/immanence. And when Catholic and extra-Catholic synthesists divide the spiritual community into two great sections, carefully verticalizing the relationship between them, they too are wrestling with, rather than resolving, an eternal problem. Nor do the two varieties within transformationism—"faith transforming history" and "history transforming faith" (both of which await our visitation)—escape an identical analytical conclusion. For when transformationists call for the rediscovery and reaffirmation of lost or neglected emphases, their views are revealed as moment-positions inside a vast gestalt of human puzzlement and striving. Transformationist views constitute special concentrations within the abiding tension of faith and history.

So it is that within a strictly descriptive frame of reference, the hyperdialectical position operates as a surrogate of history, that master of all temporal effort and judgment. This means that from the vantage point of its own

willing if painful acceptance of the twofold human condition the hyperdialectical view successfully reminds us of the ineluctable historicity of all
moral endeavor and all moral understanding.

Yet this universal insight does not immunize the hyperdialecticians
against all critical judgment. Descriptive behavior is never the whole of
human assessment, nor even its center. Sooner or later, descriptiveness
must be supplemented and in a sense completed by valuative decision.
Lamentably or happily, what is is not equatable with what ought to be. The
problem of faith and history, or what in the immediate context we may call
the fact of our two-world condition, is not reckoned with in full responsibility
until we reach beyond phenomenological commentary, and venture into
moral commitment. It is here that the hyperdialectician is kept from possessing any advantage over the rest of us. Among the legitimate concerns we
may have for hyperdialectical companions is the worry that their grasp of the
clear predicament of all humankind and of all normative images, together
with special hyperdialectical insights into the bleakness and insolubility of
the human condition as such, may open up the temptation for them to abdicate the moral struggle. Spokespersons for transformationist and other
images may then ask these people: Are you behaving as responsibly as you
could be behaving? In a word, human oughtness creates an odd democracy
in which all parties of all persuasions face equal challenges because all parties are living in the one boat. The solitary question addresses everyone:
How are we going to channel our radical freedom creatively and responsibly
amid and despite the fateful exigencies of time and place?

9

Faith Transforming History

WE take up the seventh of our normative images, the first of two transformationist positions: "Faith transforming history."

I

"Christ the transformer of culture" is H. Richard Niebuhr's summary expression for this point of view. Alternately, he labels it "the conversionist type." Writing as he does out of strictly Christian presuppositions, Niebuhr indicates certain major continuities and discontinuities between the type and the other types in his schema:

(1) The "faith transforming history" view is allied with "Christ against culture" ("faith against the world") in making the Christian gospel its point of departure and in holding fast "to the radical distinction between God's work in Christ and man's work in culture." However, this does not entail Christian separation from the world. "The function of the gospel is not conceived to be the establishing of a new society so much as the conversion of existent society."

(2) As against "the Christ of culture" ("faith for the world"), conversion implies "a radical revolution" which, ultimately, is metaphysical as well as moral. Conversionists are not prepared to modify "Jesus Christ's sharp judgment of the world and all its ways."

(3) This view resembles the other median positions of "Christ above culture" and "Christ and culture in paradox" in recognizing "a dual mediation of divine values and imperatives." Yet in contrast to "Christ above culture" ("faith above history"), the natural law as apprehended by human reason "is not the true law of God mediated by nature but the law as apprehended by a corrupted reason."

(4) In distinction from "Christ and culture in paradox" ("history and faith in tension"), moral "imperatives are not imperatives for a corrupted order but corrupted imperatives" issuing from "a true order." Again, conversionists do

not settle for "mere endurance in the expectation of a transhistorical salvation." They are more positive and hopeful toward culture than are dualists. They offer affirmative human responses to God's ordering of the creation. "The Word that became flesh and dwelt among us, the Son who does the work of the Father in the world of creation, has entered into a human culture that has never been without his ordering action." On the other hand, in their understanding of sin conversionists are much closer to dualists than to synthesists. But yet human nature is not "bad"; indeed, the problem is that an essentially good human nature has become corrupted. It is "warped, twisted, and misdirected. . . . It is perverted good, not evil; or it is evil as perversion, and not as badness of being."

(5) The values that reason acknowledges in the world apart from Jesus Christ are yet true values for God and not just relative to the world. However, human reason and culture tend to disorder these values, detaching them from God and attaching them to some temporal or dubious end.

(6) The imperatives that issue from the Christian gospel and from Jesus Christ do not replace the imperatives that stem from nature and reason. But neither are the values that the gospel apprehends of the same order as those apprehended by reason. Gospel values "are truly final imperatives, final values."

(7) Most distinctively, "the vision of the good in Christ and the reception of the final commandment through him are to be used for the restoration of the corrupted order in nature-culture, for the reinterpretation of the natural imperatives. As in the case of knowledge revelation does not take the place of reason but restores it, so in the moral life the vision of eternal good in the gospel does not take the place of temporal good but puts this in its proper place and leads to restoration of the true order of values in the world." Of course, no easy transvaluation is possible, for the power of sin in fallen man is unrelenting and the corruption of the moral and rational life is deepseated. "The problem of culture is therefore the problem of its conversion, not of its replacement by a new creation; though the conversion is so radical that it amounts to a kind of rebirth."

(8) Because of this book's special concern with the issue of history, I quote verbatim H. Richard Niebuhr's summation of the conversionist view of history in contrast with his other types.

> For the exclusive Christian, history is the story of a rising church or Christian culture and a dying pagan civilization; for the cultural Christian, it is the story of the spirit's encounter with nature; for the synthesist it is a period of preparation under law, reason, gospel, and church for an ultimate communion of the soul with God; for the dualist, history is the time of struggle between faith and unbelief, a period between the giving of the promise of life and its fulfillment. For the conversionist, history is the story of God's mighty deeds and of man's responses to them. . . . The conversionist, with his view

of history as the present encounter with God in Christ, does not live so much in expectation of a final ending of the world of creation and culture as in awareness of the power of the Lord to transform all things by lifting them up to himself.[1]

The apostle Paul seems to Niebuhr to prepare the way for the conversionist view (contra my presentation in chapter three above). With some qualification, the Fourth Gospel is held to be representative of the position. Augustine of Hippo appears as its advocate, though we are advised that the bishop fails, or refuses, to draw the universalist consequences implied by his own conversionism. The conversionist motif is prominent in the thought and practice of John Calvin. Additional exponents include John Wesley and Jonathan Edwards. A notable and most consistent advocate is the nineteenth-century theologian F. D. Maurice. A recent influential representative is Karl Barth.[2]

Probably no empirical instance of faith-oriented transformationism contains all the characteristics marking that normative image as a whole. Yet the cases we shall consider are united in and through a conviction that *within the realm of faith and grace there lives and moves a power to transform the whole historical order to the glory of the divine righteousness.* Our exposition and assessment fall into two major divisions: aspects of Islam; and political theology and the struggle for liberation within parts of Christianity.

II

Our inclusion of modern Islam finds a certain methodological authorization in a point made early in chapter seven: H. Richard Niebuhr's affirmation that the ultimate moral question is between God and man, rather than between Christ and the world. This view opens the way to the moral relevance and indeed to the attributed integrity of extra-Christian theistic faiths. (It will be noted that the affirmation cited from Niebuhr does not quite jibe with his own claim as a conversionist that history is to be construed as "the present encounter with God in Christ.") If Christian thinking/praxis ought not turn away from the historical fortunes and claims of the Jewish community, an analogous point may be made (if with relatively less fervency and directness) concerning the world Muslim community, with special reference to at least two weighty facts: Islam's loyalty to the one God, and its taking of history with intense seriousness.

If the question, What is Christianity? is elusive, in the question, What is Islam? the elusiveness is compounded. For as in Judaism, there is no single (or even moderately plural) authority to adjudicate, or to seek to adjudicate, the matter of identity. The allusion to Judaism may, however, suggest a useful entry into the identification of Islam,[3] for, in many respects, though not at the point of empirical-historical linkages, these two realities are closer to each other than either one is to Christianity. Numerically, of course, there is no comparison, since an estimated 850 million Muslims make the Jewish entity appear tiny indeed. Perhaps of greatest similarity, the Islamic community has always shown a doublesidedness of faith and peoplehood that characterizes the Jewish community as well—a condition offering perennial testimony that religion means no less than *secularity* of the "right" sort. From its inception Islam has, with Judaism, overridden any bounds that religion may arbitrarily try to set, an overriding that has been implemented not merely through historical fortune but also out of conviction and design. For in neither instance is there much sense in applying such a descriptive category as "church," particularly once that reality is juxtaposed with "state." However, Edward Mortimer's judgment, that the community of believers created by Muhammad (570–632) "was, from the beginning, what we should call a state," needs qualification. That qualification is peoplehood-religion. The great truth in his judgment is that Islam is clearly "a political culture," which in general "sanctifies political action." Yet as Mortimer himself observes, while it is so that Islam and Judaism alike "derive historically from a community that was political as well as religious," only the stubborn preservation of a religious tradition has enabled the survival of group identity and culture. Accordingly, we adjudge that Islam is "a way of life, a model of society, a culture, a civilization." Again, both the Islamic and the Jewish communities are uncompromising in their monotheism. Both emphasize the observance of divine law (Arabic, *shariʿa*).* Both reject the intervention of a priestly caste between humankind and God. And both attribute great authority to the scholar-teacher-sage-interpreter of the law (Arabic, *alim*: learned man, Islamic scholar; pl., *ulamā*).[4]

To take Islam as an empirical totality and assign it exclusively to "faith transforming history" would be most misleading. Islam, which has been required to adapt to widely variant cultures, is suffused with diversity of both teaching and praxis. Within the overall House of Islam (*dār al-Islām*) are to be found such variables as revolution and status quo-ism, progress and retrogression, tolerance and intolerance, democratic freedoms and coercive authoritarianism, private property and nationalization, interest-free loans and the equivalent of interest, social justice and exploitive libertarianism. Edward Mortimer's *Faith and Power* shows well the ways in which given Muslim societies in given times reflect multifold political interpretations of Islam. There are among Muslims enormous discrepancies concerning the explicit and specific political-social-economic content and goals of their faith.

---

*The *ulamā* (learned men) gradually elaborated the rules of the Koran and the Sunna (Tradition) into the *shariʿa*, God's way of life for humankind. The *hadīth* is the recorded tradition (collected in the ninth century A.D.) concerning the words and praxis of Muhammad and his companions.

A few instances may be tendered from within experiential Islam of continuities with normative images other than "faith transforming history." In
chapter seven passing mention is made of Sufi mysticism as an embodiment
of "faith against the world." Muslims discern spiritual and moral lessons in
Muhammad's withdrawal in 622 from pagan Mecca to Medina. There have always been world-negating elements in Islam. The Koran "does not deduce
the laws of history, it judges them," 'Abd Rabbih declares. "The Koran is
truthful even if it contradicts history." In contrast, much in Islam is reminiscent of rabbinic Judaism's concretions for everyday life. As examples, the
Koran bans cheating in commerce, provides for guarantees in legal transactions, empowers governmental intervention in cases of exploitation and
hoarding, authorizes means of communication and transportation, and sanctions the punishing of criminals. Again, there is the linkage of human rationality to "faith for the world" (as we accentuated in chapter six above). The
rationalist tradition of Islam easily rivals that of Judaism and of Christianity.
The Koran "appeals constantly to man's rational faculties. It urges him to
seek knowledge." A central Islamic concept is *ijtihād*, independent judgment/
reasoning, especially in interpreting the Koran and the Sunna (Tradition).
Sayyid Ahmad Khan, a nineteenth-century Indian Muslim reformer, finds no
conflict between the Koran and Western science. For him, "Islam is Nature,
and Nature is Islam"; i.e., revelation and natural law are identical. How could
there be any contradiction between the Word of Allah (Koran) and the Work
of Allah (the universe and its laws)? If many Christians find that human reason is corrupted and if they have doubts that reason is still capable of mediating the Law of God in unspoiled fashion, this finding and these doubts are
made empty from the standpoint of true Muslim reason. A "Christ of culture"
is here paralleled, and perhaps even excelled, by an "Allah of culture," or
what Yvonne Yazbeck Haddad refers to as Muslim acculturationism.[5]

Finally, reminders are present within Islam of "history and faith in tension." For 'Imād al-Dīn Khalīl, life itself is perennial tension and struggle. As
the Koran teaches, the central locus of the struggle is the unceasing conflict
between man and Satan. The scope of the battle encompasses the entire
universe and all of nature. Even the perfect society "is not a utopia on earth,
but one that is achieved and maintained by perpetual personal and collective struggle." Within ancient Islamic tradition there is the eschatological
suasion that one day a divinely-guided leader, the Mahdi, will come and restore the authentic Muslim order. The tension of history and Islamic faith is
nowhere more evident than in the collision between nationalist impulses
(often encouraged and supported by Muslim teachings themselves, e.g.,
within the Arab world) and spiritual-moral distinctiveness and universality.
Most of the modern and contemporary Islamic movements described by Edward Mortimer manifest an ambivalent relation to nationalism. On the one
hand, most Muslims identify a Muslim state as one governed, at least in
principle, by Islamic law; furthermore, much nationalism is present in the

Muslim world. On the other hand, Islam as a faith clearly transcends nationalist identity and loyalty.[6] Withal, there remain great symbolic and political
implications in the testimony that when God resolved to embody his very
own Word, he chose no language but Arabic.

Wherever the Islamic claim to the reception of God's truth combines with
political-moral responsibilities and interests, the historical and practical
consequences can be far-reaching. We move, accordingly, to the discrete
theme of Islam and image seven.

III

When religious faith approaches the political order its effects may be relatively modest. However, a *reformist* "faith for the world" (cf. the Christian Social Gospel) may turn into, or be countered by, a *revolutionary* "faith
transforming history." Historians will continue to wrangle over the political-
revolutionary stance versus the nonpolitical and nonrevolutionary stance of
Jesus. There is no room for any such disputation respecting Muhammad. And
the Prophet was a military leader as well as a political one. Further, the early
caliphs assumed that the main function of government was to ensure obedience to the divine law of the Koran. "The history of Islam, especially its first
few centuries, is full of movements that sought simultaneously to restore
what they saw as the true doctrine of Islam and to overthrow the existing political order. . . . [It] is unlikely that in their own minds the leaders of these
movements made any distinction between these two objectives."[7] Orthodox
Muslims have always maintained that the Islamic state "would protect and
propagate Islam, would strive for the realization of Islamic ideas, and would
apply Islamic laws."[8]

Certain basic features of and influences within the Muslim Anschauung may
be singled out for their special place in Islamic versions of "faith transforming history."

The central Islamic concept through which, in Haddad's phrasing, "everything is to be perceived" is unicity (*tawhīd*), "the integrating factor of all life."
Tawhīd

> is the means by which man assumes his vicegerency on earth and is able to
> function as an agent of God's will. . . . It denotes the freedom from submis-
> sion to any being, ideology, or power other than God, as well as the libera-
> tion from servitude to the self and to others. It is the emancipation from the
> fear of the powers of evil. *Tawhīd* makes possible the integration of the
> whole personality in both thought and conduct.
>
> *Tawhīd*. . . also operates in the community's affirmation of its commitment
> to the way of God. Thus the unity of God endows the faithful community
> with a unity of identity, of function, of destiny, and of purpose. Together the
> community commands the good and forbids the reprehensible, aiding in
> the eradication of falsehood and ungodliness from the earth.

> Thus a community operating within the framework of unity strives to bring
> about an order which is in accordance with God's will for mankind. It en-
> dows the community with an apprehension of reality that allows no division
> between sacred and secular.[9]

Muslim transformationism is not discontinuous with the Jewish prophetic-
Pharisee-rabbinic assurance that in and through the realization of justice the
historical order fosters the will of God. And the reality of *tawhīd* manifests
continuities with, as we shall see, the basic thrust of the Christian theology of
liberation. However, Islam is marked by *absoluteness of claim*, and in ways that
are not mitigated as much as is the case in Christianity and certainly in Judaism. The eternal, inerrant, and unalterable Word of God, the Koran, is "the
normative criterion by which all reality has to be measured and judged." For
the overwhelming majority of Muslims, the revelation made to Muhammad
in the Koran acted to complete and to supersede those revelations "given
to all earlier prophets," and it "is valid for all humanity and all time."[10] In
Sayyid Qutb's words, the Koranic method "is not a way of thought and
knowledge, rather, it alone possesses the correct interpretation of human
history."[11] A singular derivative of this persuasion within the Islamic world
itself is that those "Muslims" who do not accept such supersessionism are
very often not considered Muslims by those who do accept it.[12] From the
perspective of today's neo-normativist Islam—described by Haddad as "a
new articulation of the faith, relevant for modern challenges but not a new
Islam"[13]—all efforts of "modernists, Westernizers, and compromisers," however much these people may pretend to be Muslim, "are an indulgence in
apostasy, a veering from the right path, a degeneration into *jāhilīyya*, the ignorance of materialism, the establishing of other norms besides God, seeking other achievements besides His glory, and creating new orders to
compete with His will for mankind." The concept *jāhilīyya* designates any un-
Islamic order; it points by contrast to the crucial need to maintain or restore
a truly Islamic society.[14]

Of peculiar pertinence to the foregoing unqualified conflict between truth
and falsehood is the phenomenon of *jihād* (holy struggle; lit., "struggle in the
way of God"). The eventuality of holy war is not to be delimited to (alleged)
Muslims versus (alleged) non-Muslims, but instead applies remorselessly
wherever the eternal line is crossed from righteousness (truth) to unrighteousness (falsehood). In a word, *anyone* at all can become a target of *jihād*—just as
he can also be, of course, the one who fires at the target. Islam has many enemies without but it also has powerful enemies within. The theoretical/moral
foundation of *jihād* is reminiscent of certain assumptions within extreme forms
of "faith against the world" and also of "history and faith in tension." For almost from the outset, the entire world lay divided between the House of Islam wherein the religious law (*sharīʿa*) was observed and the one true God was
worshiped, and the House of War (*dār al-harb*), the rest of the world wherein

Islam was either not paramount or was denied and where people ignored or failed to engage in authentic worship.[15] *It is the duty of the Muslim to wage war upon War*, so that the whole world may be transformed into *dār al-Islām*. As ʿImād al-Dīn Khalīl formulates Muslim obligation as posited in the Koran, there are two necessary principles: ethical commitment together with corporate praxis, and *jihād*. This second principle "is Islam's continuous activity in the world to bring down the errant 'Jahilī' leadership and to make freedom of belief possible for every person wherever he may be, regardless of time, space, race, color, tongue, education, or allegiance. In fact it is the justification of the existence of the Islamic community in every time and in every place, the key to its role in the world and its ideological goal. . . . Without this *jihād* movement, the justification is eliminated and the key is lost. The Muslim community loses its capacity for unity, cooperation, and continuity."[16]

An additional and related consideration is that the Koran concerns itself with the totality of life. Sayyid Qutb describes the all-comprehending character of Muslim doctrine (*ʿaqīda*): It is the only example in human history "that is all-comprehensive to include every effort of man in all aspects of life. It does not restrict itself to one area or to a single trend. It does not give Caesar what is Caesar's and God what is God's. For what personally belongs to Caesar . . . belongs in its totality to God." In this connection, as ʿImād al-Dīn Khalīl and others emphasize, Islam permits no duality or polarity between the realms of spirit and matter. All existence is a unity, and past, present, and future are treated as a creative, dynamic whole. It follows that Islam is a missionizing faith through-and-through. Anwar al-Jundī writes that the purpose of Islam "is to arrive at the universal [dissemination] of the message since it is the only force capable of implementing human unity, equality, and freedom."[17]

The foregoing superficial introduction to Islam leads logically into the indispensable factor of human responsibility and accountability. It is affirmed above that *tawḥīd* enables man to fill the role of vicegerent of God. According to Islamic teaching, history is in God's hands. This fact in no way obviates, but instead serves to establish, human responsibility for history within the plan of Allah.[18] Rashīd al-Barrāwī attests that God makes his grace "contingent on human will and endeavor which points to the fact that He has endowed humans with capacity for such an endeavor, the responsibility for the condition they are in and the one they will achieve. . . . Thus man is responsible for his action. He cannot place the responsibility for his error on outside agents."[19] The Koran teaches man's "total freedom in the area of decision-making, planning, and execution. It is this freedom that renders man accountable."[20] The ascription of responsibility shakes loose "the process of human liberation from determinism and total resignation to the forces of destiny and the vagaries of human life."[21]

Edward Mortimer remarks: "the idea that all Muslims are fatalists is one of many Western misconceptions about Islam."[22]

We may allude to one further ideational consideration of relevance to Muslim "faith transforming history." The great power of tradition within Islamic socio-political policy and action means that the praxis of social change, even revolutionary change, is one and the same with a resurrecting of the past. Muslim versions of the seventh normative image redirect us, in one limited but significant sense, to "faith for the world"—not the awful pagan world (and surely not the Christian and Jewish worlds) but the ideal Islamic world. Present, future, and past are to be reconciled. For once the present and the future are right-fully transformed, the rightful past is thereby restored. Put differently, Islamic variations upon "faith transforming history" join other such interpretations in presupposing a humanly corrupted state of affairs, a kind of "fall." Had human society never betrayed its moral, God-willed structure, present transformationist effort would be quite redundant. However, a relative difference appears between Islamic and non-Islamic views. Islam tends to be unqualifiedly historical in its remembered vision of ideal life. Once upon a time there *was* an ideal social order: the *umma* (community) of Muhammad in Medina. "The ideal and perfect Islamic community is that of Medina where the *umma* lived under divine guidance through the mediation of the Angel Gabriel and the Prophet Muhammad." To Muslim traditionalists, the "Medinan ideal" can be and ought to be re-created in every way. Those advocates of an Islamic response "to the crisis of the present want not only to recapture the potency of the past, but to affirm that the potency cannot be recaptured outside of the prototype of the Medinan state as established during the life of the Prophet. It is not only a spirit of the age that needs to be recaptured, but a whole social and ethical order that needs to be re-created and reestablished."[23] (Of course, not all Muslim authorities accept as a fact past historical perfection.)

A ready illustration of *the identity of revolution and return* may be cited: the place of women. This issue is most often dealt with by Muslim spokespersons of today in the frame of reference of (reputed) "Western" interference, decadence, and evil. The Koran declares: "Men are in charge of women, because God has endowed the one with more, and because they spend of their property for their support. Therefore the righteous women are the obedient, guarding in secret that which God has guarded" (S. 4:34). What, then, does it mean to ensure the liberation of women? Speaking for "contemporary writers," Yvonne Yazbeck Haddad replies:

> Islam does not say that women are inferior, rather that they are different. They have been created for a specific function in which they can excel. Liberation should not mean acquiring male characteristics or performing masculine functions, which is reprehensible. Rather, liberation for the woman is being herself and fulfilling the destiny to which God has created her. Liberation is not freedom from obedience to men, or freedom from the restrictions of the faith; rather, liberation must be freedom from the corruption

and alienation that have been brought about by Western impingement on the East. It must be a liberation from measuring up to Western standards that erode the basic foundations of the community of God, a liberation from colonial status and imperialistic politics, a liberation to be oneself as God has willed for the welfare of humanity within the Umma of Islam.

... Obedience to the husband does not demean the woman or detract from her self-respect, for that is the order of things.

Accordingly, the present and future liberation of woman entails the reaffirmation of, and the revolutionary return to, an ideal previously actualized historically by the will of Allah himself. This fact serves to remind us of how and why distinctively Muslim social revolutions are through-and-through conservative (= conservationist). Nevertheless, from an Islamic perspective in the presence of fresh contemporary challenges and situational pressures, "the reaffirmation of the old becomes new." The old, eternal answer is a progressive one "not because it changes but because it is equipped to cope with all change."[24]

The conversionist image as we have encountered it in Islam is summed up in the understanding by ʿImād al-Dīn Khalīl and others of the meaning of true religion: "a dynamic, active involvement in the material world... that seeks to reform and transform the world into that which God intended it to be."[25] The motif of "faith transforming history" as identifiable within Islam will hardly replicate the extra-Muslim characteristics listed at the start of this chapter. But the Muslim conversionist view does convey the decisive conviction italicized at the end of section I of the chapter: the historical order ought to be and can be transformed to the glory of God's righteousness. In the Islamic case the conversionist stance has been significantly strengthened of late by an upsurge of Muslim traditionalism and by Islamic consciousness-raising over recent decades, particularly as a response to reputed threats from the non-Muslim "West." With such developments in mind, let us review briefly one major contemporary embodiment of Islamic transformationism.

It is paradoxical and ironic that the Islamic national revolution of 1978–1979 in Iran—upon which Professor Haddad is wholly and curiously silent—should have taken place in a Shiite Muslim land, whereas most other Islamic countries are predominantly Sunni. Minority Shiites are regarded as heretical by majority Sunnis, yet it was the Shia tradition that provided the ideology of the Iranian revolution and it was Iranian revolutionary leaders who acted to implement politically and socially a radical-restorationist Islam in ways not ventured by, or not possible for, their more "orthodox" colleagues elsewhere.

Although the extant form of Shiism in Iran encouraged the ulamā to stay outside politics, that very fact helped them to maintain an integral corporate structure and to be a potential political force. Actually, during the nine-

teenth and twentieth centuries the Iranian *ulamā* conducted themselves independently of, and even in opposition to, the monarchy, amid the latter's
capitulation to foreign encroachments. It should be noted as well that
Twelver Shiism is in part based upon Muʿtazilite rationalism, which stresses
the justice of Allah, the rationality of his work of creation, and human free
will and responsibility for the conditions under which people live.[26]

Thus was the path already opened for the coming of the Ayatollah Ruhol-
lah Khomeini and company.

In an early publication future events are portended when Khomeini declares that while "the intellectuals want progress," what they fail to realize is
that Europe offers "not civilization but savagery." He continues: "These
schools mixing young girls and young passion-ridden boys kill female hon-
our, the root of life and the power of manly valour, are materially and spiritually damaging to the country and are forbidden by God's commandment. . . .
These wine-shops and liquor-producing organizations wear off the brain of
the youth of the country and burn away the intellect, the health, the courage
and the audacity of the masses; they should be closed by God's commandment. . . . " With respect to remedies, "if the Islamic law of retribution, blood
money and punishments is put into practice even for a single year, the seed
of injustice, theft and unchastity will be eliminated from the country. Anybody wanting to extirpate theft from the world must cut off the thief's hands,
otherwise such imprisonments [as those imposed by secular courts] would
only help the thieves and promote larceny." The "calamity of the country is
that it possesses such divine laws and yet extends its hands to the countries
of the foreigners, and is seeking to execute their artificial laws which have
emanated from selfish and poisonous ideas."[27]

By 1969 Khomeini was giving lectures advocating the political "guardian-
ship of the jurist," which meant that he had ranged himself against the traditional Twelver Shiite position of avoiding direct participation in the running
of a state. Islam, Khomeini argues, is either political or it is nothing. The Koran has "a hundred times more verses concerning social problems than on
devotional subjects. Out of fifty books of Muslim tradition there are perhaps
three or four which deal with prayer or with man's duties towards God, a few
on morality and all the rest have to do with society, economics, law, politics
and the state." The laws of God "concern the whole life of the individual
from conception to the grave." And in response to those who reproach him
for being a "political cleric," Khomeini asks, "Was not the Prophet, God's
prayers be upon him, a politician?"[28]

The label that Said Amir Arjomand assigns to Khomeini is "revolutionary
traditionalist."[29] We have earlier noted that in Islam, revolution means commitment to a resurrecting of the past, a re-creation of presumed historical
perfection. Pure Islamic government is not only possible but necessary. In
Khomeini's words, "Islamic government is the government of the people by
the divine law." The supreme head of government is to be a jurist—an ex-

pert in the divine law that the government is called to enforce. Thus, we have a perfectionism of the present, in the sense that, as Khomeini avows, Islamic law possesses the answer to everything: "from penal codes to commercial, industrial and agricultural law," and also to national defense. But the Ayatollah is no mere narrow nationalist; his vision extends to the obligations of Islamic universalism. "Indeed to him the division of the *umma* into 'several separate nations' is itself something to be deplored, the work of colonialism and of 'despotic and ambitious rulers.' [A task of] Islamic government will be to restore the unity of the *umma*, 'to liberate its lands from the grip of the colonialists and to topple the agent governments of colonialism.'"[30] But all in all Khomeini wholly typifies Islamic conversionist doctrine: To observe and enforce the *shariʿa* is to reconstitute the ideal society.

From among the many moral questions that can be broached respecting transformationist Islam, we may select three.

1. Are human weakness, intransigence, and the work of Satan all-sufficient explanations for the immense amount of conflict and disagreement that permeates the Muslim community? Is the unicity (*tawḥīd*) of truth actually an objective truth, or is it interpretable in prevailing respects as an ideological strategy? Were authentic truth in reality one, would we not be confronted by much greater harmony among its recipients at the points of thinking and of advocated courses of action? As matters stand, unicity appears as a contemporary-historical will-o'-the-wisp.

2. Is it possible to be authentically Islamic and authentically modern? Must there always be warfare between these two sets of ideals?

3. What are the morally responsible ways of dealing with opponents? Such studies as Haddad's *Contemporary Islam* and Mortimer's *Faith and Power* point up that Islam today is faced here with a serious ethical challenge. With special reference to Haddad, it appears that a conspiracy theory of history is dominant within the *umma*.[31] Are there no alternatives to the silencing, prosecution, or liquidation of enemies and apostates? I do not imply that the answer can be a simple one or is to be found in a single point of view. For example, a supreme interpreter of Muslim law and a highly revered Islamic leader, Mufti Sheikh Saʿad e-Din elʿAlami of Jerusalem, recently ruled that any Muslim assassin of Syrian President Hafez Assad would be granted the status of an Islamic martyr and would be "assured of a place in Paradise for eternity." The Mufti asserts that Assad has "murdered many Muslims" and that "Islamic law is that such a person must be killed."[32] Sheikh elʿAlami is entirely correct about Assad's behavior; according to Amnesty International, in one year alone between 5,000 and 25,000 "fundamentalist" Muslims have been slaughtered by the Syrian government.[33] So let's hear it for the Mufti!—perhaps in memory of Dietrich Bonhoeffer who resolved on Christian grounds to take part in an assassination plot against Adolf Hitler. However, there is a stumbling block. What of those persons who are not guilty of the inhumanity of Hafez Assad and his cohorts but whose transgressions are

of a quite different quality? Are these people to be treated in the same or similar fashion? In Muslim Pakistan today the drinking of alcohol is punishable by eighty lashes. In post-revolutionary Iran homosexuals face a firing squad and adulterers are stoned to death; the Bahai religion has been banned and many of its adherents killed. Thousands have lost jobs, homes, and belongings. This group is considered apostate from Islam.[34] The charge of apostasy is not without a strong foundation (for instance, the Bahais teach sexual equality and the reconciliation of religion to modern ideas). There is a Koranic prayer, "Lord, leave not one single family of infidels on the earth." Must this mean that "believers" are themselves obliged to do the liquidating of infidels? As Haddad points out, for Muslims the existence of the State of Israel is "a sign that the forces of darkness and immorality, of wickedness and apostasy have for reasons yet unexplained taken the ascendancy in the world."[35] One shudders to think what would happen were the absolutist praxis referred to above to be left free for implementation respecting treatment of the State of Israel, located as it is "in the heart"[36] of the Muslim Arab world. In the name of the Allah of justice and mercy, are there not integrally Muslim moral alternatives to the destruction of enemies? Khalid Ishaq, a Karachi lawyer and well-known Islamic scholar, contends: "If you have strict Islamic law, you must have respect for human rights."[37]

Within pages that seek to give voice to Islam, perhaps the final words ought to be in behalf of that faith. Two testimonies are included. In both instances the perspective upon the nature and treatment of evil cuts in a rather different direction from the tendency referred to above in point three. In a recent article, Haddad speaks of the fact that today a number of Muslims are writing of Islam as "the Religion of Liberation."

> For them, Islam's mission is to maintain a constant revolution against man-made systems, whether capitalist or communist, that seek to enslave humans to the dominion of other beings .... [Radical monotheism is] the rejection of all alternate claims to obedience whether of state, political party, social group, etc.; it transcends them to assume the role of leadership in the world ....
>
> The *umma* is urged to strive in the way of God against all powers and principalities of oppression and injustice in the world. This mission is bound to elicit the hostility of the forces of evil who invariably have opposed the prophets throughout history. The believers must sustain each other in righteousness and unwavering zeal for the cause of God. God's liberating victory is inevitable. As omnipotent, he is the Lord of History and shall vanquish all forces of oppression. As merciful, he calls men to renounce their ways and seek his forgiveness. Then Islam will prevail, Islam—the religion of peace.[38]

Second, there is in Shiite Islam the doctrine of the concealed Imam, who has "withdrawn from human sight until the fullness of the time when he will return as the Mahdi, 'the divinely guided one' who will usher in a period of righteousness and peace before the end of the world and the last judgment."[39] A young Iranian sociologist, Ali Sharīʿātī (1933-1977), was led to identify the Shiite teaching of imamate with leadership in the struggle for human liberation. For Sharīʿātī, the revolt of Ali, Muhammad's son-in-law, against the Umayyads in the first Muslim century is an abiding lesson in the duty to defend justice against tyranny and oppression. In a way reminiscent of the Jewish mystical idea of Lamed-Vov, Sharīʿātī finds that "the Imam, though Hidden, is not necessarily absent at all: he lives in the real world, and he has his 'feet on the ground.' We may even meet him without recognizing him: he might be the farmer in that field over there, or that merchant in his shop in the bazaar."[40]

These two testimonies may serve as a transition to our next sub-heading. The finding that transformationist Islam means, in essence, a conservationist return to the past brings up the question of whether it is possible for a "faith transforming history" to have consequences different from that kind of return.

IV

We come to the second and longer exemplification and treatment of "faith transforming history": liberation theology, or political theology and the struggle for liberation, within contemporary Christianity. Almost needless to foretell, such Christian application of faith-oriented transformationism will be much more compatible with H. Richard Niebuhr's exposition of conversionism than is the Islamic absolutist transformationism just reviewed. (This is not to ignore the continuities. Thus, in reporting that "for the conversionist, history is the story of God's mighty deeds and of man's response to them," Niebuhr could be introducing an Islamic tract.)

We bear in mind that the task of this chapter is solely to represent "faith transforming the world." That subject is vast enough in its moral and theological aspects to force us to pass over collateral factors of great import. An example of the latter is technical-economic analysis, a decisive element in effecting at the practical level any theology of human liberation.

Let us attend to possible understandings of "liberation theology" and of the concept "liberation."*

The Second Vatican Council (1963–1965), under the impetus of Pope John XXIII and with its great emphasis upon the importance of transforming this world, is a significant force behind contemporary expressions of "faith trans-

---

*"Liberation theology" and the "theology of liberation" are strictly shorthand for "the theology of liberative praxis," while "political theology" and the "theology of politics" are strictly shorthand for "the theology of the political realm and of political action." The danger is ever present of the politicization of Christianity, as in the Faith Movement of German Christians. The concept "political theology" may not be wholly free of such debasement.

forming history" in general and liberation theology in particular. The Council's *Gaudium et Spes* speaks of the mission of Jesus Christ as breaking the power of evil "so that this world might be fashioned anew according to God's design and reach its fulfillment."[41] In the theology/praxis of liberation the dualism of "faith above history" is put out upon the dung heap, or at least that intention is paramount. Thus, there is immense historical significance in the fact that liberation theology, particularly in its Latin American forms, is considerably Roman Catholic.* Further, while the theology of liberation primarily instances Christian "faith transforming history," it is yet not devoid of affinities to "history transforming faith." For liberation thinking, the domain of historical life is received as a holy reality. Gustavo Gutiérrez, leading thinker of the movement in Latin America, states that to look concretely at the historical process is to apprehend the presence therein of the Lord himself.[42] We can even say that for liberation thinking, history, viz., the history of the oppressed, serves as a primary moral-theological reference point, in the way that the general theological doctrine of man serves for the Christian realism of Reinhold Niebuhr.[43] However, both the meaning and the content of this concentration upon history elicit a deontological program to transform the human condition—with Christian understanding and devotion as the power and the incentive for all such restructuring.

Of the two orientations, "faith transforming history" and "history transforming faith," on balance the former achieves precedence within liberation theology. We shall see how this is so. As made clear in *The Power of the Poor in History*, Father Gutiérrez is particularly concerned to avoid contracting the Christian gospel into social service, purely human advocacy, or mere forms of political activity. "Christ's liberation cannot be reduced to political liberation"—yet that liberation "is present in concrete historical and political liberating events."[44]

The continuity of liberation theology and "history transforming faith" is further exemplified in an affirmation of Juan Luis Segundo that concrete historical experience conditions the moral concerns of those who call themselves Christians, and conditions as well the ecclesial structure of Christianity. Segundo holds that Christian theological affirmation is markedly shaped by historical relativity. Specifically, the shared prescription within today's liberation theology that the cries of the oppressed be determinative of Christian praxis shows the moral link between this point of view and "history transforming faith." Not without significance, Segundo cites H. Richard Niebuhr's presentation of historical relativism in support of the judgment that history conditions faith.[45] But of course Niebuhr represents the alterna-

---

*But the contemporary attack upon "faith above history" within Catholic circles is independent of, and indeed has provided inspiration for, liberation theology. Latin America has no monopoly upon the "theology of liberation." We deal with Latin American thinking here for its major exemplification of that way of doing theology. It is important to remember that Latin America is the only Third World continent that is prevailingly Christian.

tive position of "faith transforming history," as does Segundo himself for the most part, along with other theologians of liberation. For none of them goes so far as to allow history to be a final arbiter of faith. The most telling consideration, in Segundo, Gutiérrez, and the rest, is that the call for the transformation of socio-historical life comes strictly from within the Christian community and is wholly inspired by certain understandings of the Christian faith, by what Gutiérrez calls "the pastoral and ecclesial nature of the Good News."[46]

This form of transformationism proposes the meanings that we ought to assign to the Christian theological enterprise. Arthur F. McGovern concludes that "the whole of liberation theology is rooted in its methodology."[47] As a corollary, social-scientific analysis is viewed as constituent to the obligations of theologizing (a conviction taken over from liberal theology and, in lesser intensity, from neo-orthodox theology). We have underscored the Hebrew Bible's insistence upon the inner identity of truth and righteousness (chap. 2). In liberation thinking the moral indispensability of *praxis* is continually stressed, a category that "points to *the ongoing interplay of reflection and action.* When we act, reflect on the action, and then act in a new way on the basis of our reflection (or when we reflect, and then act, and then reflect in a new way on the basis of our action)," we give reality to praxis.[48] Praxis is action guided by thought. It honors the dialectic between theory and deeds; as the Protestant thinker José Míguez Bonino expresses it, "action overflows and challenges the theory that has informed it; and thought, projecting the shape and future of reality, pushes action to new ventures. . . . This dialectical interplay seems to be the necessary presupposition for political ethics."[49] The concerns of liberation theology are here markedly continuous with not only the Hebrew Bible but also the New Testament admonition to "do the truth" (John 3:21). Ordinarily, truth is thought of as simple honesty or as knowledge, or as something "out there" to be discovered. Significantly, in the Fourth Gospel the doing of truth is set in opposition to the doing of evil (3:20). Thus, truth is not just something that "is" or is spoken; it is a reality the doing of which means fostering righteousness. And truth is more than simple accuracy or some objective, static condition; it is something that *happens*, that realizes itself within human history. This linkage of the truth of God with praxis points up the persisting lesson of the Epistle of James: if faith has no works, it is dead (2:17).

The world in which some of us try to do moral philosophy and theology is pain-wracked with hunger, terror, murder, racism, sexism, international rivalry and anarchy, social strife, and economic crisis. The liberation theologians tell us that in such a world "pure theology," or what they often label "academic theology"—identifiable as thinking apart from deeds—is an obscenity. Within the proclaimed context of identification with oppressed peoples, authentic Christian theology becomes, in the words of Gutiérrez, "critical reflection in and on historical praxis in confrontation with the word of the Lord lived and accepted in faith. It will be a reflection in and on faith as liberating praxis. It will be an understanding of a faith which has as its starting point a commitment to create a just and human society. . . ." It will "not stop with reflecting on the world, but [will try] to be part of the process through which the world is transformed."[50]

Near the start of chapter three I allude to John Line's phrasing, "truth is in order to goodness." Added reference to his exposition will point up further the epistemology and methodology underlying liberation theology, yet at the same time bring to the fore, willy-nilly, the important question of what, if anything, makes that theology distinctive. "The words 'in order to' denote. . . an internal relation; truth and goodness are of one being, and one implicates the other not by relativity but by essential identity." It is of the essence of the truth of God to embrace goodness. Truth and the good born of it stand in "generic unity." Love and love's deeds are seen to be "germane to truth and knowledge, not suitable addenda." According to Christian faith, if we do not love, we do not know God (I John 4:8). "Knowledge and truth, love and goodness" share a single "richness of connotation."[51] The teaching that "truth is in order to goodness" contrasts sharply with a form of truth that seeks to remain aloof from or uncontaminated by the affairs of this world, as it also contrasts with a form of goodness for which truth is no more than a means to an end. Thus, this alternative teaching avoids both otherworldly abstractness and too-worldly instrumentalism. Truth is "in order to goodness," not in an exclusively non-integral sense and not in a purely pragmatic sense, but because (insofar as it is the truth of God) it *wills* to devote itself to the service of goodness.

Now my choice of John Line's essay for summarization in this context has involved a small trick. (Writers can be tricky people.) In truth (*sic!*) Line's piece appeared over forty years ago. This was almost a quarter of a century before the advent of the movement we know as liberation theology. Accordingly, one could reasonably interject, Was not the liberationist testimony to the unity of truth and goodness put forth way, way back—in social Christianity? In considering liberation thinking, are we not dealing simply with a revivified or warmed-over Social Gospel? Although John Line himself remains free of the unhappy proclivity found in some versions of Christian Liberalism to construe religious faith in a wholly instrumentalist way, nevertheless his emphasis upon public (and personal) rectitude as constitutive to religious truth reminds us that the Social Gospel had already bulldozed out much of the foundation area upon which the theology of liberation has come to erect its home.* Again, the theology of liberation wholly carries forward the insistence we have noted in Reinhold Niebuhr that the pursuit of justice by Christians has only one avenue: engagement in the political order. Niebuhr

---

*Be it remembered, however, that the Social Gospel was very largely a phenomenon of the North upon Planet Earth.

learned this from his experience under the oppressiveness of uncontrolled American capitalism; many of the liberative thinkers have learned it under the oppressiveness of Third World life (and death), which is itself very largely the outcome of capitalist exploitation.

The analysis so far has done little more than suggest that liberation theology stands in continuity with much earlier Jewish and Christian reflection. Does this mean that nothing distinctive is offered by liberative thinking/praxis? The answer is a qualified No. The basis of this answer is found within a singular form of advocacy amid a broadly accepted and familiar understanding of "liberation." On its one side liberation is the honoring of human dignity and rights. Everyone is to be treated as the equal of everyone else. On its other side, liberation is the actualizing of responsible freedom for the oppressed as also for their oppressors. These two component sides have equivalent force and validity. Normatively speaking, in responsible freedom or the responsible life (Verantwortlichkeit, accountability) self-defensiveness and self-justification are overcome in principle. It is a life "in which one freely gives because he freely receives." Christian faith proclaims the reality of forgiveness as, among other things, a form of empowerment. That is to say, insofar as persons have been themselves forgiven, they are enabled to live "a life of forgiveness and gratitude, a life that changes [their] relationships to others."[52] Liberation is the freedom to serve righteousness, through serving others. Of course, this is to speak in an ideal manner. Expressed in psychological terms, liberation seeks and offers resources that help to overcome destructive forms of repression.[53] Theologically put, in liberation there is deliverance from idolatry. If authentic freedom cannot be achieved without the honoring of dignity and rights, it follows that to choose a truly righteous fast (Isa. 58:6) is "to loose the bonds of wickedness" and to see to it that "the oppressed go free." But liberation theology further argues—here we come to the crucial element—that oppression will not end apart from an attack upon the present socio-political structures of wrong, upon the *systemic* evils of this world.

Thus does authentic liberation mean not alone a victory over internal or subjective alienation, but a conquest of external or objective socio-political oppression. To be sure, the theologians of liberation stand in the apostolic succession of Walter Rauschenbusch, Reinhold Niebuhr, and company. But the transformation of the world must involve socio-political revolution—not the relatively mild, structure-accepting reformism of the Christian Social Gospel (which failed to grapple with the political dimension in any determining way, and was in any case largely beholden to liberal theology in ways that liberation thinking is not[54]), and certainly not a reinstituted perfectionism of the past as in revolutionary-traditionalist Islam, but instead a radical overthrow of the principalities and powers, of "the world rulers of this present darkness" (Eph. 6:12) that now afflict human beings. The true *jihād* is not one of "believers" fighting "unbelievers" but one of the disinherited,

women, blacks, et al., fighting their destroyers. "Religion" is fulfilled and redeemed by righteousness. But the meaning of revolution within and for the
theology of liberation must be identified with care. *Revolution does not mean
mere religious legitimation of armed or ruthless secular-political revolutionary action. True
revolution involves the transformation of the social order for the sake of a universal justice
and, insofar as possible, by means that are consistent with humaneness and shalom and
respect for the rights of all.*

Father Segundo laments the ideological tendency "to assimilate revolutionary language to the prevailing idiom of the status quo."[55] In the present
frame of reference liberative thinking/praxis is nothing apart from radical
socio-political revolution to free oppressed people in genuine ways. Were
the theology of liberation only reformist, it would have no distinctiveness at
all. Liberation theology assails us with shattering questions: Do not your acts
of civil goodness fail to address the structural injustices of society and
thereby fail to satisfy the categorical demands of social righteousness? Are
not your vaunted acts of "love" and "compassion" mere band-aids upon
monster wounds, accepting and perpetuating injustice? *The one path to the
praxis of justice, which is the weapon of love, is the praxis of revolution.* The divine righteousness has no other means to incarnate itself. Thus is the theology of liberation a theology of revolution. Here is the uniqueness of liberation
thinking within our treatment of normative images. Whenever the gospel according to God's righteousness fails to flesh out in social and political ways
the apodictic demands for justice, its news is not good but bad. The failure
betrays the ideal: the divine righteousness stays disincarnate, is rendered
futile.

A comprehensive understanding of "liberation" may be summarized with
aid from three reciprocally interpenetrating levels of liberation as delineated by Gustavo Gutiérrez: (a) The aspiration of human beings for freedom
from oppressing political, social, economic, and religious structures. (b) Liberation from the ideological prison which denies that people have either the
capability or the right to alter their historical condition (cf. the Islamic stress
upon human responsibility and accountability, as noted above). "True liberation can only be achieved through human beings who make their own history."[56] (c) Liberation from sin as brought by Jesus Christ. At Medellín,
Colombia, the General Conference of Latin American Bishops (CELAM) declared that God sent his son that he might liberate all people from the evils
to which sin had subjected them, including hunger, misery, oppression, and
ignorance.[57] In the words of Gutiérrez, sin is "the final root of all rupture of
friendship and of all injustice and oppression. Christ makes us truly free,
that is to say, he enables us to live in communion with him, which is the basis of all human brotherhood." Without human community, authentic human
freedom is impossible. The third level of liberation admonishes us that
liberative theology "is not a theology of political liberation," not a mere ideology of revolution, while yet reminding us, dialectically, that social and po-

litical liberation is intrinsic to salvation.[58] With respect to the oft-heard criticism that liberation theology reduces faith to politics, the best answer to this charge is that politics is the *consequence* of faith. Christian faith gives meaning to political action. Yet it transcends politics, just as does human liberation itself.

Liberationist thinking/action is by no means antipathetic to "normal" historical life (in contradistinction to "faith against the world"). This theology's demands for justice in the here-and-now dissociate it from Christian otherworldliness. In the measure that the theology of socio-political liberation is struggling from within the church against entrenched wickedness, yet doing so in the stubborn hope that the battles for righteousness may really be won within human history (in much contrast to "history and faith in tension"), that theology is compellingly representative of "faith transforming history." And insofar as the resultant, even if only fragmentary, transformations exert in turn an impact upon the church, a bond is forged with the eighth normative image, "history transforming faith."

To conclude this preface to the theology of liberation, a word is in order upon the subject of *ideology*, an issue that receives much attention in liberation thinking. The new historical situation—"new" in contrast to the premodern world—is one in which the horror of human suffering that is associated with socio-economic causes and structures has attached itself weightily to issues of international relations and world political conflict. This was the womb in which ideology in the modern sense was born. In chapter five I speak of ideology as a directing of ideas and idea-systems to the service of self-interest, especially collective self-interest. In religious ideology God and the divine purpose become a function of social status and class interest. It is a fateful question whether theology and theological ethics are forced to remain captive to ideology. If they are, does not such a program as "the theology of liberation" become internally contradictory and impossible of application? Well, for one thing marginated people are fully aware that it is not so much theological biases as it is social and political biases that undergird a great deal of Christian exegesis and theology.[59] In addition, Míguez Bonino argues for an understanding of ideology that is more comprehensive than mine, one that takes into account the insistence by new countries and classes engaged in revolutionary struggle that ideology can be received in a positive sense. He cites a finding of the Geneva Conference on Church and Society that ideology "is the theoretical and analytical structure of thought which undergirds successful action either to realize the revolutionary change in society or to undergird and justify the status quo."[60] It may thus be possible to distinguish "bad ideology" from "good ideology" (the "bad" and the "good" being identified, needless to say, in relation to a particular standpoint), and, beyond this, even to have a comprehensive, and hence in a sense neutral, understanding of ideology as encompassing human idea-systems as such. Thus can we conceive ideology in three different ways: negatively, as "false consciousness"; positively, as "true consciousness"; and theoretically or generically, as any *Weltanschauung* that expresses the values and goals of one or another social grouping. Of course, as Reinhold Niebuhr protests, collective self-interest is irremovable. But my contention here is that the moral quality of self-interest can vary infinitely, depending upon the causes to which it devotes itself. Ideology can have a non-pejorative connotation. The question then becomes, How may Christian theology and praxis be reconstituted so as to escape or redeem bad ideology or false consciousness? With Reinhold Niebuhr still in mind I submit that the above comprehensive refinement of ideology has no power wholly to obliterate the sin that can and does corrupt the finest of causes—not excluding "neutral" understandings of ideology. The only ultimate remedy for sin, in principle, is repentance and grace. "Search me, O God, and know my heart! Try me and know my thoughts! And see if there be any wicked way in me, and lead me in the way everlasting!" (Ps. 139:23-24). We have to say "in principle" because even repentance and grace can be utilized in the corrupting of (good) causes. Here is one meaning of "the demonic," the transfiguration of exalted goodness into evil.

Once the above warnings have been issued, it is felt in liberative circles that ideology can yet make a constructive contribution within a normative framework of "faith transforming history." It is the expectation of Segundo that ideology, construed as "a historical system of means and ends" in relation to real-life challenges, will be of great aid in constructing a bridge between our conception of God and concrete historical realities. Without ideologies (of necessity, provisional in character) "the faith of today is as dead as the faith alluded to in the Epistle of James (2:17), and for the very same reason: its complete impracticality."[61] On identical reasoning, ideology may have positive use—as I hope to develop—within the image of "history transforming faith." In this frame of reference, *deideologization* is to be identified as the struggle against bad ideology or false consciousness.

V

The specific, urgent problems addressed by political and liberation theology today are many in number and vast in range. They include: class struggle; the exploitation of women; racism and racist violence; ethnic, national, and religious oppression; structural unemployment; ecological wastage and destruction; war and the fear of human obliteration; and hunger and impoverishment. Neither secular-authoritarian nor secular-liberal reformism has conquered these problems.

In what follows, concentration falls upon the liberation of the disinherited (Arabic, *mustazʿafin*). This liberative cause is tied closely to such other causes as the liberation of blacks and the liberation of women: untold numbers of the disinherited are blacks, and a majority of these are black females.

Today some 500 million people are severely hungry and many of them will die soon. One of eight persons in the world is hungry most of the time. Between fifteen and twenty percent of the planet's children do not have enough to eat. Some 40,000 children die each day from hunger or disease, an average of one every two seconds. Most of these children are in the poorer nations of Africa and Southern Asia. (It is wrong, of course, to turn our backs upon the poverty and oppression that continue within the North, despite all its "development" and wealth.) Worldwide there is no scarcity of food; the chief cause of world hunger is poverty and inequality of income.

In almost every Latin American country five percent of the population controls eighty percent of the wealth. Huge landed estates are owned by a small minority. Most people who have work (there are countless unemployed) labor for a pittance. There is strong anti-union sentiment. About two-thirds of the population are undernourished, and disease is rampant. In many countries three-fourths of the people are illiterate. At the same time, foreign investors amass great profits to be transferred out of Latin America. As the Catholic bishops of the continent long since pointed out, the entire area is largely dependent economically upon outside monopolistic powers; the foreign, neo-colonialist imperialism and the economic dependency are root causes of the universal poverty.[62] (The people of the United States, comprising some six percent of the world's population, consume some forty percent of the world's resources.)

The theme of the liberation of the disinherited is incredibly complex, with unnumbered aspects. We shall venture upon just two sub-topics: (1) On taking sides; and (2) On the meaning and challenge of socio-political revolution.

(1) To all appearances, the severity of the divine wrath is aimed at the poor and the oppressed. But the theology of liberation intercedes: No, these appearances are wholly deceiving. The sufferings are brought about by human oppressors. These sufferings are, as a matter of fact, the devil's own praxis, the opposite of God's will. In point of truth, God will have no truck with the evildoers. He ranges himself* against them, and we (= responsible Christians and others, not excluding the legions of us who are among the evildoers) are called to do the same.

Is this to say that God is "prejudiced" and that Christians are therefore to be "prejudiced"? *Does the Christian faith take sides?* In a certain sense, yes. Let us return to the argumentation of Gustavo Gutiérrez, now in the frame of reference of "class struggle."[63] Gutiérrez himself is quite aware of a poignant dilemma: How are we ever to reconcile the *universality* of gospel charity with commitment to a *particular* social class?[64] Four points may be made.

In the first place, Gutiérrez and his brothers and sisters in Christ possess the confidence that the only real path to the universalization of righteous-

---

*Ironically, much liberation theology has not abandoned sexist God-language.

ness is a "preferential option for the poor"[65] and the extirpation of the class struggle. To take part in this battle "not only does not oppose universal love; such a commitment is today the necessary and inescapable means to love's concretion. Such participation leads to a society without classes, without owners or dispossessed, without oppressors or oppressed. From a dialectical perspective, reconciliation means the conquest of conflict. The communion of paschal gladness passes over confrontation and the Cross."[66] As Arthur F. McGovern has it, the way to love oppressors is to liberate them "from their inhuman condition as oppressors."[67]

In the second place, any idea of social neutrality is a moral chimera, a contradiction in (human) terms. If Christian theology and praxis are not prepared to fight the status quo, they then bless things as they are. Here is the truth in Juan Luis Segundo's overly simple but compelling implication that there are just two kinds of theology: a species of academic profession doing obeisance to the socio-political status quo (all the while quite oblivious to its own conditioning by the surrounding society) and a wholly contrasting form of revolutionary praxis, as in the prophets and Jesus.[68] I say that Segundo's implication is overly simple because there can be a reformist theological ethic (e.g., the Social Gospel) that is anti-status quo and yet not radically revolutionary.

In the third place, it is a fact that God herself takes sides: this is the biblical persuasion. There is no such thing as "equal justice" in the prophetic literature. The bias of Scripture in favor of the poor (*anawim*) and the downtrodden is undeniable. Yahweh, the liberating God, will surely punish those who "trample the heads of the poor into the dust of the earth, and turn aside the way of the afflicted" (Amos 2:7a). Krister Stendahl writes that the question

> is not how one balances off mercy and judgment, but for whom is judgment mercy and for whom is it threatening doom. For God's people God's judgment is salvation. But who are God's people? Is it not consistently true in the Bible that the only time that language about "God's people" really functions, *the only time it is allowed to stand up without the lambasting critique of the prophets*, is when it stands for the little ones, the oppressed, the suppressed, the repressed? Is it not true that all language about a chosen people becomes wrong when applied outside the situation of weakness?

Jesus never said "man shall not live by bread alone" to a hungry person; he said it to the devil (Matt. 4:1-4).[69]

From hundreds of eligible biblical passages we may single out two favorites of liberative theologians, the one attributed to Jesus' mother and the other a citation by Jesus of the prophet Isaiah.

> And Mary said, . . .
> "He has shown strength with his arm,

he has scattered the proud in the imagination
  of their hearts,
he has put down the mighty from their thrones,
and exalted those of low degree;
he has filled the hungry with good things,
and the rich he has sent empty away."
                                    (Luke 1:46, 51-53; cf. I Sam. 2:1-10)

"The Spirit of the Lord is upon me,
because he has chosen me
to preach the Good News to the poor.
He has sent me to proclaim liberty to the captives,
and recovery of sight to the blind;
to set free the oppressed,
and announce the year when the Lord will save his people."
                                    (Luke 4:18–19, Isa. 61:1–2)

These are liberative praxises for the wretched of the earth, yet they climax
in a theocentric form of deliverance. No "hidden God" here! As the theologians of liberation recall for our sake, in Jesus of Nazareth, his teachings and
his deeds, no split is tolerated among faith (the domain of the spirit), morality (the domain of responsible justice and love), and politics (the domain of
power). A false spiritualization of Jesus and his praxis has prevailed in the
church for almost twenty centuries. In truth, Jesus was carrying ahead the developing tradition of Torah-cum-Prophecy Judaism: "The Lord executeth
righteousness and judgment for all that are oppressed" (Ps. 103:6, KJV).[70] In
this respect, the theology of liberation perpetuates Jesus' hope for, and expectation of, the transformation of the world. (Gerald F. Moede cautions
against a too-facile rendering of Jesus' usage of Isaiah 61: We must not forget
the millions of people who will never see or walk, or be healed of genetic
and degenerative disease.[71])

In Robert McAfee Brown's exposition of Gutiérrez, "it is an expression of
God's *universal* love that . . . God will provisionally take sides with some and
against others, so that present inequities may be overcome and the full possibilities of personhood opened for all. To say that God loves *all* people,
means that those who thwart love must be opposed, so that their ability to
perpetuate structures of oppression, which keep people separated from
love of one another and of God, can be overcome."[72]

In the fourth place, since God takes sides, we are summoned to do the
same. Some 3,000 biblical verses speak of human responsibility to the poor.
Gutiérrez shows how Jeremiah's theme that to know God is to do justice and
righteousness (22:15–16) suffuses the entire biblical story. This means "sid-
ing with the oppressed, which means opposing the oppressors, which means
involvement in conflict, which means 'taking sides' in order to affirm rather
than deny God. It is all of a piece." The Christian church "has always 'taken

sides,' almost invariably with the rich. What is needed now is for the church
to 'change sides,' switching its allegiance from a subtle but thoroughgoing
option for the rich and the status quo, to an overt and equally thoroughgoing
option for the poor and the need for radical change on their behalf." If Christian praxis fails to be the praxis of the poor, Christian thinking gets trans-
muted into a non-threatening, middle-class ideology. For Segundo, "Jesus
seems to go so far as to suggest that one cannot recognize Christ, nor, therefore, know God, unless he begins with a certain commitment to the oppressed."[73] We have noted (chap. 4) that for Jesus the transformation of the
world is to be the result of God's catastrophic intervention. By contrast, advocates of liberation theology bring to the forefront the peculiar responsibility and praxis of human beings—of the Christian community yet also of
others—undergirded, it is agreed, by divine grace.

When all is said and done, all four of these points are hard sayings for
multitudes of Christians—Liberals and Conservatives together. Rodney
Booth speaks to the condition, acknowledged or unacknowledged, of countless Christians in the North: "Many Christians in [my country of] Canada are
carrying an incredible load of guilt simply for being who they are. When the
Good News keeps coming at you as bad news you have either to be a maso-
chist or deeply committed to stay with it."[74]

(2) Yet how are the necessary "radical changes" ever to be made? We are
impelled to face up to practical issues of social and political revolution.
Once the wretched of the world learn, as they are learning, that they do not
have to be wretched—a process called *concientización* (consciousness-raising)
by Paulo Friere—there can only be hell to pay.

As we have seen, at the heart of liberation theology is social-revolutionary
praxis. The one way "to humanize a dehumanized social order that creates
non-persons" is revolutionary transformation.[75] But this stance creates a be-
wildering problematic of, at once, *the what* and *the how*: on the one hand, the
concrete form and content of the social revolution along with the meaning of
righteous, responsible human existence; and, on the other hand, methods of
consummating the revolution. The following five points (a–e) are offered for
their relevance in the effort to cope with this massive problematic.

(a) Preliminarily but comprehensively, political reason and political praxis
have become, in the wording of Gutiérrez, "the universal determinant and
the collective ground of human fulfillment. . . . Nothing lies outside the political domain." The historical-moral consequence is that the only means for
fighting alongside the oppressed is through political engagement against
evil social structures.[76] When Christians seek to evade politics, "they have
made a pact with the devil."[77] A corollary of this, as Segundo has it, is that
"all theology is political, even the kind that does not speak or think in political terms."[78] It is essential to know that in liberation thinking, "political"
does not mean mere public power struggle but, in Gregory Baum's phrase,
participation in the world-building process. (This is how liberation political theology

is able to embody "faith transforming history.") Political engagement for social change occurs on two levels: political action and cultural transformation.
The church makes its (wider political) contribution at the second level. Liberation theology "concentrates on the spiritual experience of Christians in
which the divine-human encounter manifests itself in the creation of solidarity and the empowerment to act in the world."[79]

(b) The Christian church seems hopeless, yet there is hope within it. We
have to proceed from the unhappy fact that the church, in its dominant aspect as a mass social phenomenon, is among the very last elements to stand
for cultural and moral transformation. By contrast, minority, grass-roots communities (*comunidades de base*) within the church, of which there may be as
many as a hundred thousand in Latin America with a membership of more
than seven million, can serve and are serving as a revolutionary, humanizing
vanguard in the task of transformation. "No cultural revolution is possible
apart from the expenditure of energy by a minority that has distanced itself
from mechanized thought and feeling, wherever these are found—even in
the people."[80] However, the repeated biblical distinction between "the many"
and "the few" (cf., e.g., Matt. 7:4; 9:37; 22:14; Mark 10:45; Luke 12:32) is not a
form of elitism. As Joseph Ratzinger interprets this matter, "God does not
divide humanity thus to save the few and hurl the many into perdition. Nor
does he do it to save the many *in an easy way* and the few *in a hard way*. Instead. . . he uses the numerical few as a leverage point for raising up the
many."[81] For Segundo, the aim is to create "new forms of energy that enable
(necessarily mechanized) lines of conduct to serve as a basis for new and
more creative minority possibilities in every human life."[82]

The *comunidades de base* are groups of a dozen or two peasants and workers
who meet regularly, sometimes with a priest, sometimes not. "They share a
liturgical life, engage in Bible study, and tackle situations of injustice, from
the unwillingness of the local *patrón* to pipe water into his village, to concerted action on behalf of political prisoners being subjected to torture.
They have become the lifeblood of the Latin American church."[83]

Hugo Assmann avows that the "commitment to liberation means introducing the class struggle into the Church itself." Christian revolutionaries know
that

> they are not *with* other Christians, but rather *in open conflict* with the majority
> of them. But they also know there is no escaping this minority opposition
> role, because they have to range themselves on the side of the exploited.
> Hence the theme of conflict in history and in present-day reality has be-
> come so central to the theology of revolution. They find themselves obliged
> to denounce the ideology of a false unity-without-conflict in the Church,
> which is a major point of difference between them and others in viewing the
> whole historical existence of the Church. They can no longer accept that eu-
> charistic conditions can automatically obtain in a Church that includes op-

pressors and oppressed. An element of tension and conflict is introduced at
the centre of the life of faith.[84]

This may not be faith-against-the-world as such, but surely it is faith
against the kind of world that has invaded the church. Nevertheless, "commitment to the church is central to practitioners of liberation theology."[85]

Assmann's criticism of automatically obtaining "eucharistic conditions"
prompts a critical-liberative judgment even against liberationism—a liberationism that, as in Gutiérrez, celebrates the Lord's Supper as "openness to
the future, full of trust and gladness."[86] If it is so, as the prophet Jeremiah
testifies, that to know God is to do justice and righteousness, then the bread
and wine of "Holy Communion" are as blasphemy unless *real* bread and
wine are also furnished. "What man of you, if his son asks him for bread, will
give him a stone?" (Matt. 7:9). In the same way, if any human being begs for
bread, will you give her or him a communion wafer? How many calories can
the "Lord's Supper" boast? The "real presence" for the disinherited is an
adequate daily diet, and it can be nothing less.

(c) The encounter between Christian faith and Marxist socialism is fundamental to our present problematic; as such, it requires the most attention
within our five points. As Arthur F. McGovern makes plain, the question of
whether Christianity and Marxism are compatible would be settled in an in-
stant were Marxism and dogmatic Communism one and the same: the in-
compatibility would be transparent. For dogmatic Communism is atheistic
and absolutist. But the truth is that while all modern Communists are Marxists, the reverse is hardly the case. A further complication is that many advocates of *socialism*—defined as public ownership of property, with special
reference to the means of production, but often, normatively speaking, in a
democratic, decentralized manner—are not Marxists. In these respects, the
general moral issue comes down to whether Marxist analysis on the one
hand and socialist goals on the other are consistent with Christian faith,
granted that Communist ideology is not.[87] But once it is adjudged that true
atheists are people who are not committed to the-poor-in-whom-God-is-
found, what does this do to the claim that the church is made up of "believers" and secular revolutionaries are a bunch of "non-believers"?

There are many additional complications into which we cannot here enter;
nor can we explore the history and inner world of Marxism. As a matter of
fact, Karl Marx has little to say on how a socialist society ought to be organized politically.[88] Himself a democrat, he spoke of revolution only on limited
occasions. His antisemitism is well known. Marx is understood and interpreted in markedly different ways, even by Marxists. Today many varieties
of Marxism are in competition, within Latin America as around the world.

Obviously, "revolution" does not have to imply "Marxism" and even
less so "Communism"; well before Marx there were uncounted social revolutions. However, in Latin America a number of recent revolutionary

movements have been Marxist-inspired and Marxist-oriented. When Christians of that continent are faced with the issue of revolutionary change, they are perforce brought to deal with some variation upon socialism, which, experientially speaking, directs the problematic to the meeting of Marxism and Christianity. For the socio-political alternatives within Latin America are, in many instances, restricted to "right" versus "left," the former of which entails capitalist transnational projects "under the centralized control of technocratic elites,"[89] and the latter of which involves Marxists and Marxist praxis.

By way of coming to grips with an enormously complex state of affairs, I first sketch elements of opposition to Marxism within the Christian community, and then survey critical openness to and acceptance of Marxism. The differences in length between the two sub-sections that follow reflect the relative weight of disparate attitudes, with special reference to liberation circles in Latin America. It must be pointed out that allusions to Marx and Marxist literature are relatively infrequent in liberationist writings by Latin American Christians. "Liberation theology is not grounded in Marxism. It is grounded in the experience of the peoples of Latin America and in faith reflection." Because Marxist thinking is pervasive in that continent, liberation theology is of course affected by it.[90]

(i) In some contrasts to Medellín (1968), the conference of Latin American bishops at Puebla (1979) was, in its explicit references to Marxism, entirely negative. "Classical Marxism" was condemned for possessing an inadequate understanding of man through (allegedly) reducing human nature to its economic dimension. "Marxist collectivism" and its dialectics of class struggle were rejected together with the ideologies of capitalist liberation and "national security." The church runs great dangers when it ignores the intimate link between Marxist analysis and Marxist ideology. Whenever Christian theological reflection has recourse to Marxist analysis, it is itself wrongly ideologized.[91]

In 1977 the Catholic bishops of France had declared Marxism and the Christian faith incompatible. McGovern observes that the latter declaration helps to pinpoint the core objection of the church to Marxism for more than a century, an objection that runs through the early encyclicals, the writings of Paul Tillich, Reinhold Niebuhr, and Pope Paul VI, and into the present:

> The objection centers on Marxist ideology. But it is not simply that Marxism as a worldview is based on atheism and materialism. Christians and atheists could learn and have learned in many parts of the world to live together. Nor is it a question of Marxist opposition to capitalism, which many Christians oppose, nor even of class struggle, if it is taken to mean a struggle against unjust structures and systems and not as a vindictive clash against persons. The core objection or fear is that Marxists will "impose" their views once in power, believing that they alone possess the "truth."

On this basis, the contemporary Christian-Marxist encounter centers upon the issue of whether true socialism can be a democratic socialism that respects a plurality of worldviews.[92] (Much argumentative energy could perhaps have been saved through the years were Marxist "materialism" identified for what it really is: not "matter-ism" but a species of anti-idealism. The anti-idealism involved embodies a close link to the biblical outlook and to Christianity before the latter came under the sway of "spirituality." We recall Archbishop William Temple's observation that "Christianity is the most materialistic religion in the world.")

(ii) A changed openness to Marxism and socialism, together with adverse judgments upon the wrongs in capitalism, has long been present within the churches, Catholic and Protestant. Thus, Pope Leo XIII and Pope Pius XI were sharply critical of capitalism (though of socialism as well), while Pope Paul VI deplored an economic system that identifies profit as the key to progress and spoke of the usefulness of Marxist social analysis, while yet lamenting the violent totalitarianism so often created by Marxist interpretation and practice of class struggle.[93] International dialogues between Christians and Marxists go back as far as the 1960s. Qualified Christian openness to socialism is typified in a statement of 1975 by the Catholic bishops of the Antilles, representing various Caribbean countries:

> The Catholic Church does not condemn indiscriminately all forms of socialism. In the past it denounced three particular aspects of socialism, namely: the denial of God and the spiritual, the insistence on the need for class warfare, and the suppression of all types of private property. In so far as these are to be found in some forms of socialism, a true Christian cannot accept them. But today there are other forms of socialism in the world and the very word "socialism" is used in many different ways. Past Church statements referring to socialism must therefore be understood in the light of these new developments. . . . [When] looking at socialism, or Marxism, or capitalism for that matter, it is important to distinguish carefully among (a) basic aspirations, (b) ideologies or systems of thought, and (c) concrete historical movements.

By "basic aspirations," the bishops mean a quest for a more just society. They reject the "ideology" of Marxism. And with respect to "concrete historical movements" and particular political parties, they say that Christian support will be contingent upon the extent to which these factors succeed in transcending bad ideology and upon what methods are utilized to realize the "basic aspirations."[94]

More than one Marxist-based revolution in Latin America has received significant support from Christians (e.g., the Chile of Salvador Allende in the 1970s[95] and, more limitedly so, Nicaragua under the Sandinistas in the 1980s). In that continent a fundamental conviction that "reformist, developmental policies had failed, and that a more radical liberation from systems of economic dependence and oppression was needed. . . . led some liberation theologians to speak out for the value of Marxist analysis."[96] Among these figures Segundo cites approvingly a letter by fifteen bishops of the Third World (written a year before the Medellín Conference):

> *In the moment that a particular system fails to secure the common good by favoring special interests*, the church must not only denounce the injustice but at the same time break with the iniquitous system. *She must be ready to collaborate with another system that is more just and is better adapted to the needs of the time.* . . . Taking into account the human need for a certain kind of material progress, the church over the last hundred years has tolerated capitalism, with its loans at accepted interest rates, and its other practices that hardly conform with the morality of the prophets and the gospel. But the church cannot help but *rejoice over the appearance of an alternative social system that is less distant* from this morality. . . . Christians are obligated to show "that true socialism is Christianity integrally lived through the just distribution of goods and in fundamental equality."[97]

The question of what it is that may specifically justify socialism as a proper alternative to capitalism, or at least as a better choice, is a difficult and controversial one. Capitalist economic structures are not the only oppressing evils in the world, while the oppression and exploitation of masses of people in such socialist countries as the Soviet Union and Poland is notorious and hardly needs elaboration here. One pertinent development within recent Christian thinking is a shift in emphasis from the affirmation of *individual* human rights (e.g., the right to protest, the right to express minority views, the right to private property) to *social* human rights, which, without any betrayal of the more individual kind of right, involves a greater concentration upon such rights as adequate housing, jobs, just distribution of goods, proper nourishment, medical care, education, and shared control of power.[98]

The foregoing paragraphs help us to understand the acceptance of socialism by some Christians, whether or not we are able to do so ourselves. The fundamental cause is human suffering, and the fundamental hope is to assuage that suffering. And so for José Míguez Bonino, Marxism becomes "a scientific, verifiable, and efficacious way to articulate love historically." For Hugo Assmann, the conflict between Christian "love" and Marxist "interest" is resolvable: In dreaming of a revolution inspired by pure love, Christians have been wanting in historical realism. Marxists recognize that the revolution "will be carried out by those who have a direct interest in its success. Historically incarnate love is in no sense removed from interests, provided 'interests' is not understood in the bourgeois, individualist sense. *The clear definition and realization of the interests of the oppressed is the historical embodiment of love.*" For Gustavo Gutiérrez and Richard Shaull, "only the transcending of a society divided into classes, a political power at the service of the great popular majorities, and the elimination of private appropriation of wealth produced by human work can give us the foundations of a society that would be more just. It is for this reason that the elaboration in a historical project of a new society in Latin America takes more and more frequently the path of socialism." And for Juan Luis Segundo, a politically-neutralist stance is to be exposed as chimera (thus returning us to our earlier discussion upon the taking of sides): "After denouncing on various occasions the inhuman consequences of capitalism for the vast majority of the Chilean people, the bishops of that land, faced with the actual conflict between a capitalist system and a socialist system, declared that the church could not choose one over the other. Why not? Because, according to them, the church belongs to all the people of Chile, and to single out one specific option in the name of justice, human rights, or the liberative plan of God, would be to exclude a certain part of the people from the church, and, on that same basis, from the best opportunities for salvation." Segundo, in specific response to the bishops' decision that they could not opt for socialism as an alternative to the existing capitalist system, asks the inevitable question: "By what strange mental process did the bishops persuade themselves that they were not choosing sides when they made such an affirmation?"[99]

Quite apart from where we may stand on socialism-versus-capitalism, most Christian theologians who opt for socialism honor the precept (contributed, historically, by Reinhold Niebuhr) that *discriminate* judgments are necessary and that no more than *relative* valuations are legitimate as between conflicting socio-political systems. These theologians repeatedly insist that the socialist alternative is "better than" capitalism, from the standpoint of overall justice in light of their particular historical situation. But they do not absolutize socialism and just about every one of them engages in some criticism of Marxism. All of this prescinds them from Communist socialism. The faith-centered orientation of liberation theologians encourages these people to avoid subservience to Marxism whenever the latter manifests unacceptable dogmatic tendencies, yet to profit from what are to them valid moral elements in Marxist thought and praxis—in short, to make "critical use of Marxist analysis with an awareness of its assumptions and limits."[100] Gregory Baum provides a decisive, clarifying point: "Marx concentrated on the industrial proletariat as the universal class. He had little sympathy for the unemployables and outcasts in the cities, the *Lumpen* as he called them. For Marx the industrial workers had the special role in the revolution and the making of the new society because they were the ones who extracted the raw materials, produced the goods, and created the wealth of society. The *Lumpen* had no destiny in society. The Marxist position is, therefore, quite different from the Christian option for the poor . . . . [which] is basically a religious and a moral decision." In this as in other respects it can be argued, accordingly, that "liberation theology presents a dialectical overcoming of Marxist theory."[101]

I think that we have to be vigilant lest we fall into either-or positions respecting "capitalism" and "Marxism." Even in Latin America, it is not impossible to work for a socio-economic order that combines free-economy elements and socialist elements. One tragedy of Latin America is the absence there of a worker-movement tradition. On the other hand, the political, moral, and theological limitations of Marxism are as crucial as, or more crucial than, its contribution. Along with certain other "isms" Marxism, particularly in its Communist apparel, fancies that human wrongdoing and alienation (*Entfremdung*) orginate in specific causes and can therefore be overcome by specific socio-economic measures. At this point, Jewish faith and Christian faith are much more realistic and extremely skeptical. Sin is a primordial, general condition within human existence, a condition that is never fully conquered. Again, and by contrast, Marxism does not really comprehend "the human sense of laying down one's life for others—so deeply relevant to revolutionary practice," nor has it really tried to see the importance of that phenomenon. Finally, we have "the Christian affirmation of victory over death, that final alienation to which Marxism can find no satisfactory answer."[102]

(d) In liberation theology the question of *violence* is existentially addressed. Professor Assmann sets the matter within a Latin American context: "The traditional concept of the ideal Christian above all as a man of 'peace,' pacifically stationed within the existing order, quietly collaborating with the rules of the game of the status quo, has virtually become a thing of the past."[103]

The reporting I am about to do necessitates a caveat: few theologians of liberation have personally followed or will follow the pathway of Néstor Paz, whose life has been epitomized via three words: "mystic, Christian, guerrilla."[104] Why, then, make reference to Paz? Because it is important to bring into the open and in a way uncorrupted by scholarly equivocation the wracking question: What does it mean to forge a bond between the Christian faith and violent revolution? As a matter of fact, much of the energy of liberation thinking/praxis is expended in diverse efforts to qualify and to question, yet sometimes to justify, the eventuality of that bond.

Néstor Paz was a member of a small guerrilla band. In October 1970 he died of starvation in the Bolivian jungle near Teoponte. He was 25. Formerly a Catholic seminarian and medical student, Paz saw his guerrilla commitment it terms of fidelity to Jesus Christ through fighting the oppression of his people and striving for their liberation. He and his wife Cecilia—she was killed by Bolivian troopers in March 1972—were influenced by Camilo Torres and by Ché Guevara. Through study of the Psalms, the New Testament, and Guevara's writings, the couple had sought to synthesize their Christian faith with Marxist thought. Devoted as he was to St. Francis of Assisi, Paz assumed the name "Francisco" at the time of joining the guerrillas as a sign of his love for the poor. Paz was neither the first nor the last Christian guerrilla to take to the battlefields of Latin America.[105] He wrote in his journal:

> Yahweh our God, the Christ of the Gospel, has announced the "good news of the liberation of humanity," and acted in accordance. We cannot sit down to spend a long time reading the Gospel with cardinals, bishops, and pastors, all of whom are doing quite well where they are, while the situation of the flock is one of hunger and solitude. This state of affairs is called "non-violence," peace, Gospel. . . .
>   "Greater love has no man than this, that a man lay down his life for his friends." This is the commandment which sums up the "Law."
>   For this reason we have taken up arms: to defend the illiterate and undernourished majority from exploitation by a minority, and to win back dignity for a dehumanized people. . . .
>   [The] struggle for liberation is rooted in the prophetic line of Salvation History. Enough of the languid faces of the over-pious! The oft-betrayed whip of justice will fall on the exploiter, those false Christians who forget that the force of their love ought to drive them to liberate their neighbors from sin, that is to say, from every lack of love. . . .
>   . . . Conversion implies an inner violence which is then followed by violence against the exploiter.[106]

Daniel Berrigan once wrote an open letter to Ernesto Cardenal, the Nicaraguan revolutionary priest, admonishing him that violence is never right, for not even the highest moral principle can justify the death of a single child. After the *guardia nacional* attacked Cardenal's monastery of Solentiname, killing several people and driving the rest into exile, including Cardenal, he replied to Berrigan: Yes, no principle is worth the life of a child—including the principle of pacifism, which, were it adhered to by the poor people of Nicaragua, would indeed keep them from defending children against murder.[107]

Father Segundo offers phenomenological insight into the reality of violence through linking it to the destiny of human love. His philosophic rationale is "the fundamental law behind all truly human existence: the law of the economy of energy with all its sorrowful consequences." The plain truth is that "love is no less violent than egotism." The Good Samaritan himself could be in a position to render aid to the man left half dead only because he had previously passed by an infinity of people in need. Otherwise, he would no longer have had a burro or money or even the ability to travel. "The economy of energy presupposes, within the very praxis of love, a certain mechanism for keeping multitudes of people at a distance from us, else we could never exercise effective love." A truly fateful consideration is that this mechanism has nothing to do with hostility; it is instead a matter of *violence*—or "at the least, the raw material of violence." For this device really *does violence*—how revealing an expression!—to these other people, at once mentally and physically. And here enters the phenomenon of "the law." The relations we have with our "neighbors," with those we consent to treat as *persons* in the deeper sense of that term, place them, in a sense, above the law. By contrast, "an intrinsic characteristic of 'the law' is that always standing behind it is coercive power, i.e., the kind of physical violence that compels compliance." All this means that we must overcome the simplistic notion that violence is a revolutionary shooting a gun. In truth, "conscious or unconscious mental tendencies can constitute a more efficient and dangerous weapon in the death of millions of people than weapons traditionally identified as such." We are brought to conclude that *"violence is a constituent dimension of all concrete love* in human history, just as it is constituent to all concrete egotism. . . . [To] try to choose between love and violence makes no sense whatever."[108]

Thus is there insistence within the theology of liberation that the dichotomy "to be or not to be violent" misrepresents the moral issue of violence. Liberative thinking carries forward the finding of Reinhold Niebuhr (in partial continuity with Karl Marx) that coerciveness is built into conflictual social situations, and further that there is no way to separate overt coerciveness and implicit coerciveness. However, Segundo's interpretation cannot avoid the issue of how and when the evils brought by violence are to be fought once the inevitability of violence within life itself is granted. Must there not be some sense in which human liberation extends to liberation from the consequences of violence? In this regard, we may return once more to Gutiérrez and to Míguez Bonino.

We come back to the matter of objective socio-political structures. The bishops at Medellín, with aid from Gutiérrez as draftsman, emphasized that quite beyond the shooting of guns, violence is already regnant in the "structural violence"—more especially, economic violence—through which the people of Latin America are condemned to suffering, despair, and death. Elsewhere Gutiérrez distinguishes among the *institutionalized violence* of today's social order; the *repressive violence* that maintains the first kind; and *counter-violence*, "the least of the evils," made necessary "when all else fails" within the oppressive violence of the status quo. For an oppressed, power-deprived people to practice political pacifism is to make impossible virtues out of reprehensible necessities. From this perspective, as Dorothee Sölle puts it, pacifists are not "peace makers" but accomplices in aggression. Nevertheless, the abiding concern of Gutiérrez is to bring about change by peaceful means wherever this is possible. The decision as to whether revolution will be violent or nonviolent rests, not upon him and his colleagues, but upon those in power. Should the entrenched forces voluntarily share that power with the poor, change will be peaceful; if not, then the oppressors themselves are culpable when recourse is taken to "the last resort."[109]

Míguez Bonino agrees that "whether Christians or not, we are always actively involved in violence—repressive, subversive, systemic, insurrectional, open, or hidden.... direct or indirect, institutional or revolutionary, conscious or unconscious." Much of the violence is simply dedicated to preserving an evil social order. Then there is the persuasion that violence may be creative, a redeemer of evil. But the biblical approach is distinctive; it associates violence with "a breaking down of the restrictions (slavery, revenge, whim, absence of defence or protection, usurpation, etc.) which leave a person, a group or a people in a state of weakness and inferiority. They are freed to be and to act as responsible (the typical instance being 'as a partner in a pact') before God, other persons and things." The Christian is ever in tribulation over "the human cost of the revolution" and ever concerned for the enemy. The Christian yearns to know "how it may be possible to humanize this struggle." The Christian must not forget *the suffering of the oppressors*—"their anxiety, their fear of being dispossessed (which in their ideological blindness they count as death because they have defined the whole meaning of their lives by their possessions) and in some cases of being physically eliminated." The encounter with the theme of violence is always "a test of the authenticity of one's faith. My violence is either obedience to or betrayal of Jesus Christ." Finally, "the substantialization of ideology is the temptation to idolatry which Christians must fight in every revolutionary process. Idols always destroy people. Perhaps that is the most important insight that the Christian has to offer—especially as self-criticism—in regard to violence."[110]

Jacques Ellul draws a radical but compelling conclusion. He offers a test for telling whether the violence we take up is genuinely *for others*:

> ...[The] Christian must change sides once his friends have won; that is, when in the aftermath of its victory the revolutionary party assumes power; for the party will immediately begin to oppress the former oppressors.... Therefore, if a Christian's participation in a violent movement was truly prompted by his concern for the poor, the oppressed, and the disinherited, he must now change camps. He must move to the side of the erstwhile "enemies"... because they are now the victims, they are now the poor and the humiliated. Taking their part shows that his earlier involvement was authentic, that the reasons he gave for his participation in the violent movement were the true reasons. If he stays on the side of the victors, he admits in effect that he was not really concerned for the poor and the oppressed in the first place.[111]

It seems to me that with this criterion Ellul manages to deideologize the "taking of sides." The question may be addressed not alone to human beings but also to God: How prepared are you to change sides?

(e) In opposition to revolutionary praxis the charge of "utopianism" is heard echoing, but to the theologians of liberation the charge is illicit on the ground of the Christian moral demand for fresh historical creations, i.e., transformations of what has been "no place" into a "someplace."

Rubem Alves protests that "utopianism" bears a positive meaning. It "is not the belief in the possibility of a perfect society but rather the belief in the nonnecessity of *this* imperfect order."[112] The distinction by Alves does not silence the question that must haunt all radical socio-political persuasion: *After the revolution, what is to be the fate of the revolution?* In different terminology, *liberation to what?* Or again: How are the presently oppressed ever going to be saved, *eventually*, from what Dorothee Sölle identifies as the totalitarian fascism of consumerism that is sweeping the world, or from what Will Herberg calls the "pre-fabricated mass-culture" that crushes human authenticity?[113] But there is obscenity in addressing questions about an indefinite future directly to people who are starving this very minute. For them, over-consumption would be paradise. Monika Hellwig, following the Spanish writer José María González-Ruiz, observes that mere efforts to get the oppressed into the oppressor position are far removed from genuine liberation, which only occurs "when the structures of society are so changed as to undo the oppression itself, not to pass it over into different hands."[114] Overall, of course, apostles of liberative praxis maintain that true revolution means nothing less than the creation of a fully cooperative, essentially just and loving community. But the very question of "possibility" is the one that remains stubbornly at issue.

It is sometimes maintained within liberative thinking that the allegation that the movement involves idealistic utopianism reflects bad ideology, or false consciousness—meaning support, perhaps unconscious, for the status quo. One response by the target of this countercharge is that the accusation of false consciousness may itself be an instance of bad ideology. The indictment of status quoism may become a means to the end of vanquishing one's opponents. This is unjust and ironic in cases where those who are discerning idealistic utopianism in liberation thinking are as much at war as anyone against the status quo.

I think that the prime issue in all this is the life of hope. Utopian expectations are most usually dismissed as nurturing false hopes. Yet does not the quality of hope occupy an indispensable place within all motivations that produce social change? Indeed, political power is one enablement of human hope, an estoppage of fantasy.[115] The transformationism of faith knows well the hardship of the divine righteousness in making its way in the world. Gutiérrez believes that it is wrong to equate eschatological promises with a particular social reality or attainment. There is no question of identifying a new socio-political order or historical dispensation (*etapa*) with the kingdom of God. The consuming duties of day-to-day praxis are actually a counterweight against all "idealism and evasion." The nature of Christian hope itself saves us from confusing the reign of God with a given dispensation. It keeps us from "all idolatry before human achievement that is inevitably ambiguous, and from all absolutizing of the revolution." Nonetheless, the promises of God do gain a kind of fulfillment within history. There can be and are connections between human life and the kingdom. "The gospel is not foreign to human designs. On the contrary, human designs and the gift of God imply each other."[116]

We may hardly equate "liberation" in any form with "ultimate salvation." "Liberation" primarily means deliverance within this life from oppression and alienation, in contrast to "ultimate salvation" beyond this world. Yet liberation has intrinsic value in redeeming human beings from evil suffering, and also in preparing them for the promise of final salvation. Paradoxically, once the power and the task of final salvation are reserved to God, human beings are set free for moral responsibility in this world. A major contribution of liberation thinking is its polemic against those Christians whose insistence upon the primacy of "salvation" means a denial of the moral demand that the oppressed be liberated. Nevertheless, there are historical limits upon human liberation *as such*. These center in the anxieties of human life *as such*. The fact that alienation and meaninglessness can and do afflict the non-oppressed (we think of the widespread resort to drugs among the middle classes and the rich) exemplifies how the revolutionary abolition of poverty—an abolition that is at once *unconditionally* required and *historically* possible—is not a cure but only a decent act of melioration, a "reasonable service" (Rom. 12:1, KJV). This non-curative condition points the revolution beyond itself and indeed beyond history to the One whose grace alone is able finally to banish alienation and overcome meaninglessness.

In some contrast to the allegation of utopianism, a much more commanding criticism of Latin American liberation theology is one that meets the position upon its own ground. (The really telling evaluations of any view are, I suggest, those that proceed out of sympathetic identification with the viewpoint in question.) I propose the phrase *utopianism of dogma*. David Tracy correctly asks whether the theologians of liberative praxis are being completely "faithful to the full demands" of *their own* praxis. Specifically, if praxis must always relate itself to a critical theory "applicable to all infra-structural and super-structural factors in human reality," why do these theologies so seldom apply this critical theory to the very theological symbols that inform them? I find that some liberation theologians are much more prepared to do this work of criticism than others, e.g., Segundo in marked contrast to Gutiérrez. Thus, while in his *Teología de la Liberación* Gutiérrez effectively brings "critical reflection on praxis" to bear against the concept of economic "development," he nowhere permits his method to judge the major Christian doctrines that undergird his own work. Tracy argues that the exclusivist and traditionalist understanding of God, revelation, and Christology serves to threaten "the ultimate value and meaning of that basic secular faith shared by all those committed to the contemporary struggle for liberation."[117] Pertinent as well is Dennis P. McCann's discernment of a fundamental dilemma within Latin American liberation theology, the dilemma of either politicization or trivialization: Insofar as these theologians determine to stay with the *method* presented in Gutiérrez's Magna Carta, they tend to distance themselves more and more from mainstream Christian life and thought, and in the end the *comunidades de base* may become mere "recruitment centers for secular liberation movements." But insofar as these theologians stay with the *content* outlined by Gutiérrez, liberation theology tends to become more and more indistinguishable from "the progressivism of Vatican II. In either case its distinctive program, the new way of 'doing theology in a revolutionary situation' is sacrificed."[118]

One major challenge in conjunction with our final normative image of "history transforming faith" will be that of a critical revisionism of Christian dogma but not at the price of the integrity of Christian faith. In the meantime, and blessedly, Felix Luna's utopia is anything but one of dogma:

> The time is coming
> Latin America my land
> When our frontiers will be borders of flowers
> And our guns weapons of wood
> You can see the dawn rising
> The light in our darkness
> You can hear the future
> As our people sing
>
> Latin America my land
> Young woman rising from sleep
> Who gave you your beauty?
> And who your bitterness?
>
> If death takes me
> It is not for ever
> I shall live in my songs
> For you I shall live for ever
> Forward the banners go
> Forward for freedom
> Sing with me
> For our freedom is here
>
> How good the days smell
> The sweet air is ripe
> And all the guitars sing
> for the morning
> I believe in a life to come
> That men call justice
> When all whom I love
> Will smile for ever
>
> The time is coming
> Latin America my land[119]

VI

In a comparative frame of reference, Frederick Herzog conveys in summary form the context, spirit, and intent of "faith transforming history" as given voice through the Christian aspects of this chapter: "Liberal theology seemed to view the gospel as man's possibility in history. It often resulted in shallow activism and finally in cynicism. Neo-orthodoxy countered that the gospel reveals itself as man's impossibility in history. . . . Liberation theology labors over the gospel as *God's* possibility in history. By divine empowerment human beings are made whole in the transformation of inimical structures."[120] But the very serious question remains of whether the thinking, policies, and deeds for which liberation thinking stands can actually be counted upon to transform history; or whether, alas, its praxises are to be grasped as preeminently reactive and diagnostic of abiding social sickness and sin. Is this the work of transformation or is it the work of desperation? To study liberation writers across the spectrum of several different areas of liberation (the disinherited, blacks, women) is to be left with the impression that however radical the revolution to be carried out, no social order could ever really satisfy these awesome transformationist demands for human happiness and fulfillment. Strange as it may sound, a link appears between "faith transforming history" and "faith against the world," faith against *any* world. It is with a certain sadness that I make this interjection. However, a like sadness menaces everyone's human hope. The issue of efficacy, of impact pursues each of us. In the nature of the case, liberation *from* and liberation *to* and *for* are equally hard to reckon with, theoretically and practically. Or it may be, indeed, that the latter forms of liberation are the harder ones. Yet as we turn at the last to the normative image of "history transforming faith" the eventuality will at least be hinted at that we may not be all alone in our endeavors, but rather that an ally abides within our forest of despair and hope. Perhaps the transformation of history rests, in the end, within the strong hands and upon the marching legs of history itself (as a tool of God?).

10

History Transforming Faith: A Prologue

HOW, if at all, may we "mend the world"?[1] In principle, there are two generic choices: through the world itself, and through something "beyond the world." Everyone expects—well, almost everyone—that the proponent of faith will opt for the second choice, and, indeed, insist upon it. But what if the representative of faith says: "Through the world itself"? Is that understanding out of the question? Is it to be ruled out? Is its protagonist being "unfaithful"?

I

Thus, do we come, at the last, to "history transforming faith," or, in terminology a bit more forceful, a Christian *theocentric historicism*, as aimed especially at the life and thought of the church. We have alluded at various points to *historicalness*, the acceptance of and response to the crucialities of time and place. Historicalness is not itself just "history," although of course decision-making takes place wholly within history. When bringing together the realities of "historicalness" and "history," we may find it useful to employ the word *historicity*.

The concept "Christian" in the phrase "Christian theocentric historicism" refers simply to Christian auspices, the praxis that is available, as a gift to the Christian community, but yet is independent of Christianity as of every other religion. Christian triumphalism and supersessionism would devastate the ethic involved.

I identify representatives of this view as "eighth people" or "people of eight."

Today many concepts vie as aids in encapsulating the intent and the hope of Christian and other thinkers: e.g., "post-liberal," "post-modern," "post-Christian," "post-secularist," and "post-conciliar" (still in gladsome memory of good Pope John and *aggiornamento*). Common to viewpoints that appropriate "post-" as a prefix, though of course not lacking elsewhere, is a felt obli-

225

gation to begin anew, to construct a living bridge between a certain spiritual past and the moral challenges and agonies of humankind today, to point the way responsibly to the future. So it is with the "post-liberal" position that I espouse. This latter usage of "post-" may, with other such usages, sound presumptuous. For the viewpoints to which "post-" wants to attach itself sometimes retain a vitality that keeps them from being sent to oblivion via the pretensions of a four-letter prefix. The "liberal" outlook may well be a case in point. Is Liberalism as dead as all that? The living gift of Liberalism is its demand that religious claims be subjected to the judgments and life of morality. To speak in behalf of a "post-liberal" outlook does not have to mean casting Liberalism away but can instead mean acting to redeem it by infusing it with a realism and a transcendence of which it still stands in need. In this respect my "post-liberal" position is a species of Christian "revisionist" moral philosophy. As David Tracy writes:

> the neo-orthodox insisted that the liberal analysis of the human situation was able to account at best for human finitude and possibility, but was utterly unable to account for those negative elements of tragedy, of terror, indeed, of sin in human existence.... With the relative strengths and limitations of liberalism, orthodoxy, neo-orthodoxy, and radical theologies in mind, the revisionist theologian is committed to continuing the critical task of the classical liberals and modernists in a genuinely post-liberal situation.... [He] is committed to what seems clearly to be the central task of contemporary Christian theology: the dramatic confrontation, the mutual illuminations and corrections, the possible basic reconciliation between the principal values, cognitive claims, and existential faiths of both a reinterpreted post-modern consciousness and a reinterpreted Christianity.[2]

In the present chapter I offer a prologue to our final normative image, the third of those images not specifically delineated within H. Richard Niebuhr's typology. Then in the closing chapters, I try to develop several major aspects of the position, including attention to some of the uncertainties and difficulties within it.

II

For the sake both of review and of the analysis still to come, it may be helpful to assay a few of the more prominent comparisons and contrasts between our eighth image and the images that have gone before.

Eighth people can be freely accepting of one or another aspect of all seven of the other points of view. Among the supports for this statement, four interrelated points may be singled out: (a) Every normative image is inseparable from human experience of one kind or another. Indeed, all the images have a place within historical determinations of faith. Even a denial of history's consequentialness cannot be made other than within time and place; thus does that denial paradoxically pay tribute to history's power. To paraphrase First John's comment on sin (1:8), "If we say we are not conditioned by history, we deceive ourselves, and the truth is not in us." All this has a disarming way of making us "members one of another." (Who among us does not *fear* infirmity and death?) (b) All the normative images we are studying are linked in one or another way to the responsibility of unfolding and representing the divine righteousness. (c) Because both "history" and "faith" are taken by eighth people to be, in principle, equally licit and commanding, this establishes continuity, of varying degrees, with most other images or types. (d) "The relativities of all things human and the mysteries of all things divine are too great ever to permit any one solution to become *the* Christian answer. That answer must be sought again and again in every particular context and time by finite men responding to the absolute God."[3]

These four reasons explain, at least partially, how people of eight can be fully open to philosophic and theological-ethical pluralism. Each item witnesses to the cruciality of history for faith. Yet history comprises no more than half the total dialectic of faith and history. And eighth people know well, as other protagonists ought to know, that within the bounds of history, no final resolution of the problem of faith and history is possible. (To acknowledge that a given faith evolves over the course of history is to honor the overall dialectic of faith and history. For the process of development involves [a] independent influences arising over time from *within* the faith, and [b] independent influences arising over time from *beyond* the faith, i.e., from external history. Thus are eighth people enabled to acknowledge the contribution of all normative images to a general theological ethic.)

Let us return to the individual images covered thus far.

The two non-dialectical views of "faith against the world" and "faith for the world." In their thinking/praxis eighth people do not support unqualified rejection of the secular order, however sorry that order's present and constitutive state. As H. Richard Niebuhr points out, around the edges of the radical movement of "Christ against culture" the Manichean heresy is forever developing.[4] On the other hand, people of eight do not accept a mere conciliation or accommodation of faith to the secular realm. They oppose any betrayal of transcendence. In Troeltsch's language, they are neither a "church-type" nor a "sect-type." They join other mediating views in a life that moves constantly, and with fear and trembling, between the world and their faith.

However, the possibility of confusing or identifying "history transforming faith" with another image is markedly greater in the case of "faith for the world" than of "faith against the world." A reason for this is discernible in or through the passage cited above from David Tracy. Within the post-liberal posture a certain reminiscence is found of the two interests of Friedrich Schleiermacher: to be both a Christian theologian and a modern person, "participating fully in the work of culture, in the development of science, the maintenance of the state, the cultivation of art, the ennoblement of family life, the advancement of philosophy."[5] (Just here are we not haunted, quite involuntarily, by the specter of the Faith Movement of German Christians?) This much cannot be gainsaid: Exactly because of their historicist leanings, eighth people are not exempt from a certain temptation, in singular ways, to assimilate their faith to history, under the power of false consciousness. Because their deontological ethic of response/responsibility is peculiarly vulnerable to the idolatries of the world, they must fight these idolatries with the same fervor that they battle moral irresponsibility.

Part of the life insurance available to people of eight consists in the fact that these people do not receive history as an absolute, after the fashion of its Hegelian or extra-Hegelian disciples, but instead in all its relativity and fragmentariness. In this regard, the demands of responsible decision-making upon the stage of history are such that certain events may have to be judged and found wanting at the hands of other events. In consequence, previously authoritative happenings may be told to abdicate their authority. That this can and does occur helps to show that the process of history is being assigned, not absolute status, but instrumental and pragmatic status. The simplest refutation of any absolutizing of history lies in the truth that history not only helps answer some of our problems, it also creates greater problems, if only by compounding the insufficiency of our responses to it.

The other part of the eighth people's insurance policy is that they have no intention of abandoning their faith in the God who judges all pretension and idolatry.

In light of "faith for the world's" constituent stress upon human reason, a word on that theme is in order. It is, after all, the presence of the instrument of human reason that enables us to identify the present work as an exercise in *moral philosophy*.* In the view of Lockean rationalism, Christian teaching may be according to reason and above reason but never contrary to reason. A historicist faith is accepting of this principle. However, the attestations of historicism extend broader and deeper than those of rationalist empiricism. It will be recalled that for Locke, reason entails deductions from the natural faculties of sensation and reflection. By concentrating upon events and the meanings of events, and, most particularly, extraordinary events, historicism goes beyond this form of rationalism. It speaks from the standpoint of a faith that is according to history and above history, though not contrary to history. There is, nevertheless, a final link between reason and history. I refer to the dimension of transcending reason, which not only examines reason itself but responds creatively and sometimes ecstatically to transcending events.

In seeking to develop the legitimacy of "history transforming faith," I shall resort both to argument and to testimony. The difficulty of balancing logical-rational discourse and existential avowal is a perennial one. The illegitimacy

---

*A "theological ethic" is grounded in a given faith. Accordingly, the dialectic of reason and faith is the dialectic of philosophy and theology.

of switching from argument to unsupported asseveration (a peculiarly tempting device whenever the going gets rough) is often pointed out. I do not envision any final victory over this condition, in literature or in life, for the difficulty ultimately defies resolution through mere human thought or action. To commend reasoned analysis or reasonableness (including "common sense") as the criterion of certain kinds of knowledge and truth cannot itself be rationally vindicated. To pretend otherwise is to beg the question because we are forced to assume the integrity of reason in the very effort to "prove" (i.e., test) that integrity. As G. K. Chesterton succinctly put it, "reason is itself a matter of faith." All arguments finally rest upon, yet also lead into, some kind of "I believe." The other side of this state of affairs is that confessions of conscience lose their imperative force when they are turned into logical argumentation. And, happily, the fact that reasonableness, if it is to be honored, must itself be accepted on faith does not necessarily negate its validity or its usefulness. All in all, the most we can manage to do is to make our subjective testimonies as objectively reasonable as possible, and our objective arguments as vitally subjective as possible.

Jesus and the kingdom/righteousness of God. A preeminent paradox is that a Christian "return into history," to Jesus and the origins of Christianity, turns us completely around, directing us to the end-time, the coming of the reign of God, which Jesus himself proclaimed. But we recall as well that in Jesus this proclamation is related to, or counterbalanced by, his ethic of Torah-cum-Prophecy. In these concrete ways the Christian church is bonded historically to Jesus. He is the foundation of Christian historicism. Insofar as Jesus points beyond himself to the reality and authority of God, his historicity is the paradigm for the Christian life. Instead of recasting the figure of Jesus to satisfy a traditionalistic "authority" for him, "history transforming faith" will seek to apprehend the "authority" of Jesus in reconciliation with the historical truth about him.

The talmudic and rabbinic tradition. We have been apprised of the dialectical ways in which this vast Jewish tradition interweaves the three categories of changing historical experience, certain advocated concretions of day-to-day morality, and a transcending Torah and faith.

Faith above history. In chapter four I maintain that the overall relation between faith and history is architectonic in the sense that history is at the foundation of human life, and that faith comes along to build upon that foundation. However, in contrast to "faith above history," the historical-moral demands and opportunities of the divine righteousness apply to *all* members of the religious community.

History and faith in tension. Eighth people freely acknowledge the sinfulness and tragedies of the human condition whereby history and faith are placed into inevitable and abiding tension. (Practitioners of "faith against the world" are anything but strangers to the knowledge of sin; yet, as H. Richard Niebuhr points out, they are tempted to exempt their own holy commonwealth from sin's dominion.[6]) We live in an unredeemed world. It is so that people of eight support the socially and politically ameliorating emphases within Christian realism. However, Reinhold Niebuhr's Christian realism tends to take the message and life of Jesus and the event of the Cross and shift their foci "from historical fulfillment to the religious problem of ultimate reconciliation with God." At this point it would appear that Christian realism does not wholly surmount the spiritualizing proclivities of traditionalist Christianity. From the perspective of today's theology of liberation, the Exodus experience of God's historical deliverance of his people from oppression is to remain paradigmatic.[7] Herein is suggested a means of avoiding "excessive spiritualization" (Gutiérrez). In this vital respect, the theological aspects of Christian realism appear paradoxically more supersessionist respecting Judaism than does liberation theology. I say "paradoxically" because Reinhold Niebuhr is in truth much more sympathetic to Judaism and the Jewish people than are today's liberation theologians (even though Niebuhr himself did not overcome all Christian triumphalism).

Faith transforming history. Because images seven and eight share a transformationist perspective and yet in constituent ways are not the same, extra attention to that relationship is appropriate. Following upon a few general comments, I shall re-introduce the theology of liberation, include brief references to feminist thinking, and comment upon H. Richard Niebuhr's conversionism.

In the first of the two transformationist positions, faith goes to work seeking to change the historical and created order. The engine of that image is revolutionary praxis broadcast to the wide human world. In "history transforming faith" the imperatives of historical events and patterns become instruments for making religious faith more responsibly moral. The engine of this image is revolutionary praxis targeted upon the *ecclesia*. A shared commitment to the reconstruction of human life makes close allies of the two advocacies. The discrepancies between them revolve around, on the one hand, the *vantage ground* and, on the other hand, the primary *object* of the praxis. Thus do they vary in their strategies.

The Christian priest in South America who concentrates his efforts upon prayer and Bible study groups (*comunidades de base*) to the end of political action, and the secular Christian who from the outset devotes herself to strictly political labor here, there, or somewhere, are doing two measurably different things, if not at all conflicting ones. In addition, eighth people are distressed when utopianism, an agathological expectation of success, comes to afflict "faith transforming history," with special reference to the grandiosity of its hopes and programs. In its tendency to lean toward a deontological ethic and an ethic of responsibility,[8] "history transforming faith" does not play up expectations of success, since "duty" and what is "right" together with what is deemed "fitting" comprise its determining moral incentives. In this regard, the very wording "history transforming faith" carries a tiny suggestion that the exigencies of time and place will ultimately have their say and their way, not simply with aid from individual human beings but at times in spite of them.

All things considered, the variations within the two tranformationist outlooks remain partial, for world and church can never be rigidly dichotomized, any more than can faith and history. As Gutiérrez states, a liberating theology concerns itself not alone with the transformation of history, but also therefore with the portion of humanity that is gathered into the *ecclesia*.[9] The latter concern is the special one taken on by "history transforming faith." The scope is much more delimited but the task is hardly easier.

Within contemporary liberation theology, traditional Christian supersessionism and triumphalism are retained at the broadly political level, and this not alone through the usual influences of historic anti-Jewishness and anti-Judaism[10] but also under the power of moral-theological persuasion. For even though history remains a struggle, yet "the promises of the Exodus paradigm" are held to be "fulfilled ultimately through the work of Christ the Liberator," as through the process of conscientization the Christian *comunidades de base* (reputedly) align their aspirations and praxis with Christ's liberation.[11] Such religious imperialism is unacceptable to people of eight.

In certain of its aspects the movement for women's liberation further exemplifies "faith transforming history." There is the oft-used symbol of Eve and Lilith standing together ready to re-create the Garden of Eden. Such symbolism represents fittingly the sort of faith that yearns to transform history. But the figure is appropriate as well to "history transforming faith," since the rebuilding of faith is vitally constituent to the rebuilding of the Garden. But the question remains: Where are we to find the weapons for rebuilding faith?

People of eight oppose spiritualization with its implied denial of the integrity of the created, historical order, the tacit dismissal of that order's relevance and value. In this respect they are at one with today's radical feminist struggle. However, in relative contrast to the skeptical, even cynical attitude within radical feminism respecting the redeemability of Western traditions of religious faith, eighth people fight hard to keep from abandoning all hope for political-moral change within traditional-institutional structures. Many of them will continue to work, however critically and while shedding many tears, from the side of the religious community. Thus may they ally themselves with Christian and Jewish reformist feminists, in some contrast to revolutionary, anti-religious feminists.

The basic differentiation between "history transforming faith" and the feminist movement as such (though never in any sense of non-support of the womanist cause) centers in the elementary disparity between *principle* and *history*. All feminism proceeds essentially under the authority and inspiration of a principle: the principle of the goodness of woman. Of course, womanist praxis cannot be dissociated from history, a history comprising in the first instance the woeful tale of patriarchalism. But the tale ought never to have happened. The truth of female goodness has not been taught by history. It is authenticated, we must say, in and through the very goodness of creation, of Being itself. People of eight tend to operate prevailingly under the promptings and often the impulsions of historical event (though not excluding the history of nature*). I have to stress that the difference is not absolute. Thus, the historicist's answerability to events can scarcely be severed from certain prevenient convictions or principles respecting the meaning of the right and the good, not to mention the very meaning of history itself. But yet it would be wrongheaded to fail to distinguish between the determining power of transhistorical principles and the commanding voice that may be heard from within one or another happening of time and place. The fact that the quality and character of the moral conclusions and prescriptions of the two parties involved may prove to be affinal and sometimes even identical will perhaps incline us to lose the point. The point not to be missed is that the advocate of our final normative image gambles upon the determinative quality of history for her or his faith-decisions and moral decisions, however shattering the outcome. Accordingly, the anguishing practical problem for people of eight is not the seriousness of history as such but instead, as we shall emphasize in chapter twelve, *the truly fearsome challenge of which patterns and events in history may be deemed crucial for day-to-day decision-making.*

The Christian conversionist type is H. Richard Niebuhr's own option.[12] (The conversionism that H. Richard Niebuhr propounds is highly dynamic. Life, the world, the church—all manifest a state of permanent revolution. Christianity itself "is 'permanent revolution' or *metanoia* which does not come to an end in this world, this life, or this time."[13]) Niebuhr it was who taught me the meaning of theocentric relativism. According to that persuasion, "it is an aberration of faith as well as of reason to absolutize the finite." But yet "all this relative history" of finite persons and movements "is under the governance of the absolute God."[14]

Must we not adjudge that the use of the term "absolute" in connection with God has today become problematic? Again, I think that H. Richard Niebuhr's individual position as an identifiably median one could be more balanced dialectically between God and world. Lonnie Kliever observes that for Niebuhr "man's relationship to God is determinative of his relationship to neighbor," which means that "theological reflection has a certain priority in the work of the moral theologian."[15] Niebuhr's tendency to "favor" God over world is reflected in the fact that his polemic against a Christianity of the world is rather more forcible and consistent than are his criticisms of Christian otherworldliness.[16]

---

*To affirm the God of creation is to assert that God is God of nature as much as of human history.

Three interrelated judgments are offered: (a) We may affirm, in equal measure, that the relationship to God is determinative of the relationship to neighbor, and that the relationship to neighbor is determinative of the relationship to God. (b) Granted that the theocentric imbalance within H. Richard Niebuhr's thinking was able to meet responsibly his own historical situation back at mid–twentieth century, we are challenged to apply the category of responsibility to the time a generation and more afterwards. (c) A possible consequence of points (a) and (b) taken together in a contemporary context—a wholly limited and relative context: let 2090 bury its own dead—is that while God and neighbor are equals when it comes to mutually determinative relations, yet, in paraphrase of George Orwell, the neighbor is for the present rather more equal. According to a talmudic witness, no less a personage than God is said to have once yearned: "Would that my children might forget me if only they remembered my commandments!" (*Chagiga* 1.7).

It is true that the mature H. Richard Niebuhr coveted a theology that combines "the radical sovereignty of God and the radical historicity of men. Only such a theology could do justice to historic Christianity and modern existence."[17] But "sovereignty" and "historicity" are not on the one level of power and priority. We have cited Niebuhr's statement that "for the conversionist, history is the story of God's mighty deeds and of man's responses to them." People of eight assent to this, but then they add two things. First, history is also the story of humankind's deeds (some mighty ones, many pitiful ones) and of God's responses to those deeds. Second, history is in addition the tale of human reaction to essentially human action and need. If the Christian conversionist looks for the transformation of culture in and to the glory of God,[18] the Christian historicist looks for the transformation of the church in and to the glory of "the least of these" our sisters anf brothers (Matt. 25:40). Yet this latter witness is no mere "faith for the world," since eighth people are aware of the poverty of the world's riches and the idolatries of the world's poverty, as they are aware too that the eschatological reign of God is the only sure *finis/telos* of all human striving and all human hope.

A few remarks respecting the church are relevant. Martin Luther rejected the claim that the church was the custodian of God's will and activity upon earth.[19] True to that Reformation witness, H. Richard Niebuhr came to abandon "expectations and exhortations for some ideally pure and united church as God's instrument of renewal." Eighth people are no more idealistic than is Niebuhr respecting the church. But the fundamental concern of this book is with *normative* images. The eighth image implies regulative demands upon the church in order that the Christian movement may do a lot more to fulfill its obligations to the world. Niebuhr does believe that "the reformation of the church and the reformation of the world must proceed apace as a permanent revolution of the world of culture (man's achievement) within the world of grace (God's Kingdom)." Here continuity is once again present between "faith transforming history" and "history transforming faith," a continuity that extends as well to the moral images represented in Jesus of Nazareth and in the rabbinic tradition. Niebuhr's own emphasis upon the reformation of the church is of constitutive influence upon the viewpoint of "history transforming faith." In all four normative images just mentioned there is agreement that responsibility to God "is incompatible with a spiritualism limited to immaterial goods, with a moralism that values only the virtuous man or nation, with an individualism that disregards mankind as a whole or its societies, and with all idolatries that substitute some finite concern for God as the center and source of life's value."[20] If humankind's worst sins are in fact religious ones, we have a necessary warrant for the permanent revolution of faith. (I hope that I do not anywhere imply that there is no support in Niebuhr for "history transforming faith.") The continuing imperative of the Christian faith is the reformation of church as of society. This means that each new generation is called to develop new sacred and secular expressions of the reign of God. *Yet there remains a basic difference between H. Richard Niebuhr and eighth people: over whether the transformation of faith is to fall primarily under the aegis of faith itself or primarily under the aegis of secular historicalness.*

III

The above state of affairs takes us into an essential difficulty in H. Richard Niebuhr's ethic: the issue of Christology. The moral fittingness (applied at various places in this study) of assessing a given point of view from *within* its own life and claims, and not simply from outside, is observed here.

H. Richard Niebuhr's Christological position expresses a double movement. Half the meaning of Jesus Christ, morally construed, is a movement "from the world to the Other." Jesus

> points away from the many values of man's social life to the One who alone is good; from the many powers which men use and on which they depend to the One who alone is powerful; from the many times and seasons of history with their hopes and fears to the One who is Lord of all times and is alone to be feared and hoped; he points away from all that is conditioned to the Unconditioned. He does not direct attention away from this world to another; but from all worlds, present and future, material and spiritual, to the One who created all worlds, who is the Other of all worlds.

The other half of Jesus Christ's meaning is a movement "from the Other to the world."

> Because he is the moral Son of God in his love, hope, faith, obedience and humility in the presence of God, therefore he is the moral mediator of the Father's will toward men. Because he loves the Father with the perfection of human *eros*, therefore he loves men with the perfection of divine *agape*, since

God is *agape*. Because he is obedient to the Father's will, therefore he exercises authority over men, commanding obedience not to his own will but to God's. Because he hopes in God, therefore he gives promises to men. Because he trusts perfectly in God who is faithful, therefore he is trustworthy in his own faithfulness towards men. Because he exalts God with perfect human humility, therefore he humbles men by giving them good gifts beyond all their deserts.

Christologically treated, then, the polar norms of "faith against the world" and "faith for the world" can offer no more than half-truths and no more than partial aid to the life of moral decision-making. For Jesus Christ is the "focusing point in the continuous alternation of movements from God to man and man to God; and these movements are qualitatively as different as are *agape* and *eros*, authority and obedience, promise and hope, humiliation and glorification, faithfulness and trust." Even if theologies fail to do justice to the double movement, Christians are aware of it. "For they are forever being challenged to abandon all things for the sake of God; and forever being sent back into the world to teach and practice all the things that have been commanded them."[21]

H. Richard Niebuhr's problem is the discord between his claims for Jesus Christ and his insistence upon an unqualified historical and revelational relativism (*relativism* understood as the foe of absolutism). In different terms, Niebuhr engages in theological-ethical equivocations upon his commitment to "radical monotheism." Ernst Troeltsch came to see, not alone that we know the absolute God solely through the relativities of history, but that we know God only in a historically relative way.[22] Niebuhr follows in this train. He finds "the great source of evil in life" to be "the absolutizing of the relative, which in Christianity takes the form of substituting religion, revelation, church or Christian morality for God." Furthermore, no genuinely critical theology can be "an offensive or defensive enterprise which undertakes to prove the superiority of Christian faith to all other faiths." Niebuhr works hard "against absolutizing *any* embodiment or concretion of faith."[23] But he does not reach the goal. For we note the absence of Jesus Christ from his list of unacceptable substitutions for God. Correspondingly, he definitely comes out implying "the superiority of Christian faith" to other faiths. For example, for H. Richard Niebuhr the Christian church "is the only community where God has fully revealed his reconciling nature and revolutionary action."[24] Niebuhr's emphases upon "the authority of Jesus Christ" vis-à-vis the authority of culture seriously qualify his insistence upon the moral perils in absolutization. True, the defense of Jesus Christ is not in itself self-defense. Yet the fact remains that whatever we defend (not excluding God himself) is never defended apart from our own self-defense. Indeed, the foregoing sentence sounds very much like one of Niebuhr's own. But he does not always listen to himself. For his strictures against defensiveness and self-defensiveness stop short of judgments concerning Jesus. Thus, in his affirmation that the *unity of humankind* is to be found in Jesus Christ, Niebuhr stays absolutist and supersessionist. When he bespeaks "that ultimate reality" which is "decisively revealed in Christ," the last thing he is talking about (from the perspective of moral consequences or interfaith relations) is historical relativism—or even "historical relationism," a term he later preferred. And when he declares as a "fact that Christ is risen from the dead, and is not only the head of the church but the redeemer of the world," Niebuhr is both absolutist and supersessionist.[25]

Interpreting H. Richard Niebuhr, Kliever writes: "Jesus Christ is that historic one in the living memory of the Christian community who was and is the mediator of a new relationship between God and men." Again, "the duality in union of God and man in the *Christ* event is the paradigmatic way that God and man are related in *every* event."[26] The stumbling block here is the word "men" in the first proposition and the word "man" at two places in the second—not in the sense of sexism (though that issue can never be ignored) but in the sense of a religious-absolutist claim. Were Niebuhr to have spoken unexceptionally of "God and Christians" rather than of "God and men/man" he would not have gone against his own confessional position. An essential consideration here is the lack of any evidence that he would ever have consented to such a linguistic change. For he believed, as his writings clearly show, in a Christ who is "the mediator" between God and humankind in a universal-objective sense and not merely within the "internal history" of the Christian church. Niebuhr's strictures against what he calls "Christomonism," or the reduction of God to the figure of Jesus Christ, do not annul the difficulty in his assigning divine and human "wills" to Jesus Christ as the unique mediator. True, a "deformation of radical monotheism in Christianity occurs when Jesus Christ is made the absolute center of confidence and loyalty."[27] Yet the issue is not met by the repeated insistence that the lordship of Christ must not be substituted for the lordship of God, for this very point is offset by Niebuhr's equal insistence upon theological affirmations respecting Jesus (including the Resurrection) that are not to be made about anyone else. When he pens the words, "some imagined idol called by his name takes the place of Jesus Christ the Lord,"[28] he ignores *his own discernment* that there is idolatry in ascribing lordship to any being other than the Creator of heaven and earth.

Involved in Niebuhr's problem is the relation between internal history (history as lived) and external history (history as seen). The stubborn presence of external history serves to keep him from the unreserved confessionalism that he sets forth as the Christian norm and goal. Internal history without objective sustenance or grounding gets reduced to pure subjectivity, as Niebuhr is well aware.[29]

To be sure, no one is enabled to confess any belief without holding to at least one presupposition that, itself remaining unexamined, comprises the foundation of all their beliefs and all their testings. Otherwise they should be forced into utter silence and the decimation of praxis. Yet certain ineluctable questions persist: How is the authority behind all our relative authorities going to be identified? How is that authority going to be authenticated? Wherein lies its legitimacy? Is there not an all-decisive moral difference between the presupposition of the God who is not an idol and the presupposition of some finite reality or principle? In a post-Auschwitz world, how is it possible for any absolutist defense still to be found for Jesus Christ? And then there is the most fateful question of all: Where is the moral justification in implying that Jesus Christ is an exception that needs some defense? Unless these questions are reckoned with constructively, the omission of Jesus from any list of non-defendables opens the defender to the charge of absolutization. We mark well that the *failure* to apply the knife of historical relativism (= anti-absolutism) to Jesus cannot be justified by protesting that such an operation would excise the *essentia* of the Christian faith. For that protest would only beg the entire moral question. The question that will not down is not a historically descriptive one but a normative one: How ought the Christian faith be identified today?

H. Richard Niebuhr's inability to carry his historical relativism to the fulfillment he himself calls for may be accounted for historically-experientially. He early came to doubt the practical power of German liberal theology and the American Social Gospel "to call forth anything more than a brotherhood of European manners, to establish anything more than a kingdom of American prosperity. . . . Their programs of human brotherhood were bourgeois because their view of God's fatherhood was sentimental. Their strategies of social transformation were parochial because their vision of God's sovereignty was uncritical." As Lonnie Kliever shows, our teacher struggled for years to fasten upon a mediating theological method that would conjoin two partially valid but unsatisfactory views, the anthropocentrism of liberal theology and the theocentrism of crisis theology—a method that would at the same time provide a theological ethic "at once distinctively Christian and culturally relevant." The element he found was Christological in substance. The anthropocentric and theocentric

articulations of Christian faith could only come together in a theology of revelation. But that revelation must be at once the mediation of God and the transformation of man in *actual* history. God must be known and served in and through the concrete histories of selves and communities without being collapsed into or separated from those histories. In *The Meaning of Revelation*, Niebuhr sketched out a way to meet those demands by bringing together sovereign God and sinful man in an unending and inescapable process of historical transformation. Here at last the reformer has a theological method to match the religious mandate that he had so keenly felt and ardently advocated for a dozen years—*reformation as continuing imperative!*[30]

Since, for H. Richard Niebuhr, Christological-revelational affirmation is what meets the entire life-and-death challenge of a theological method adequate to the demands of contemporary Christian history, it would perhaps be too much to expect that he subject his chosen criterion to the remorseless critical judgment of an unqualified historical relativism. But by exactly the same reasoning, insofar as the demands of our time differ from those of the 1930s and 1940s we may be called to explore alternative theological methods and alternative theological criteria (as is being done in these pages and of course in many other places). However, the required mandate ought to carry forward Niebuhr's own advocacy of reformation as continuing imperative, for otherwise his relativist-relationist position would not any longer be recognized for its great truth and met on its own ground. To deal responsibly with his unremitting query of "what God is doing and requiring in concrete cases and circumstances," and to be in accord with Niebuhr that "responsible theology is responsive theology, reponsive to God but always to God in a particular situation,"[31] means that we have to face theologically the actual conditions and the real needs and great events of our own time.

IV

In accordance with the two previous sections, there is the challenge of how to evade the kindred faults of *spiritualization, absolutization,* and *supersessionism.* A threefold program may be proposed (to be developed in succeeding chapters): (a) We carry forward liberation theology's indispensable campaign for the kind of deideologization of the Christian corpus that is essential to the struggle against spiritualizing and absolutizing the Good News. (b) In opposition to false spiritualization, we accept liberation theology's apodictic call to transform the real social world, to wipe out the "limit-situations of oppression"(McCann). At the same time, (c) we maintain the continuity of Christian realism (chap. 8) with the people Israel's teaching that the world of humankind and of nature yet remains unredeemed. The essential distinction between "liberation" and "salvation" is preserved—all false utopianisms and absolutisms are precluded—but preserved as well is the assurance that the God who hides herself in human history is known and worshiped through the doing of justice. It is the God of history who undergirds the cruciality of historicalness for the moral life. For the significance of history is not self-authenticating.

In each of the above ways, but especially via the third, the Christian church is rebonded to the Jewish community, and the Christian absolutism and supersessionism that culminated in the *Shoah* (Holocaust) are fought.

James Cone declares that black theology "will accept only a love of God which participates in the destruction of the white enemy."[32] People of eight may agree with this—but on the proviso that we must not stop there. A historicist Christian theology will accept a love of God that destroys the white enemy, the rich enemy, the male enemy, the Christian enemy, the black enemy, God the enemy, Christ the enemy, the Holy Spirit as enemy, and on and on all down the line. In and through the war against every enemy and thereby the dissolution of enmity itself, liberation is apprehended as universally and comprehensively victorious over oppression, with the result that the love-justice of God gains, in principle, the final victory. Abstractness and partiality are together overcome, programmatically speaking. The "undefined universalism" that rightly disturbs James H. Cone is vanquished.[33] We stand for a rigorous and responsible *defined universalism*. This form of a neo-liberation theological ethic is equivalent to a historicist theological ethic or a historicist Christian moral philosophy.

It can be interjected that this eighth genre of ethics is scarcely new. Endeavoring as they are to reassert in some meaningful way a biblical-type witness, people of eight need not be deterred by the point. For their effort at recapitulation actually serves to mark them off from those many parties who do not always seem to be re-living a biblical-type witness, at least not with respect to its radically historicist side.

How, then, may we summarize the theological and moral advocacy of people of eight? "History transforming faith" is a critical response, but not a wholly rejective one, to the autonomism of humanity that is grounded in the Renaissance and the modern era. That response endeavors to serve the values of human dignity and freedom. Yet in opposition to any elevating of humankind to practical sovereignty over God, eighth people posit history as a tool of God in her abiding synergy, her righteous love affair with human beings. (See Figure 4.) It appears to be our lot to live in a time of special revelations. This means that the sacred keeps taking on the visage of the secular. The trick is how to discern within secular history—the experiential history of the world—some clues to the rightful conduct of human life. Accordingly, "what I say to you I say to all: Watch" (Mark 13:37). There will be uncertainties, wrong turnings, sins, unresolved anguish. Withal, the responsible maturing of faith consists in a permanently transforming political praxis with special concentration upon a transforming of the house of faith. Eighth people distinguish themselves from other representatives of dialectically median views through their testimony that *history does not abolish faith; it transforms it*. The fresh worldliness of these protagonists is not secularistic; it is secular. It may not appear to be very "religious." It lives upon secularity, at the very moment that it is casting out secularism. It suggests a radical form of incarnationism. It is, dialectically speaking, a "genuine worldliness" or even, daringly, a "Christianity without religion" (Dietrich Bonhoeffer).[34] These are its rallying cries. Thus do the people of eight stake out an autonomous claim within the unending dialectic of faith and history.

I have avoided and avoided an unavoidable question: Is our eightfold imagery really the most comprehensive one that we can have? Or are there eventualities of ninth, tenth, etc. normative images? (How about these: "The world for faith"? "History above faith"? "Faith transforming faith"?) A coherent historicism ought to allow room for progress beyond its own schemas. Were historicism to try to stop history, it would be committing suicide.

Figure 4

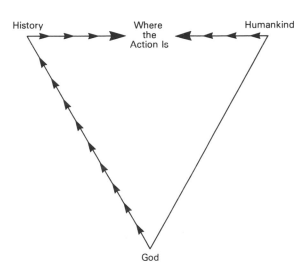

The potentiality of an additional image of "faith transforming faith" is actually hinted at in this book. I refer to the transformation of Christianity through the teachings and power of an abiding Judaism and abiding Jewishness. But there are at least two problems. First, I am unsure that this would mean an integrally alternative type, since Jewishness is already representative of a worldly historicism as much as a religious faith. Second, how could Christianity ever be reduced to Judaism?

V

From among the unnumbered discrete challenges that eighth people face, I propose that in the last part of the book we attend to three:
1. From the point of view of theocentric historicism, what may we assert respecting the general human (philosophic and theological) problem of faith and history? What perplexities does this eighth approach induce? The issue of faith and history is of course integral to all normative images, but it is particularly critical within any avowal of religious historicism. If, as I maintain near the start of chapter two, differing positions in Christian moral philosophy arise out of the normative substratum of "history under command and judgment," where exactly

is the legitimacy in advocating the transformation of faith by history? Should no such legitimacy be producible, the image of "history transforming faith" becomes an imposter. (Here is the subject matter of chapter eleven.)

2. Which history is to be our history? It is apparent, logically speaking, that the category of history-as-history lacks any self-transcending capacity to supply us with criteria for deciding that *this* event is morally decisive while *that* event is not morally decisive. In the course of addressing this question, we shall grapple with three major events and processes of recent history: the *Shoah*; the return of the Jewish people from political powerlessness; and the rise of religious pluralism (chapter twelve).

3. In light of the moral demands of historical liberation, what is to be the fate of faith? What does it mean, if it still means anything, to confess the Covenant? To speak of Incarnation, of the Cross, of Resurrection? Is God to be put on trial? Can there be redemption for God? (chapter thirteen).

The burden we bear is whether there can be any blessing for human life in a world after modernity, a world after Auschwitz. Is it still possible to speak of hope? Is it still possible to confess the ancient words, "for righteousness' sake"? The counsel of a "return into history" is a forbidding one. The major existential and substantive reason for this is that historicalness is so fragile, so precarious. There is the "terror of history" (Mircea Eliade). Subjected to history's travails, we laugh—but only that we may hold back the tears, or pretend that there are no tears. Who wants to live their one and only life suspended over an abyss of contingency, of evident happenstance and coincidence and fortune? And yet, hauntingly, the memory has not been wholly lost to some human beings that the way of historical precariousness opens as well a possibility of blessedness: "He did not create [the earth] a chaos, he formed it to be inhabited" (Isa. 45:18). Ultimate destruction or ultimate promise—here is the terror yet here as well is the hope that history holds out to us.

III. *People of Eight*

Challenges and Uncertainties

11

Historicalness: Opportunities and Perplexities

FOR hundreds of years the Christian church has sought to shield itself, along with its message and even through the power of its message, from the uncertainties and vulnerabilities of history. Such a stance is plain enough as we study early and medieval Christianity. Yet we see it too in Reformation Christianity with that movement's recourse to the scriptural Word of God that, confessedly, alights from beyond history. But the effort to rise above historical limitation and thereby in a sense to subdue history appears as well within the modern era, in such developments as Christian subjectivistic pietism and Christian Liberalism in its pristine version. The first of these latter movements sought to "save souls" within and from a fallen and troublous world. And the second movement, in the more idealist and idealistic aspects of its ethic, endeavored to overcome historical fatefulness by envisioning and fabricating an ideal world of universal peace and "brotherhood."

Eighth people march to other rhythms. We ask, from their point of view: What judgments are to be made within the abiding, overall dialectic of faith and history? What quandaries do such judgments evoke? Through this chapter and the two that follow we shall have especially in mind two tantalizing questions: Can there be conciliation among the dimensions of history, faith, and human liberation? And are there ways to reconcile traditions of religious obedience and the integrity of freedom?

The exposition in the present chapter singles out four themes. In developing them, I wish also to bring to greater focus some of the moral affirmations I have suggested or implied in previous pages.

I

Historicalness and people of eight. I have made reference at different places to the quality of historicalness, that spatio-temporal mode of being which strikes and wounds and heals us, and which mediates singular demands to us. Although a return into historicalness is not identical with a return into history, the two are inseparable. The difference and the relation are clarified via a single sentence: Historicalness means to take history with infinite seriousness; it is our historical *response*, our peculiarly human reply, to the raw materials and experiences of history, to the fate-opportunities of time and place. History is the objective diathesis of human life. Our responses to history may themselves be conjoined historically with, and even come to foster, the partial authoritativeness of history within our lives, yet often in ways not expected or sought. The Jewish, Muslim, and Christian witness to historicalness not only confirms the general human apprehension of historicity but itself wills to live with, if also to go to work upon, the historical scene.

We may reflect upon David Tracy's treatment of the religious dimension as not just "another super-everyday, super-natural life but rather a final, a limit-dimension to the whole of everyday life itself."[1]

It is so that under the conditions of our epoch, human decision-making does not escape a painful and lonely individualness. However, our responses and decisions are much more than personal ones. Tracy observes that "we are authentic selves only in direct proportion to our ability to be affected by and related to other selves. The substance-self of the classical tradition is at best an abstraction. I am the person I am precisely because of my relationship to this history, this family, these friends, these mentors, these ideas appropriated and experiences shared. I am, in a word, a profoundly relative not substantial being." Again, as H. Richard Niebuhr writes, while the present moment is the time of decision-making for the responsible self, the present never comes to us without a past or without an impact upon the future. "The self does not leave its past behind as the moving hand of a clock does; its past is inscribed into it more deeply than the past of geologic formations is crystallized in their present form. As for the future, the not-yet, it is present in my now in expectations and anxieties, in anticipations and commitments, in hopes and fears. To be a self is to live toward the future and to do so not only in the form of purposiveness, but also of expectation, anticipation, anxiety, and hope." Accordingly, the human self in its personal as in its social dimensions is, so Niebuhr concludes, radically historicized.[2]

But does not a plea for a return into history *on the part of the church and its spokespersons* compromise the probity of a transcending Christian faith? That problem asserts itself throughout the present exposition of "history transforming faith." At this juncture I submit three comments.

(a) Reasoned moral analysis testifies in support of the mutual integrity of faith and of history. It would not be right to subject all religious affirmation to the compunctions of historicalness. True, persons of faith are historical beings with historical obligations. But yet it is in the very avowal of overarching religious truth that the integrity of history is asserted—through, primarily, the doctrine that the divine creation is good. The very declaration of

the integrity of history presupposes a transcending reality that affords history its meaning. Transcendence and historicity are linked by abiding tension and interpenetration.

(b) The above kind of reasoned moral analysis reflects *theōría*, a form of
disinterested contemplation. But such disinterestedness is easily infected
by irresponsibility. The hour and the day then move in to interpose their
special demands.

> New occasions teach new duties;
> Time makes ancient good uncouth....[3]

The moral crisis under which we live is so all-pervading and so devastating
that the reasonable balance of faith and history is blown away. In opposition
to the timeless leisure and spaceless serenity of *theōría*, we are driven into
new occasions and new praxises in all their heartrendingness. We are called
to take sides. Yet this is not to subvert truth, for truth is "in order to" goodness, our "reasonable service."

(c) Nevertheless, concern for and dedication to concrete historical causes
and interests has to be ever wary of absolutization. This caveat cannot be repeated too many times. In the measure that historicity gets infected by absolutization, recourse must be had to the courts, the courts of truth, that is, to
the One who judges and smashes the idols. History is not an ultimate; it is
simply the flooring for praxis, the occasion for responsible historicalness.

This third point prompts a reactive comment upon the inglorious connotation that is often attached to the concept "historicism." Emil L. Fackenheim
observes that historicism as a philosophy "fails to philosophize about itself:
it asserts the historical relativity of all things, those philosophical included;
yet it claims or implies that it is itself exempt."[4] The brand of historicism ad-
vertised in this book is self-critical, or struggles to be. Its self-critical character is made possible and underwritten by its *theocentrism*. And the practical
theology it conveys is a revisionist one. This contemporary revisionism has
as a chief distinguishing characteristic "the central demand for the continuing refinement of genuinely critical theory and for its universal applicability
to all experience and all symbol-systems"[5]—yet with the proviso that in
both instances "all" is restricted to "our own" history, the history of our community. In sum, I agree with Will Herberg's apprehension of historicism as a
positive concept which in its depth and breadth enables it to be, in Bernhard W. Anderson's words, "the touchstone, or criterion, for determining theological authenticity."[6]

II

The fragility and the potentialities of faith's return into history. Rubem Alves pleads
for an understanding of faith opposite to the claim of eternal certitudes.
Alves apprehends faith "as a radically historical mode of being, as 'accep-

tance of truly historical existence.' " From this point of view, the language of faith is required to "express the spirit of *freedom for history, of taste for the future, of openness for the provisional and relative.*" Paul Tillich concedes that in the course of relating theology to culture—or, in our terminology, of relating faith to history—the substance of the Christian message may get lost. Yet this danger must be risked. "Dangers are not a reason for avoiding a serious demand."[7]

To acknowledge that the very being of humanness is pierced by history, that history is humankind's determination-destiny (*Bestimmung*) and hence its own potentiality-power (*Wirkungsvermögung*)—an acknowledgment that contrasts sharply with the spiritual orientation that has prevailed in such a land as India—is to be true to a simple, shared condition: human beings are born, live for a time, and die (as is the case too, just slightly less microcosmically, with every civilization). We are advised that the sea can never really be conquered but only survived.[8] The difference between the sea and life is that life is not once survived, much less conquered. The raging ocean turns out to be, by contrast, a friendly little puddle. At the same time, we have to affirm the dimension of freedom in opposition to fate (*moira*). This may be done in two ways: through (a) the dialectic of human determination-cum-destiny, and (b) the dialectic of God-cum-history.

(a) Humankind's existential awareness of its historicalness stays vital as long as people do not, in one or another way, turn their backs upon reality (*die Wirklichkeit*). This latter prodigious fault is made possible, even inevitable, by the truth that, in Arthur A. Cohen's aphorism, "man is a creature whose freedom tempts his reason." The awareness of historicalness is first of all ontological-anthropological, that is to say, this awareness accompanies and suffuses the human condition as such. The Bible, among its other qualities, labors to depict this overall condition of humanity. It is natural, therefore, that the biblical literature should confirm and unfold humankind's historicity. Will Herberg points out that in Scripture "the self and history come into their own, for in biblical faith it is man's 'essential dignity' that he is a self and 'can have a history.' Indeed, the two are really one: in biblical faith, human history is instrinsically personal, and the self is a historical structure.... The message biblical faith proclaims, the judgments it pronounces, the salvation it promises, the teachings it communicates, are all defined historically and understood as historical realities rather than as timeless structures of ideas or values."[9]

In the context of the problem of history, the question of human moral and metaphysical responsibility is seen to be the question of the reality and limits of freedom. Within Western culture as a whole the prevailing or practical consensus has been to reject both unqualified determinism and unqualified human self-determination. Accordingly, history gets construed as an indeterminate mixture of necessity and freedom. Humankind both determines history and is determined by history, is at once history's creator and history's creature. In Reinhold Niebuhr's conceptualization, freedom can be realized in history because human intelligence adds "various artifacts to nature's original minimal force of social cohesion," yet there is no absolute freedom within history, since "every choice is limited by the stuff which nature and previous history present to the hour of decision."[10] Accordingly, it is in principle always possible that human beings will *either* be overwhelmed by historical eventualities; *or* somehow manage to bring events—including even monstrous catastrophes—within their overall universe of meaning and partial control, learning from them and thus in a sense profiting from them; *or* achieve or even fall into some kind of mixture of the other two extreme possibilities. In sum, any interpretation of history that dictates either humankind's hegemony over the spatio-temporal process or its subjection to events beyond its control has not grasped the dialectical character of humanity's actual relation to history.

It is in the name of a return into historicalness, and hence as a pathway to the prospering of rightcousness, that the Christian church may be bidden to return into history. In and through that very summons, we may perhaps make a contribution to the church's own history, the history out of which the church may continue to live.

(b) The inexorable tale of birth-life-death may force the conclusion that, at base, the historical flux has no meaning at all. But yet faith (trust) in the power, providence, and love of the God of history and of eternity is able to transmute meaninglessness into meaning, fragmentariness into wholeness, despair into hope. The possibility is opened up of life beyond subjection to fate. Within a theological frame of reference, "choice, design, is what determines the shape of events"[11]—however much we may have to grant that God's choices can be incitant of fateful consequences. The *determination* of God may be held to mean just that: determination (will), freedom, the contrary of determin*ism*. Correspondingly, the prophet Jeremiah is given the assurance, "If at any time I declare concerning a nation or a kingdom, that I will pluck up and break down and destroy it, and if that nation . . . turns from its evil, I will repent of the evil that I intended to do to it. And if at any time I declare concerning a nation or a kingdom that I will build and plant it, and if it does evil in my sight, not listening to my voice, then I will repent of the good which I had intended to do to it" (Jer. 18:7–10). From God's side (*kiveyakhol*) and perhaps to some degree therefore from humanity's side, the future is always open. Such openness is among the warrants of authentic freedom. This is not to imply that the ways of God are transparent to human understanding. As Abraham J. Heschel declares, "in the realm of theology, shallowness is treason." Thus is the psalmist (36:5–6) "overwhelmed by the sublime grandeur of God's righteousness and the unfathomable depth of His judgments. They are like mighty mountains beyond the reach of man, like the abyss too deep to fathom. Only His love and faithfulness are everywhere." Again and again, perplexity afflicts the biblical writers and prophets.[12]

If history is ever to be won over or (theologically put) redeemed in ways that will vanquish death and sin, suffering and tragedy, this may occur through One who, authoring and encompassing the entire life and morphology of history, yet also stands beyond and beneath history as its judge and fulfiller. All of life in history is marked by sacredness because it "carries the property of eternity."[13] Paralleling, undergirding, and penetrating the birth, life, and death of human beings and civilizations, as also of all nature, there is manifested (so faith teaches) a certain patient but tireless drive toward a sublime and new creation-judgment-redemption. The truth of God wills itself into goodness by impelling itself, through love, into history. Through the praxis of grace, divine truth frees itself to become radically historical. Historicalness is not left at sea; it is empowered to gain direction in and through the transcending power that undergirds all history. The truth and the faith that derive from the transcendent being of God orient themselves to historical life, for the sake of the wellbeing of creatures who live in given times and places. The historicalness that may be recognized and potentiated by humankind is already present in the very life of God. In God, "truth is in order to goodness."

The human apprehension of the eventual divine victory is what is meant by *hope*.

When it is acknowledged, then, that history is our assigned and true lot, and when the consequent, shattering question intrudes of where, if anywhere, meaning is to be found, perhaps we may respond by, so to speak, marshalling history against history, i.e., by calling to witness events and processes within our own history that we apprehend, compellingly if fallibly, as originating from beyond history or from out of the very ground of history. Whatever our uncertainties, we may testify that just here is centered the dialectic of history and faith—that poignant relation between the dramas of time and place and the avowal of religious truth and meaning.

III

The impotence of history in the vindication of faith. We can agree with the oft-repeated aphorism of the great British historian James Parkes: "You cannot build good theology upon bad [i.e., false] history." This means that our attestations of faith are not permitted to contradict what we know of actual history. To plead otherwise is to open ourselves to an ideology of double truth. Any committedly historical faith will be exceedingly circumspect in its handling of history, particularly its own history. But what are we to say respecting a more ambitious, companion proposition, "You *can* show the validity of faith through resort to good history"? When we ensconce historicity in the front office of our moral and theological business, are we perhaps insinuating thereby that the declarations of faith find justification within history, and are even vindicable through recourse to history? For the Muslim scholar

Maḥmūd al-Sharqāwī, any nation that succeeds must by definition be righteous and be following the religion of God. Yvonne Haddad comments that "for the committed Muslim, history provides authentication of God's constancy."[14] But can the same thing be said by the committed Christian and the committed Jew?

As one way to wrestle with this issue, I suggest that we look at a particular aspect of the phenomenon of historical catastrophe.

A conviction that the calamities suffered by one or another transgressing nation or human being furnish a more or less definite measure of the wrath and punishment of God, while the blessings enjoyed by other (or the same) collectivities or individuals comprise a sign of God's approval, marshalls some surface plausibility. It is supported in parts of Scripture. Thus, the theology of history in the Book of Judges devolves around the neat idea that whenever Israel defects from Yahweh and worships idols, it is punished by him through subjugation to and oppression by another people; but whenever Israel returns to Yahweh, begging for deliverance, Yahweh saves his people (by raising up another judge). This understanding is carried forward within some of the prophetic literature, e.g., in Isaiah 1:19–20.

In a modern frame of reference we may recall Victor Hugo's classic treatment of the Battle of Waterloo in *Les Misérables*:

> Had it not rained on the night of the 17th of June, 1815, the future of Europe would have been changed. A few drops of water, more or less, prostrated Napoleon. That Waterloo should be the end of Austerlitz, Providence needed only a little rain, and an unseasonable cloud crossing the sky sufficed for the overthrow of a world....
>
> Was it possible that Napoleon should win this battle? We answer—no! Why? Because of Wellington? Because of Blücher? No! Because of God....
> It was time that this vast man should fall.... When the earth is suffering from a surcharge there are mysterious moanings from the deeps which the heavens hear.
>
> Napoleon had been impeached before the Infinite and his fall was decreed.
>
> He vexed God.
>
> Waterloo is not a battle; it is the change of front of the universe.[15]

Very moving. Very touching. But....

Prophetic preachments of the Judges-Isaiah-Hugo genre are often called upon by would-be prophets of today in discerning, if through a glass darkly, the status and impending fate of collectivities of divergent moral worth, and in bringing to these collectivities needed demands for repentance or, it may even be, needed words of assurance. Again, most people appear to believe that relative moral assessments respecting different nations and groups are quite in order: This people's way of life and behavior is "better" (or "worse") than that people's, and hence is more deserving of reward (or retribution).

But the question is: Are the ways of God to be comprehended through a similar disposition? Is it licit, even within the general frame of reference of theocentric obedience, to have recourse to the historical-moral dimension in order that we may secure "proof" of the authenticity or nobility of specific faith-claims? I suggest four points.[16]

(a) We are met by the perplexing fact that unvarnished ethical-spiritual character often clashes with the demands of socio-political responsibility. How are we ever to be free of this constraint? A government or other collectivity that, through fear of compromising its moral standing or even its fealty to God, would refuse to "make friends" for itself "by means of unrighteous mammon" (cf. Luke 16:9) may well prove itself remiss in its duties to its own people and perhaps even to the wider human community.

Biblical prophetism sometimes addresses itself to the specifics of politics, including what we would today call international politics. Isaiah holds in derision "the rebellious children" of God who seek protection from Egypt and ignore the truth that "the Egyptians are men, and not God; and their horses flesh, and not spirit. When the Lord stretches out his hand, the helper will stumble, and he who is helped will fall, and they will all perish together" (Isa. 30:1–5; 31:1–3). Jeremiah subsequently decries reliance upon Egyptian aid against Babylon, although his counsel is not heeded (Jer. 37). In still later years Ezra leads the exiles back from Babylon without accepting a military escort, since he is shamed by his earlier declaration that the hand of God "is for good upon all that seek him" (Ezra 8:21–23). Again, in opposition to political alliances a prophetic oracle counsels alliance with God:

> Call not alliance what this people calls alliance,
>   and fear not, nor stand in awe of what they fear.
> But with Yahweh of hosts make your alliance—
>   let him be your fear and your awe. (Isa. 8:12–13, NAB)

An all-too obvious difficulty here is the naïveté of rendering the divine "protection" as though it were of the same order as the physical protection that soldiers can provide (though supposedly stronger in its power). Even were the naïveté absent, a deeper lesson would be present. As Reinhold Niebuhr writes, "the sublime unconcern of the prophets for political destiny represents a point of religious transcendence where religion and politics stand in contradiction."[17] In other language (to repeat a point made in chapter eight), there is no way perfectly to reconcile responsible power and untainted goodness within human history. Whenever an ultimate religious perspective is attained, religion and socio-political morality reach a denouement: the knot is untied. The prophetic assurance that spiritual and moral regeneration, as against "entangling alliances" or other practical measures, is what will save a nation from destruction can hardly be subscribed to as the unilateral foundation of political policy. To fail to remember this is to provide a religious sanction for moral irresponsibility and futility.

(b) The preachment that the anger of the Lord (the Lady?) brings nations to naught really tells us nothing, morally-historically speaking. The stern fact is that all nations are soon or late destroyed. To be sure, the transcending explanation of the collapse of any given nation may well be its sinfulness: the wrath of God is the abiding complement of human sin. But the final temporal outcome is the same among all nations. Thus, the preachment before us says no more than does that universal strophe of history, "Nations finally fall."

In a sermon delivered shortly after the Second Great War began, a noted American clergyman proclaimed with homiletic satisfaction that when the Assyrians conquered Israel and the people afflicted were tempted to cry that this proved the power of the Assyrian gods, the prophets of Yahweh replied that what the event actually proved was that Israel had sinned. But did it really prove that? Relations between peoples and between humankind and God are far too complex for any event conclusively to "prove" anything. In point of fact, the conquest of nation A by nation B may well be the consequence of the truth that A sinned *much less than* B, the real imperialist and aggressor.

Herbert Butterfield writes: "Judgment in history falls heaviest on those who come to think themselves gods, who fly in the face of Providence and history, who put their trust in man-made systems and worship the work of their own hands, and who say that the strength of their own right arm gave them the victory."[18] Two related difficulties are present here: (i) Is it in fact the case that retributive judgment in history—granted the actuality of that phenomenon—so markedly outstrips vicarious action and suffering? That would be exceedingly difficult to show. The words "do not" can be readily substituted within each of Butterfield's clauses: "those who do *not* come," "who do *not* fly," etc. (ii) Everything depends upon the length of the time span we are to admit as having evidential relevance. Butterfield goes on to speak of the great and rapid tragedy that Adolf Hitler brought upon the world. Quite so. But the Hitler movement was also to help make Western Germany especially vigilant against a recurrence of totalitarianism (a development that, needless to say, does nothing to justify Nazism). A trouble with simplistic renderings of history, particularly in the long run, is the good that may eventually follow upon evil (together, of course, with the evil that may eventually follow upon good).

Many ruthless empires endure for centuries while some nations that produce generous portions of political and economic justice and righteousness in internal and external affairs—the only criteria we have for judging collective worth—may perish in their youth. There is no simple correlation between the temporal survival of a nation and its moral and spiritual health. The lament of the psalmist, "we are consumed by thy anger; by thy wrath we

are overwhelmed" (Ps. 90:7), is a universal cry. But this is a religious conviction, which is only secondarily historical. Such *indiscriminate* confession of sin
is considerably removed from the *discriminate* moral and historical help that a
distinction between the fate of "good" and of "bad" nations is supposed to
provide us.

(c) The Judges-Isaiah-Hugo preachment that uprightness means divine
favor, while "the way of the ungodly" must perish (Ps. 1:6), runs the danger
of treating God purely as a means to human interests and ends. Psalm 1
and related biblical passages rightly remind us of the ultimate denouement of faith versus sin: all the plots are to be at the last resolved. For the
writer of Hebrews, Jesus "endured the cross, despising the shame, and is
seated at the right hand of the throne of God" (Heb. 12:2). Correspondingly, in the fulfilled reign of God "the way of the ungodly" will already
have perished. Hence, to take Psalm 1 in a purely literal-historical way is,
on the one hand, to cause confusion in the presence of data that contradict the Psalm both historically and morally, and, on the other hand, sacri-
legiously to employ God as "omnipotent servant," butler to our moral
expectations.

The persuasiveness of avowedly human convictions concerning the relative goodness or evil of nations is thrown into question before the God who
"knows the secrets of the heart" (Ps. 44:21) and who raises up a faithful remnant from among those whose "righteousness is as filthy rags" (Isa. 64:6). The
preachment we are considering thus has a certain pertinence in testifying to
the power of God as she holds the fate of the nations in the palm of her
hand. This message may very well perform a cathartic and homiletic function
and induce repentance. But it may be used with propriety only when the
complications we have pointed to are honestly admitted.

(d) The foregoing difficulties combine to teach us a formidable lesson:
History as such cannot be convincingly utilized to interpret or explain history. Here is an all-decisive, constitutive restriction upon the place of history
within the dialectic of history and faith. As human beings gifted with a moral
sense we are obliged to offer relative moral judgments between individuals
and between collectivities, and to use these judgments as a basis of moral
and political praxis. But this is quite another matter from any attempt to rely
upon *history*—including the history in Scripture, wherein prophets warn of
doom and demand repentance—as a finally authoritative method for com-
prehending how history proceeds.

The temptation to presuppose that history can interpret history is so
great that some of the very theologians who caution us against it do not
entirely escape it themselves. Reinhold Niebuhr repeatedly and wisely
warns against ignoring the disjunctures between time and eternity, history
and superhistory, and (accordingly) politics and religion. In *Faith and History* Niebuhr points out that "the processes of historical justice are . . . not
exact enough to warrant the simple confidence in the moral character of

history which both secular and religious theories frequently ascribe to it." He is fully cognizant that analyses of the fate of nations and civilizations offer almost undecipherable complexities. And yet, Niebuhr himself seeks to show that the Christian paradox of life through death and death through life can be at least partially validated through analysis of the collective life of humankind.

> The death and famine in the life of man's social institutions and cultures is ... never so much the fruit of a natural mortality as the consequence of a vain delusion which seeks to hide the contingency and mortality of every power and majesty in human history.
>
> But there is fortunately another possibility in history. The powers and majesties, the institutions and structures of human contrivance do not always meet the challenge of competitive forces by increased rigidity and idolatry. Sometimes the competitive challenge serves to moderate the idolatrous claims. Judgment leads to repentance. There is not as clearly defined an experience of repentance in the life of communities and social institutions as in that of individuals. Yet there is a possibility that old forms and structures of life may be renewed, rather than destroyed, by the vicissitudes of history. These experiences establish the validity of the Christian doctrine of life through death for the collective, as well as for the individual, organism.[19]

In truth, when one looks to an event or trend in history as a means of validating faith, it is not the history as such that offers the real support. Or if one facet of history appears to provide support, another does the opposite. The work of "validation" is always a matter of personal and group interpretation through the eyes of faith. If it is so that faith precedes the analysis and interpretation of history (however much it is the case that those who come to have faith do so by virtue of their own history), the fact remains that history cannot validate faith. The nonbeliever is unable to find any convincing representation of the Christian life-death paradox in historical events, or if she does discern some sort of paradox, she will account for it in naturalistic or other extra-Christian terms. She certainly will never agree that historical events can disclose, even in a fragmentary way, a judgment or work of God. This disagreement is neither perverse nor stupid. The nonbeliever simply approaches history with presuppositions alternative to those of the Christian. On *the ground of historical analysis and experience alone*, she is no less right than the Christian.

In one place Roger L. Shinn gets into the same difficulty as Reinhold Niebuhr. Shinn knows very well the absurdity of trying to discern a simple pattern within the course of history. He stresses that "the sovereignty of God is not obvious in history" and that "the Christian doctrine of providence in its deeper forms cannot be primarily a theory of historical causation." Nevertheless, Shinn contends that we can detect certain limited evidences within the "cumulative process" of history for an affirmation of divine providence. Thus, he refers with evident approval to Herbert Butterfield's attestation that providential judgment is made manifest in the way that history breaks the power of lopsided ambition. Shinn discerns further support in Reinhold Niebuhr's avowal that divine grace is shown in the chance a society is given to repent of its sins.[20]

Is it not incumbent upon us to point simultaneously to the truths that unambitious men go down and that relatively "good" societies tend to see little reason for repenting? The point is that the choice of certain historical eventualities as supporting data for a doctrine of providence without equal attention to contrary historical possibilities is an arbitrary choice. Apart from allusion to these alternative considerations, any universally convincing application of our understanding of providence is precluded. Yet once the other considerations are brought into the picture, as they must be, the original claim that particular aspects of history sustain a conviction of the operation of divine providence loses its force.

In *Christianity and History* Professor Butterfield claims to discern the operation of a "moral factor in history," a certain nemesis that "makes itself apparent within the course of history itself," a judgment upon evil. There may be elements of truth in this kind of empiricism, but its force is contravened by the empirical need to recognize an equal, or greater, immoral factor in history, a judgment upon good, and to acknowledge that the flow of history is far too intricate to single out specific events and trends and denominate them (as Butterfield does) a "judgment of God." Butterfield does not attend sufficiently to his own intimations of a providence that appears as an accomplice of cunning and immoral power, and to his own confession that we "cannot introduce the idea of judgment into history without quickly meeting with situations of a paradoxical kind." None of this refutes his modest conclusions that "moral defects have something to do with" actual catastrophes, and that "at bottom it is an inadequacy in human nature itself which comes under judgment."[21]

Roger Shinn criticizes Karl Löwith for denying the "meaning of history" while trying to preserve the "meaning of life in history." This surrender of the meaning of history, Shinn alleges, is a departure from biblical faith.[22] A response different from Shinn's is suggested. Would it not be equally correct, or more correct, to affirm that, while there may well be a divinely supported meaning to certain events of history, we simply do not know what that meaning is? Or, better, while we are assured by the scriptural witness that God's purpose is to reconcile to himself the humankind that lives in history, it is not given to us to fathom the exact relation between the course of history and ultimate salvation. It is true that once we attest to a God who is active within history, we can hardly rule out divine judgments upon history. Yet (unhappily?) it does not follow from this that we can stipulate just what those judgments are. Here the hiddenness of God remains the stumbling block together with its special accomplice, the incredible complexity of the historical drama. Roger Shinn is quite aware that the only way we can apprehend meaning in history is through the eyes of faith. But he does not recognize sufficiently that the transcendent perspective of faith in the God whose thoughts and ways are not ours makes impossible any and every interpretation of how and why history moves as it does. Faith is primarily *pistis* (confidence, devotion) rather than intellectual *gnosis*.

We may agree and disagree with Karl Löwith. He is right that the pattern of history is inscrutable. Yet, in a way reminiscent of Marcion, he also denies, from the standpoint of Christian faith, the emphasis of the Hebrew Bible upon God as sovereign over world history. He states categorically that "Christians are not a historical people."[23] We may respond that Löwith's first conclusion does not necessitate his second one. The cause of much confusion in Christian interpretations of history is a failure to distinguish the question of a discernible "pattern" of history from the avowal of the hidden sovereignty that God exercises over all history. Once this confusion is present, Shinn and Niebuhr can criticize Löwith for denying the meaning of history, and Löwith can criticize Shinn and Niebuhr for imagining that history partially discloses a Christian meaning.

The Christian interpretation of history naturally implies and needs a theology of history. But it cannot simply ground itself upon the facts (events and trends) of history. When it does the latter, it opens the door to the subjection of faith to history, with the difficulties we have noted under points (a)–(c). The prophetic preachment we have analyzed, together with various other attempts to rely upon history in order to interpret history, come down to a form of rationalism that is quite different from faith, not excepting a fully historicist faith. These efforts comprise, in effect, a *philosophy* of history as against a *theology* of history. Unfortunately, philosophies of history finally run up against historical facts that upset all rational schemes, and moral and religious obligations that not only disappoint moralistic expectations but require such "faith, hope, and love" as put history to shame as at the same time they may begin to point the way to its redemption. (The philosophic aspect of interpretations of history is never wholly absent, however, for the simple reason that whenever we try to understand and explain events, we have to resort to a theoretical scheme of some kind.[24])

A final paradox of life is that there is no redemption within human history as such, but yet that we are called to act within history if we are to be responsible beings. Religious faith is crucial at both these points—by directing us to a salvation that will ultimately redeem and fulfill history, but a salvation that will gather up into the strange work of God the decision-making of human beings. Here is the sense in which Herbert Butterfield is quite right in arguing that "for those who have faith," Christianity transforms the meaning of history's story "and the mode of experiencing it even though the course of the world's events remains the same as before." (This act of transformation applies as well with Judaism and Islam.) Perhaps the most redoubtable paradox of all is that we are forbidden to divinize history but are yet impelled to avow history as the theater of divine action and revelation. Will Herberg asks: "How do we know God? The answer is that we know God precisely in the same way that we know other persons, that is, historically. The theme of the Bible is that God discloses himself in a 'shared history' remembered and confessed by the believing community. . . . This is what *Heilsgeschichte* means."[25]

I have strong reservations about the use of the concept *Heilsgeschichte* (lit., "history of salvation") insofar as it tends to connote some kind of realized eschatology or salvation within history. Liberation is one thing; salvation is something else. However, Herberg is cautious in his treatment of the term *Heilsgeschichte*.[26] To affirm "redemptive history" within a world that yet remains unredeemed requires us to speak in an unqualifiedly proleptic way. We are simply expressing the faith that, for all its distress and sin, the history of our world is not unrelated to a redemption that is to come.

That the normative image of "history transforming faith" should be put forward within an epoch of great historical disruption and crisis (the horrible wars of the twentieth century; the discovery/revelation of thermonuclear energy; the annihilation of the Jews of Europe; the return into history of the remnant of the Jewish people via the State of Israel; the postindustrial technological revolution; etc., etc.) cannot in itself work to support the position of people of eight. I repeat: history does not prove or validate faith. This applies as well to a historicist faith that proclaims the need for a historical transformation of faith. (There is a sense in which it is faith that validates history, through attributing meaning to history from an eschatological perspective.) However, while history cannot vindicate faith, our existential confrontation with history helps open the way to a Yes (or a No) respecting the claims of faith, including the possible necessity for the revision and deideologization of those claims. The one way in which history offers something enduring for faith is through providing raw materials for faith's response and through affording concrete opportunities for responsible human-moral decisions and praxis. *The return into historicity is to be apprehended strictly as a means to a coherent fulfillment of moral obligations deriving from a particular faith, and not as an apologetic instrument for the vindicating of faith.*

The question of the relation between human history and religious faith has momentous consequences for all the issues of morality with which the present study is concerned. Our negative judgment upon the possible employment of the historical process to validate faith (yet along with, paradoxically, a stress upon the cruciality of history for people of faith) thereby poses serious questions respecting the convincingness of one influential theoretical ground of ethical motivation. I refer once again to an agathological (or teleological) type ethic, with its great hope of realizations of "the good" within time and place.

IV

History and the hiddenness of God. The foregoing acknowledgment of the impotence of history to authenticate faith, when put side by side with the avowal of Will Herberg and others that we know God historically, supports the recognition that God remains hidden within history. What, then, can it mean to say that we know God? I offer five propositions, each of them of relevance to the overall dialectic of history and faith.

(a) To speak in general terms, the teaching of the divine hiddenness bears directly upon our human status in relation to nature, to history, to the divine purpose, and to sin. These several elements are helpfully addressed in a single passage from Reinhold Niebuhr: When prophetic religion attests "that life and history are under the sovereignty of a hidden God" it declares that they are to be understood "in terms of a dimension deeper and higher than the system of nature, that there are obscurities and contradictions in the 'behavior' of history which can be clarified only if the unique purpose of God is more fully disclosed; and that human explanations of this behavior must be corrected since they contain sinful elements." These sinful elements within the human knowledge of God are especially serious "because they involve the pride of the finite self seeking to understand . . . the eternal ground and source of existence in terms of itself."[27]

(b) Any truly transcending God who is believed to disclose herself amid the spatio-temporal flux can do so only as a hiding God. I speak quite literally here of an objective restrictiveness upon the divine power or ability. Were God either to remain above or beyond history, or to be essentially immanent to history, the entire basis of the faith-history relation would, objectively speaking, disintegrate. God's hiddenness is, so to speak, the price that has to be paid for the kind of divine revelation from beyond history that does not at the same time so dazzle and overwhelm the domain of time/space that the integrity of history is annihilated (and with that, the integrity of revelation itself). If it is so that history and this world are not themselves God, how could God ever operate within them without obscuring or camouflaging herself? From this perspective, there is nothing esoteric or strange about the hiddenness of God within history; it is a simple epistemological-ontological necessity. This makes cogent a contention of Carl Michalson: "The doctrine that God is hidden is probably the most pertinent Christian witness about God for our time.... The nature of God's presence is that God is so solely and completely God in his presence that he cannot but remain hidden.... For transcendence does not mean God is so far away that he is hidden but rather he is so near that he is hidden."[28]

(c) It follows that a recognition of the hiddenness of God is just what creates all the perplexities that beset the relating of faith and history.

Any and all efforts to ascertain the will of God are shot through with ambiguities and uncertainties. Dennis P. McCann writes that the vision of God as hidden "requires the theologian to be sensitive to the vicissitudes, the ironies, even the paradoxes of historical experience," to "the difference between religious 'truth' and the 'vain imaginings' that obscure it." The theologian "must be ever alert to the possibility of self-deception. For if God is a hidden God, then things are never quite as they seem." The theologian must be ever vigilant "regarding the myths, symbols, and images taken for granted in society." And "if such a task is to be politically relevant, those images—the idols of the marketplace—will have to be criticized not simply for their religious disorders, but also for their ideological distortions. In other words, the practical theologian will have to address the concerns of critical social theory as well as therapeutic psychology. Otherwise his or her personal intuitions regarding the truth or falsity of religious images will remain incommunicable and without effect."[29]

The above listing by McCann of the demands upon theologians is a tall order. No one will do more than approximate a satisfaction of these demands. However, the "impossible possibilities" (Reinhold Niebuhr) of the Christian life are themselves of important help in facing such demands. For religion teaches people to find God by loving their brothers and sisters, and to love them because they have themselves found God.[30] In such ways the hiddenness of God is qualified—for those who have eyes to see and ears to hear.

It is said that Ernst Troeltsch "was the epitome of the tendency in liberal theology to discern God's presence in history (past and present) through some measure or criterion arising within contemporary experience itself."[31] The trouble with any polemic against this kind of theology is that, alas, we are all simply bereft of measures or criteria other than experiential ones. Here is a constituent part of the human plight. At this point, "liberal theology" is not being prescriptive but simply descriptive. Does this end the argument? No. There can be all the difference in the world between *this* measure or criterion and *that* measure or criterion. We make our decisions on the basis of what seems right, or less wrong, and of what seems most fitting, or relatively less unfitting.

(d) There is the consequent and staggering question: *How can we ever say what the hidden God is doing?* A serious problem for "history transforming faith" is the nature of the proportionate relations among divine action, human action, and the action of nature within the total historical process. The problem is occasioned by the very emphasis of eighth people upon God's utilization of history. In this context "history transforming faith" is affinal to the inherent skepticism of the hyperdialectical outlook (chap. 8): there is no way finally to resolve the tension between history and faith. But the fact is that no normative image wholly escapes this limitation.

We simply have to concede the absence of any instrument for prescribing when or if "God does this," "people do that," and what the difference is.* This unresolvable enigma is already hinted at by Paul: "You must work out your salvation in fear and trembling; for it is God who works in you, inspiring both the will and the deed, for his chosen purpose" (Phil. 2:12–13, NEB). One contending reply to the question of what God is doing—a reply that is hardly original—entails a continuing recourse to chosen testimonies of different parties within the story of faith. In the search to apprehend the divine will, we turn for aid to theological interpretation, religious discernment, the stubborn happenings of every day, and the biblical witness. For example, the writer of Luke records the Magnificat of Mary in celebration of her pregnancy. The account in turn testifies to an ancient prayer of Hannah. The Magnificat is cited in the exposition of liberation theology in chapter nine above: the deranging of the proud and the mighty is juxtaposed with the exalting of the lowly and the feeding of the hungry (Luke 1:51–53; cf. I Sam. 2:1–10). It will be noted that the varied praxises of God are here made matters of the past. This fact at once poses a problem and suggests a resolution of the problem. I have been arguing that it is illicit to call upon history in order to validate faith. Does such an argument mean that the Magnificat and like passages are not accessible to theological-ethical application? No. This negative answer may be explicated via a commentary by Robert McAfee Brown. The context is a real-life occurrence: his account of the singing of the Magnificat at the end of a session in theology for lay people in Lima, Peru:

> [The Magnificat] is attributed to Mary, a lovely, spiritual person, as we all know, the humble handmaiden of the Lord. Tame, safe stuff up North. Dynamite down South. For the humble handmaiden of the Lord turns out to be the greatest revolutionary of them all. The *real* marching orders come straight from her. The police cannot stop a bunch of Catholics from singing a hymn by the Blessed Virgin. But listen to the words: I had never really heard them until that day. . . . The humble handmaiden of the Lord has set the agenda for the next half century of Christian activity in Peru.[32]

Did the praxises of God *in fact* all lie in the past, these Peruvian Christians would obviously require no agenda at all, since their whole socio-economic plight would have been abolished by God a long time ago. The alternative is to receive the Magnificat as a marching order for a future that can begin in

---

*We can never say, experientially or scientifically, that God must be *there*. For God is, after all, the hidden God. But to adjudge that God is *not there* is to surrender the God of history. A dialectical alternative is to affirm that the God who is hidden is *nevertheless there*, morally speaking, if only as the One who is ultimately accountable for evil as for its rectification to the end of righteousness. It is at this juncture that truth and goodness converge. To be sure, faith in God cannot be demonstrated through historical experience. And yet, if there are no "exaltation-liberation events" (William R. Jones), faith becomes empty and nonmoral. Perhaps within this dialectic lies one viable way to bear the unbearable question of "faith and history."

this very moment: God *wants* to scatter the proud, she *wants* to put down the mighty, she *wants* to exalt those of low degree, she *wants* to fill the hungry, she *wants* to send the rich away empty. She yearns to do all these things right now. *The only problem is where she is going to find the people who are willing to help her bring it off.*

Robert McAfee Brown is simply saying that, with other Christian revolutionaries, these Peruvian Christians have ranged themselves upon the side of God's future. Our own testimony to *their* testimony can be a similar declaration of hope and resolve. In this regard, the definition of Christian theology that was put forward in Lima may be compared with some others: Christian theology is "a matter of reflecting from a Christian perspective on what one is doing *in the world* to transform social structures for the benefit of the poor."[33]

(e) A historicist faith remains a hazardous venture, an attempt to live responsively/responsibly in the (hoped-for) presence of the divine hiddenness. It is infinitely more becoming to speak of knowing the *effects* or the *traces* of God, than to claim to know the majesty of God herself. The ongoing, agonizing summons to make some kind of sense of the relations among God, history, and the human condition is to be lived with, not through ultimate solutions fashioned by the human mind, but with aid from two questions linked together: What are the moral responsibilities we are to honor? And what is the praxis of faith? The first of these questions is addressed throughout this book. The second is helpfully addressed via a commentary upon Martin Luther by Wolfhart Pannenberg: "What Luther in his later years said of theology, is primarily true of his concept of faith: it seizes us and puts us outside ourselves, lest we rely upon our own power, conscience, perception, person and works, and it makes us rely upon that which is outside ourselves, namely, upon God's promise."[34] From this point of view, history, humanity, and even God herself comprise the foundational elements—sometimes harmoniously, ofttimes conflictingly—out of which our moral decision-making is ventured, in reliance upon God's promise. This orientation is quite alien to any effort to reach exact or final answers to questions of historical meaning and destiny.

It may at first appear that the call to return to historicity (in the meaning of historicalness plus history) is undermined by the admission that we can never overcome uncertainty respecting God's praxis within history. Such a conclusion does not pay sufficient attention to the nature of historicalness and of history. The return to historicity is not a method of ensuring certainty or of "proving" something. It is an effort to implement human responsibility and faithfulness to God within a world where there are no final certainties. To be sure, such responsibility and faithfulness may themselves help to implement and strengthen faith, but this will happen only as a natural accompaniment and fulfillment, and will not take the form of objective demonstration.

The massive moral and theological issues that have assailed us in the chapter here ending (together with those that meet us all through the book) are thus part and parcel of the life of historicalness itself, and do not imply its refutation or abandonment. The overall problem of history-humankind-God is to be treated heuristically, dynamically, and in openness to the future. The analysis within the present chapter has suggested that both of the variables within the dialectic of "history" and "faith" are attestable all right, but that serious difficulties yet obtain in any effort to resort to history as a means to the intellectual authentication or moral vindication of religious faith. However, this latter form of negative conclusion does nothing to dissolve the specific challenge, brought forward by eighth people, respecting the role of historical event in the actual moral transfiguration of faith. It is in this sense that the problems reflected upon in this chapter provide background and a certain foundation for the remainder of the volume. *We are in a position to be much more positive now than we have been, for we have set history free to come into its own—yet in most chastened form—as finite, prudential, and pragmatic judge, not alone of humankind but perhaps even of the divine life itself.*

There is no such thing as a pure or complete "history transforming faith." For the historical events we choose as decisive, and the meanings and significance we assign to them, are never wholly independent of some kind of faith-decision. This consideration brings us to the subject matter of chapter twelve.

12

Which History? Whose History?

IN a Christian context, as in a Jewish and Muslim one, the *principle* of "history transforming faith" seems sensible enough, once we agree that human history is a scene of the divine praxis. But this does little if anything to spare us perplexity or uncertainty. Our difficulties appear even to be compounded. For how are we ever to link concretely the unfolding of the divine righteousness and the processes of history in all their particularity? Which events, and which kinds of events, may we embrace as decisive or compelling? Which events and kinds of events may we exclude, or at least ignore? Which history is to be our history? Whose history is to be our history? These are inescapable questions for historicists, due precisely to their historicism.

In "faith transforming history" the standing ground tends to be restricted to a particular faith. By contrast, in "history transforming faith" there is a relatively greater willingness to expand the horizon beyond a given faith, and often beyond religion itself. The history that is to transform faith can well appear as secular in character.

I

At least three caveats are in order. (a) While it is true that any affirmation of the objective conditioning of faith under the power of various human events, processes, and patterns suggests a need for careful historical analysis, we cannot here pursue such strictly historical work. This is due to the delimited moral and phenomenological concerns of the present volume. (b) Although it is the case that "history transforming faith" tends to be my own view, that position is much more than a personal or idiosyncratic one. Accordingly, as has been the case with the other images, I treat this one with the aid of varying amounts of exemplification and documentation. In chapter ten I list several moral-historicist norms as being desirable: deideologization, antispiritualization, and antisupersessionism, together with a recognition of the unredeemedness of the world. Such advocacy is permitted in a book like this only in the measure that it mirrors a publicly identifiable movement within moral philosophy and theological ethics. As a matter of fact, eighth people are growing in numbers. However, I think it doubtful that others who tend to adhere to this overall way of thinking/praxis would be happy with my labels "historicist" and "historicism." Those labels are quite controversial. (c) We cannot repeat too often that it is wrong to stuff human life into rigid conceptual categories. Thus, a number of the illustrative materials I have introduced all along the way could be placed, arguably, under alternative normative images, at least in one or another of their aspects. On the other hand, the choice of exemplifications is not, or ought not be, an arbitrary or random one. For such choices involve us as deciding human beings and as scholars.

The transforming of faith under the impact of history is amenable to all sorts of illustrations and all kinds of documentation. We could concentrate, for instance, on the effects of science and technology upon faith and morality, or on the impact of modern secularism and hedonism upon religious ethics. The areas I have chosen are receiving increasing representation in the contemporary scene:

—The contemporary Christian and Jewish "return into history" via a "return" to the historical-political reality of Israel, with the implicit and explicit consequences that this has for faith.

—The experience of the American people, together with trans-American influences, as opening the way to the development of, and an existential rapprochement with, religious and cultural pluralism.

Points of departure for a "return into history, return to Israel" may be found in two twentieth-century figures, Dietrich Bonhoeffer and Choan-Seng Song. In one of his prison letters Bonhoeffer writes:

> Unlike the other oriental religions the faith of the Old Testament is not a religion of salvation. Christianity, it is true, has always been regarded as a religion of salvation. *But isn't this a cardinal error*, which divorces Christ from the Old Testament and interprets him in the light of the myths of salvation? Of course it could be urged that under Egyptian and later, Babylonian influence, the idea of salvation became just as prominent in the Old Testament—e.g., Deutero-Isaiah. The answer is, the Old Testament speaks of *historical* redemption, i.e., redemption on this side of death, whereas the myths of salvation are concerned to offer men deliverance from death. *Israel is redeemed out of Egypt in order to live with God on earth.*[1]

On the basis of this passage, at least two queries direct themselves to us: First, are the categories of worldly liberation versus eschatological salvation (as we have earlier distinguished them) really sufficient? No less than three concepts seem to vie for attention: liberation, redemption, and salvation. "Salvation" as something otherworldly may be excluded all right—or at least postponed! But "redemption" is authorized. However, it is authorized only because it points to something *historical*. Once this latter, essential qualification is made, *redemption* and *liberation* may be more or less equated. Second, and much more fatefully, if the redemption of Israel (within which, Bonhoeffer is implying, Christianity finds its own meaning) entails Israel's life with God upon this earth, what are we called to say and do when Israel is threatened with extinction? (By participating in an assassination plot against Adolf Hitler, Dietrich Bonhoeffer played a frontier role in the contemporary Christian return into history. It is recognized that Bonhoeffer never overcame certain elements of anti-Jewishness.[2])

Eighth people are benefactors of contemporary liberation movements within and beyond the church. And they are in accord with the stress within liberation theology, echoing Bonhoeffer, upon Israel's worldly redemption out of Egypt as a paradigm for the moral life. (One of liberation theology's shortcomings, as we have intimated at a few places, is its proponents' failure to stand behind the full logic of redemption from the slavery of Egypt, viz., life for the Jewish people of today within a promised land of freedom.)

"History transforming faith" goes beyond paradigms from the past. It endeavors to appropriate and to apply lessons taken from specific epoch-making events of today. This distinguishes it, but does not separate it, from other advocacies of liberation.

Choan-Seng Song has written an essay with the seemingly non-apposite title "From Israel to Asia—A Theological Leap." To prepare the way for our encounter with him, let us phrase a question: What is the ground, if there is one, for adjudging that the re-creation of Jewish sovereignty in the country of Israel in 1948 is for us a "different" kind of happening from the coming of Communism to the country of China in 1949, even with all our remembrance of the latter's "resolute rejection of Christianity"?[3]

Song characterizes the Exodus from Egypt as God's *violent revolution* in history *par excellence*. Nevertheless, he opposes any forcing of God's redemption into the history of the nation of Israel and of the Christian church. According to him, the prophetic tradition itself refuses to equate the history of Israel "with the totality of God's acts in the redemption of his creation." Song goes so far as to argue (very controversially) that Israel was not to be "the nation through which God's redeeming love would be mediated, *but* to be a symbol of how God would also deal redemptively with other nations." Here then is the fittingness of Song's title: Other nations may learn from the experience of Israel "how their histories can be interpreted redemptively. . . . An Asian nation will thus be enabled to find its place side by side with Israel in God's salvation."[4]

In light of Song's own rendition of universalism, the judgment he reaches becomes that much more paradoxical and that much more significant. He insists that human beings, lacking as they are in the power to comprehend the prodigiousness of history-as-such, are obliged and even summoned to cope with the regnancy of time/space by means of the peculiar instrumentality of

existential history. Perhaps we may be permitted to make something of a functioning virtue out of what Song holds to be a moral necessity. To him, the
"Western theologian" really has no business invading a history other than
his own. Western theology still finds it hard to emancipate itself from the
ideologization of faith; Asian and African cultures and histories are subjugated, in effect, to the history of the (Western) church. Song advises us that
"the question is not what God is doing through the church but what he is
doing in the world. . . ." This makes Song's subsequent conclusion nothing
short of astonishing. For what and where is the "world" to which he then bids
us turn?

> Western theologians must first address themselves to their own situations,
> and wrestle with the question of how Israel can be existentially related to
> suffering and hope in the West today. *Israel must become their existential experi-
> ence. . . .* Let us recognize that one cannot do theology for those who live,
> suffer and die in a society with different cultural, socio-political demands
> and responsibilities. The most one can do is give mutual support and en-
> couragement through sharing of theological experiences and interpretations
> of human suffering and hope in given situations. . . . Theology cannot deal
> with the question of what God *is.* Its task is to come to grips with what God
> *does—and we cannot know what God does apart from events and realities in which we are
> involved existentially. . . .* Freedom from external theological inteference, the
> conscious effort to become true to a particular situation, and *liberation from
> the claim to universal validity*—these make theology become alive, useful, dy-
> namic and, above all, authentic. An ecumenical theological community must
> be built on the foundation of situational authenticity.[5]

The history that is eligible to transform faith is resolutely existential history. The theology that accompanies such transformation is a *theology of existence*; the philosophy that accompanies it is a *philosophy of existence.* An
implication is that since there are many such histories, and many such theologies and philosophies, the door to moral and intellectual pluralism is already opened. As Song affirms, once theology is set free from claims to
universal validity, it can become authentically alive and humanly responsible.

Our living options, then, are not between history-as-such and something
ostensibly nonhistorical, but rather between a given historical genre and
other historical genres—and this in a confessional, ideally nonapologetic
way. There is to be no subservience to some reputedly "main stream of salvation history" (*Heilsgeschichte*).[6] To insert an analogy, human wedlock does
not mean a choice between the universal of "marriage" and its presumed
opposite, but instead involves a choice between *this* potential marriage partner and *that* one. The history that transforms a given faith will tend to be a
special history, a specific history—in at least two respects: It is concentrated
within a certain spatio-temporal continuum and context; and it does its work

within and through the moral choices of human beings who either stand within that history or make that history somehow accessible to their own lives. To continue the analogy of marriage: The truth that one's own marriage may be, existentially speaking, undeniably good does not say anything one way or the other respecting the fortune or quality of other marriages. It certainly does not raise invidious questions about the integrity of such marriages; by implication, it even supports them (through its celebration of itself).

In and through the contentions of Dietrich Bonhoeffer and of Choan-Seng Song another of many caveats is suggested: The Christian return to Israel contravenes Christian imperialism. There are serious moral temptations in any return into a particular history that is not one's own property. The challenge is how to be part of something without trying to dictate what that something is or ought to be. Accordingly, the possibility of Christian imperialism directed to the Jews and Israel hangs as a Damoclean sword over the exposition to the very end of this book. There is the haunting thought that the very insistence upon Judaism and Jewishness as the foundations of Christian faith may only compound antisemitism and Christian supersessionist imperialism. The power of this thought is part of the demonic price still being exacted for almost two millennia of Christian denigration of Jews.

The Christian church spent nineteen hundred years trying to negate Israel as the people of God. Today some Christian theologians are moving to the opposite stance, but one with comparably lamentable moral implications: Jews are made into special witnesses to God whether they like it or not. They are subjected to religionization from outside. The question is: When will the Jewish people be received and treated simply as human beings? (That the intentions of these theologians are of the best does not help.) This much may be insisted: We are to avoid any "Christian theology of the people Israel." Such an effort is implicitly presumptuous, a form of lingering triumphalism. It is an essentially pre-*Shoah* undertaking, and it ought to be abandoned.[7] The only licit theology of Israel as a people is a Jewish one. Jews alone are the arbiters of their identity. Let us reflect a little further upon this point.

To speak of the Jewish people as the "people of God" is to offend many Jews who simply do not think of themselves that way. But to speak of Jews as *not* the people of God is equally offensive. It perpetuates Christian anti-Judaism and antisemitism. Thus it is that the option of silence on this matter offers itself as an alternative course for Christians. Yet in the contemporary world, would not such silence inhibit Christian moral responsibility to the Jewish people? Is it possible to achieve a purely confessional, non-imperialist rendering of "people of God"? Such an understanding could perhaps take its departure from the historical-theological truth that the Jewish people, and particularly Jesus, have made it possible for certain other people, now known as Christians, to be "brought to faith" in God. However, this approach is not without serious problems. The most fateful pitfall is that, implicitly, Jews are being treated as a means to a Christian end. Perhaps the least of various evils is to think of "people of God" as referring to those people, the Jews, who are *traditionally* the people of God. The historicity behind that reference can hardly be denied.

A most anguishing dilemma for Christians is whether they are permitted to affirm the Covenant (apart from which their faith may face dissolution) without falling into presumptuousness respecting the Jewish place in the Covenant. Were they eventually forced to decide that there is no way to connect the Jewish people with the Covenant without contributing to destructive Christian imperialism, the dissolution of the Christian faith as an independent reality would indeed be the more responsible choice. If God himself can, *kiveyakhol*, yearn "that my children might forget me if only they remember my commandments!" the "forgetting" of Christianity is seen, in contrast, to be hardly a big deal. However, were any such Christian dissolution to take place, would this not mean that the special bond of Christians with Jews would also be dissolved? Probably the answer depends upon the measure in which Christians will really have taken Jewishness into themselves. Insofar as they are able to do so, the bond can endure—as suggested in the simple fact that the bond of Jew with Jew is not contingent upon any kind of religious affirmation or denial. It is a strictly human bond. Within a Christian context here is one possible way to apply Bonhoeffer's conception of *religionless* Christianity.

If a "Christian theology of the people Israel" is morally out of the question, we are instead called, on the one hand, to "Christian *moral responsibility* to the people Israel" (or "a Christian ethic of the people Israel"); and, on the other hand, to learn "lessons for Christians from the people Israel." Yet nothing above is to be taken as excluding the fact of Christian benefit from Jewish testimony to Israel as people of God. Such testimony, an inspiration to Christians, remains uncorrupted by Christian imperialism or supersessionism.

The history that serves to transform faith is always a specific history and a specific form of historical-existential testimony.

II

To turn to a further and related consideration, the Christian historicism that is joined to the history and life of Israel has as its cornerstone the Jew Jesus of Nazareth. In and through the actual event of Jesus there is manifest the essential historicity that marries the Christian community to Israel, the objective authorization for declaring that historical Israel is the root that supports the church (Rom. 11:18). Those who have been "strangers to the covenants of promise, having no hope and without God in the world, . . . are no longer strangers and sojourners, but . . . fellow citizens with the saints and members of the household of God" (Eph. 2:12, 19). Here, for Christians, is the all-decisive meeting place or convergence of faith and history. Once such confessions as these are deideologized, i.e., monotheized, they become the spiritual counterpart and authentication of Jesus-historicity. The primary Christian obligation today is not so much to demythologize the tradition as to deideologize it. The opening of the Covenant to those outside Israel helps to implement the promise that Abraham and his posterity would be a source of blessing to all the peoples of the earth, as repeated a number of times in Genesis (12:3; 18:18; 22:18; 26:4; 28:14).

The opposite proclivity (though a deeply related one) to the practice of dehistoricizing Jesus for the sake of a theologism, a theological idea, is the equally woeful effort to dehistoricize him for the sake of an alleged moral-spiritual "universality." Thus is Jesus fabricated into a black African, a Mexican *campesino*, a saint of India, an American business man, etc., etc. On the contrary, Jesus must remain what he was: a Jewish man of first-century Galilee, Samaria, and Judea. To speak of Jesus as other than a Jew is no longer to speak of him. Father Sloyan declares: "To be faithful to Jesus Christ as the New Testament speaks of him is to be in full continuity with him in his Jewishness."[8]

True, different references and tributes to Jesus today entail radically diverse reactions, meanings, and decisions. But really to speak of Jesus is to say to everyone (not excluding skeptics, cynics, and detached observers) that Christianity is a historicist faith, a way of historicalness. For the bedrock of the church is an event: the birth, life, and fate of a particular human being. At this vital juncture the calling of the Christian historicist replicates (as suggested in chapter four) the interests of "the quest of the historical Jesus," since the basic concern of that quest "is the decisive importance of the historical Jesus for Christian faith."[9]

The historical-existential sources of Christianity reach infinitely deeper than the life of a solitary figure. For what is the history of a human being apart from the history of his or her people? A house rests upon a foundation, but the foundation is in turn supported by the earth beneath, as perhaps by bedrock. The foundation of the church's foundation is a certain historical collectivity with its enormously diverse societal ways, its politics, its fortunes, its faith, its lapses from faith. This foundation-of-the-foundation is Jewishness, which involves historical peopleness (*laos*), a laic reality.

The broad foundations of the Christian tale come to focus in a dialectic between Jesus of Nazareth and the people from whom he originated and to whom he ministered. And if it is so that the Covenant between God and her people remains unbroken—"How can I give you up, O Ephraim!" (Hos. 11:8a)—then the Christian church is called to pledge itself, *morally speaking*, to the truth of that Covenant. For at stake is nothing less than the church's own relation to God as a hoped-for part of the Covenant. Catholics and Protestants have been learning anew—so writes David Tracy—"how Jewish a religion Christianity finally is."[10]

The all-crucial reason why the Christian reaffirmation of Israel and Jewishness will mean a return into history is that the reality of Jewishness is forever breaking out of religiousness into the world. It is in this way that the religion called Christianity may itself be, paradoxically, carried beyond "pure" religiosity. In and through a historicist Israel the Christian church may be empowered to carry out its worldly obligations and to be saved from falling into otherworldly spirituality. For the Jewish *laos* is wholly "secular" in an all-decisive respect: a people wholly of the world (*saeculum*) is present among us. The Jewish phenomenon is epitomized in James Parkes's characterization of the Jewish people as a *natural community.*[11] Much contemporary liberation thinking has so far failed to develop essential links with this historical foundation and root of Christianity. A consequence is an inability to grasp the mutuality of citizenship between Christians and the Jewish people.

Jürgen Moltmann has criticized the churchly pretension of attempting, through the device of impartiality, to realize a universalist potential: "Only in and through the dialectic of taking sides does the universalism of the Crucified become a reality in this world. The phony universalism of the church is something very different. It is a premature and untimely anticipation of the *Kingdom* of God."[12] The "taking of sides" with Israel constitutes a discrete, historical application of a fundamental principle of liberation theology. However, this particular commitment means not alone self-transcendence but also self-fulfillment. Through love of the neighbor who is not a Christian neighbor, the ideological taint of Christian self-concentration is fought. But at the same time, Christians are fulfilling themselves through returning to their own ancestral home and family. (Here is involved the ultimate foundation of Christian unity.)

To counsel a Christian return into history is to speak *selectively, normatively,* and *critically.* We should never be able to reappropriate "a total past." But we can reaffirm the foundational unity of certain aspects of the Jewish-Christian tradition (a primarily selective element), the historicalness of biblical faith (a primarily normative element), and a way of thinking that ventures to call upon history to judge history and thereby to judge itself (a primarily critical element). Historicalness is an attitude to history that seeks out resources for living; it implies anything but a fulfilled or static system. Indeed, it may well be our responsibility to utilize one or more events of post-biblical history as instruments for assessing, and perhaps even casting aside, events of earlier history. This is not out of accord with the Christian teaching that the Holy Spirit—"the finger of God with which divinity touches history"[13]—may guide us into new apprehensions of truth and responsibility. "The task of contemporary Christian theology," writes David Tracy, "demands the critical correlation of the meaning and truth of the interpreted Christian fact (including therefore the texts, symbols, witnesses and traditions of the past and pre-

sent) and the meaning and truth of the interpreted contemporary situation."
A fundamental thrust here is the ongoing relevance and value of tradition,
yet in ways that offset the dogged tyrannies of tradition. Historicalness encompasses, in Uriel Tal's exposition, on the one hand "a means of selecting
the essential from the historical continuum, thus strengthening the continuity of tradition under changing traditions," and on the other hand "a critical
factor revealing the historical needs which tradition aims to fill, thus relativ-
izing that tradition."[14]

A moral and theological recourse to the history and reality of Israel is not
to be understood in apologetic terms. There is no attempt to "prove" the
objective "truth" of something. And there is no necessarily adverse criticism
of human beings who move in an alternative direction. We are grappling with
the question of existential history. Yet there is a common challenge: how to
realize a third way to knowledge and truth (beyond sheer subjectivism and
sheer objectivism). In the concentration camp Viktor Frankl was kept from a
breakdown and from death by thinking constantly of his wife. Frankl made
no claim of having *the* truth. But he was also kept from the despair of having
no truth. Here is an entirely new reality. To respond to Frankl: There is no
question of either coveting his wife or of rejecting the healing power of his
wife for him. Instead, the man who is blessed with a wife can say to Frankl:
"Yes, I understand what you are telling me. My wife brings me wholeness in
essentially the way that your wife has done for you. I am granted human liberation through the history, through the very presence of this woman." So
too with the covenantal marriage of the Christian community and Israel.
Within none of the liberation movements we have made reference to is
there total emancipation from treating the Jewish people as the church's historic "other." In authentic liberation all this is changed. The partner is no
longer "the other" but becomes the one through whose historical presence
the church of "the teaching of contempt"[15] for Jews is delivered from its
moral perdition. Herein is found the power of a third way to knowledge and
truth, the way of We-Thou, the way of living history.

To sum up: We ask, "What is happening in the world?" and then we ask, Is
there a "fitting response to what is happening?"[16] The return into history, an
inexorable but thankfully received consequence of any genuine acceptance
of historicalness, means the quest for a distinctive, selective history that
may help recapture meaning and nurture responsibility within human life.
With aid from this quest, the Christian church and its adherents are helped
to assess and to revitalize their own historical condition, to the end of meeting their moral obligations and for the sake of a yearned-for redemption. A
fitting and viable Christian "choice" directs itself to the abiding history of
Israel. The "choice" is not a new one (hence the inverted commas). It consists in an existential reaffirmation of a very old choice. "For where you go I
will go ... your people shall be my people" (Ruth 1:16). Hence, neither is
the choice a radical one. Yet in another respect it has to be radical, because

of the separations of almost two thousand years. It is radical in the original sense of a return to roots or origins (*radix*, root), which means that it is conservative as well. But it can never be idealist or utopian. Perhaps all that is necessary to offset any perfectionist temptations here is to remember the continuing history of Jewish male chauvinism, within the country of Israel as outside it. Through the Christian "choice" of Israel in all of Israel's ongoing historicalness, the church today may meet constructively the counsel of Choan-Seng Song, as also that of Dietrich Bonhoeffer. In such a way the church can live with the necessary exigencies of historical life, as at the same time it moves to transcend its own self-obsessions and idolatries. For Christianity, Israel constitutes, in one aspect, "the world." But yet, in Israel as traditional wrestler with God the church's own life and meaning are present. Herein is focused a fundamental challenge for contemporary Christianity. Within and through this challenge the church's participation in historical-secular reality is granted preeminent, concrete form. Here is an essential history-secularity that acts permanently to transform faith. All together, the church is thus brought to honor the inseparability of religion, history, morality, and politics.

It is fitting, therefore, that the title and contents of Professor Fackenheim's work *The Jewish Return into History* should have helped fashion my own expressions from the Christian side, "the return into historicalness" and "the return into history."

III

The beginnings of a new Christian reattestation of Israel extend back a half century or more. Much of the original impetus lay in an acknowledgment that antisemitism is a chronic disease within the life of the church. Today the Christian "return to Israel" crosses denominational, confessional, and national boundaries.

An exemplar. The Christian return into history through a return to the independent reality and meaning of Israel is embodied in Nes Ammim (lit., "miracle of the peoples"), an international Christian cooperative settlement of upwards of 150 inhabitants in Israel. Almost a third of the residents are children. Nes Ammim is located in the coastal plain of Asher between Acre and Nahariya, on land purchased from a Druse sheikh. Started in 1962 by European Protestants, the settlement is mainly constituted of Dutch Christians. It identifies itself as a sign of the collective solidarity of the churches within different countries. The single motivating principle of these people is "lived solidarity with the people and State of Israel." In the words of Johan Pilon, a physician and founder of Nes Ammim, " 'solidarity' here involves a world of meaning, which is seen throughout both the Old Testament and the New Testament. It connotes a basic spiritual unity—rediscovered in our time—after a history of nearly two thousand years, during which period the gentile church wrongfully came to believe that it was not only the branch, but the tree and roots as well."

This special act of returning into history is bound up, critically and paradoxically, with the long history of Christianity. Thus, in explaining the motivation behind their effort the people of Nes Ammim list "a few points from church history": an Easter sermon by Bishop Melito of Sardis (ca. 190) accusing "the Jews" of deicide, a term that "has echoed through history and caused many murders of Jews"; the slaughter of Jews in the Crusades, including driving the Jews of Jerusalem into the synagogue and burning them; death at the stake for Jews in Spain at the hands of the Inquisition; Martin Luther's demand to set fire to synagogues and expel "the Jews"; and the killing of six million Jews in Nazi-dominated Europe, "a civilization shaped by centuries of Christianity." The historical listing ends: "In 1948, after this hell, the resurrection broke through; or, in Jewish terms, another Exodus from the house of slavery took place. But on the very day of its rebirth, the new state was attacked by all the Arab countries. Since that date, Israel has fought four wars for her existence. And in our time she is more and more pushed into isolation and driven into a ghetto, after Zionism was equated with racism by the United Nations Assembly (November 1975). The anti-Zionism of today shows a dangerous affinity to antisemitism."

The people of Nes Ammim explain that they came to the country of Israel not to say something but to do something. "Everything that can be said, or must be said, finds its natural base in this 'life as it is lived' (*gelebtes Leben*)." Human solidarity means nothing until it takes "a concrete form." Dedicated to fostering the life of Israel through capital investment, economic activity, and technical know-how, Nes Ammim engages in the cultivation and sale of roses and avocados, including foreign sales, and more recently in the production of customized staircases (constructed from wood imported from Africa). The policy of Nes Ammim is to develop forms of business enterprise that can subsequently be turned over to Israelis, thus advancing the principle of Christian diaconal service. Much of the work is non-profit. (Many young Christian volunteers come from different countries, including the United States, on work-and-study programs.) The traditional church policy of missionary effort among Jews (*Judenmission*) is steadfastly fought here. The Nazis decreed the annihilation of the Jewish people in *eine körperliche Endlösung* (physical Final Solution). A Christian missionary stance would mean *eine geistliche Endlösung*, a spiritual Final Solution, with equally grave and immoral consequences. For body and spirit are inseparable. In truth, it is through the Jewish people that Christians may "participate in the spiritual wealth of Israel."[17] The fundamental Christian attitude to Jews must be one of indebtedness and gratitude.

Under the aegis of the manufacture of wooden staircases in *this* time and *this* place the faith of the church is enabled to undergo historical transformation. Here is where the action is. But more is involved than the reconciliation of Christians and Jews. At Nes Ammim and under its auspices, Jews and Arabs (including Muslims) meet in free and open encounter.

IV

Among contemporary eighth people within the Christian and Jewish communities, three historical realities stand out and are receiving a great deal of attention: the Holocaust (HaShoah, the Destruction); the re-emergence of the Jewish people from powerlessness; and the rise and influence of religious and cultural pluralism. Each of these is given varying measures of attention in the following pages, in brief and selected ways. In the present generation Christians may be especially bonded to the Jewish people through two historic events, the Shoah and the restoration of the State of Israel.

The tremendum. This is Arthur A. Cohen's expression for the Holocaust. The term Holocaust refers exclusively and equally to two realities: the murders by German Nazis and others of some 5.8 million European Jews, of which some 1.5 million were children; and the intended and planned annihilation of the Jewish people as a whole. The Shoah is thus at once *fact* and *intentionality*, the latter referring to the resolve to rid the world of every Jew.

The existential-historical singularity of the Shoah for the Jewish people hardly requires elaboration. What about the singularity of this event for the non-Jewish world and especially the Christian world? Increasing numbers of Christian thinkers and churchpersons in North America, Germany, and elsewhere are apprehending the Holocaust as a world-determining event within Christian reality itself.[18] This is exemplified by the American Catholic theologian David Tracy:

> The post-Rosenzweig Jewish "return into history" must be matched, on the Catholic side, with a Catholic return into history. . . . Any purely realized eschatology (including those informing purely incarnationalist theologies) can maintain itself only at the price of ignoring two central realities: first, the clear presence of the eschatological "not yet" in the New Testament itself, and second, the stark negativity of the radical not yet in our age disclosed in all its horror by the Holocaust.[19]

> . . . To think theologically in a post-Holocaust situation is to live and think historically. . . . To think historically . . . is to develop a hermeneutics of suspicion focussed upon the illusions and the not-so-innocent theories of both ourselves and our predecessors. Only through such radical suspicion is retrieval of any tradition possible. . . .
> When even those Christian theologians most committed to thinking in relationship to the frightening history of our age (especially most liberation and political theologians) ignore both the Holocaust and the history of Christian anti-Semitism, something is profoundly awry. When the subject of the tremendum becomes a subject only discussed in the context of the "Jew-

ish-Christian dialogue," then the subject is quietly trivialized by Christian
theologians as an inner-Christian theological challenge. No less than for
Jewish theology does the *tremendum* and the caesura demand new Christian
theological reflection. Our classic and our contemporary theodicies are now
speechless. Our serious theological reflections on the reality of God must
now occur within the uncanny realm of a recognition of the *tremendum*.[20]

The American Protestant historian Franklin H. Littell characterizes the Holocaust as "the major event in recent church history."[21] What are the grounds
of this characterization? For one thing, the Jewish people and Judaism stand
as the foundations of the Christian faith. Their God is adopted as the Christian God. And had Jesus of Nazareth been "available," he would have been
sent to a death camp—simply because he was one of "those Jews." Second,
at issue in the *Shoah* is the moral credibility of a Christian faith that could
contribute so powerfully and so culpably to the unparalleled suffering of a
specific collectivity of human beings: the Jewish people. The vast bulk of the
victimizers within and beyond Germany were themselves Christians. There
is no coincidence in the fact that the people whom the Nazis identified as
the Evil of the world had long since been identified in Christendom as the
devil's special agents. However numerous and complex were the causes that
gave rise to Nazism, and however strong its anti-Christian interests, Nazism
carried forward, and gave practical implementation to, the anti-Jewish ideology and praxis of Christianity. As the Christian theologian Helmut Gollwitzer
of the Free University of Berlin observes, "the so-called absoluteness of
Christianity together with the specific form it assumed in medieval sacra-
mental piety" was eventually to spell the doom of the Jews of Europe.[22] All
in all, the Holocaust poses the most fundamental questions of moral, theological, and psychological motivation and causation. (To put the two foregoing points together, the dread thought is hard to dispel that the ongoing
wish of Christians to rid themselves of the moral and spiritual demands of
Jesus is, through the psychomoral mechanism of displacement, targeted
ever and again upon Jesus' own people.) However, at the level of final deci-
siveness, the *Shoah* is a Christian event because of the church's participation
in the reality of Israel. What happens to Jews happens to Christians. It is thus
fitting that each year Yom HaShoah observances now take place in large numbers of American churches. The past is made present for the Christian community.

The present stage of our exposition will focus upon the controversial and
currently lively question of the *Shoah* as transcending event.

In applying to the Holocaust the concept *tremendum*, Arthur Cohen is striving to "think the unthinkable," to speak meaningfully of something that
makes a mockery of all meaning.[23] Can there be "demystification" of such a
phenomenon? *Unless some resolute effort is made in the direction of demystification, it
appears impossible for us to construe the Holocaust as a faith-transforming event and as a*

potential impetus to moral regeneration. As Emil L. Fackenheim points out, only when historical events "are assimilated by the historical consciousness of succeeding generations are they capable of transforming the future." In this way such events "become historical in the deeper sense."[24]

It is proposed in chapter ten that by virtue of a concentration upon extraordinary happenings and their meaning, the form of historicism represented in the present volume goes beyond Lockean rationalism. To repeat part of the wording in that chapter, historicism "speaks from the standpoint of a faith that is according to history and above history, though not contrary to history. There is, nevertheless, a final link between reason and history. I refer to the dimension of transcending reason, which not only examines reason itself but responds creatively and sometimes ecstatically to transcending events."

The above passage contains the seed of a possible interpretation of, and response to, the *Shoah*. But the word "ecstatically" demands clarification. The Holocaust meant anything but "rapture"—except perhaps, and diabolically, to the victimizers. Derivationally, the word "ecstasy" is comprised of "displacement": it is a matter of being driven "outside ourselves" or even of being "beside ourselves" (as in certain kinds of madness). Thus, the intended connotation here has nothing to do with joy or enjoyment; on the contrary, an ecstatic condition may derive from a confrontation with horror. Transcending events can be apprehended by reason (as well as by faith) and certainly in ways that are not "contrary to" history. However, such events drive us "outside ourselves." In this respect they are transrational, above mundane history.

To Yehuda Bauer, a historian of the Holocaust, there is a widespread, current tendency to mystify the *Shoah*, and this smacks of obscurantism.[25] He argues against the mystification of the event. "If what happened to the Jews was unique, then it took place outside of history and it becomes a mysterious event, an upside-down miracle, so to speak, an event of religious significance in the sense that it is not man-made as that term is normally understood." On the other hand, Bauer is quite sensitive to the historical and moral failure, or refusal, to face up to the Holocaust as it actually occurred. He asks, If that event is not at all unique, where then are its parallels or precedents?[26] To turn one's back upon the singularity of the *Shoah* is to violate the integrity of the event and to assault implicitly the dignity of its victims. But to identify the Holocaust as absolutely inexplicable and incredible may have, paradoxically, these very same consequences.

In the interests of responsible demystification, let us try to bring the category of transcending event to bear upon improper mystification. By coming to terms with different understandings of "uniqueness," we may seek to cope with the enigma of the *Shoah*'s uniqueness.

It was Wilhelm Windelband who first applied the terms "nomothetic" and "idiographic" to two modes of epistemological activity within the human mind. In nomothesis, attention is directed to the generality of things and to what they have in common. Upon that foundation the abstractive and symbolist asseverations of certain dominant forms of science are put forth today. In idiography, by contrast, stress falls upon the distinctiveness of the individual happening and the individual case. Quantitative considerations are supplemented and sometimes replaced by qualitative ones.[27]

The practical question before us is associated with the idiographic extremities of the continuum of nomothesis-idiography. Three discrete meanings of uniqueness are suggested, the sequence of which drives us farther and farther into particularity and incomparability: ordinary uniqueness, unique uniqueness, and transcending uniqueness.

(1) In opposition to our memorable high-school indoctrination with the idea that "history repeats itself," it is apparent that all historical events are unique, by which is meant simply that they are qualitatively different from each other. The philosophic grounding for this practical observation derives empirically from the shifting conditions of the spatio-temporal flux and is, accordingly, twofold: Succeeding events must perforce occupy physical locales that are alternative to those that earlier events have occupied; and succeeding events take place within temporal frames of reference that are alternative to those that previous events involved.

From within this initial and very prosaic point of view, the unqualified proposition that the Holocaust is a unique event is judged to be at best a truism and at worst an excrescence. A like judgment applies to the proposition that the Holocaust could occur another time—as long as that proposition is left similarly unqualified.

(2) Since all happenings within space-time bear unique marks, the concept of uniqueness has to be elaborated and qualified if we are to grasp the fabric of uniqueness in its manifoldness. As the mind reviews the dramas of human history and seeks after the meaning of that history, it quickly resorts to the continuum of insignificance/significance. The mind freely concludes that while many happenings appear to be more or less trivial, others are possessed of singular importance and may be characterized as, in truth, "epoch-making": they *make* the epoch in which they transpire. We find ourselves captivated and even dominated by the great watersheds of history. Some of these epochal events are constructive while others are catastrophic, but all are regarded as decisive within the story of the human race.

That the Holocaust of the Jews is a uniquely unique event scarcely requires argument. It is noteworthy that for all his polemic "against mystification," Professor Bauer insists upon the need to distinguish "Holocaust" and "genocide":

> Clearly, what was happening to quite a number of peoples in Nazi Europe was genocide: their institutions of learning closed, their political leadership decimated, their language and national .culture discarded, their churches

eliminated from a free exercise of their functions, their wealth despoiled, and subjected to killings of groups and individuals as the Nazis pleased. . . . The difference between that and the Holocaust lies in the difference between forcible, even murderous, denationalization, and wholesale, total murder of every one of the members of a community. Contrary to legend, there never was a Nazi policy to apply the measures used against the Jews to other national communities. . . . [There] may be no difference between Holocaust and genocide for the victim of either. But there are gradations of evil, unfortunately. Holocaust was the policy of the total, sacral Nazi act of mass murder of all Jews they could lay hands on. Genocide was horrible enough, but it did not entail *total* murder if only because the subject peoples were needed as slaves. They were indeed, "subhumans" in Nazi terminology. The Jews were not human at all.

The Holocaust was an unprecedented event. "[For] the first time in history a sentence of death had been pronounced on anyone guilty of having been born, and born of certain parents. . . . This Nazi decision was based on an ideology in which the Jew was defined as the anti-race, . . . as that mixture of characteristics that could be described, in Nazi terms, as an absolute evil." Accordingly, Nazi policy toward Jews could contrast sharply with Nazi policy toward the Gypsies, as it did with the earlier Turkish slaughter of the Armenians. Significantly, Bauer emphasizes that the failure to recognize that the Jewish situation was unique is itself an instance of the unhappy mystification of history—equally as mystifying and unfortunate as the assertion that the Holocaust is inexplicable or that it bears no parallels at all to other murderous events.[28]

(3) Nomothetic science may not desire to concern itself with uniquely unique events, or it may wish, for the sake of its own operations and purposes, to abstract from the realm of the uniquely unique those elements or characteristics that are ostensibly shared by more than single events. But there is nothing within nomothetic science to rule out a priori the actuality of uniquely unique events or data. The scientist and the historian are able to live under a common roof without going at one another's throats. However, with our third eventuality, a certain conflict appears unavoidable within the community of disciplined thought.

Let us turn our eyes to just one of many scenes within the camps of death. In Auschwitz little Hungarian Jewish children saw with their own eyes the murders by fire of other children, and they knew that they themselves would shortly be burned alive. This evil is more terrible than other evils.[29] But much of the terror in it is that it partakes of absolute universality: *The intention of the Holocaust is that there is never to be another Jewish child.*

When on May 5, 1985, the president of the United States *determined* to go to Bitburg, Western Germany, and honor, among others, Nazi SS murderers of Jews—claiming that the killers had long since "met the Supreme Judge of right and wrong"[30]—he was striving to annihilate the historical-moral singularity of the Holocaust. He was seeking to escape from, indeed to gain control over, the truth of history. The massive opposition to his act—an opposition involving untold numbers of non-Jews—reflects a widespread recognition of the absolute singularity of the *Shoah*. Neither theology nor faith nor human praxis can escape judgment by the truth. For history is not helpless: it will not forget this deed of the American president. It knows too well that murderers are not victims, and victims are not murderers.

The concept of transcending uniqueness refers to events that are received as essentially different from not only ordinary uniqueness but even unique uniqueness. With transcending uniqueness the quality of difference raises itself to the level of absoluteness. ("Absoluteness" does not necessarily rule out subsequent, absolute events.) One way to situate the qualitative shift to transcending uniqueness is to speak of a radical leap from objectness to subjectness,* a total existential crisis and involvement for the party who makes one or another affirmation of transcending uniqueness. This extraordinary about-face is accompanied by a marked transformation in modes of language.

Now, in place of relatively calm, descriptive references to the merely unprecedented character of the Holocaust or to its singularly catastrophic nature, the witness to transcending uniqueness is heard to testify that this event is beyond belief. The witness asks, How could there ever be such an event as this one? Often this person will plead that the only really sensible response to the Holocaust is a kind of holy, or unholy, awe and even a consuming silence. Many times it is the survivors of the Holocaust who have reacted in this way (cf. the works of Elie Wiesel). But sometimes nonsurvivors are caught up in the same spirit, taking into themselves the very abyss of the *Shoah*. Thus, Dalton Trumbo, the well-known writer of screenplays, tried for no less than sixteen years to create a novel on the Holocaust and died with the work yet unfinished. A non-Jew, Trumbo was conscience-stricken and overwhelmed by the ultimate horror and incomprehensibleness of the Holocaust.[31]

The condition now is not the simple unique uniqueness of the Jew as victim but rather the question of how could it be that, alone among all the inhabitants of this planet, the Jew is singled out for obliteration. *For no one else is to be totally obliterated.* The German Nazis' decree was *die Endlösung der Judenfrage*, the *Final* Solution of the Jewish question. In these few short words the transcending uniqueness of the Holocaust-event is conveyed. For there is something in this event that marks it off as transcending, even when it is placed, as it can be, within the dreadful company of other great catastrophes

---

*I resort to the terms "objectness" and "subjectness" instead of the more traditional "objectivity" and "subjectivity" in order to offset the usual connotations of "arbitrariness" or "illusoriness" or "personal taste" within the popular-academic usage of "subjectivity." The proponent of transcending uniqueness will simply deny that he has sold objective (real) truth for the pottage of mere whim or individual preference.

and genocides of human history. The transcending quality of the *Shoah* rests upon the special identity of its victims. *Only the Jew, only the Jew, only the Jew.* By this is obviously not meant that only Jews were victims, for that is not true. Very many non-Jews were destroyed. But *any playing of a numbers game has nothing to do with the Holocaust.* As Elie Wiesel has said, not all victims were Jews, but yet all Jews were victims. Herein lies the infinite qualitative difference. Of no other people was it ever decreed that its *being* demands *nonbeing.* This is the transcending uniqueness of the *Shoah. Only the Jew. Only here is only all, and all only.* As God is transcending in uniqueness, so too is the Holocaust.

The response that finds in the *Shoah* a transcendent, crushing mystery points to the dimension of the numinous, as described by Rudolf Otto in *Das Heilige.* That mental/spiritual state called the numinous by Otto presents itself as *ganz andere,* wholly other, a condition absolutely *sui generis* and incomparable, whereby the human being finds himself utterly abashed. There is a feeling of terror before an awe-inspiring mystery, but a mystery that also fascinates infinitely. The difference between an affirmation of unique uniqueness and an affirmation of transcending uniqueness is that the latter revolutionizes the being and meaning of human lives. Those lives will never be the same again.

V

We are obliged to do what we can to demystify the mystery of the *Shoah* while yet avoiding the sacrilege of despoiling the mystery itself. Considerations of space preclude a full, continuing attempt to meet the question of how the concept of transcending uniqueness may meet the canons of empirical and rational comparison and discourse. I shall make brief reference to just one factor of marked relevance, the relation of historic antisemitism and the *Shoah.* (A number of additional considerations are adduceable.)[32]

The connection of the Holocaust to the long history of antisemitism—a linkage that appears self-evident—suggests that nomothesis and idiography may be construed dialectically, each side presupposing and driving toward the other. In the nomothetic method, particular realities or events are understood through being assigned to a more comprehensive category. In the present instance "Holocaust" may be placed, all too obviously, within the larger category "antisemitism." But this very act impels us in the direction of the extremities of idiography because antisemitism, as it has manifested itself within the whole history of the West, is itself a markedly unique phenomenon. This phenomenon is radically discontinous with ordinary forms of human "prejudice," such as in race and religion, forms that have their occasions and their locales and then atrophy or are superseded. Antisemitism is the one perennial malady of its kind within the history of the Western world, and it is spread universally within the entire geography of the West but yet also beyond the West. Distinctively, it is pervasive in time as in space.

Thus may the peculiar generality of antisemitism be wedded to the peculiar particularity of the Holocaust.

In concluding this fragmentary exposition in response to the *tremendum*, we may remind ourselves that moral obligation can fill the role of arousing convictions of absoluteness respecting a given event even should the event itself fail to manage to attain authentic philosophic categorization as something transcendently unique.

Reference may be made to Gertrude Stein's famous sentence, "Rose is a rose is a rose is a rose." We are given three choices. One is to subject all roses to an abstract fate, in good nomothetic fashion. Second, we may select out one rose from all other roses and concentrate upon its unique uniqueness within time and space. But, third, we may establish a moral-existential relation with *this* rose, perhaps determining to do what we can to fight against the unhappy transitoriness of so fragile and beautiful a thing. Thus, if fortunate enough to be blessed with requisite talent, we may resolve to embody for others the being of this rose by means of artistic representation so that, in a sense, the rose will not have to die. The tie between moral obligation and the philosophic quest appears at this third level of choice: this rose differs transcendently from all other roses because of our human relationship to it. We yearn that it not become a victim.

The singularity of the *Shoah* is measured by the specific identity of its victims. It is from within the context of historic and abiding Jewish victimization that the moral peculiarity and challenge of the Holocaust may be said to emerge. This state of affairs itself exemplifies the dialectical character of nomothesis-idiography: "Holocaust" is here assimilated to the more general concept "Jewish victimization." Moral claims do not take form apart from specific historical conditions and milieux. The Jew has been the traditional enemy and scapegoat of Christendom and, subsequently, of the secularizing West. Even the international readiness after World War II to sanction a land of refuge for the miserable remnant of the Jews of Europe cannot be comprehended apart from the social psychology of victimization. And the widespread and concerted opposition to Israel over some years, not excepting the identical parties that supported the United Nations' partition of part of Palestine, bespeaks an ongoing refusal to tolerate Jews and to have compassion for them in any place other than that of victim or underdog.

The challenge of the *Shoah* is addressed concretely to the Christian and Western worlds, although this is hardly to exclude the non-Western world from all blame. The singular relation that Christians and other Gentiles have to Jews, a psychomoral relation of victor to victim, takes us beyond many forms of unique uniqueness, including its most epochal forms. Those who continue to identify themselves with the Christian community are confronted by certain transcendent questions, questions of absolute moral import: "Am I my brother's keeper? I can, to be sure, renounce my place in and my allegiance to the Christian community. But if I choose to remain within that community, do I not thereby take upon myself, in tacit yet positive and ineluctable ways, the burden of the church's guilt for the antisemitism that helped make the Holocaust inevitable? And am I not then faced with the obligation to engage in such thinking and action as will help purge away that guilt?" (It is absurd to maintain that Christianity was the only cause of Nazism and the Holocaust. But this does nothing to lessen Christian culpability.)

The historic relationship that the Christian church bears to the Jewish community demands a revolution within those Christian doctrines that are still promulgated today, most especially a critical transformation in teachings that are traceable directly to the many anti-Jewish elements in the church's prevailing authority for faith, the New Testament.[33] In the struggle against "the ugliest of all Christian crimes—our crime against the Jews," and to the end of Christian transformation, there must be, says John B. Cobb, Jr., a re-Judaization of Christianity.[34]

Were we to seek to characterize the Holocaust as transcendingly unique in any objective, impersonal sense, mystification would certainly enter as a fault. My hope is that by keeping ourselves free from objectiveness and impersonalism, we may help counteract such mystification as we yet continue to observe the Holocaust's transcending mystery. The transcending uniqueness of the Shoah is made manifest in an existential way by virtue of the special relation that many human beings have to that event. (A woman I know, formerly a Christian, says that she became a Jew to replace one of the six million. She lives now in Israel.) The Shoah ruptures history but does not destroy it: we confront now a ruptured history.[35] It is at this place that a social ethic for the post-Holocaust era converges upon a sociology of knowledge applied to the Holocaust. Herein lies the uniqueness of the Shoah, in an existentially absolute sense, for our time.

In chapter thirteen we further pursue the possible transformational implications of the Shoah for faith and morality. The other two events/processes we shall consider in the present chapter are interpretable as historical-moral reactions to the kind of Christian triumphalism that issued in the Holocaust—the one, by virtue of a specific movement of human liberation; the other—religio-cultural pluralism—by virtue of special conditions and ideological influences within countries that were, paradoxically, products of Christian culture.

VI

The Christian church and the movement of Jewish liberation. In our world, there is no Jewish survival apart from Jewish power.[36] In this respect, Jewish liberation simply typifies any and all forms and necessities of human liberation. (We have already argued that historical events do not vindicate religious faith; if valid, that reasoning must apply to the restoration of a sovereign Israel.)

How may eighth people and others respond to Zionism, the human liberation movement of Jews, and to its consequence, the twentieth-century State of Israel? James Cone asks: "Why is it that the idea of *liberation* (inseparable from the biblical view of revelation) is conspicuously absent among theological discussions about the knowledge of God?"[37] In part, Cone's question has over the years been met constructively; human liberation is by no means as absent today from the theology of the knowledge of God as it used to be. Yet the same is hardly the case respecting a parallel condition: Why is it that the liberation of the Jewish people (inseparable from the biblical outlook) remains conspicuously absent among many Christian theological-ethical discussions about the *life* of the God of Israel?

What does it mean to speak of "a secular Christian ethic of Israel"?[38] The question of a responsible Christian theology of politics applied to Israel is a special case of the effort to relate faith and history, to link religious conviction and the events of time and place. Part of the Christian failure here is traceable to a recidivist splitting of the sacred and secular realms. Another part of the failure is associated with the eclipse of the historical Jesus. We can envision a twentieth-century Jesus of Nazareth, somehow spared the hell of Belzec or Sobibor, as a faithful citizen of the State of Israel, committed to justice for its people and resistance to its enemies (cf. chap. 4).

One point of departure for addressing the issue of a Christian ethic for empirical Israel is to make reference to two widely divergent Christian views that nevertheless together threaten the political integrity of Israel, the one by questioning her legitimacy in principle, the other by supporting her on grounds that may be either dubious or indefensible. However, both these positions sustain a certain plausibility and appeal.

There is, first, the phenomenon of "liberal"-universalism. I use quotation marks to avoid confusion with genuine forms of liberalism. Within authentic liberalism Jewry possesses the entire right to make its own decisions respecting what Jewishness is to mean. But "liberal"-universalism visits special demands upon Jews. Christian representatives of the "liberal"-universalist viewpoint set the universalist possibilities of faith in hearty judgment upon the alleged temptations and evils of Jewish particularity. The modern roots of this outlook are traceable to the Enlightenment, entailing a fervent opposition to "nationalism" through denominating "humanity" as a center of value. "Nationalism" becomes the single, most formidable enemy of universal, "spiritual" norms. National identity and loyalty are identified as barriers to ideal human relationships and goals. A truly enlightened people of God will transcend all such barriers.

The attraction of this position lies in the honor it gives to the anti-parochial reaches of human moral endeavor. In point of fact, the modern history of Judaism itself has not been wholly devoid of "liberal"-universalist ideology. Thus, in one period the Reform movement was forcefully anti-Zionist, specifically on the ground that the Jewish people are emancipated, or ought to be, from all nationalist proclivities. Jewish laic particularity was here subverted in principle. Jewishness was assimilated to a gestalt of human religiousness: Jewish identity was reduced to adherence to the religion called Judaism. It was only through bitter, real-life experience at the hands of antisemites and non-Jews hostile to Zionism that the Reform leadership was driven back to the truth that there is much more to Jewishness than religiousness, and indeed that universalistic moral and spiritual norms, when not fleshed out via the particularities of existence, comprise a menace to human life itself. "Citizens of the world" are inevitably subversive of legitimate human-collective needs and values. Particularity is, in reality, the *sine qua non* of universality. The alternative is fascist and totalitarian homogeneity, wherein the discrete elements that make up human collectivities are subjugated and even destroyed for the sake of the "whole." The very survival of the religion of Judaism, a faith that boasts many universalist aspects, is paradoxically threatened whenever provision is lacking for the secular-laic identity of Jews. The Jewish community in its entirety has long since repudiated false universalism.

Within the Christian camp, forms of anti-Zionism and anti-Israelism that derive from "liberal" sources have behind them an influential tradition. According to that tradition, the great moral heritage of the biblical prophets is held to be violated whenever and wherever "nationalism" becomes dominant. No form of idolatry is more serious or more destructive than that stemming from nationalistic pretensions. However, it is essential to keep before us that while Christian "liberal"-universalism views itself as emancipated from narrowness of interest, it in fact exhibits the antithesis of its own moral norm. For when it is confronted by the actual conflicts of human life, the universalist norm is very often revealed as mere ideology (in the Christian realist and Marxist sense): moral ideas and ideals are taken captive by collective self-interest. In a great many cases it is the custodians of regnant power who are preaching to the afflicted the evils of nationalism. Such counsel becomes, in effect, an instrumentality for depriving the oppressed of justice.

If "liberal"-universalism is readily placed in the service of less-than-universal causes, its primary import in the present context is its betrayal of Jews as a historical, particular people. Yet we cannot neglect the element of truth within the warnings of "liberal"-universalists against nationalist idolatries.

To turn to a second and quite discrepant position respecting Israel within Christian circles, there is a point of view that, at first blush, appears to have consequences quite different from those of "liberal"-universalism. It arises from within the Christian right. Now, in place of criticism or even outright rejection of the Jewish national cause, we hear expressions of sympathy for and solidarity with Israel. The overall category here is Christian Zionism.

Christian Zionists as a group are distinguished by an insistence that the return of the Jewish people to Zion is to be comprehended in positive theological terms. The establishing of the Third Jewish Commonwealth is received as a special work of God, a sublime act constitutive to the story of divine salvation (*Heilsgeschichte*). Beyond this shared assumption there are many varieties and conflicts of conviction. However, two major types predominate: a surrogate religious apologetic for Israel on, confessedly, the latter's own terms; and a subjecting of Jewish historical fortunes to the Christian imperium.

In the one version the will of God is insinuated unqualifiedly into the political process, but without any necessary insistence upon Christian or Christological sanctions. Some evangelicals and fundamentalists do not seek to qualify Israel's legitimacy through peculiarly Christian demands or dogma. Thus a group called Evangelicals United for Zion has sought "to stimulate real interrelation between the Evangelical Christian and Jewish communities based upon a biblical bond of love for God's land and His people, Israel."[39] Insofar as such people maintain the traditionalist promise that Abraham and his children's children are to inherit Eretz Yisrael,* they naturally incline to sustain the socio-political cause of Israel.

The other form of Christian Zionism is dominated by Christology. The return of the Jewish people to their land is construed instrumentally, in accordance with certain alleged timetables of heaven. The renewal of Israel becomes part of a divinely scheduled preparation for the Parousia, the return of Christ in glory. Thus does Carl F. H. Henry assure a "Conference on Biblical Prophecy" meeting in Jerusalem: "We live already in the last days because of the Resurrection of the Crucified One. The dramatic and unmistakable message of the New Testament is that the very last of those days is soon to break upon us."[40] The restoration of Israel in 1948 is often regarded as proof that the Parousia is imminent. And many times that restoration is held to open the way to, and perhaps even to ensure, the Jewish acceptance of Jesus Christ. In an article in *Eternity* it is held that if God has indeed acted to resettle the sons of Isaac in Eretz Yisrael, the sons of Ishmael, i.e., the Muslims, can scarcely be expected to dislodge them. The writer goes on to attest that although the Jews have not returned to the Land "in faith," tomorrow they will "look upon Him whom they pierced," and the entire nation of Israel "will be converted in a day."[41]

Philip Culbertson evaluates triumphalist Christian Zionism: Israel becomes a tool "to further the reign of Christ, rather like a whore to be used and then discarded when she has serviced her patron."[42] However, a major appeal of Christian Zionism as a whole lies in its refusal to exclude God's

*On this view, the thrust of the Exodus is no mere redemption from slavery but entry into the Land. This is implied hermeneutically in the promise of the Land well before the sojourn in Egypt (Gen. 12:1).

active will from the common life. Further, there may be discernible here a vital judgment against those Christians who either remain indifferent to the collective fate and destiny of Jews or are positively hostile to Zionism and the State of Israel. Christian Zionism's support of Israel constitutes a theological, moral, and practical denial of the pretensions of "liberal"-universalism and its "spiritual" demands. This suggests that on balance Christian Zionism is morally superior to "liberal"-universalism. It is better to be practically (politically) right for relatively wrong reasons than to be practically (politically) wrong for comparably wrong reasons. However, the "liberal"-universalist concentration upon the moral perils in nationalist dedication points, functionally speaking, to serious faults within Christian Zionism. The question is: Can Christian Zionist testimony be allowed to slide into, and take control of, the political domain?

The overall trespass of Christian Zionism is its theologizing of the political order. (Not all Christian Zionists do this.) There are several paradoxical effects, all of which are baneful. The foremost of these is an eroding, however unintended, of Israel's collective integrity. Scattered all through the Christian tradition is the allegation that the fall of Jerusalem in 70 C.E. and the "dispersion" of the Jewish people comprise the judgment of God upon an unbelieving Israel. (In point of truth Jewish communities existed outside Palestine well before the advent of Christianity.) Now along come the Christian Zionists to turn up the opposite side of the identical coin. They proclaim that the contemporary return of Jews to their land is a special sign of God's mercy and even an intimate disclosure of his own singular plans. But the fabricators of God's mercy have joined in the same game played by the historicizers of God's judgment. Both parties misappropriate the events of history. The implication is as ominous as it is obvious: There would be no way to receive Israel's physical destruction tomorrow other than as a sign of God's returning wrath, or at least as the hiding of the divine face. If it is the Lord that gives, it is the Lord that must take away (cf. Job 1:21). This is the sort of predicament we arrange for ourselves when we fancy that the events of history can contribute to or exemplify the truths of faith—in contrast to a more acceptable biblical teaching that the Sovereign of history assigns her own final meanings to the exigencies of time and place.

Another consequence of Christian Zionism is the exacerbating of human strife at the hands of religion. As James M. Wall writes, "the use of religious validation to settle secular conflicts is a misuse of religion and a disservice to politics."[43] One quite logical counter to the claim that Yahweh gave Palestine to the Jewish people is the protestation that Allah has since transferred the Land to his true people, the Muslims, as embodied today in and through the Arab nation. The Muslim rejoinder is not unlike the traditional anti-Jewish affirmation of the Christian church that the "New Covenant" replaces the "Old Covenant." Indeed, a chronologizing theology may have little choice but to award the gold medal to the Muslims (over Christians as well as

Jews)—for having come in last. Last is first. Such theologizing constitutes, of course, a political *reductio ad absurdum*. The expectable or natural reaction to its Muslim version on the part of Israelis has been to *fight*. Yet there is a sense in which the pragmatic-theological and psycho-theological advantage stays with the Muslims, because the Jews simply lack any counterpart to the *jihād* (holy struggle) of the Koran and of subsequent history, including today.

An equally serious consequence of Christian Zionism's assimilating of the political world to the assertions of faith is its paradoxical undermining of the integrity and credibility of the religious order. Authentic religion functions as a pointer to the transcending, mysterious ways of God. "For my thoughts are not your thoughts, neither are your ways my ways, says the Lord" (Isa. 55:8). In Christian Zionism the thoughts and ways of God are massively domesticated, a procedure that is more properly reserved for human life with cats and cows. Various parties, Jewish or Christian, may continue to believe that the establishing of the Third Jewish Commonwealth brings special evidence and assurance of God's grace and perhaps even contains the seeds of ultimate redemption. Such testimony may be granted a hearing as an instance of strictly confessional celebration. I do not question the affirmation of God's presence within the common life. "History transforming faith" rests upon that very presupposition. (In this latter, delimited context, there is no necessary or principled conflict between Christian Zionism and eighth people.) But it is one thing to glimpse, in a wholly existential-historicist way and as through a glass darkly, the hand of God within the happenings of history, and quite something else to mobilize that witness of faith (and hope) for apologetic or polemic purposes, with the ultimate outcome of a theocratizing of political structures. The *Deutsche Christen* of the Nazi era politicized their theology; the Christian Zionists of today theologize their politics. The result is one and the same; the integrity of the religious order is undercut.

The identical effect occurs by virtue of an insistence upon a religiously absolutist rendering of Israel's right-to-be. Once God is fashioned into a weapon of geopolitical claims, the opposition is furnished with an excuse to cry "Idolatry!" And this reaction is not unjustified. The desacralizing of political claims is an ever-present essential of peace among nations.

We see today a move within right-wing Protestantism to honor moral-political obligations, a cause first made vital to some of us through the Christian Social Gospel. But if the evangelical position on the politics of the Middle East is any harbinger, evangelicalism may be better advised to return to its "pure gospel" of personal salvation. Christian Zionism is a transparent instance of how the combining of social action with the dictates of religious absolutism engenders a flawed political theology.

Despite their evident disparity, "liberal"-universalism and Christian Zionism are marked by a shared failure to offer responsible political counsel. For, significantly, it is not alone the Christian right but also the "liberal" left that theologizes the political order—the one by imperializing the particularities of human affairs, the other by nullifying them. The evangelicals fabricate Israel into *a political church*, a theocratic tool. The "liberals" force Jewish identity onto the Procrustean bed of *an apolitical church*, a strictly "spiritual" entity. In both instances the Jewish people are ideologically forbidden to be what they are, a laic reality with all the limited rights of any collectivity of this world. Thus is the integrity of Israel menaced from opposite directions.

VII

Our problem becomes: How are the elements of appeal within the "liberal"-universalist and Christian Zionist positions to be given due heed as at the same time we seek to avoid their temptations and errors? Generally speaking, possible responses to this question may be grounded in a historicist-secular ethic, i.e., an ethic oriented to this world, the human order. As a means to that end, and as a way of further bringing out the reasoning behind the above critiques as well as of mediating between the two positions, I include six points (anything but an exhaustive listing). The necessity of making relative, less-than-ideal moral judgments, with all the perplexities these entail, is present here as everywhere. This is another way of saying that I do not necessarily recommend all these points without qualification. I believe that they merit careful reflection. And when added together, their force is considerable.

(1) The particularity of Israel (as of any nation or country) may be comprehended under the "orders of creation" (*Schöpfungsordnungen*), or at least as "emergency orders" or "orders of necessity" (*Notordnungen*).

Emil Brunner characterizes "the orders" as ways in which the will of God meets us, if only in fragmentary and indirect fashion. The orders encompass the family, economic life and labor, the community of culture, the law, and the nation-state. Helmut Thielicke utilizes the phrase "emergency orders," thus speaking more cautiously than Brunner. The orders offer "physical spheres of existence" that help protect human beings in a fallen world. They are orders of "preservation."[44]

To apply Brunner's reasoning, "liberal"-universalism ranges itself against the divine creation. In opposing Jewish national sovereignty, the "liberals" reject a certain incarnation of the ways of God for human existence. To apply Thielicke's reasoning, every people requires political sovereignty to protect them from the will-to-power of others. This need applies especially to smaller groups. "Liberal"-universalism thus carries a threat to human welfare within our far-from-perfect world. On the other hand, Christian Zionism wrongly concentrates only upon Israel, to the implicit exclusion of a concerned policy respecting other peoples and nations. A linking of the nation-state to the protective authorization of God is not an argument for Israel *qua* Israel; yet, unless we are to fall into a double standard, the right of Jewish sovereignty is apprehended as one instance of a universal right.

(2) Within the real world—the world of political relations—the legitimacy of the State of Israel is a matter of the moral-historical-juridical rights of the Jewish people within the larger area known as Palestine.

The original British Mandate of Palestine extended through present-day Jordan; Israel today encompasses only twenty-five percent of the total area. Objectively speaking, the right of Jews to their land matches, and in many comparisons surpasses, the claims of any sovereignty in the world. Emphasis here falls upon the unbroken character of Jewish residency in the Land for more than three millennia. As James Parkes observes, the real title deeds were written by the "heroic endurance of those who had maintained a Jewish presence in the Land all through the centuries, and in spite of every discouragement."[45] (As Parkes shows, Palestinian Arabs have comparable rights, if not with as lengthy a historical support.[46])

The historical and moral attainments of humankind need not be antithetical to the attested will of God—provided that God is apprehended in humanizing, creative, and providential terms. This principle applies everywhere. Thus, one tenable response to a possible allegation that America really belongs to the Indians and ought to be given back to them is that such a demand does not take into account the "white man's" stewardship of the country over a fair period of time. This is not to ignore elements of false consciousness in the "white man's" claim, nor is it to forget our terrible treatment of Native Americans or the need for continuing acts of justice and restitution in behalf of these people. The state of affairs within Palestine is a comparable one. Israel's stewardship of the land easily approximates that of the United States in North America. This stewardship has been marked by the creating of a democratic social order which contravenes various forms of tyranny, including religio-political forms. Furthermore, in contrast to the fate of Native Americans at the hands of the European invaders, Jews did not displace a local population.[47]

The United Nations' recognition in 1947 of the legitimacy of the Jewish claim was applied, of course, only to a restricted part of a division of the section of Palestine that lies west of the River Jordan, with a Palestinian Arab polity being equally recognized. But the admission of the State of Israel into the United Nations in 1949 (six years before Jordan's admission) was underwritten in total independence of the Arab rejection of the UN vote concerning partition. Significantly, the acknowledgment of Israeli sovereignty was not made at all conditional upon the Arab response to the Plan of Partition. Thus was the traditional Jewish moral-historical claim capped by the juridical factor of unqualified assent by the international community.

This second point may be epitomized via the declaration of a group of Dutch Protestant and Catholic theologians that to separate the Jewish people, in thought or in deed, from the Land of Israel is tantamount to disdaining their integrity as human beings.[48] Authentic "Zionism" from the Christian side may be defined as an insistence by Christians upon the right of Jews to be Zionists.

(3) Arguments from the "orders of creation" and from historical right powerfully support as well the political rights, integrity, and liberation of the Arabs of Palestine.

Lest this seem like a departure from the subject, I should argue that it is irresponsible to contend for or to consider Israeli rights while ignoring Palestinian Arab rights.[49] The lesson of the Holocaust for Jews—powerlessness opens the way to death—is not the private property of the Jewish people. The Arabs of Palestine do well to learn from it, and they have learned from it, not alone with respect to their vis-à-vis with the power-possessing State of Israel but with respect to their oppressed condition in the frame of reference of the surrounding power-possessing Arab world. With the exception of their relatively happy status in Jordan and Israel, the Arabs of Palestine remain pariahs.

Today's lingering tragedy of the Palestinian Arabs was occasioned by the Arab side's rejection of the United Nations' proposal of the partition of Palestine—a proposal that, ironically enough, would today quite meet the yearnings expressed by unnumbered Palestinian Arabs. All that most of these people cry out for is the right to live freely on their own land. They ask no special privileges. As the Peel Commission of 1937 had declared, the overall situation of Palestine clearly involved a "conflict of right with right." It is sometimes contended that because of the refusal of the UN plan, the Palestinian Arabs forfeited their own claim. This argument does not wash, because, among other things, the decision was not sanctioned through any form of plebiscite. However, we do have to concede that the moral validity and political workability of a given proposal of international geopolitical partition is always contingent upon the readiness of each principal party to acknowledge the other's legitimacy. The problematic of such mutuality continues on as a foundational issue of the Arab-Israeli conflict. Finally, the presence of the State of Jordan (which used to call itself Transjordan) is most pertinent. (After Transjordan conquered and annexed the so-called West Bank, it changed to the name Jordan. The annexation was recognized by only two states, Pakistan and Great Britain. The notion that Israel ought to "give back" the "occupied" territory of the "West Bank" thus poses a fundamental issue in international relations. To whom is the territory to be "given back"?) The majority of the population of Jordan (which extends to large parts of traditional Palestine) is Palestinian Arab. Here is the source of the contemporary argument over whether it would be right to approve a "second" Palestinian Arab state.

(4) It is well that we observe the moral relevance and applicability of the liberation principle of "taking sides"—*not*, to be sure, theologically but morally and politically.

The only way that an authentic return into history can take place is through specific moral commitments and deeds. Otherwise, such a "return" is not a real commitment. It remains only an idea, an abstraction, at most an intention. In employing the words "*not*, to be sure, theologically but morally and politically" in conjunction with the taking of sides, I speak in anthropocentric terms. However, I do not mean to exclude the eventuality of God taking sides. That is to say, some liberation theologians and others call upon us to treat the divine praxis as being itself heavily politico-moral in character, and hence as exempt from or beyond such traditional theological charges and worries as idolatry and absolutization. (Interesting query: Can God be licitly idolatrous?) Perhaps this is a place to reintroduce the notion of *kiveyakhol* vis-à-vis God. God may not, *kiveyakhol* (= in a manner of speaking), desire to be subject to the warning edicts that moral theologians are always issuing. It is attested, traditionally speaking, that Israel is, after all, the people of God and that God does not renege on his promises (Gen. 17:13, 19; Lev. 24:8; Ezek. 37:26; etc.). To put it as simply as I am able, God can do as she pleases. (Of course, there is no way around the fact that human beings are the ones expressing such a possibility in behalf of God.)

The meaning here may be clarified with the aid of a reference to James Cone and the black theology of liberation: "If God is not for us and against white people, then he is a murderer, and we had better kill him." We must "reject any conception of God which stifles black self-determination by picturing God as a God of all peoples. Either God is identified with the oppressed to the point that their experience becomes his or he is a God of racism." We recall too a question put by William R. Jones: Is God a white racist?[50]

The parallels are clear and elementary: If God is not for Jews and against those who seek to destroy Jews, he is a murderer. We have to reject any conception of God that stifles Jewish self-determination. Either God is identified with the vilified State of Israel to the point that Israel's experience becomes his or he is an antisemite.

Along the same line, Professor Jones rejects as morally obscene any theodicy of blacks as God's contemporary suffering servant. Such an eventuality would simply turn God into a white racist. On identical moral reasoning, any *theological* demand that the State of Israel comport itself in ways that are morally self-sacrificing or morally superior to other nations turns God into an antisemite—or, to say the same thing in other terminology, into the devil. The traditional theodicy of Israel as the Lord's powerless and suffering servant (cf. Isa. 53) is seen to be evil, particularly in the shadow of the *Shoah*. There is infinite moral difference between the suffering of an individual (ofttimes knowingly or deliberately taken on) and the suffering of a people (which inevitably includes children). No one has the right to demand that an entire collectivity sacrifice itself.

If God has taken sides with the disinherited, with blacks, and with women, has she not taken sides as well with the oppressed people of Israel? If God is *not* the God of the rich, *not* a white racist, *not* a sexist, then neither is she an antisemite. It is sad that in an epoch when God has become poor and black and female, she has not yet become Jewish.

But it is one thing to entertain the possibility that God may wish, *kiveyakhol*, to defy theological "universalism" and the various fears of idolatry by taking sides with *this* party, and quite something else to authenticate our own taking of sides. Are we not forbidden *theologically* to do any such thing? That is to say, a historicist rendering or transforming of faith must be ever on the watch against the absolutizing of what is relative. (This caveat would seem to apply to every one of our normative images.) The "sins" that God may wish to commit cannot be justified for our own commission. Having cleared that away, we are yet bound to a *moral* taking of sides. Otherwise, the moral life is made irresponsible and it is robbed of meaning. The taking of sides is not like concurring that two plus two equal four rather than five. It can be argued that assent to such a simple arithmetical truth is the very opposite of taking sides. For to take sides morally is to be caught up in controversy. ("Why the Jews? Why not the Irish?") To take sides is to *cast one's lot* with a cause. We do this all the time. We vote for *this* candidate against *that* one. Again, a mother or father will take the side of their child. In the context of the Jewish-Christian relation, a more accurate simile would be children taking the side of their parents. That our chosen cause may "lose out" is always very much a possibility. Yet the moral commitment persists. The moral demand is not silenced.

In a word, Christians are, of all people, particularly called to solidarity with and support of Jews. The "preferential option for the poor," for blacks, and for women is reproduced in the preferential option for oppressed Israel. Hypocrisy is not entitled to anything, but the very last thing it can be allowed is to subvert decisional praxis. If it is hypocritical to lament the suffering of the poor without a support of power for the poor, to bewail black persecution without a support of black power, to deplore female oppression without a support of female power, so too it is hypocritical to talk of Christian repentance for the Holocaust without supporting the State of Israel.

However regrettably, some human beings will be hurt in the process, as occurs in all acts of liberation. Such is the fate of the rich, of whites, of males—and of the opponents of Jews and Israel. If the ethic of liberation is to remain fairminded, the Jewish people will not be subjected to special reprobation for this unfortunate fact of life. In fact, a major test for ascertaining whether the non-Jew has actually overcome his antisemitism is the absence/presence of such reprobation.

(5) A Christian position on Zionism and the State of Israel may profit from the prevailing Jewish position.

The dominant persuasion among Jews and Israelis avoids any theologizing of politics and any religious apologetic as such. The contemporary Jewish commonwealth is an increasingly secular reality. The main trunk of the tree of Israel, as it lives and grows today, bends neither to the theological left nor to the theological right. The last thing most Israelis would tolerate is a theocracy.

(6) Having suggested several pathways toward a secular Christian ethic of Israel, I have to offer a qualifying point, in part lest one or another of the other proposals assume a countenance of perfectionism.

The relation of the religious order and the political order will continue to manifest varying degrees of tension. This fact may be viewed both positively and negatively—positively in that each of the sides is possessed of integrity, negatively in that each side is conditioned by the demands of the other. From a theological-ethical viewpoint, judgment is to be rendered against any political order that absolutizes itself or its claims. From a political standpoint, judgment is to be levied against any spiritualizing of the traditional people of God, whereby the wardrobe of its "whole armor" is limited to truth, righteousness, and faith (Eph. 6:11–17) and fails to include military defense and praxis: guns and bombs. Eugene B. Borowitz counteracts all such spiritualization: The equating of justice and love (*agape*), as in the ethic of Joseph Fletcher, means that the laying down of my life permits you to "continue in your sinfulness. The appeal of such a doctrine of love to all exploiters and oppressors of the weak is a commonplace of social and historical analysis." This is why "justice looms so large" in the biblical prophets[51]— justice as an *instrument* of love, never to be confused with love itself.

Within this world there is no ultimate peace, no final resolution of human conflict, no end to the struggle between moral claims and human will-to-power, and hence no wholly consummated union of the sacred and the profane. The very persistence of the duality of religion and politics is itself a reminder of this. The truth that the reestablished Jewish commonwealth has not succeeded in wholly dispelling the untidy dualism of religiousness and the state helps underscore the point. This dualism manifests itself in every human collectivity.

The seer John finds no Temple in the heavenly Jerusalem because there and then God will be all-in-all (Rev. 21:22). Only in that transcendent time/ place will the separating categories of life be reunited, for that is the Day of the Messiah. A secular theological ethic is a needed corrective to such enticements as the two major ones reviewed and criticized in section VI above. But this ethic cannot put an end to enticement as such, for any hope of that sort ignores the tension of the two orders. The people of Caesar and the people of the Sovereign of the world do not march to the one drummer.

In sum, while the movement *toward* a secular Christian ethic of Israel may offer a summons to us, pointing to ultimate norms and hopes, a fully realized secular ethic of Israel is not achievable in the present dispensation. Abraham and his children's children are obliged to search unendingly for the secular city "whose builder and maker is God" (cf. Heb. 11:10).

VIII

The course and the cause of pluralism. Our treatment of exemplifications of a "return into history" is concluded in and through a third phenomenon, which, like the other two, will be handled in highly limited and selected fashion. The relation of Christians and Jews has been at once enriched and complicated by the rise and influence of religious and cultural pluralism. However, this new section carries us beyond the Christian-Jewish relation. A transformation of the Christian faith may become possible—we have been intimating—by virtue of the permanently revolutionary history of Israel. But the Christian church within the United States lives (as indeed the Jewish community and other communities do) within a peculiar moral-historical milieu: the American "system" respecting the relation between the secular order and religious faith, the American version of religio-cultural pluralism—in remarkable and sharp contrast to early American society. This ethos is constitutive to the existential history of indigenous Christians, Jews, and others. (The dynamic encounter among all eight of the normative images we are studying itself offers a complex paradigm of pluralism at work within an intellectual-moral frame of reference.)

The origins of Western pluralism are ultimately traceable to the breakup of medieval culture occasioned by two forms of revolt: the fourteenth-century Renaissance and the sixteenth-century Reformation.[52] By the end of the Second Great War, the state-church arrangement of colonial America had quite fully evolved into its opposite of religious pluralism. The process, involving great conflict, was made possible by a variety of conditions, including political suspicions of theocratic states, the inability of any single church body to have its way in the new nation, the weakness of organized religion at the country's inception, the majority demand for freedom *from* religion, and a minority demand for freedom *for* religion (the last of which meant pressing for freedom from government interference in religion). "The compromises of the intellectuals of politics and the proponents of religious tolerance" could give rise to the historic separation of church and state. That separation was aided by the influential values of liberalism and pluralism, by the strengthening of nonconformism in conjunction with the First Great Awakening, by the sheer variety and number of religious groups, and by the power of voluntarism (self-support and self-perpetuation) within most such groups.[53]

The presence of religious diversity in the United States has been constituted by several major historical processes: a huge influx of immigrants (largely Roman Catholic); the divisive effects of sectionalism and the Civil War upon American religion and culture; doctrinal divisions and schisms within the Protestant churches; the coming of Jews to the country, develop-

ing into an influential (though small) minority; the growth of indigenous religious groups and sects; and the democratization of Roman Catholicism in
America, in contrast to its traditionally authoritarian and antidemocratic
ethos.[54]

The ongoing process of pluralism has inevitably helped to transform the
Christian community and even its proclaimed Christian dogmas, in North
America but elsewhere as well.

The depth of American amorphousness and perplexity, and the critical
function of the American arrangement, are together suggested in a recent
proclamation in the *National Lampoon*. Beneath a tableau of a monster Easter
Bunny being resurrected from its tomb, a sight before which two Roman
soldiers fall in consternation, these words are found:

> Alleluia! Upon the occasion of this year's Vernal Equinox, when we com-
> memorate the Mystery of the Resurrection, the most basic tenet of what is
> (if the word of the President of the United States is anything to go by) our
> state religion, it behooves each of us, Fundamentalist and un-American
> alike, to doff our Easter bonnets and contemplate that age-old question:
> Are you washed in the blood of the Lamb? the Rabbit? the Baby Chick? a
> Druse? a Nicaraguan? a Grenadian? What this nation, under God, needs is a
> good oldfashioned Christian bloodbath! Say Amen, somebody![55]

Any and every social system produces evil as well as good. Pluralism is no
exception. Its contribution to social and moral complacency and the status
quo is a conspicuous case in point. One exemplary caution among many
needed cautions is offered by John A. Colemen: "In cases of religious pluralism, the symbols of the civil religion, if they are to function as a powerful
moral reference, must be both concrete enough to provide some meaningful
content and direction to national identity and general enough so that civil
religion does not become a serious alternative rival to particular religious
groups within the nation."[56] (Coleman defines civil religion as "the religious
dimension of the national political experience.") Or as Ted Peters has said,
we have to be very wary of pluralism when it "becomes an ideology presupposing its own theory of truth." One serious eventuality here is a loss of universal or common humanity through the dissolving of the human into purely
manifold essences and expressions. "When the concept of a universal humanity is missing, the door to dehumanization is wide open."[57] With this
kind of danger in mind, we may nevertheless point up a few of the positive
values within pluralism that are especially pertinent to the present study.

(1) Pluralism is a judgment upon, and a social protection against, religious
imperialism and self-idolatry.

Despite its Christian majority, the United States is not a Christian country
in any political or legal sense. It is a secular-pluralist nation, carrying in its
Constitution, its laws, and its ethos built-in preventives of religious exclusivism and tyranny. The American outlook and system have received recent ex-

pression in the American Indian Religious Freedom Act (1978), the text of which follows:

> Whereas the freedom of religion for all people is an inherent right, fundamental to the democratic structure of the United States, and is guaranteed by the First Amendment of the United States Constitution;
>
> Whereas the United States has traditionally rejected the concept of a government denying individuals the right to practice their religion and, as a result, has benefited from a rich variety of religious heritages in this country;
>
> Whereas the religious practices of the American Indian (as well as Native Alaskan and Hawaiian) are an integral part of their culture, tradition and heritage, such practices forming the basis of Indian identity and value systems;
>
> Whereas the traditional American Indian religions, as an integral part of Indian life, are indispensable and irreplaceable;
>
> Whereas the lack of a clear, comprehensive and consistent Federal policy has often resulted in the abridgement of religious freedom for traditional American Indians;
>
> Whereas such religious infringements result from the lack of knowledge or the insensitive and inflexible enforcement of Federal policies and regulations premised on a variety of laws;
>
> Whereas such laws were designed for such worthwhile purposes as conservation and preservation of natural species and resources but were never intended to relate to Indian religious practices and, therefore, were passed without consideration of their effect on traditional American Indian religions;
>
> Whereas such laws and policies often deny American Indians access to sacred sites required in their religions, including cemeteries;
>
> Whereas such laws at times prohibit the use and possession of sacred objects necessary to the exercise of religious rites and ceremonies;
>
> Whereas traditional American Indian ceremonies have been intruded upon, interfered with, and in a few instances banned. Now, therefore, be it
>
> Resolved by the Senate and House of Representatives of the United States of America in Congress assembled, That henceforth it shall be the policy of the United States to protect and preserve for American Indians their inherent right of freedom to believe, express, and exercise the traditional religions of the American Indian, Eskimo, Aleut, and Native Hawaiians, including but not limited to access to sites, use and possession of sacred objects, and the freedom to worship through ceremonies and traditional sites.
>
> The President shall direct the various Federal departments, agencies, and other instrumentalities responsible for administering relevant laws to evaluate their policies and procedures in consultation with native traditional religious leaders in order to determine appropriate changes necessary to protect and preserve Native American religious cultural rights and practices.[58]

We observe here part of the genius and the moral contribution of American democracy: its capability for replacing unjust laws with approximations of just laws.

A pluralist, democratic social order is an effective antidote to the intolerance and religio-political tyranny that have dogged historic Christianity through most of its history. Thus, while many American Christians may continue to *preach* anti-Jewishness and supersessionism vis-à-vis Judaism, they are limited by the American "system" from putting their hopes and designs into practical effect within the moral-political domain. Theologically expressed, the American socio-historical structure may be said to reflect, among other things, a judgment of God upon the idolatries and sins of the very people who claim to be special representatives of the divine will and truth. The American "experiment" itself rests, paradoxically enough, upon certain spiritual foundations, including, especially, prophetic Judaism and a Christianity that, in the very face of its own idolatrous absolutisms, has somehow managed to keep Jewish prophetism alive.[59]

Religious pluralism means a good deal more than a historical (divine?) judgment against Christian supersessionism respecting Judaism. It is a judgment against all forms of Christian imperialism toward many other religious faiths and peoples. The universalistic claims of Christian faith are a species of false universalism. The moral necessity of this finding lies in the church's traditional insistence upon the ultimacy of its own particularist form of divine truth at the expense of other discrete apprehensions of the divine. Pluralism counteracts morally and politically this false universalism of Christianity, and thus aids the continuing transformation of the church into an effectively confessional, nonapologetic faith.

(2) Pluralism is an aid to group rights and freedoms, and thereby to individual rights and freedoms.

Ethnic and religious pluralism is an antidote to the totalitarian homogeneity implied in "liberal"-universalism. The American ethos supports the integrity of such distinctive historical-cultural phenomena as Jewishness. It does this from two equally weighty sides: freedom of and respect for religion; and the honoring of discrete ethnic identities. Pluralism helps foster the free decision-making that is constituent to a living faith and a living community. Among the happier consequences of pluralism is its contribution to the self-confidence and creative social status of minorities.

Several years ago the president of Hadassah wrote: "As free people living in a free country, we take directions from no one. When we react, we do so out of shared priorities and common destiny, not at the behest of any government, including that of Israel. Independence also means independence from rote subservience to whatever administration happens to occupy the White House at a given time."[60] These words speak not alone for Jews but for all Americans. Group self-interest fills a justifiable, constituent, and even honored place within a pluralist, democratic social order. The Jewish community has learned that precisely because competing and conflicting self-interest is justifiably integral to the American ethos itself, there can be no moral legitimacy in forbidding Jewish forms of self-interest while condoning other forms.[61] Thus, "the Jewish vote" joins "the black vote," "the labor vote," "the Hispanic vote," "the business vote," "the Catholic vote," etc., etc., in an implementation and celebration of American rights and American responsibilities.

Hopefulness respecting the future of Jewish wellbeing in the United States (in considerable contrast to many other countries) is grounded in the truth that legally and morally, if not always traditionally, there is no such thing as an ideal or normative American. That is to say, Americanness is substantially a hybrid phenomenon because the country is a band of immigrants—unlike, say, Frenchness in France. Jewishness is as American (and as trans-American) as Irishness and Germanness, Russianness and Chineseness, Catholicness and Protestantness. Accordingly, in the United States the traditional antisemitic charges of Jewish "internationalism," "separatism," or "universalism" fail to possess the same evil power that they marshall in certain other lands, because all Americans bear the mark of greater or lesser universalism and particularism.

(3) Pluralism is consistent with formidable limitations upon the human apprehension of the truths of God, but also is reconcilable with the bearing of a truthful religious witness.

In I John the rhetorical question is raised, "Who is the liar but he who denies that Jesus is the Christ?" (2:22). To this, the voice of religious pluralism responds, in effect, "Who is the liar but he who is claiming that the denier of Jesus Christ is a liar?" As David Hartman points out, one moral advantage of contemporary life is the ease of meeting persons of other faiths who, by differing with us, mirror our limitations. "There is nothing healthier for restoring humility to the human spirit than confronting people who disagree with you with dignity and conviction." For "no human being can transcend the limitations of human finitude and comprehend the infinite reality of God." Despite their problems, the secular democratic world and secular liberal society "have created conditions for the emergence of religious humility and help restrain man's propensity to universalize the particular."[62]

On the other side of the ledger, religious pluralism is entirely compatible with religious affirmation, and it even requires such affirmation for the sake of its own integrity. As Reinhold Niebuhr writes,

> the main role of all religious communities in a pluralistic but increasingly secular culture which subjects all historical and natural events to empirical [i.e., scientific] scrutiny, is to bear witness to the necessity of the realm of the transcendent, even if it must be interpreted symbolically. For it is in the sphere of the transcendent that the meaning of life is established, the integrity and unity and uniqueness of the individual soul is emphasized, and

the mystery and meaning of the growth of human freedom over nature is appreciated. A culture without a penumbra of mystery surrounding its realm of meaning robs both man's history and man's individuality of meaning. . . . The superior vitality of pluralistic cultures which have retained the religious sense of mystery and meaning . . . lends basic security to fragile men who are exposed to the vicissitudes of life and its natural and historic evils.

An additional function of religious communities within a pluralist culture is, according to Niebuhr, the moral one of imbuing responsibility for the welfare of the neighbor, a norm that arises, not from the rational, scientific self, but from the integral self, as biblical faith comprehends the human person. "The great virtue of biblical faith is that its sense of a divine mystery does not prevent it from affirming unambiguous moral principles." To Niebuhr, the Christian theologian, it is *"only in terms of Judaism"* that it is possible "to comprehend the unity of the person, despite the incongruity of his involvement in and transcendence over nature and history." It is noteworthy that the essay in which these words are found should be the final published writing of Reinhold Niebuhr.[63]

The foregoing passages from Niebuhr serve to remind us of necessary moral limitations upon history, even a history that is given the right to transform faith. Now faith is asserting its own abiding integrity and independence. If it is so that faith stands *under* the judgment of history, it is equally so that faith stands *in* judgment upon the temptations of historical experience (not excluding scientific experience), most especially the ever-present temptation to fall into idolatry—the idolatry against which Judaism stands as a solitary witness.

To conclude this chapter: Among the unnumbered and sorely perplexing intellectual and moral problems that beset eighth people none surpasses this one: If history is among the instruments of God's intention, how in the last resort are we to settle upon the essentiality and significance of *this* event as against *that* one? I suggested in chapter two that in just eight words from the prophet Isaiah, "the Holy God proves himself holy by righteousness," an entire theology for a time of anguish is brought forth. Righteousness is the proof, the test of holiness. *Herein is contained the primary foundational and functioning criterion for any assessment of the events and processes of history, including both those that relate to human beings and those that relate to God.* Yet, at the end, the most shattering of all challenges confronts us: Can the righteousness that is sustained by faith survive once faith is itself put on trial—for nothing less than capital crimes—and once God is put on trial on the same charge? We are brought to a final chapter.

13

Trial of Faith, Trial of God

THE transition to our last chapter may be assisted by a few further words upon (a) the problem of absolutes in history; and (b) the quest for Christian liberation.

(a) In chapter eleven I proposed that when faith does no more than ground itself upon the facts (events and trends) of history, it opens the way to an unhappy subjection of faith to history. Do we subject faith to history when we receive as existentially absolute such an event as the Holocaust?

Here are a few suggestions for grappling with this question: First, it is faith in the God of history that permits the testimony that the hidden God may be seeking to say something through a particular historical event. It is in the midst of historical exigency that we try to do what is right. We try to "do the truth."

Second, although history may not be used to validate faith, it can serve as critical partner of a morally responsible, viable faith. As Irving Greenberg writes, the credibility of religious and other systems rises or falls "in the light of events which enhance or reduce the credibility of their claims."[1] An event of history can be so crushing that it brings to judgment faith in its present form and calls for its reformation. Quite possibly, faith will be wiped out in the process.* The event of the Shoah is a judge and transformer of faith. To speak of it as in any way sustaining of faith would be obscene. If there is a sense in which the Holocaust can be construed as a "revelatory" event, the

---

*A surface logic would appear to suggest that if history cannot demonstrate faith, neither can it disprove faith. Life is at once larger and more contingent than such logic allows. We live in a world where many times failure outstrips success, suffering and catastrophe overbalance happiness and peace, and human sin is victorious over goodness. Faith is assailed by history. However, in one crucial respect ongoing experience is not always decisive. Assumptions concerning religious faith and trust in God are very often in place before historical fortunes come to intervene. Accordingly, faith/unfaith will serve as an instrument for coping with new experiences. The retention of faith tends to be an "in spite of," whereas the renunciation or absence of faith tends to be a "because of." There is the further complication that one or another aspect of faith may be surrendered and another aspect kept or gained.

"revelation" must remain a critical and regulative one. For the *Shoah* seeks to destroy everything in its path: life, ideals, hopes, beliefs. However, the claim that a devastating historical evil just may issue in possibly "good" consequences presents no substantive difficulties to Christian (or Jewish) thinking. For the church, an authoritative prototype is found in the "good" outcome of an "evil" Crucifixion. Once a particular faith has been revolutionized, it may then, ideally, succeed in reasserting and maintaining itself amid and despite the assaults of history. This is one way in which the dialectic of faith and history is moved along. But the history through which faith is transformed for good may be the most evil history imaginable.

Third, to identify the Holocaust as a moral absolute is not to absolutize history. There is an essential disparity between *an absolute criticism* (= a regulative principle) and *an absolute claim*. The former does not absolutize history or itself; on the contrary, it acts to reject historical absolutization. In and through the *Shoah* an ultimate critical judgment is instituted against Christian faith for having fallen into the absolutization of its own history.

Fourth, sometimes an unrelieved concentration upon the question of what God may be saying and doing will, regrettably, take human minds and hearts off the vital question of what *they* ought to be saying and doing.

(b) From the perspective of "history transforming faith," some of the otherwise praiseworthy liberationist motifs within "faith transforming history" appear deficient at the very point of liberation. This is shown in the failure of much Christian "theology of liberation" to grapple with the event of the *Shoah*, to surmount Christian absolutism and imperialism, and to restore creatively the rootage of Christianity in Israel. William Jay Peck attests that in a "structural sense, the whole of Christianity was responsible for the death camps." In consequence, any "denial of such involvement will doom the message of the church to remain at the level of shallow and impotent argumentation."[2] Some Christians are prepared to confess the culpability of Christianity in the *Shoah*. But comparatively few express a willingness to repudiate, or even to lament and criticize, the structure of dogmatic teachings that, objectively considered, helped bring the Holocaust to pass. Accordingly, Peck's fear that the message of the church is doomed and futile retains its force. One severe lesson of the *Shoah* is its exposure of the pretense that there can be anti-Judaism without antisemitism. Defamations of the human spirit become the deaths of human bodies.

The problem of morality and the problem of meaning are inextricable. As the twentieth century wanes a truly revolutionary challenge addresses us. Within a world where history turns faith as such into ashes, what can it mean still to have faith? But this challenge creates an additional one: Is there perhaps left to us the opportunity for a faith that opens itself to history? Are there any ways to restore faith, once history has shattered faith, by continuing to struggle with and against history, upon the stage of history itself? If we can once muster the courage to meet straight on the power of history—that nemesis of all faith—we just may be able to keep open the pathway to human liberation.

Finally, there are senses in which the very history that serves as the ground of deliverance from idolatry and imperialism needs itself to be cleansed constantly of false consciousness and bad ideology. In its ultimate reaches, *liberation* is the redeemed righteousness that weds God and human-kind. How are the antiliberative elements within a reputedly liberative the-ology ever to be transcended and deideologized? Can there be versions of Christian faith that, at least in principle, achieve freedom from idolatry, supersessionism, and triumphalism? Can the truth claims of Christianity be reconciled with moral requirements of goodness and justice? A distinguish-ing mark of those who are doing Christian post-*Shoah* philosophy and theol-ogy is the moral revulsion that is their meat day and night. Herein may lie much of the critical power, and eventually constructive power, of that work.

I

At several places we have alluded to the moral evil implicit in the reli-gious exclusivism and imperialism of Christianity. At this juncture, a more discrete assessment of determinate Christian doctrine is in order. Stress will fall upon the Resurrection. It should be kept in mind that the potential transformation of Christian faith vis-à-vis the Jewish people and Judaism has many implications and lessons for the wider problematic of Christian life and faith in relation to all peoples and faiths.

The focal Christian teachings of Incarnation-Crucifixion-Resurrection com-prise the building blocks of anti-Judaism and antisemitism. (It is sometimes argued that a *theologia crucis* is able to exorcise the demon of triumphalism. Neill Q. Hamilton contends that Mark's theology of the cross overcomes tri-umphalism.[3] The stumbling block here is that Mark evidently accepted the actualized Resurrection of Jesus [Mark 16]. The eligibility of a *theologia crucis* for removing triumphalism turns upon where the advocate stands on the Resurrection.)

Within Christendom the yearly occasion of Holy Week has been a time of special fear for Jews and of persecution of the Jewish people as the Christian rites move on to Good Friday and the reenactment of the death of Jesus, the latter reputedly at the hands of Jews. Nor is this ideological condition just a thing of the past. The Gospel of John, most dear to Christian piety of all New Testament books, remains, as the Christian scholar Ulrich E. Simon has put it, in and of itself an incitement to corporate murder through its defamation of the Jewish people.[4] Today's Oberammergau Passion Play in Western Ger-many (based as it is on the Gospel of John) and increasing numbers of pas-sion plays in other countries regularly promote among hundreds of thousands of people the false myth of deicide—as do unnumbered Chris-tian sermons around the world. Nevertheless, from the standpoint of the enduring social, psychological, and theological power of Christian anti-Jewishness, the proclaimed Resurrection of Jesus Christ remains easily as crucial as the Crucifixion, or more crucial, though in much more indirect and much more subtle ways. For the ultimate problem is not Good Friday but Easter. Indeed, had there been no first Easter, the Crucifixion would quite probably never have been able to develop its contribution to human hatred. Belief in the Resurrection of Christ was the moving force behind the entire life and mission of the early church. Without that belief, there would have been no Christianity in separation from Judaism.

The prime mover in the subtlety, obliqueness, and ultimate demonry of the Resurrection-factor as a contributor to Christian imperialism is linked to the truth that so much of the focus of Resurrection-teaching goes in a direction diametrically opposed to evil. That direction is typified in passages from David Tracy: Just as "the cross discloses to the Christian the suffering love of God's own self by its intensified focus on that love as the ultimate, binding, eternal relationship of the divine and the human," so the Resurrection "vindicates, confirms, and transforms that journey in and through its negations of the negations of a suffering love. The resurrection of Jesus by God grounds our hope in a real future for all the living and the dead where pain shall be no more." The symbol of the Resurrection reveals that "the Crucified one is the Risen One, that Jesus has been accepted and received by God as the surest ground for our hope in the transformation of our compulsions, alienations and oppressions, as the ground of a total hope—for history and nature, for the living and the dead, and their acceptance by the same God of suffering love who raised the crucified Jesus from the dead."[5]

Thus does the Resurrection appear to function in an ecstatically and wondrously soteriological way—so sublimely and, accordingly, so innocently. On the above testimony, not alone Christians but all human beings may receive hope. But can this be the same Professor Tracy who has called us to the cruciality of the Holocaust for Christians, and who demands *a hermeneutics of suspicion* respecting the various Christian doctrines? It is noteworthy that Tracy nowhere applies his hermeneutics of suspicion to the dogma of the Resurrection. It appears that the thought just never occurs to him. How is that possible? Has he been beguiled by all the hopefulness, all the sublimity, all the innocence? Surely the obligation of a truly post-*Shoah* Christian theology is to go behind and beyond everything that is true and beautiful and good, to seek out, with a broken heart, its falsity, ugliness, and evil.

Gregory Baum asks: "Is it possible to purify the Christian message of its anti-Jewish ideology without invalidating the Christian claims altogether? This is the frightening question." For Baum, Auschwitz reveals to the Christian community *"the deadly power of its own symbolism"*—teaching and preaching that have incarnated themselves in social attitudes and political behavior, a species of vilification that translates itself "into genocidal action of monstrous proportions."[6] And could this not happen again? Once the Resurrection is identified as a special act of God, a divine event or divine fact, how can Christian vilification, imperialism, and supersessionism vis-à-vis Judaism and the Jewish people ever be vanquished? For the issue between the two sides is seen to be, not a relatively harmless disparity of mere human symbolism, spiritual conviction, or "religious experience"—probably amenable to the soothings of "relativization" or "confessionalism"!—but a matter of saying Yes or No to God himself, the Sovereign of all things.

We do not get anywhere by trying to distinguish *forms* or *kinds* of the Resurrection—"bodily," "spiritual," "spiritual body," etc., etc. That is not the issue. Nor is the issue primarily one of interpretation or understanding. The issue that counts is whether the Resurrection is a divinely wrought fact: Did God raise Jesus from the dead?

Wolfhart Pannenberg declares that since Jesus has *in fact* been raised from the dead by God, Jesus' claim to divine authority "has been visibly and unambiguously confirmed by the God of Israel." In and through the Resurrection, Judaism is abolished.[7] The Resurrection is proclaimed as an objective historical event embodying the divine praxis and divine truth—and not *kiveyakhol!* Those who affirm the truth of the Resurrection of Jesus, but who oppose the way in which Wolfhart Pannenberg assimilates the Resurrection to Christian imperialism, are challenged to show how their own affirmation avoids supersessionism. With the teaching of the Resurrection Christian triumphalist ideology and psychology reach a substantive fulfillment that cannot be surpassed. Just here the numerous human and divine claims that make up the church's theological and moral structure are crowned by an event that is exclusively "God's" and thus vindicates eschatologically every other claim. The apostles of this ideology announce, in effect: It is not the Christian theologian to whom you Jews are to give heed. He is, after all, a fallible, sinful human being. He can be quite wrong, again and again. So you are infinitely better advised to pay attention to *God* and to what he does and has done. Let God decide the matter! But note well the nature of God's decision and God's act: His decision and act are on the Christian's side, and against yours. God has raised Jesus from the dead. The Christian community is proved right, and you and your community are proved wrong. It pains us immeasurably to have to tell you this, for we have the utmost respect for you as human beings and even as Jews. You were, after all, the people of God's old Covenant while we are only poor adopted sons and daughters. Yet the truth must stand. In the Resurrection of Jesus Christ, God has confirmed the Christian hope, the Christian gospel, the Christian cause. Who are we—and who are you—to go against the Truth?[8]

Jean Daniélou expresses the final logic of Christian anti-Jewishness: The offense of the Jews is that "they do not believe in the risen Christ."[9] For there is no "Resurrection of Jesus Christ" without "Christian resurrectionism," the transfiguration of a claimed historical event into an ideology. Accordingly, we have to say that in the Resurrection, Christianity is brought to trial. The offense is the church's, not Israel's. And God is brought to trial as well, since in the New Testament view responsibility for the Resurrection appertains exclusively to God.

The "deadly power" of the Resurrection dogma—as of other aspects of Christology—is beginning to be acknowledged within contemporary Christian thinking. However, it is exceedingly questionable whether a straightforward denial of the Resurrection or an out-and-out attack upon it would be anything but futile, since the Resurrection of Jesus Christ as a historically actualized event will doubtless continue to be central to Christian teaching. It is unrealistic to expect Christians to surrender their conviction that Jesus Christ has been crucified and raised from the dead for their sake. In the traditional Christian mythos the event of the Resurrection is, indeed, the judge of all truth and all history. Yet none of this is able to silence the question: Is there a message from Auschwitz to the dogma of the Resurrection? Does not *this* history stand in judgment upon *that* history? Is there a way to subject the Resurrection to historical-moral valuation? Is there a way to redeem the Resurrection? Or has the church worked itself into a corner where truth is not "in order to" goodness?

II

A few proposals may be reviewed. I do not perforce agree (or entirely disagree) with these approaches with respect to their possible effectiveness. They all share a commitment to history as in some way utilizable in the transformation of faith; hence their appropriateness to this chapter.

(1) The Resurrection of Jesus construed as a non-event.

I ventured to suggest above that the denial of an actualized Resurrection of Jesus is futile. However, this does not annul the relevance of the Resurrection as an alleged non-event. For were the event rejected as an actual historical happening, the Christian supersessionism or triumphalism over Judaism that is associated with Resurrection-teaching would clearly be subverted. The truism here is elementary.

This first position may range from a simple rationalist-historicist-scientific disclaimer of the possibility that dead persons *can* be brought back to life to a more modest disavowal that in this particular case Jesus *was* brought back to life. But to be a rationalist or historicist, or to take a scientific point of view, does not necessitate any such categorical denial. Any effort to "get rid" of the Resurrection of Jesus Christ as an objective truth of God, i.e., a truth that obtains whether or not certain persons recognize or honor it, and to do so through recourse to a negative, *doctrinaire* historicism, i.e., by means of an a priori denial that a given event or certain kinds of events could ever occur in history, is not tenable. For the refusal is question-begging. How could we ever dub a supposed event "impossible" when we remain in the vulnerable condition of not being able to establish final criteria for adjudging what can and cannot occur in history as in nature? In point of truth, no human being can say absolutely what is possible and impossible in our world. Thus is a *doctrinaire* historicism unable to refute the possible fact of the Resurrection.

At least two pathways remain open for the proponent of this initial point of view. (a) She can proceed "confessionally," rather than "apologetically" or "polemically." One prevalent way that recent theology has handled phenomenologically the *affirmation* of the Resurrection is to render it as a form of community confession. Similarly, any *disavowal* of the Resurrection can, potentially, develop into a like instance of community confession. The affirmation and the disavowal share a certain independence of historical-scientific disproof/proof. Religious faith may very well come to build a certain viability and power upon *denials* (of idolatry, of polytheism, etc.). (b) If the foregoing appraisal suggests that the problematic of the Resurrection is not resolvable through historical-intellectual argument, neither does such argument have any jurisdiction over the abiding demand to assess the Resurrection from the perspective of moral good and evil. The latter demand cannot be dismissed or quelled through resort to extra-moral criteria.

The eligibility of this first position for placement under "history transforming faith" remains evident, since any assigning of the Resurrection to the category of non-event would constitute a negative-historical determination of what it is that faith ought or ought not affirm.[10]

(2) The alleged impotency of the Resurrection in advancing human liberation.

William R. Jones seriously questions Jesus' Resurrection as *the* event of universal human liberation, on the moral ground that black misery, slavery, and oppression are all *post*-Resurrection phenomena. In a critique of J. Deotis Roberts, Jones enumerates two fateful issues: the ostensible definitiveness of what he here calls the Cross-Resurrection; and, second, its presumed universality. Jones declares: "If in Christ humiliation and exaltation are combined, what are the tangible events in the lives of blacks that manifest that the Resurrection has in fact occurred in power? If the surplus of black suffering [which Roberts poignantly describes] still persists after the alleged event of God's 'victory,' how then are we to regard the Cross-Resurrection" in light of Roberts's description of its historicity as authenticating God's providence and his salvific work among men? For Roberts, at the cross love gains the victory over hate, and at the empty tomb life triumphs over death. In Roberts's words, "A new age has come into being, God's new age. The climax of a struggle for justice and righteousness in history has occurred and the victory belongs to God. . . . The resurrection is the basis of a black hope secure in the God of the resurrection, who is a God of love and power, who promises to be with us always and to make all things new."

This is Jones's response:

Two lines of argumentation are open to Roberts here: He could follow the
example of Jewish theology and challenge the decisive character and
salvific singularity of the Resurrection. That is, the Resurrection may be an
important occurrence in man's salvation history, but the conditions in the
alleged New Age suggest that the Messiah is yet to come. We do not have
realized eschatology yet. Good theology but bad psychology?

Another option would retain the decisive aspect of the Resurrection but
question whether blacks are the intended recipients of its saving grace. This
approach frontally challenges the universality of the Resurrection. Roberts
has argued that the superfluity of black suffering nullifies the theodicy of
deserved punishment. What theological principle prevents this conclusion:
the same surplus makes problematical the universality and/or the definitive
character of the Resurrection—except the assumption of God's intrinsic and
universal benevolence?[11]

Parallels between the hapless black experience and the hapless Jewish
experience scarcely require elaboration. However, in the frame of reference
of the Cross-Resurrection, the black experience referred to by Roberts and
Jones becomes infinitely more ironic and poignant than the Jewish experience. For, in principle, Christian blacks are *believers* in the power of the Cross-
Resurrection. As nonbelievers in that power, the Jewish people do not face
the same disillusionment that Jones reflects.

Unlike the initial alternative already considered, this second position
does not necessarily deny the historical actuality of the Resurrection.

(3) A Christian thrust against the historicizing of eschatological reality,
against the absolutizing of one or another historical event.

To historicize the eschatological domain is not the same as putting forward an eschatological view of history according to which history appears to
point beyond itself to an unrealized eschaton. One can reject the former attempt while holding to the latter. To sing

> Soon I will be done with the troubles of the world,
> Going to live with God . . .,

is not at all to historicize eschatology while it does imply the eschatologizing
of history. Indeed, through an assigning of meaning to history, despite all its
fragility, as the place where the hidden God is somehow met, we are enabled to justify a transforming of faith by history, and the liberating of faith
through a liberating of the divine righteousness.

This brings us to Rosemary Ruether's position on the Resurrection.
Ruether states: "The self-infinitizing of the messianic [Christian] sect that
empowers itself to conquer all mankind in the name of the universal" is essentially a "false messianism." In concrete application of this protest,
Ruether argues that at the root of Christian antipathy to Jews and Judaism is
the church's traditional effort to historicize eschatological reality. Accord-

ingly, the one answer to Christianity's *Tendenz* of imperialism and supersessionism with respect to the Jewish people is to reject all such historicization, all endeavors to incarnate the finality of things within the historical process (even where this is done with reservations). From Ruether's critical point of view, it is wrong, therefore, to permit the Resurrection to embody a historicizing of the eschatological. For her, "only by reading the Resurrection in a paradigmatic and proleptic way can the church avoid making the absolute claims about itself which are belied by its own history." The Resurrection "is not the final happening of the eschatological event, but the proleptic experiencing of the final future."[12]

Ruether's purpose is the highest and best: to expunge from the church's message, once and for all, the demons of Christian oppression and injustice. She is striving, not against mere flesh and blood, but against the kind of Christian imperialism that is given formulation by, as examples, the German Protestant theologian Jürgen Moltmann and the Dutch Catholic theologian Edward Schillebeeckx. Moltmann presumes that on the date of Jesus' Resurrection "the eschatological era begins." Schillebeeckx acclaims the New Testament word "that the one 'suffering righteous man,' the one unique and eschatological 'suffering prophet,' Jesus Christ has saved the whole world." To Schillebeeckx, the "definite salvation" that comes from God for each and every human being, past, present, and future, living and dead, is found "in Jesus of Nazareth." And the Resurrection? It is "God's yes to the person and the life of Jesus."[13]

Does Ruether's remedy rise to the level of her critical intention? The problems posed by the two extreme views we have already sketched are pertinent to a response to this third remedy. Elsewhere Ruether asserts that Jesus is an "archetype" for us, through whom "the evil powers are already conquered in principle."[14] Yet just when or where were "the evil powers" conquered by Jesus—even in principle? We are back with our old question: What is to be the relation between *theological avowal* and *historical event*? I suggest that Ruether's concept of prolepsis (anticipative praxis) tends to confuse the matter. In the nature of eschatological reality, there is no such possibility as the qualifying of its historicization. It can be qualified on the basis of its partiality or even its fragmentariness, but we are prevented from qualifying it in kind. That is to say, eschatological reality is either historicized or it is not. The absolute or definitive quality of the Christian Resurrection turns, not upon its partial or its nonpartial character, nor upon how human beings decide to treat it, but solely upon its essence as a special act of God. God either performed that act or he did not perform it; no third or other alternative is possible. Whatever one's decision respecting the Resurrection, there is just no way to deny that the New Testament reports of it (the only record we have) make it wholly a divine deed and not at all a human one. (Here we are aided by common sense: What human being has the power to raise himself from the dead?)

The conclusion is evident: If the Resurrection of Jesus has not yet occurred, any reason or need to characterize that claimed event in paradigmatic and proleptic terms disappears. But if the Resurrection of Jesus has in fact taken place by a special act of God, its association with the categories of "paradigmatic" and "proleptic" does not really annul an asserted historicizing of eschatological reality. The risen Christ would still remain the unique "first fruits of those who have fallen asleep," the one through whom "all shall be made alive" (I Cor. 15:20, 22). Even if the Resurrection is received as, at most, an earnest of the Reign (B*asileia*) of God that lies essentially in the future of space/time—this is in truth the New Testament confession—we are not thereby spared a historicizing of the eschatological dimension.

To reject the historicity of the Resurrection of Jesus would obviously mean escaping the historicizing of the eschatological. (The consequence would be the same were his Resurrection deferred to the future.) Such a rejection would also speak to the problem of liberation/nonliberation that is posed by William R. Jones. But the obstacle stays with us that the negating of an actualized Resurrection of Jesus and its eclipse from Christianity appears as impossible as it is futile. For many, any such denial would constitute a betrayal of the Christian faith itself. If Ruether is right that the basic sin of the Christian church respecting Judaism and the Jewish people centers in its historicizing of the eschatological dimension, is it yet possible to affirm the Resurrection of Jesus as an actual event, a historical act of God, without committing that very trespass? This brings us to a fourth proposal.

(4) An effort to secure the Resurrection within its originative home.

This book has become involved in various kinds of side-taking. If it is so that God is on the side of the poor against the rich, and of Jews against their persecutors, what may we say concerning a conflict between the Sadducees and the Pharisees? We are given to understand that the Sadducees insisted that there is no resurrection (e.g., Matt. 22:23)—contra Pharisee teaching. To introduce a light note (and perhaps therefore an especially serious one): We are advised that the One who sits in the heavens is not above laughing certain parties to scorn (Ps. 2:4). What would be a better joke on those reactionary Sadducess than for God to raise her own Pharisee-liberal Son from the dead! She would be having a go at one of her dearest truths, and would also be giving at least a few of her people a foretaste of the things that are to come. Maybe best of all, she would be reminding the Sadducees exactly what she thought of them, meanwhile assuring her good friends the Pharisees that she was on their side. . . .

Perhaps a happy thing about the above little tale is that it works to keep the Resurrection in the family, where it originally belonged. Let us carry this orientation a little farther via a recent recorded conversation between two Christians:

PAUL: I hardly have to repeat that a lot of people—Christians, Jews, others—consider that fealty to Jesus' Resurrection is what, more than anything else, makes a person a Christian.

MARY: Yes, but doesn't this point to a basic trouble with Christians? Where did we ever get the right to take over the Resurrection from Jesus and his people? Let's put ourselves in the place of the Jew. Consider our Israeli colleague Pinchas Lapide. He has said: "I do not exclude the possibility of the bodily Resurrection of Jesus from the grave on the first Easter."[15] Pinchas is, as you know, an Orthodox Jew.

PAUL: Yes, and many of his friends and relatives in Israel and elsewhere will have decided that he's either sold out to the goyim or simply gone bananas. Perhaps you've read the reaction of another colleague of ours, Rabbi Peter Levinson in Heidelberg: "Lapide's statement is a terrible shock. He has overstepped the bounds of Jewish theology. If I believed in Jesus' Resurrection, I would be baptized tomorrow."[16]

MARY: All right, all right. Pinchas contends as well that however Easter be interpreted, one thing remains certain: "Since all the witnesses of the resurrected Jesus were sons and daughters of Israel, since, moreover, he appeared only in the land of Israel, his Resurrection was a Jewish affair which must therefore be judged by Jewish standards if we are to gauge its authenticity."[17] Also, don't forget that those of Pinchas's conviction will yet have no truck with the notion that Jesus, resurrected or not, was *the* Messiah of Israel or the divine Son of God.[18] And remember too that belief in Jesus' Resurrection would not have offended most non-Christian Jews of New Testament times.

PAUL: You mean to tell me that Jews can actually take a positive view of . . .

MARY: Please! Let me speak for the Jewish people here. To the testimony that Jesus was raised from the dead, the Jew may well respond: "What else is new? Jesus wasn't the first, you know.[19] A major reason why we Jews have bypassed this teaching is that you Christians long ago took that one episode and blew it up out of all proportion. But the worst thing is the way you've used it against us. It's not unlike what you did to our conception of sin. You appropriated that from us too, only to push the teaching to inhuman extremes. (There's scarcely any need to mention your grand larceny of the entire *Tanak*—including the travesty of making it over into the 'Old Testament'!)"

PAUL: I agree with the contention about the Bible.

MARY: "The point is," the Jew will continue, "that you Christians have done your damnedest to turn Jesus' Resurrection into a seal of the Messiah and a warranty of your so-called truth. In *real* truth, the Resurrection ought to be allowed to stand or fall on its own. It's about time Christians quit their coveting of it and their monopoly on it."

PAUL: Let me see if I can restate what you are implying: Christians have no business running off with Jewish property. There's no necessity that the Resurrection of Jesus promote a "theology of substitution,"[20] so long as Christians stop misappropriating and misrepresenting the Resurrection

by turning it into a possession of the church. Once the Resurrection is
grasped as an event strictly between God and the Jewish people, the
awful triumphalism of Christians will be dealt a mortal blow.

MARY: You've got it.

PAUL: Come to think of it, aren't you simply representing the original history
of the New Testament? I'm also reminded of a line from Gerald
O'Collins: "Only those who have known him during his earthly ministry
can acknowledge the risen Lord . . . to be one and the same person as
Jesus of Nazareth."[21]

MARY: Leave it to a male to want to make Jesus lordly. Why don't we just
stick with the Resurrection?[22]

The Dutch Protestant theologian J. (Coos) Schoneveld, active in the movement to oppose Christian supersessionism, asks: "Is it possible for me as a
Christian, from the depth of my faith commitment to Jesus Christ, to affirm
the Jewish people and Judaism sincerely, really and truly, instead of rejecting, if not the Jewish people, then at least Judaism?" Schoneveld's answer falls within our fourth category. Just as Jesus, son of Israel, remained
faithful to God unto death, so God remained faithful to Jesus unto life. More
concretely, the Resurrection is a vindication of Jesus' utter commitment to
God's Torah. Jesus had properly and courageously obeyed the essence of
the Torah, which is the call to do justice, to love kindness, and to walk humbly with God. The Resurrection "means that the path of the Torah is the right
one, that the word of God . . . can be trusted," that it discloses a future and is
a source of hope for us.

What does this mean with regard to the Jewish people? Jesus did not abolish the Torah, but fulfilled its deepest intention. The resurrection means
that Jesus was vindicated as a Jew, as one who was faithful to the Torah, as a
martyr who participated in Jewish martyrdom for the sake of heaven (*Kiddush
ha-Shem*). What else can this mean than that the Torah remains valid, and
the Jewish people are vindicated as God's beloved people. By resurrecting
Jesus God affirms his promises as well as his commandments to the Jewish
people. . . . I see the Jewish people in the light of the resurrection. The survival of the Jewish people throughout the centuries I see in the light of what
the resurrection means, namely: the affirmation of the Torah, the affirmation
of Israel, and the affirmation of the meaning of Jewish existence. Therefore,
a Christian-theological affirmation of the Jewish people ought to belong to
the very center of the Christian faith. If I nowadays see that the Jewish people get a new chance to survive and to revive, presently through the existence of the State of Israel, I must see this in the light of the resurrection of
Christ, and praise God for his faithfulness to the Jewish people, and his purpose with humanity.[23]

The sum and substance of this fourth position is that Resurrection imperialism is best fought from within, by Christians who, just because they will to

live and die in historical solidarity with the Jewish people to whom the Resurrection belongs, are thereby permitted to affirm the Resurrection themselves.

The issue that here arises is thus not whether the integrity of the Jewish people and Judaism is to be affirmed. There is no disagreement about that. The real issue is whether or not the Christian Resurrection militates, in and of itself, against Jewish integrity. In this regard I think that we have little choice but to keep before us the question: What has been the fate of the Resurrection in the course of history? What has been *done* to it? I submit four historical-moral comments. They are interrelated.

(a) In the very process of bonding the Resurrection of Jesus to Jewish integrity, Dr. Schoneveld has no choice but to observe that other people before and after Jesus have, without doubt, lived lives according to the Torah. Indeed, Schoneveld contends that it was in conjunction with the many deaths of Jews as martyrs that the belief in a future resurrection as vindicating the power and justice of God became strong in Pharisee and other circles.[24] We must ask then: Why was Jesus singled out for Resurrection?* That Jesus' Resurrection should be elevated to preeminence in the presence of other contemporary, faithful Jews inevitably suggests something unusual or distinctive about Jesus. It already smacks of Christianity. And this fact in itself can hardly be separated from the truth that soon, in Christian history, the proclaimed Christology was no longer that of a Jew from the Galilee who was obedient and faithful to God's Torah but rather that of One who displaces the Torah and becomes *the* Word, *the* Torah, who himself demands obedience to, and faith in, himself.

(b) In all inadvertence, to "return" the Resurrection to the Jewish community is condescending, objectively speaking. Something that is a pearl of great price for the Christian community is anything but that for the Jewish community. Remorselessly, history exacts its tolls. From the Jewish side, the goods that were once misappropriated simply do not possess, if they ever did, the indispensable worth that Christians attribute to them. Of course, the Resurrection of Jesus was a strictly Jewish affair, once upon a time. But for years on end it has not been that. Pinchas Lapide's reappropriation is anything but representative of the Jewish community. It is an anachronism—a winsome gesture but an anachronism. For what *could* have been a normally accepted historical datum for Jews—the resurrection of a Jew of the first century—has fallen under the sway of bad ideology, of false consciousness. Its reality and meaning are fatally flawed. There are gas chambers now, and crematoria.

---

*To be sure, Scripture records other resurrections, but the point is that Jesus was, reputedly, *the* martyr of his generation to be raised from the dead. Little notice has been given by the church to the act of collective resurrection reported in Matt. 27:52–53, and even that act is assimilated by the evangelist to the great event of Jesus' Crucifixion. The other resurrected bodies are left nameless.

(c) The damage has been done. Are not the consequences beyond consolation? The goods that were stolen have been long since corroded by evil.
Just as for many Jews the Cross of Jesus seems more like a *Hakenkreuz* than
anything else, so too the Empty Tomb cannot but represent a church and a
world emptied of righteousness. In addressing the oft-made appeal to Jesus'
Crucifixion-Resurrection as a supposed means of coping spiritually with the
Holocaust, Robert E. Willis points out that the passion of Christ has become
part and parcel "of the very evil it seeks to illuminate."[25] Responsibility for
the entire problem centers in the very symbolism and praxis that are being
put forward as a cure. Thus, the theological notion that Jesus suffered for all
humankind (therefore for Jews too) is turned on its head in the *Shoah*. The
Jews are made to suffer for Jesus. (Elie Wiesel has Shlomo, a blind *Hasid*,
meeting Yeshua on the day of the Crucifixion. Shlomo said: "You think you
are suffering for my sake and my brothers', yet we are the ones who will be
made to suffer for you, because of you." A man named Moshe then responds
to the story: "If only you could have made him laugh, things would have
been different now."[26]) In the same way, the endeavor to restore the Resurrection to its original home comes too late in world history to provide the
rectifying power that is so sorely needed.

(d) The fourth orientation does not address itself at all to the ambivalence
that possesses so many Christians of today respecting the Jewishness of the
New Testament and Christianity. This ambivalence is the creation of Christian history.

The first two of the four positions on the Resurrection that we have singled out are primarily negative in substance and impact; the intent of the
second two is primarily one of positive rectification. Yet neither of the latter two succeeds in dissociating the Resurrection from the Christian imperium. In contrast to abortive efforts such as these to deliver the
Resurrection from false consciousness, Christian liberation is made authentically incarnate through trust in and love for the God of Israel, and
the love for human beings that is realized through justice. Exclusivist religious claims are a primary means to the oppression of humankind. Thus,
Wolfhart Pannenberg's agreement with Martin Luther that genuine human
freedom and identity can only be obtained by faith in Christ[27] constitutes
sacrilege against the *imago dei*. In opposition to the Luther-Pannenberg ideology, we may testify that true liberation is freedom, not alone from being
oppressed, but from oppressing. It is deliverance from idolatry, triumphalism, supersessionism, and other forms of arrogance. This is to imply that
there is still much hope for the Christian faith. That faith can be redeemed
from its sinfulness. However, the knowledge of and commitment to such
possible transformation cannot be allowed to nourish pretentiousness and
self-righteousness among eighth people. Indeed, some of the foregoing critical comments upon the endeavor to link the Resurrection to its originative
home may be turned into a deeper critical question, to be addressed to the

entire presentation in chapter twelve above: Do we not have to face the eventuality that the very Christian effort to "return into history" via a "return to Israel" is itself incapable of vanquishing Christian imperialism? An immediate and concrete way of realizing the nature of this fear is through the entirely licit objection of more than one Jew: "In light of the last 1900 years, isn't it about time that you Christians just let us alone?" Accordingly, nowhere is the title of part three of this book more imperative than just here: "People of Eight: Challenges and Uncertainties."

We are forced to conclude that the trial of the Christian faith—not excepting our eighth normative image of that faith—remains (to use legal parlance) under continuance. Meanwhile, the contemporary Israeli will wish to make sure, *kiveyakhol* but perhaps more than this, that his Uzi is never quite beyond reach. Comparable precautions have to be taken by other non-Christians.

III

In the same courtroom where the Christian faith continues to stand trial, the trial of God is held. For from our reflections so far in this chapter, it is evident that the two trials cannot be kept apart. (A third trial is simultaneously in process in the identical courtroom—a very busy place: the trial of human beings who are Christians. The proceedings of that third trial are given voice throughout the two final chapters of the present work. Indeed, those proceedings are hinted at upon more than one page of this volume as a whole.)

I include one caveat here. If an ever-pressing danger within traditional theology is to reduce humankind to a means to divine ends, a patent danger for "history transforming faith" is to reduce God to a means to the ends of humankind. People of eight have to work hard to avoid both these pitfalls but especially the second. To this purpose, they may attest that God is at once end and means for human beings, just as human beings are end and means for God. In short, both parties are members of a family.

Nevertheless: A special indictment is entered against God, from the side of the Jewish people. There is the traditional Jewish conviction that "for our sins were we exiled." But how are human ashes fluttering through the air ever going to be described as heading for exile? How *could it be that this Destruction is visited upon Israel?* In solidarity with the Jew, the non-Jew stands at the partner's side. Yet are not identical questions to be asked in the name of all piteous sufferers of the world? I saw on 60 *Minutes* a dear young lad who was a victim of leukemia. He said that when he dies he is going to ask God *why*—"and if he doesn't give me an answer, I'm going to punch him in the mouth." The majestic thing was the boy's childlike/adult implication that if God will only *answer* him, this will somehow be enough to annul the retribution against God.

"Rabbi Elisha ben Abuyah, the Talmud relates, foreswore belief in God after witnessing the death of one innocent child. One cannot but understand if faith breaks after having witnessed the death of six million innocent men, women, and children."[28] The question here is anything but the theoretical one of whether there is a divine providence in history that works things out for good. (There is no theoretical resolution of that theoretical question.) The real question is one of life and death. The Holocaust bears witness that human history is a place where things work out for evil—indeed, where absolute evil is done for absolute evil's sake (Emil L. Fackenheim). Here is the very reason why our course of action must be to marshall history against history itself. And this is how the pathway is opened, not for intellectual or theological reflection upon this or that view of God, and surely not for weighing argumentatively the relative fortunes of "good" and "evil" in the world, but instead for bringing the God of history before the bar of justice—due precisely to his own standards and requirements of justice. Accordingly, the venue of a university or theological school classroom is disallowed. The confrontation must take place in a courtroom. The participants are not mere scholars, mere professors, mere students. They are accusers, witnesses, those who must testify, those who must judge. Yet they are impelled to take the witness stand only because their hearts have been broken—by the torment of the history of their religious faith as by the very history of God.

In the Kingdom of Night the Judges-Isaiah-Hugo theodicy of goodness-means-reward-and-evil-means-punishment is smashed into pieces. This is not to say that it is reversed, for goodness-means-suffering-and-evil-means-reward is smashed as well. In place of these possibilities, there appears the figure of Dr. Joseph Mengele of Auschwitz. It is solely in and through him that the decision is made to send *these* persons to the right and *those* persons to the left. All theodicies are brought to a fateful crisis by the "Angel of Death," who would be more aptly named Satan. Justice as such is obliterated, not excepting justice invaded by injustice. T*his* (human?) will is beyond all justice. That is what makes it satanic.

There remains, however, the effort of Pharisees and their heirs to overcome the Judges-Isaiah-Hugo theology of history.* On this alternative, it cannot be said that everything evil that happens to Israel is divine punishment. For, on the contrary, God suffers with his people and goes into exile with Israel. In any event, the theological-ethical question of the *Shoah* has nothing to do with the traditional query of what the "word of God" may consist of upon the occasion of a given historical event, nor with a query of whether

---

*A revisionist, post-*Shoah* rendering of the blessing/retribution ideology of the Book of Judges—virtue is rewarded, wickedness is punished—need not cancel out such a duality in the sphere of some kind of ultimate reckoning. But the decisive consideration in the present context is that post-Holocaust thinking tends, without rejecting a blessing/retribution frame of reference, to shift the issue from human praxis to divine praxis. If God is virtuous, he deserves to be honored; if he is blameworthy, he deserves to be cast away.

the Holocaust is "revelatory" or not, nor with the enterprise of creating a theologically correct "theodicy." The only question is the one addressed to God: Are you or are you not a worthy being? What is the link, if there is one, between "for thy name's sake" and "for righteousness' sake"? Accordingly, to bring God to trial, in a post-*Shoah* time, may be the one way left for there to be obedience to God, the one way left to praise God. For is not righteousness the crucible of holiness? An answer of Yes is the compound testimony of all biblical prophecy. Judith Plaskow contends that "if the model of sacrificial obedience is destructive on an inter-human level," it "may also be destructive as a model for the human relationship to God."[29] Perhaps, then, we may commend a *self-accepting obedience* to God.

The trial of God is under way.[30]

According to a survivor of Auschwitz, a certain story was told in that camp of death about a hasidic *rebbe* who argued with a disciple in this wise: "You know, it is possible that the *rebbono shel olam* [Master of the Universe] is a liar." "How can that be possible?" asked the disciple in dismay. "Because," the *rebbe* answered, "if the *rebbono shel olam* should open his window now and look down here and see Auschwitz, he would close the window again and say, 'I did not do this.' And that would be a lie."[31]

Why would God be lying? Eliezer Berkovits writes (strictly in the frame of reference of the *Shoah*): "God is responsible for having created a world in which man is free to make history."[32] This sentence is possessed of frightful power, of numinous power. The remainder of this final chapter comprises a modest *midrash* upon these sixteen words. By virtue of a single sentence Rabbi Berkovits is consigning to perdition any protest that Auschwitz is only the sin of men and not at the same time the sin of God. No *human being, no death camp victim—yet how are we to exclude the victimizers?—ever asked to be born or had anything to do with being born.* The *Shoah* is a final (= existential) refutation of the religious notion that human beings have no right to question God and the ways of God. (There is no answer to the charge that to seek to bring God to task is the ultimate human betrayal, save through the possibility that this human effrontery is itself somehow bonded to God's will, that God herself has a stake in developing daughters and sons who stand on their own two feet as human beings with dignity, even if need be at God's expense.) To silence such questioning is to commit sacrilege against the *imago dei*: "My God, my God, why hast thou forsaken me?" (Ps. 22:1; Mark 15:34). And not alone the psalmist and Jesus but Abraham lives again, now in the shadow of the fires and the gas chambers: "Shall not the Judge of all the earth do right?" (Gen. 18:25). Job as well is here in the courtroom: "I will defend my ways to his face" (13:15b). And so is Habakkuk: "Why dost thou look on faithless men, and art silent when the wicked swallows up the man more righteous than he?" (1:13).

The sentence of Eliezer Berkovits cuts in more than one way. It is an ontological sentence, not a historical one. Therefore, could not the same declaration have been made previous to the *Shoah* or independent of that event? I shall try to grapple with this question. If sin remains a primordial factor within human suffering (of course, not the sole factor), does not a like state of affairs obtain with respect to suffering brought by God? Yet this kind of question was raised long before the Holocaust.* The hasidic rabbis of earlier centuries sometimes brought God to trial for permitting unjustified anguish to afflict his people. They often ruled that God stood guilty.

Three parts of a brief are about to be submitted. Each part assumes the standpoint of divine/human righteousness in the presence of—*kiveyakhol?*—the divine sin.

(1) The *Shoah* is beyond consolation.

It is to no avail to protest that not all Jews were destroyed in the Destruction and that Israel still lives. I cite Professor Fackenheim:

> The pious men ... in the Lodz Ghetto spent a whole day fasting, praying, saying psalms, and then, having opened the holy ark, convoked a solemn *din Torah* [legal hearing], and forbade God to punish his people any further. (Elsewhere God was put on trial—and found guilty.) And in the Warsaw Ghetto a handful of Jews, ragged, alone, poorly armed, carried out the first uprising against the Holocaust Kingdom in all of Europe. The rabbis showed religious piety when, rather than excuse God or curse him, they cited his own promises against him. The fighters showed secular piety when, rather than surrender to the Satanic Kingdom, they took up arms against it. *The common element in these two responses was not hope but rather despair.* To the rabbis who found him guilty, the God who had broken his promises in the Holocaust could no longer be trusted to keep any promises, the messianic included. And precisely when hope had come to an end, the fighters took to arms—in a rebellion that had no hope of succeeding.

Fackenheim then proposes what I believe to be the only possible conclusion: "Every explanatory connection between the Holocaust and the State of Israel has broken down, the causal historical kind in part, the teleological religious kind entirely, and even the hope connecting the one with the other competes with despair." Does this mean that no bond exists between the two realities? No, there is such a bond, and it is unbreakable. But the bond is not a causal one, neither is it a bond of theological meaning. The bond is manifest in and through the *human response* to the *Shoah*, only there, yet necessarily there. "It is necessary because the heart of every *authentic* response to the Holocaust—religious and secularist, Jewish and non-Jewish—is a commitment to the autonomy and security of the State of Israel."[33] *Nevertheless:*

---

*At one place in Hosea it is implied that God has terminated the Covenant because of the "great harlotry" of Israel. A child is to be named "Not my people" (1:2–10). (Subsequently, the judgment is reversed.) On identical grounds, Jews of the *Shoah* can say "Not our God." May that judgment be reversed too? In any case, apodictic norms destroy themselves when they fail to attain universal applicability—to God as to humankind.

There is no consolation for the Holocaust. For the deed is done. The infants, the children, the women, the men, and the old people are dead. "Rachel is weeping for her children; she refuses to be comforted for her children, because they are not" (Jer. 31:15). And many of those who survive are among the living dead. To interject that the Ruler of the universe looked upon the abomination of desolation in Treblinka or Maidanek and resolved to return some of her offspring to Eretz Yisrael contains an obscenity. "The dead do not praise the Lord" (Ps. 115:17a). No, all consolation is absent here. The one choice is to grasp Israel as an act of defiance, whereupon Jewish life is taken wholly into the hands of the Jewish people. We are met with what Irving Greenberg calls "the third era of Jewish history,"[34] which stands for the essential rebirth of political power to replace the hell that powerlessness made possible. (The two previous eras are identified as the time before the Destruction of the Temple, and the period between that catastrophe and the Shoah.) In the day of the Shoah a paradoxical truth comes to human beings: To leave everything to God is to betray God; to do everything themselves (even against God) is to serve God. For the latter reason, as Greenberg has it, "we are living in the age of the renewal of the Covenant."[35]

I do not believe that it follows from the above that the Torah is dead. Is there a sense in which the corpus of commands to the Jewish people to live as Jews remains morally legitimate? Yes, on the stipulation that the Jewish people maintain sovereign political power. Otherwise the command is indefensible. In principle, the dilemma of Torah apodicticity vis-à-vis human dignity is thereby resolved. (This is in ruling accord with biblical prophecy, which presupposes that Israel is possessed of collective laic integrity. How is it possible for Abraham J. Heschel to dedicate his classic work on the biblical prophets to "the martyrs of 1940-45"? For did not the absolute demands of these men—as Stellvertreter of Yahweh—contribute eventually to the martyrdom? I do not see any way to save those demands from immorality other than by balancing them against political independence.)

(2) The nature of the Holocaust's intention—to kill every last Jew—bears tellingly upon the complicity of God.

Accusations of "Holocaust-myopia" are being brought these days, charges that certain Jews and certain Christians have taken the Holocaust and made it into an obsession chopped off from the history of Jewish and other suffering. One response to the accusers is that they have betrayed the absolute singularity of the event: the intention of the Holocaust. The accusers would do well to reflect upon a remorseful letter that Adolf Hitler felt compelled to write just before his suicide. In the letter Hitler apologized for not having exterminated the Jews. Six million Jews were dead, yet Hitler knew that he was a total failure. By comparison, other acts of destruction against Jews have always been successes.

It is particularly at the point of intentionality that the Shoah cannot be dissociated from what it was that made the event possible in the first place, namely, the Covenant, the setting apart of Jews as "a kingdom of priests and a holy nation," a light to the peoples of the world (Exod. 19:6; Isa. 42:6). If it is unjust to demand that children suffer because their parents sin, it is comparably unjust to demand that people suffer because their ancestors made certain promises. The Covenant is the one reality that serves to make the *Shoah* revelatory, *kiveyakhol.* The intentionality of the Covenant and the intentionality of the *Shoah* are what unite the two realities. They are blood brothers. Presumably, God is anything but uncaring of the future, and he ought to have had the sense to foresee the consequences of his own methods and decisions. To be sure, God is the culprit behind all sufferings of Jews-as-Jews. But the Nazi intention to kill every Jew brings to light the monstrousness intrinsic to the Covenant that was not previously evident. This is shown in the question of a young madman: "How does God justify Himself in His own eyes, let alone in ours? If the real and the imaginary both culminate in the same scream, in the same laugh, what is creation's purpose, what is its stake?"[36] *In the Holocaust the holy nation is turned into excrement*: this is the program's purpose. Therefore, after the *Shoah* collective Jewish martyrdom would only make feces of the name of God. The one way left for Jews—other people too?—to serve God is to have children and to keep them safe.[37] Human suffering is the enemy.

(3) A third element of a brief in behalf of the norm of divine/human righteousness takes us back to the relation between human integrity and apparent sacrilege. I restrict myself to what could be called the unforgivableness of forgiveness and the forgiveness of unforgivableness.

Elie Wiesel describes the genesis of his play *The Trial of God*: "Inside the Kingdom of Night [the *Shoah*] I witnessed a strange trial. Three rabbis—all erudite and pious men—decided one winter evening to indict God for allowing his children to be massacred. I remember: I was there, and I felt like crying. But there nobody cried." As the drama moves along, only a solitary individual can be found who is ready and willing to serve as defense attorney. In the interest of those who have not yet read or seen the play, I shan't reveal that party's true identity. I mention only his name. It is Sam.

The burden of Sam's argument is this: While the events are not to be disputed, they are irrelevant. For who is to blame for them? Human beings, and human beings alone. Why implicate God? God's ways are just and beyond reproach. Our duty is simple: to glorify him, to love him—in spite of ourselves. (*Just who in our world today would be distributing that kind of theological-moral advice?*) By contrast, the prosecutor argues that if our truth is not God's as well, then God is beneath contempt—for giving us the taste and passion of truth without apprising us that such truth is in fact false. He may very well persist in his destructive ways. This does not mean that we have to give our approval. "Let Him crush me, I won't say Kaddish [the mourner's prayer]. Let Him kill me, let Him kill us all, I shall shout and shout that it's His fault." Let the priests chatter on about God's suffering. He is big enough to take care of himself. We do better to pity other human beings.[38]

Jesus said: "If you are offering your gift at the altar, and there remember that your brother has something against you, leave your gift there before the altar and go; first be reconciled to your brother, and then come and offer your gift" (Matt. 5:23–24). But what are we to do if we have murdered our brother? The way to reconciliation is blocked. And God? Forgiveness for God may be conceivable if he can still somehow manage to leave his gifts at the altar and go and be reconciled to his human children. He has sinned against life, and life can only be vindicated through life.

How, then, is God to be saved? Two possibilities suggest themselves. First, he can seek out human forgiveness. In Wiesel's work *Souls on Fire* Rabbi Levi-Yitzhak reminds God that he had better ask forgiveness for the hardships he has inflicted upon his children. That is why, so the tale goes, the phrase *Yom Kippur* appears also in the plural, *Yom Kippurim*: "the request for pardon is reciprocal."[39] Second, God can act to redeem herself. One way to do this is to make certain that the victims of the *Shoah*—indeed, all human victims—are raised to eternal life. This suggests to us that the final disposition of the *trial* of God will turn upon the *future* of God.

Yet our own special obligation remains that of human beings. The trial of God moves to its denouement. The verdict is given: Guilty as charged. Eliezer Berkovits concludes that within the dimension of time and history, the ways of God are simply unforgivable.[40] But what is to be God's sentence?

IV

Courtroom sentencings are determined by historical situations: the identity of the judges, the witnessess, the lawyers, the jury, the nature of the evidence, the circumstances, the time and place, the legal system, the applicable moral standards, etc., etc. In the present case an analogy is called for. Simon Wiesenthal gives us a true story titled *The Sunflower*. He recounts a personal experience. A dying Nazi soldier in a makeshift army hospital one day begged Wiesenthal to grant him forgiveness for the young man's crimes against the Jewish people. Wiesenthal found that he had to leave the bedside without giving any reply—save the reply of silence.[41] One possibly compelling reason for such silence is that no human being is justified in forgiving wrongs done to other human beings.

What gives a human being the right to forgive God, especially when the person is not a victim and is perhaps in fact an associate of the human victimizers? The actual victims, dead and living, may well wish to oppose all such forgiveness, and this upon impregnable moral grounds. (The effrontery of the non-victim here is perhaps only equalled by his having called God to task for the sufferings of other people. Yet does not this latter act at least reflect the human obligation to be a keeper of one's sisters and brothers?) The protests of some actual victims mean that in the present historical instance there is no way to forgive God without committing some kind of sin against certain people. This truth has to be kept at the forefront with respect to the remainder of our discussion. The right to forgive God appertains at most to one's own life and experience. (For that matter, the testimony of Rabbi Berkovits that the ways of God are unforgivable cannot possibly be a representative one. He is able to speak only for himself.) A large part of the present study is representative of collective opinion; the remaining paragraphs of this chapter are of necessity personal. (That does not annul the need for forgiveness—of the party involved and also of God.)

In his powerful *oeuvre* upon the Holocaust, Arthur Cohen brings honor to those who are aware of the abyss of the *tremendum* in all its horror, yet whose own being "is elsewhere—on the bridge, in fact, over the abyss."[42] The complication is that every bridge points in at least two opposite directions. Which direction is to be mine?

Permit me to start out in one direction. I find it overwhelming that Wiesel's *Trial of God* should be set on the Feast of Purim, an occasion when, as the innkeeper Berish observes (the very chap who plays the role of prosecutor): "Everything goes." And we are to wear masks on the journey, since Purim is a day for fools, children, and beggars.[43] Perhaps, then, we can at least play together (before the dark comes). Here is one little gem for entertainment along the way:

> A rabbinical student is about to leave Europe for a position in the New World. He goes to his rabbi for advice, and the rabbi, a great Talmud scholar, offers an adage which, he assures the younger man, will guide him through his life: "Life is a fountain."
>
> The young rabbi is deeply impressed by the profundity of his teacher's remarks, and departs for a successful career in America. Thirty years later, hearing that his mentor is dying, the younger man returns for a final visit.
>
> "Rabbi," he says to his old teacher, "I have one question. For thirty years, every time I have been sad or confused I have thought of the phrase you passed on to me before I left for America. It has helped me through the most difficult of times. But to be perfectly honest with you, rabbi, I have never fully understood the meaning of it. And now that you are about to enter the World of Truth, perhaps you would be so kind as to tell me what these words really mean. Rabbi, why *is* life like a fountain?"
>
> Wearily, the old man replies, "All right, so it's *not* like a fountain."[44]

I include this story only for the purpose of pointing up a stark contrast to it: In *The Gates of the Forest* the dancing and singing of a certain *hasid* remain his way of telling God: "You don't want me to dance; too bad. I'll dance anyhow. You've taken away every reason for singing, but I shall sing. I shall sing of the deceit that walks by day and the truth that walks by night, yes, and of the silence of dusk as well. You didn't expect my joy, but here it is; yes, my joy will rise up; it will submerge you."[45]

The one direction of the bridge thus seems to end in a wall of stone. The playing, the singing, the dancing, the joking—none of these can any longer be done for the sake of joy, but only in behalf of outrage, of defiance. As Julian Green said, After Auschwitz, only tears have meaning. The *rebbe* who tells the story of the singing and dancing *hasid* has to grant that the song merely cloaks "a dagger, an outcry." The humor and the joy only fall upon their swords. And, worse, the Feast of Purim appears powerless before an ice-hot awareness that should the unforgivableness of forgiveness ever become the final word, despair will in a single moment gain dominion over all things. The visit by the character Gregor to the storytelling *rebbe* climaxes in a pitiful request, "Rabbi, make me able to cry."[46]

But perhaps there is a door in the wall of stone. If so, will not laughter at least help carry us to the door? And might it be that beyond the door lies forgiveness? Cullen Hightower has written that "there are people who can talk sensibly about a controversial issue without taking sides; they are called humorists."[47] (Humor is a good friend of pluralism.) In authentic humor we all, in a way, stand forgiven.

Therefore, let us not be too hasty to abandon the way of Purim: Abraham J. Heschel emphasizes the "overwhelming sympathy with the divine pathos" that the prophet Isaiah developed.[48] Why do we not just don the mask of Isaiah? The play's the thing: no one will stop us. Contrary to Berish the prosecutor, to be sorry for God and for human beings is never an either/or: the two deeds sustain each other. For me, the penultimate height of faith—not the final height, for that would be salvation, the last reconciliation of humankind and God—the penultimate height of faith is to find oneself genuinely sorry for God (*daath elohim*, sympathy for God).

The psalmist testifies:

> My tears have been my food
>   day and night,
> while men say to me continually,
>   "Where is your God?" (42:3)

After the night of the *Shoah* is not this the word of God:

> My tears have been my food
>   day and night,
> while the heavens say to me continually,
>   "Where are your children?"

Before the *Shoah* the prophet is sent by the Lord "to bind up the brokenhearted" (Isa. 61:1). Is it not so that after the *Shoah*, the remnant of humankind is sent to bind up the broken heart of God?

I think that all this is what lay behind my outrageous suggestion way back in chapter one that God is, *kiveyakhol*, a klutz. Yes, this is the very worst thing we could say, and—for that reason, *but much more in the presence of Auschwitz-Birkenau and Belzec and Chelmo and Maidanek and Sobibor and Treblinka*—we are condemned/blessed to say it: God is the ultimate klutz. She would have to go and make herself a world. Now he is stuck with it, and with us, and she is left with little choice but to keep on undergoing the agony of it. For no divine sin is possible without human beings, just as no human sin could ever eventuate apart from God. (Yet without human beings, how could the story of God ever be told? What could be more sad than the total aloneness of God?) And by revealing and making normative for humankind certain apodictic requirements, God opened the way to being held unmercifully to account before the very same requirements—and, of all things, at the hands of that upstart, humankind. The Creator of all the universes made radically assaultable, and under his very own sponsorship! If this is not the essence of klutzyness, then I do not know what that concept means. But were God a *total* klutz, how could we ever be enabled to behold the faces of children? However: I think I am prepared to suggest a deal (perhaps moved by the palliation induced by more or less having finished the book). I am willing to substitute *vulnerability* for klutzyness.

It is so nevertheless: God remains unforgivable. Rabbi Berkovits is right. Yet I believe that it is also right to forgive God. A transfiguration of roles here takes place: Once upon a time, God was responsible for human beings. Once upon today's time, her people are responsible for God. Who is there to take the side of God if we do not? Who is there to go to his side, in her aloneness? Dietrich Bonhoeffer taught that God does not appreciate "cheap grace."[49] Yet maybe we *can*, when it comes to God. Does that make us inferior to God? Well, it hardly makes us superior: it is not we who originated forgiveness. Forgiveness is a gift of God. And if it is so that on the Feast of Purim our own grace has to go for cheap, to go, indeed, for no price at all, this is because all the available currency was burned up in the *Shoah*. To lapse into more sophisticated language: If God is to be God, perhaps this will have to be established *despite* theodicy—*via the very impossibility of any divine vindication.*

Why do I believe that we ought to forgive the unforgivable God, and without any price and without any conditions? The answer comes down to whether we love God, in all his unforgivableness. And there is a special justification: Does not God herself yearn that we be free? (Cf. David Tracy: "Perhaps it need not always be the case that the God of the Scriptures and the God of the philosophers are irreconcilable. In that revolution in theological reflection upon the meaning of God called process thought, perhaps that chasm has at last been bridged."[50] One consideration that may help save Christian and Jewish historicism from despair and meaninglessness before the fact of such an event as the *Shoah* is the "process" conviction of a God who works up through history, *against* human beings but also *with* human beings in their own freedom. To associate God with "process" need not be to deny God as person, that is, as one who possesses the twin qualities of personhood: structure and freedom. The basis of identifying God as a person is the conviction that God "embodies both the structure of being and a transcendent freedom."[51]) Further, as Paul Tillich has it, "a person experiences an unconditional demand only from another person. The demand becomes concrete in the 'I-Thou' encounter. The content of the demand is therefore that the 'thou' be accorded the same dignity as the 'I' [and, we may add, that the 'I' be accorded the same dignity as the 'thou']; this is the dignity of being free.... This recognition of the equal dignity of the 'Thou' and the 'I' is justice.... Justice is the true power of being."[52] Or—can we not substitute?—*love* is the true power of being, for at this place love and justice appear as united, within the praxis of a most strange equality.

It was the very same prophet who knew sorrow for God who also insisted that "the holy God proves himself holy by righteousness" (Isa. 5:16). On the assumption that the *imago dei* and the *imitatio dei* somehow converge here, human beings too prove themselves holy by righteousness. But righteousness can never come finally into its own until it is forgiven, until everyone begins to smile and then breaks up in laughter, in joy. This is how the righteousness of God is itself set free. Love between God and humankind is always having to tell the partner that one is sorry. Laughter is sorrow, sorrow is laughter.

I have heard it said that at the conclusion of one of the many trials of God, after the accused had been adjudged guilty as charged, a certain *hasid* rose before the assembly and said: "Let us pray." And it is told, at the close of *The Gates of the Forest*, that Gregor, whose real identity was that of Gavriel but whose faith had been carried off in the transports to the East, came to pray. He prayed for, among others, the soul of his father. And he prayed as well for the soul of God.[53]

Could it be that the return of the *Shekhinah* from exile is under way?

People of eight have had their say. Let people of nine et seq. take their turn. (Authentic Christian historicism welcomes, even celebrates, that right of succession—a new "apostolic succession"?) During the moments that the ninth people are assembling their instruments and their arguments, and donning their masks, a few last words may be heard from the historicist camp: The redeeming of God[54]—as of the Christian faith—empowers the laughing of special kinds of laughter. Perhaps it is by virtue of such laughter that "from time to time the Creator, Blessed be Her Name," will "set forward the clock of the Last Judgment by one minute." For it is in accordance with this same laughter that, as testified by Rabbi Nachman of Bratislav, "nothing is so whole as a broken heart"—provided that the heart is broken for righteousness' sake.

Epilogue

Consider the Animals

Platero is a small donkey, a soft hairy donkey: so soft to the touch that he might be said to be made of cotton, with no bones. . . . I call him softly, "Platero?" and he comes to me at a gay little trot that is like laughter of a vague, idyllic, tinkling sound.

—Juan Ramon Jiménez,
Platero y Yo

THIS book has focused upon human-divine obligation. Yet human beings are hardly the only creatures on Planet Earth. Human exploitation and mal-treatment of other life, often called speciesism, is affinal to such evils as ra-cism and sexism. Peter Singer and others stress the parallels between the oppression of humans and the oppression of animals. By way of a last testi-mony against exclusivism, I include a brief word about the "higher animals" as representative of other creatures of God.[1]

"Higher" suggests something distinctive. From one point of view, the ani-mals represent simply one more level within the complex structures of na-ture. Yet they are also set apart from the rest of nature. They resemble us, as we resemble them.

The animals transcend the natural world through, among other things, the menace of distress. This makes them sisters and brothers of human-kind, as it makes us sisters and brothers of the animals. It is here that good and bad, even right and wrong, intrude themselves. To toss a stone into a pond is not, in and of itself, a moral act. And, as the Japanese and others teach us, when human beings arrange plants and flowers in careful concert they enable these objects to reach a fulfillment they could not at-tain were they left to thrive haphazardly, "free" of human interference. However, such fulfillment is much more aesthetic than it is moral. The boundary between the amoral and the moral domains is drawn by the eventuality of distress. This is why the arbitrary removal of an animal from

326

its erstwhile habitat is quite a different kind of act from the dislocating of rocks or plants. Now the query becomes especially poignant: Do we really have the right to force that change?

To express the case philosophically, the question of what is "right" is determined by the question of "being." From the standpoint of "being," of what "is," we behold in the higher animals a sort of miracle, the miracle of independent movement and sentience. In contrast to "lesser" forms of nature, a new kind of being confronts reality and us, a creature that gathers impressions all its own and matures into rudimentary self-consciousness and self-identity. Here are creatures who are eligible for deprivation and pain, but capable as well of a certain childlike companionship together with its fateful partner, loneliness.

It is said that there are dangers in this line of observation, dangers of sentimentalism and anthropomorphism. Humans are reputed to be "a little lower than the angels"; this ensures our distance from God. So too the animals are a little lower than humans, i.e., they are innocent. The remembrance of this fact helps keep us from the above dangers. Of course, humankind is itself an animal. But humans are animals with a qualitative difference. One way to define humankind is to say that it is the animal that puts other animals into zoos. But the definition is too narrow. For humans are very strange animals: They often wonder whether it is they who are behind the bars of the cage. Humanity knows the higher suffering of anxiety, of meaninglessness, of conscience.

To scold the family puppy for being a "bad dog" is in fact to insult him. In a later moment, when reason returns, we are capable of confessing our anthropomorphic lapse. Clearly, it is convenient to teach our pets "civilized" habits; they are readily "conditioned" to behave this way rather than that way. Yet, at most, it is only a primordial kind of accountability that begins to surface in the animals. In them nature has evolved into, yet is constrained by, spirited nonresponsibility. Here at once is their opportunity and their confinement. The household pet remains marvelously self-possessed and self-contained. This becomes alarming only in human beings. We are made apprehensive by the eating habits of our children, and we reprimand them for their messiness. But morality and psychology are pushed aside as we relish vicariously the innocent gluttony of our pets. Human beings justify their lives through a healthy tension between "is" and "ought"; the animals vindicate themselves merely by "being." Animal beastliness is circumscribed and blessed by innocence.

Lamentably, the innocence does not keep pathos away, either for the animals themselves or for us in their presence. One man, noting the distress of another man, may adjudge, with good reason, that the other "had it coming." And when affliction strikes his own life, he may even receive the grace to apply to himself the same conclusion. Contrast here the vexation and impotence many of us have known when binding up the wounds of bird or beast.* We are met by the poor creature's inchoate bewilderment before a world where "good" and "bad," "right" and "wrong," lack substantive or rational meaning and are hence incapable of offering any consolation. At best, such categories, for the animal, are like the fleeting shadows known to some persons afflicted with blindness.

The lot of the animals is not a tragic one, for tragedy entails accountability. The animals' plight is one of pathos. The heart of this pathos is the absence of comprehension. Thus, the beauty of the animals within this world that frames their portrait remains a beauty they themselves can never know. As Jiménez tells his donkey, "Your eyes, which you cannot see, Platero, and which you raise humbly to the sky, are two beautiful roses."

One consideration helps to temper the pathos. We are not God, yet something in our life with the animals points to the divine life. Attention to and even concern for the human neighbor is still a fixation upon our own species. Love for other humans may reach sublime heights. But it is never entirely liberated from *eros*, mutual or self-fulfilling love. The most unselfish intrahuman deed may only induce praise from the other, thus bolstering our self-esteem and self-interest.

Happily, love may be more than *eros*; it can become *agape*, wholly other-regarding love. Other beings are now ends in themselves and not means. The ideally redeeming quality of our life with the animals rests upon the truth that, *rationally speaking*, the animals cannot respond as persons. Yes, they may grope vaguely for the accountability, the gratitude, that comes to flower in humanity. But the groping remains a pitiable thing, too embryonic to be telling. The animals are simply incapable of manifesting authentic gratitude, despite all the superficial parallels with human behavior. The parallels are deceptive. To assert the opposite would be *real* sentimentality.

It is the non-personal nature of the animals that grants majesty to humankind's love for them. Be it remembered that even the divine love does not preclude the suffering and destruction of the creatures of God. (There ought to be a world in which animals [including humans] do not prey upon each other. It is not right.) The behavior of the "higher" animals, including the "affection" they show us, is not the love that personal freedom can alone make possible. And yet we humans are enabled to love these creatures. It follows—I offer a bold analogy—that we thereby learn a little of what it is like to stand in the place of God in a universe where for one or another reason human beings do not comprehend God's love.

*Some eighty million birds die each year in the United States by crashing into window panes. That number can be greatly reduced through various protective devices.

Notes

1. Beginnings

1. Cf. H. Richard Niebuhr, *The Responsible Self: An Essay in Christian Moral Philosophy* (San Francisco: Harper & Row, 1978), p. 45.

2. Lonnie Kliever, *H. Richard Niebuhr* (Waco, Texas: Word Books, 1977), p. 184. On the concept "center of value," see H. Richard Niebuhr, *Radical Monotheism and Western Culture with Supplementary Essays* (New York: Harper & Brothers, 1960), pp. 100–113.

3. Walter Rauschenbusch, *A Theology for the Social Gospel* (New York: Macmillan, 1918), pp. 101–102.

4. Van A. Harvey, *The Historian and the Believer: The Morality of Historical Knowledge and Christian Belief* (Philadelphia: Westminster, 1966), p. 137. See also Friedrich Gogarten, *The Reality of Faith*, trans. Carl Michalson and others (Philadelphia: Westminster, 1959); Larry Shiner, *The Secularization of History: An Introduction to the Theology of Friedrich Gogarten* (Nashville: Abingdon, 1966).

5. Uriel Tal, "German-Jewish Social Thought in the Mid-Nineteenth Century," in *Revolution and Evolution: 1848 in German-Jewish History, aus Schriftenreihe Wissenschaftlicher Abhandlungen des Leo Baeck Institute*, 39 (Tübingen: J.C.B. Mohr [Paul Siebeck], 1981), p. 300n.

6. Frederick E. Crowe, *The Lonergan Enterprise* (Cambridge, Mass.: Cowley Publications, 1980), p. 82.

7. H. Richard Niebuhr, *Christ and Culture* (New York: Harper & Brothers, 1951); Ernst Troeltsch, *The Social Teaching of the Christian Churches*, 2 vols., trans. Olive Wyon (London: Allen & Unwin, 1931).

8. H. R. Niebuhr, *Christ and Culture*, pp. 32–39.

9. Ibid., pp. 43–44.

10. Herbert Butterfield, *Christianity and History* (London: G. Bell and Sons, 1954), p. 81.

11. David Tracy, *Blessed Rage for Order: The New Pluralism in Theology* (New York: Seabury, 1978), p. 243.

329

12. H. Richard Niebuhr, "Types of Christian Ethics" (mimeographed conspectus, n.d.). This conspectus was distributed to students in Niebuhr's basic course in Christian ethics at the Yale Divinity School in the early 1940s.

13. Ibid.

14. Ibid.

15. Ibid.

16. H. R. Niebuhr, *Responsible Self*, pp. 60–61.

17. Cf. ibid., p. 136.

18. Dorothee Sölle, "Mysticism, Liberation and the Names of God," *Christianity and Crisis* 41 (1981): 183.

19. Krister Stendahl, *Paul Among Jews and Gentiles and Other Essays* (Philadelphia: Fortress, 1976), p. viii.

20. Heinz Moshe Graupe, *The Rise of Modern Judaism: An Intellectual History of German Jewry* 1650–1942, trans. John Robinson (Huntington, N.Y.: Robert E. Krieger, 1978), p. 249.

21. For a brief but helpful exposition of the way in which the rationality of traditional Christian theism may be defended, consult Basil Mitchell, *The Justification of Religious Belief* (New York: Oxford University Press, 1981). On the question of God with special reference to moral philosophy, consult Lenn Evan Goodman, *Monotheism: A Philosophic Inquiry into the Foundations of Theology and Ethics* (Totowa, N.J.: Allenheld, Osmun/Oxford Centre for Hebrew Studies, 1981).

22. Lawton Posey, "Paul Tillich's Gift of Understanding," *The Christian Century* 98 (1981): 968.

2. Human History and the Divine Righteousness

1. Cf. Edwin S. Shneidman, ed., *Endeavors in Psychology: Selections from the Personology of Henry A. Murray* (New York: Harper & Row, 1981), p. 275.

2. James A. Sanders, "The Bible as Canon," *The Christian Century* 98 (1981): 1250, 1253, 1254, 1255.

3. James A. Sanders, "Hermeneutics of True and False Prophecy," in Burke O. Long and George W. Coats, eds., *Canon and Authority: Essays in Old Testament Religion and Theology* (Philadelphia: Fortress, 1977), pp. 40–41.

4. Mitchell, *Justification of Religious Belief*, p. 145. On the problem of biblical inspiration and authority, see ibid., pp. 152–156.

5. Sanders, "Bible as Canon," pp. 1251, 1252.

6. Gabriel Josipovici, "The Irreducible Word," *European Judaism* 15 (1981): 20.

7. "Good," "Truth," *A Theological Word Book of the Bible*, ed. Alan Richardson (New York: Macmillan, 1952), pp. 99, 269–270; Abraham J. Heschel, *The Prophets*, Vol. I (New York: Harper Colophon Books, 1969), p. 57; Bernhard W. Anderson, *The Eighth Century Prophets: Amos-Hosea-Isaiah-Micah* (Philadelphia: Fortress, 1978), p. 42.

8. "Know, Knowledge," *Theological Word Book*, p. 121; Heschel, *Prophets*, I, p. 57.

9. Heschel, *Prophets*, I, p. 57.

10. Ibid., pp. 200–201, 210.

11. "Moses," *Encyclopaedia Judaica* (Jerusalem), XII, p. 371.

12. Scholars differ over the actual dating, origins, and distinctiveness of the Decalogue and its reception. On recent scholarship, see Walter Harrelson's summarization in *The Ten Commandments and Human Rights* (Philadelphia: Fortress, 1980), pp. 19–48. There is a tendency today to earlier dating of the "Ten Words." Harrelson adjudges that "the Ten Commandments as a series are from Moses" himself (pp. 42–43).

13. Ibid., p. 42.

14. Ibid., p. 46; see also pp. 53–54.

15. James Parkes, *The Foundations of Judaism and Christianity* (London: Vallentine, Mitchell, 1960), p. xv.

16. Gerard S. Sloyan, *Is Christ the End of the Law?* (Philadelphia: Westminster. 1978), pp. 27–28.

17. Harrelson, *Ten Commandments and Human Rights*, pp. 23, 24, 25–26.

18. Bernhard W. Anderson, *Understanding the Old Testament* (Englewood Cliffs, N.J.: Prentice-Hall, 1957), p. 55.

19. Harrelson, *Ten Commandments and Human Rights*, p. 17.

20. Gene M. Tucker, "The Role of the Prophets and the Role of the Church," *Quarterly Review* 1 (1981): 14.

21. Anderson, *Eighth Century Prophets*, pp. 1, 2.

22. Tucker, "Role of the Prophets," p. 18.

23. Heschel, *Prophets*, I, p. 33.

24. Anderson, *Eighth Century Prophets*, pp. 15, 22.

25. Heschel, *Prophets*, I, p. 25.

26. Anderson, *Eighth Century Prophets*, p. 43.

27. Heschel, *Prophets*, I, pp. 218–219.

28. Sloyan, *Is Christ the End of the Law?*, pp. 22–23.

29. Anderson, *Eighth Century Prophets*, p. 59.

30. Ibid., p. 66.

31. Ibid., pp. 66–67.

32. Heschel, *Prophets*, I, pp. 198, 216.

33. Harrelson, *Ten Commandments and Human Rights*, pp. 53, 20, and *passim*.

34. Hans Werner Wolff, "The Day of Rest in the Old Testament," *Lexington Theological Quarterly* 7 (1962): 76, as quoted in Sloyan, *Is Christ the End of the Law?*, p. 27.

35. Heschel, *Prophets*, I, p. 110.

36. *The Confessions of St. Augustine*, trans. E. B. Pusey (London: J. M. Dent & Sons, 1907), bk. i, ch. I.

37. Cf. Harrelson, *Ten Commandments and Human Rights*, pp. 173–193.

3. Faith against the World

1. H. R. Niebuhr, *Christ and Culture*, chap. 2.

2. John Line, "Truth Is in Order to Goodness," *Theology Today* 2 (1945): 160–174.

3. Eugene B. Borowitz, *Contemporary Christologies: A Jewish Response* (New York: Paulist, 1980), pp. 158–159.

4. Troeltsch, *Social Teaching of the Christian Churches*, I, p. 339.

5. "Essenes," *Encyclopaedia Judaica* (Jerusalem), Vol. VI, pp. 899–902; "Dead Sea Sect," Vol. V, pp. 1408, 1411; Geza Vermes, *The Dead Sea Scrolls: Qumran in Perspective*, rev. ed. (Philadelphia: Fortress, 1981), pp. 88, 117, 125, 126, 171, 172–174, 179, 180, 181; Hyam Maccoby, *Revolution in Judaea: Jesus and the Jewish Resistance* (New York: Taplinger, 1980), pp. 73, 226. Very many scholars agree that the identification of the Qumran sect with the Essene community is to be preferred to any other ("Dead Sea Sect," pp. 1418–1419; Maccoby, p. 73; Vermes, pp. 126–130).

6. Vermes, *Dead Sea Scrolls*, p. 165.

7. Ibid., p. 167.

8. Ibid., pp. 167–168.

9. Rick Hordern, "Paul as a Theological Authority," *Union Seminary Quarterly Review* 33 (1978): 133.

10. H. R. Niebuhr, *Christ and Culture*, pp. 159–167, 196, 170.

11. Cf. Vermes, *Dead Sea Scrolls*, pp. 218, 219.

12. See below, note 29.

13. W. D. Davies, *Paul and Rabbinic Judaism: Some Rabbinic Elements in Pauline Theology,* 4th ed. (Philadelphia: Fortress, 1980), p. 285.

14. H. R. Niebuhr, *Christ and Culture,* p. 193.

15. E. P. Sanders, "Paul's Attitude Toward the Jewish People," *Union Seminary Quarterly Review* 33 (1978): 185.

16. Clark M. Williamson, *Has God Rejected His People? Anti-Judaism in the Christian Church* (Nashville: Abingdon, 1982), pp. 50, 62.

17. Cf. Lloyd Gaston, "Paul and the Torah," in Alan Davies, ed., *Antisemitism and the Foundations of Christianity* (New York: Paulist, 1979), p. 51.

18. Williamson, *Has God Rejected His People?,* p. 62.

19. Ibid., p. 63; E. P. Sanders, *Paul and Palestinian Judaism: A Comparison of Patterns of Religion* (Philadelphia: Fortress, 1977), pp. 543, 517.

20. Stendahl, *Paul Among Jews and Gentiles,* pp. 80, 93; Williamson, *Has God Rejected His People?,* p. 54.

21. David Flusser, "Paul of Tarsus," *Encyclopaedia Judaica* (Jerusalem), Vol. XIII, pp. 190, 191.

22. Sanders, *Paul and Palestinian Judaism,* pp. 435–442, 482–495; "Paul's Attitude Toward the Jewish People," p. 175; Davies, *Paul and Rabbinic Judaism,* pp. 221–223; Stendahl, *Paul Among Jews and Gentiles,* p. 27 and *passim.*

23. Sanders, *Paul and Palestinian Judaism,* pp. 441–442.

24. Stendahl, *Paul Among Jews and Gentiles,* pp. 26, 2, 9, 130, 40, 34.

25. Ibid., pp. 22, 84, 88–89; see in general pp. 78–96.

26. Ibid., p. 132.

27. Sanders, *Paul and Palestinian Judaism,* p. 496.

28. Stendahl, *Paul Among Jews and Gentiles,* p. 15.

29. Sanders, *Paul and Palestinian Judaism,* p. 442; Stendahl, *Paul Among Jews and Gentiles,* pp. 28, 85–86; Sanders, "Paul's Attitude Toward the Jewish People," p. 179; Richard L. Rubenstein, *My Brother Paul* (New York: Harper Torchbooks, 1972), pp. 122–126.

30. Sanders, "Paul's Attitude Toward the Jewish People," p. 180; Stendahl, *Paul Among Jews and Gentiles,* p. 4.

31. Sanders, "Paul's Attitude Toward the Jewish People," p. 181.

32. Ibid., pp. 181–182; see also Sanders, *Paul and Palestinian Judaism,* pp. 449, 470–472, 492–495, 544f.

33. Sanders, "Paul's Attitude Toward the Jewish People," p. 183; cf. pp. 176, 179–180. For a reply by Stendahl to Sanders's critique of him, see Krister Stendahl, "A Response," *Union Seminary Quarterly Review* 33 (1978): 189–191. I think that Stendahl's response does not meet Sanders's objections.

34. Sanders, *Paul and Palestinian Judaism,* p. 497 (italics in original). On the question of why God gave the Law, see *loc. cit.;* also pp. 472f., 488–491. For Sanders's summary-conclusion, consult pp. 543–556, which include his comments on Paul's views in relation to those of the Dead Sea community.

35. E. P. Sanders, *Paul, the Law, and the Jewish People* (Philadelphia: Fortress, 1983), pp. 207–208.

36. Sanders, *Paul and Palestinian Judaism,* p. 474.

37. William Baird, review of Sanders, *Paul and Palestinian Judaism,* in *Perkins Journal* 32 (1979): 39.

38. Howard Clark Kee, Franklin W. Young, and Karlfried Froelich, *Understanding the New Testament,* 3d ed. (Englewood Cliffs, N.J.: Prentice-Hall, 1973), pp. 151, 153.

39. E. P. Sanders, "Given the Christian Claims . . . How Should Christians Think of Themselves and of the Jews in Light of the Continuation of the Jewish People?" in Josephine Knopp, ed., *International Theological Symposium on the Holocaust October* 15–17, 1978 (Philadelphia: National Institute on the Holocaust, 1978), p. 62.

40. A. Roy Eckardt, *Elder and Younger Brothers: The Encounter of Jews and Christians* (New York: Scribner, 1967), pp. 55–58.

41. In this latter connection, see Charlotte Klein, *Theologie und Anti-Judaismus, Eine Studie zur deutschen theologischen Literatur der Gegenwart* (Munich: Chr. Kaiser Verlag, 1975), espec. chap. 3.

42. Cf. Sloyan, *Is Christ the End of the Law?*, pp. 94–98.

43. Sanders, *Paul and Palestinian Judaism*, p. 544.

44. Sanders, "Paul's Attitude Toward the Jewish People," p. 184.

45. Sanders, *Paul and Palestinian Judaism*, p. 552.

46. Kee et al., *Understanding the New Testament*, p. 212.

47. Rubenstein, *My Brother Paul*, p. 42.

48. Sloyan, *Is Christ the End of the Law?*, p. 182.

49. H. R. Niebuhr, *Christ and Culture*, pp. 65–69.

50. Ibid., pp. 76–82.

51. Ibid.

4. The Kingdom/Righteousness of God: Jesus of Nazareth

1. Cf. H. R. Niebuhr, *Christ and Culture*, pp. 12–27, 29.

2. Ben Zion Bokser, *Judaism and the Christian Predicament* (New York: Knopf, 1967), p. 208.

3. Nicholas de Lange, "Who is Jesus?" *Sidic* (Rome) 12 (1979): 9.

4. Will Herberg, *Faith Enacted as History: Essays in Biblical Theology*, ed. Bernhard W. Anderson (Philadelphia: Westminster, 1976), p. 192.

5. Rudolf Bultmann, *Jesus and the Word*, trans. Louise Pettibone Smith and Erminie Huntress (New York: Scribner, 1934), pp. 3–4.

6. My treatment of the titles of Jesus corresponds to the outline-exposition of Geza Vermes, *Jesus the Jew: A Historian's Reading of the Gospels* (London: Fontana/Collins, 1976), pp. 83–225.

7. Ibid., p. 84.

8. Ibid., pp. 88–90; see also A. E. Harvey, *Jesus and the Constraints of History* (London: Duckworth, 1982), pp. 57–65, 135; and Michael Grant, *Jesus* (London: Weidenfeld & Nicolson, 1977), pp. 74–75, 80–81.

9. Vermes, *Jesus the Jew*, pp. 103, 127, 121, 126, 123, 125; Martin Hengel, *The Charismatic Leader and His Followers*, trans. James Greig (New York: Crossroad, 1981), but keeping in mind the problems Hengel emphasizes in any denominating of Jesus as "teacher" or "rabbi" (pp. 46–51).

10. Vermes, *Jesus the Jew*, pp. 130–140.

11. Ibid., pp. 144–145, 254.

12. Ibid., pp. 140–143, 149; see also Grant, *Jesus*, pp. 95–102; Harvey, *Jesus and the Constraints of History*, chap. 6.

13. Cf. Vermes, *Jesus the Jew*, pp. 160–161.

14. Ibid., pp. 185, 162, 168, 176, 186; cf. also pp. 188–191.

15. Geza Vermes, "Jewish Studies and New Testament Interpretation," *Journal of Jewish Studies* 31 (1980): 15–16.

16. Vermes, *Jesus the Jew*, pp. 202–211.

17. Grant, *Jesus*, pp. 117–118.

18. Vermes, *Jesus the Jew*, p. 209.

19. Ibid., pp. 201–202.

20. Harvey, *Jesus and the Constraints of History*, p. 157; cf. John 10:31–38.

21. Vermes, *Jesus the Jew*, p. 225.

22. Grant, *Jesus*, p. 79; Geza Vermes, *Jesus and the World of Judaism* (Philadelphia: Fortress, 1983), chap. 3; John Riches, *Jesus and the Transformation of Judaism* (London: Darton, Longman & Todd, 1980), p. 87, and in general pp. 87–111; Harvey, *Jesus and the Constraints of History*, pp. 66–97; Hengel, *Charismatic Leader*, p. 53.

23. Vermes, *Jesus and the World of Judaism*, pp. 33–35.

24. Wolfhart Pannenberg, "The Revelation of God in Jesus of Nazareth," in *Theology as History*, ed. James M. Robinson and John B. Cobb, Jr. (New York: Harper & Row, 1967), p. 113.

25. Grant, *Jesus*, pp. 18–19.

26. Maccoby, *Revolution in Judaea*, p. 206.

27. Vermes, *Jesus and the World of Judaism*, p. 53.

28. Williamson, *Has God Rejected His People?* p. 14.

29. Grant, *Jesus*, pp. 30, 33, 26, 45, 76.

30. Harvey, *Jesus and the Constraints of History*, pp. 112–113; Grant, *Jesus*, pp. 20–21, 40.

31. Harvey, *Jesus and the Constraints of History*, pp. 115–118.

32. Grant, *Jesus*, pp. 22–23.

33. Cf. Gustavo Gutiérrez, *Teología de la Liberación* (Salamanca: Ediciones Sígueme, 1977), 8th ed., chap. 13: "Pobreza: solidaridad y protesta."

34. Vermes, *Jesus the Jew*, p. 224; see also Grant, *Jesus*, pp. 52ff.

35. Grant, *Jesus*, p. 24.

36. Joel Carmichael, "The Jesus Story and the Jewish War," *Midstream* 25 (1979): 63.

37. Consult, e.g., S.G.F. Brandon, "Jesus and the Zealots: Aftermath," *Bulletin of the John Rylands Library* 44 (1971): 53–55; *Jesus and the Zealots* (Manchester: Manchester University Press, 1967), espec. chaps. 1, 5; *The Trial of Jesus* (Naperville, Ill.: Allenson, 1970); Carmichael, "The Jesus Story and the Jewish War," pp. 62ff.; Haim Cohn, *The Trial and Death of Jesus* (New York: Harper & Row, 1971); and Paul Winter, *On the Trial of Jesus* (Berlin: Gruyter, 1961).

38. Brandon, *Jesus and the Zealots*, p. 20. Examples include Matt. 5:9, 39; 26:52; Luke 6:27–29; Matt. 10:34f.; 21:12–13; Luke 12:51f.; 19:45–46; 22:36; and Mark 11:15–16.

39. Vermes, *Jesus and the World of Judaism*, pp. 35, 156.

40. Grant, *Jesus*, pp. 43, 88, 10 (italics added); see also pp. 11, 34, 41, 44, 48.

41. Gutiérrez, *Teología de la Liberación*, pp. 236–241; Carmichael, "The Jesus Story and the Jewish War," p. 68.

42. Grant, *Jesus*, p. 21; also Riches, *Jesus and the Transformation of Judaism*, p. 160.

43. See Brandon, *Jesus and the Zealots*, pp. 17–18, 280–282; Gutiérrez, *Teología de la Liberación*, pp. 297ff.

44. Hengel, *Charismatic Leader*, pp. 38ff.

45. John H. Yoder, *The Politics of Jesus: Vicit Agnus Noster* (Grand Rapids: Eerdmans, 1972), p. 108.

46. Riches, *Jesus and the Transformation of Judaism*, p. 100.

47. S.G.F. Brandon, as cited in Maccoby, *Revolution in Judaea*, p. 100.

48. Carmichael, "The Jesus Story and the Jewish War," p. 67.

49. Brandon, *Jesus and the Zealots*, p. 355.

50. Maccoby, *Revolution in Judaea*, pp. 56, 78–79, 66. But Brandon points out that Zealotism was closely linked to Messianic expectation (*Jesus and the Zealots*, pp. 112–113).

51. John Townsend, "Jesus, Land, Temple," unpublished paper at Princeton University, 1981. Cf. I Cor. 1:23 and the many passages where Paul refers to Jesus' death by crucifixion.

52. Maccoby, *Revolution in Judaea*, p. 145.

53. Brandon, "Jesus and the Zealots: Aftermath," pp. 64, 65–66; Maccoby, *Revolution in Judaea*, pp. 69, 90.

54. Yoder, *Politics of Jesus*, p. 50.

55. Brandon, *Jesus and the Zealots*, pp. 16, 203; see also pp. 20, 316, 317, 340–341.

56. Maccoby, *Revolution in Judaea*, p. 157.

57. Grant, *Jesus*, p. 117; see also pp. 51, 101.

58. James P. Mackey, *Jesus the Man and the Myth: A Contemporary Christology* (New York: Paulist, 1979), p. 65.

59. Brandon, "Jesus and the Zealots: Aftermath," p. 66.

60. Cf. Tracy, *Blessed Rage for Order*, p. 220.

61. Joseph Klausner, *Jesus of Nazareth: His Life, Times, and Teaching*, trans. Herbert Danby (New York: Macmillan, 1946), p. 390.

62. Yoder, *Politics of Jesus*, pp. 242, 100, 102 (emphasis added).

63. J. C. O'Neill, *Messiah: Six Lectures on the Ministry of Jesus* (Cambridge: Cochrane, 1980), p. 58.

64. Cf. Brandon, *Jesus and the Zealots*, pp. 316, 340–342, 355.

65. Vermes, *Jesus and the World of Judaism*, p. 38.

66. Rubenstein, *My Brother Paul*, p. 39.

67. Vermes, *Dead Sea Scrolls*, pp. 220–221.

68. On Jesus, the Deuteronomic tradition, and the Torah; also on the closeness of the Sermon on the Mount to the Decalogue, see Harrelson, *Ten Commandments and Human Rights*, pp. 161–164; also section on "Law and Gospel," pp. 164–172. In addition, see O'Neill, *Messiah*, pp. 27–43; Sloyan, *Is Christ the End of the Law?* pp. 38–69; and Vermes, *Jesus and the World of Judaism*, pp. 46–48. On the general problem of Jesus' relation to the Law, see Harvey, *Jesus and the Constraints of History*, pp. 36–65.

69. Williamson, *Has God Rejected His People?* pp. 13, 16. William E. Phipps argues that Jesus "was a Pharisee who engaged in intense interaction with other Pharisees" ("Jesus, the Prophetic Pharisee," *Journal of Ecumenical Studies* 14 [1977]: 17–31). See also Vermes, *Jesus and the World of Judaism*, p. 31; *Jesus the Jew*, pp. 55–57; Philip Culbertson, "Changing Christian Images of the Pharisees," *Anglican Theological Review* 64 (1982): 539–561; and John T. Pawlikowski, *Christ in the Light of the Christian-Jewish Dialogue* (New York: Paulist, 1982), chap. 4.

70. Carmichael, "The Jesus Story and the Jewish War," p. 64. The Pharisees would not object at all to Jesus' cures on the Sabbath; his "method of healing involved no breach of the Sabbath law" (Maccoby, *Revolution in Judaea*, pp. 63–64).

71. Riches, *Jesus and the Transformation of Judaism*, pp. 97, 168, and *passim*.

72. See, e.g., chap. 6, "Jesus and the Law of Purity," in Riches, *Jesus and the Transformation of Judaism*. Throughout, Riches reflects the highly questionable methodological assumption that where Synoptic materials are close to other Jewish materials, they are secondary (cf., e.g., p. 151).

73. Cf., e.g., Harrelson, *Ten Commandments and Human Rights*, pp. 161–164.

74. Harvey, *Jesus and the Constraints of History*, p. 93.

75. Ibid., p. 56.

76. Consult Salo W. Baron, *A Social and Religious History of the Jews*, 2d rev. ed., Vol. II, Part II (New York: Columbia University Press, 1952), pp. 73–75.

77. Riches, *Jesus and the Transformation of Judaism*, p. 159; Matt. 19:26; Mark 10:27.

78. H. R. Niebuhr, *Responsible Self*, p. 167.

79. Gutiérrez, *Teología de la Liberación*, p. 307.

80. H. R. Niebuhr, *Responsible Self*, pp. 167, 178.

5. Concretions of Righteousness and Goodness: Glimpses of the Rabbinic Tradition

1. Sloyan, *Is Christ the End of the Law?* p. 180.

2. Jack N. Lightstone, "Problems and New Perspectives in the Study of Early Rabbinic Ethics," *The Journal of Religious Ethics* 9 (1981): 199–209.

3. Adin Steinsaltz, *The Essential Talmud*, trans. Chaya Galai (New York: Basic Books, 1976), pp. 3–4.

4. David Hartman, "On the Possibilities of Religious Pluralism from a Jewish Viewpoint," *Immanuel* (Jerusalem) 16 (1983): 108.

5. Riches, *Jesus and the Transformation of Judaism*, p. 97.

6. Steinsaltz, *Essential Talmud*, pp. 95–96.

7. Williamson, *Has God Rejected His People?* pp. 13–16; in general, Ellis Rivkin, *A Hidden Revolution* (Nashville: Abingdon, 1978), espec. part 2.

8. *Genesis Rabbah* 1.6; *Leviticus Rabbah* 36.4; *Taanit* 3b; Lionel Kochan, *The Jew and His History* (London: Macmillan, 1977), p. 7.

9. Harold J. Berman, as cited by Norman Solomon in *Ends and Odds* (Arundel, West Sussex), No. 24 (1981): 3. See also Berman, *The Interaction of Law and Religion* (Nashville: Abingdon, 1974).

10. Williamson, *Has God Rejected His People?* p. 20.

11. Abraham Joshua Heschel, *The Sabbath*, p. 69, as quoted in Irving Greenberg, *Guide to Shabbat* (New York: National Jewish Resource Center, 1981), pp. 26–27.

12. Greenberg, *Guide to Shabbat*, p. 27.

13. Ibid., p. 19.

14. Steinsaltz, *Essential Talmud*, pp. 110–115.

15. Greenberg, *Guide to Shabbat*, pp. 9, 12.

16. Ibid., pp. 1, 4, 5–6 (emphasis added).

17. Ibid., pp. 13–16.

18. Ibid., pp. 22–24.

19. James O'Toole, as cited in *U.S. News & World Report* (March 14, 1983), 81.

20. From Mekhilta de-Rabbi Ishmael, *ba-hodesh* 5, as cited in Hartman, "On the Possibilities of Religious Pluralism," p. 118.

21. Morris Adler, *The World of the Talmud*, 2d ed. (New York: Schocken Books, 1963), pp. 69, 75; Z. H. Chajes, *The Student's Guide Through the Talmud*, 2d rev. ed., trans. & ed. Jacob Shachter (New York: Feldheim, 1960), pp. 157, 29–30; hereinafter cited as *Guide Through Talmud*.

22. "Decalogue," *Encyclopaedia Judaica*, V, pp. 1442–1443; Chajes, *Guide Through Talmud*, p. 20; Steinsaltz, *Essential Talmud*, p. 165.

23. As cited in Judah Goldin, ed. & trans., *The Living Talmud: The Wisdom of the Fathers* (New York: New American Library, 1957), p. 22.

24. Steinsaltz, *Essential Talmud*, pp. 167–168; "Decalogue," *Encyclopaedia Judaica*, V, p. 1443.

25. Steinsaltz, *Essential Talmud*, p. 168.

26. Ibid., pp. 172–173.

27. Ibid., pp. 169–170, 172.

28. Greenberg, *Guide to Shabbat*, p. 14; Steinsaltz, *Essential Talmud*, pp. 145, 155, 172.

29. Steinsaltz, *Essential Talmud*, pp. 155–156.

30. Ibid., pp. 145–146, 153.

31. Ibid., p. 172.

32. Eugene B. Korn, "Ethics and Jewish Law," *Judaism* 24 (1975): 206–207.

33. Adler, *World of the Talmud*, p. 134.

34. Steinsaltz, *Essential Talmud*, pp. 199–200; Goodman, *Monotheism*, p. 99.

35. Steinsaltz, *Essential Talmud*, pp. 149, 157, 201–202.

36. Ibid., p. 200.

37. Ibid., p. 203.

38. Chajes, *Guide Through Talmud*, p. 131.

39. Goodman, *Monotheism*, p. 114.

40. Ibid., chap. 3.

41. Ibid., pp. 89–90.

42. Goldin, *Living Talmud*, pp. 140, 44, 48, 49; Goodman, *Monotheism*, pp. 90, 91, 92.
43. Goldin, *Living Talmud*, p. 65.
44. Goodman, *Monotheism*, pp. 93, 117.
45. Hermann Cohen, as cited by ibid., p. 93; italics in source used.
46. Chajes, *Guide Through Talmud*, p. 131.
47. Goodman, *Monotheism*, pp. 94, 118–119.
48. Adler, *World of the Talmud*, pp. 127–128.
49. Vermes, *Jesus the Jew*, p. 92.
50. Steinsaltz, *Essential Talmud*, p. 27.
51. Goldin, *Living Talmud*, pp. 226, 150.
52. Chajes, *Guide Through Talmud*, pp. 133, 131, 132.
53. Goodman, *Monotheism*, p. 94; Grant, *Jesus*, p. 28.
54. Steinsaltz, *Essential Talmud*, p. 237; Goldin, *Living Talmud*, pp. 147, 148.
55. Chajes, *Guide Through Talmud*, pp. 30, 31, 124, 80; Adler, *World of the Talmud*, pp. 116–118.
56. Korn, "Ethics and Jewish Law," pp. 207–209.
57. Goldin, *Living Talmud*, p. 183; Adler, *World of the Talmud*, pp. 81, 98.
58. Steinsaltz, *Essential Talmud*, pp. 230, 246, 64, 56, 95.
59. Rubenstein, *My Brother Paul*, p. 134; Steinsaltz, *Essential Talmud*, pp. 259, 261; more generally, chap. 33; Goldin, *Living Talmud*, p. 81; Greenberg, *Guide to Shabbat*, p. 12; Chajes, *Guide Through Talmud*, p. 202.
60. James Parkes, *The Interplay of Judaism and Jewish History* (Southampton: The University, 1967), p. 7.
61. Harrelson, *Ten Commandments and Human Rights*, pp. 179–180 (italics in original).
62. *Tanna d'bei Eliyahu*, p. 48, as cited in Adler, *World of the Talmud*, p. 129.
63. Harrelson, *Ten Commandments and Human Rights*, pp. 180–181; italics as in original except for their added use with the words "All must keep Torah."
64. Hartman, "On the Possibilities of Religious Pluralism," pp. 110–112.
65. Ibid., p. 115.
66. Ibid., pp. 115–116.
67. Ibid., pp. 116, 117.
68. Vermes, *Jesus the Jew*, p. 197.
69. Steinsaltz, *Essential Talmud*, p. 198.
70. Ibid., p. 194; in general, pp. 193-198.
71. Goldin, *Living Talmud*, pp. 119–120; Chajes, *Guide Through Talmud*, p. 121.
72. As quoted in Adler, *World of the Talmud*, p. 69.
73. Abraham J. Heschel, *A Passion for Truth* (New York: Farrar, Straus and Giroux, 1973), p. 40.
74. As expressed in James Parkes, "Christendom and the Synagogue," *Frontier* 2 (1959): 276.
75. Goldin, *Living Talmud*, p. 36.
76. Ibid., pp. 174, 179.
77. As cited in Adler, *World of the Talmud*, p. 75.
78. As cited in Steinsaltz, *Essential Talmud*, p. 127.
79. Ibid., p. 107.

6. Faith for the World

1. H. R. Niebuhr, "Types of Christian Ethics"; *Christ and Culture*, pp. 41, 83.
2. Ibid., pp. 92, 93, 94, 84.
3. Ibid., chap. 3, espec. pp. 85, 88, 84, 94, 98; "Types of Christian Ethics."
4. Borowitz, *Contemporary Christologies*, p. 164.

5. Hermann Cohen, *Religion of Reason Out of the Sources of Judaism* (*Religion der Vernunft aus den Quellen des Judentums*), trans. Simon Kaplan (New York: Frederick Ungar, 1972); *Begriff der Religion im System der Philosophie* (Giessen: A. Toepelman Verlag, 1915), pp. 137–138.

6. Borowitz, *Contemporary Christologies*, pp. 160, 164; H. R. Niebuhr, *Christ and Culture*, p. 91.

7. Paul R. Mendes-Flohr and Jehuda Reinharz, eds., *The Jew in the Modern World*: A Documentary History (New York: Oxford University Press, 1980), p. 452; Borowitz, *Contemporary Christologies*, p. 101.

8. Graupe, *Rise of Modern Judaism*, p. 247; "Cohen, Hermann," *Encyclopaedia Judaica*, V, p. 676; Eliezer Berkovits, *Major Themes in Modern Philosophies of Judaism* (New York: Ktav, 1974), p. 30.

9. Martin Buber and Hermann Cohen, "A Debate on Zionism and Messianism," in Mendes-Flohr and Reinharz, eds., *Jew in the Modern World*, p. 450.

10. Graupe, *Rise of Modern Judaism*, pp. 247, 246; David Novak, "Universal Moral Law in the Theology of Hermann Cohen," *Modern Judaism* 1 (1981): 103.

11. Berkovits, *Major Themes in Modern Philosophies of Judaism*, pp. 35–36.

12. Buber and Cohen, "Debate on Zionism and Messianism," in Mendes-Flohr and Reinharz, eds., *Jew in the Modern World*, pp. 449, 451.

13. Ibid., p. 450; Graupe, *Rise of Modern Judaism*, p. 296n.

14. Mendes-Flohr and Reinharz, eds., *Jew in the Modern World*, p. 452.

15. Borowitz, *Contemporary Christologies*, pp. 101, 102.

16. Cohen, *Religion of Reason*, pp. 330, 54, 159.

17. "Rabbi Jacob Emden's Letter," trans. Harvey Falk, *Journal of Ecumenical Studies* 19 (1982): 110, 111.

18. Berkovits, *Major Themes in Modern Philosophies of Judaism*, pp. 19, 33, 16.

19. Ibid., p. 25.

20. Borowitz, *Contemporary Christologies*, p. 161.

21. John Locke, *The Reasonableness of Christianity with A Discourse of Miracles and part of A Third Letter Concerning Toleration*, ed. and abridged by I. T. Ramsey (Stanford: Stanford University Press, 1958).

22. H. R. Niebuhr, *Christ and Culture*, p. 91; "Types of Christian Ethics."

23. Locke, *Reasonableness of Christianity*, p. 48.

24. Robert L. Wilken, *The Myth of Christian Beginnings: History's Impact on Belief* (Garden City: Doubleday Anchor, 1972), pp. 177–178.

25. Locke, *Reasonableness of Christianity*, pp. 76–77.

26. Ibid., pp. 73, 71, 75–76.

27. George W. Forell, *Christian Social Teachings: A Reader in Christian Social Ethics from the Bible to the Present* (Garden City: Doubleday Anchor, 1966), p. 243. These distinctions of Locke are contained in *An Essay Concerning Human Understanding*, Bk. IV, Ch. 17, para. 23.

28. Locke, *Essay Concerning Human Understanding*, Bk. IV, Ch. 18, para. 2, as cited by I. T. Ramsey, Editor's Introduction to Locke, *Reasonableness of Christianity*, pp. 10–11.

29. Ramsey, Introduction to *Reasonableness of Christianity*, p. 11. Locke's other identification of faith, as cited here, is from the *Essay Concerning Human Understanding*, Bk. IV, Ch. 17, para. 24.

30. Locke, *Essay Concerning Human Understanding*, Bk. IV, Ch. 19, para. 13.

31. Ramsey, Introduction to *Reasonableness of Christianity*, pp. 11–12; Locke, *Essay Concerning Human Understanding*, Bk. IV, Ch. 19, para. 15.

32. Ramsey, Introduction to *Reasonableness of Christianity*, pp. 12–13.

33. Ibid., p. 13.

34. Ibid., pp. 13–14, 14–16. Of importance are Locke's *Discourse of Miracles* and his *Third Letter on Toleration*, which are included (the *Discourse* in its entirety) in the edition of *The Reasonableness of Christianity* here cited.

35. Ramsey, Introduction to *Reasonableness of Christianity*, p. 16.

36. Ibid., p. 19.

37. Locke, *Reasonableness of Christianity*, pp. 50, 44–45, 40; *A Discourse of Miracles*, published with *Reasonableness of Christianity*, pp. 83–84; *Reasonableness of Christianity*, p. 67.

38. Locke, *Reasonableness of Christianity*, pp. 68–69, 33, 70.

39. William A. Clebsch, *From Sacred to Profane America: The Role of Religion in American History* (Chico, Cal.: Scholars Press, 1968), p. 21.

40. H. R. Niebuhr, *Christ and Culture*, pp. 100-101.

41. Rauschenbusch, *Theology for the Social Gospel*, p. 146.

42. Ibid., pp. 24, 25, 26.

43. Ibid., pp. 5, 95, 96, 167, 7.

44. Ibid., p. 97.

45. Ibid., pp. 46-47, 50, 53, 48, 99.

46. Ibid., pp. 51, 42–43, 59, 67, 61, 57.

47. Ibid., pp. 50, 51–52, 67, 81, 62, 66, 72–73, 78.

48. Ibid., pp. 72, 86, 87; *Prayers of the Social Awakening*, in Benson Y. Landis, compiler, *A Rauschenbusch Reader* (New York: Harper, 1957), p. 36.

49. Friedrich Schleiermacher, *The Christian Faith*, as cited and trans. by Rauschenbusch, *Theology for the Social Gospel*, pp. 92–93.

50. Rauschenbusch, *Theology for the Social Gospel*, pp. 90, 91.

51. Ibid., p. 53.

52. Ibid., p. 54.

53. Ibid., pp. 155-159.

54. E.g., ibid., pp. 159–161, 186, 217, 248–254.

55. Ibid., pp. 159, 8, 15, 178. On Rauschenbusch and socialism, see *Christianizing the Social Order*, in *Rauschenbusch Reader*, pp. 47–62.

56. Rauschenbusch, *Theology for the Social Gospel*, pp. 133–137, 178.

57. Ibid., pp. 138, 105, 14, 20, 139–143, 207, 145, 226; *Christianizing the Social Order*, in *Rauschenbusch Reader*, p. 62.

58. Rauschenbusch, *Theology for the Social Gospel*, p. 279.

59. George Rupp, *Culture-Protestantism: German Liberal Theology at the Turn of the Twentieth Century* (Missoula, Mont.: Scholars Press, 1977), pp. 9–11 (italics added).

60. Kliever, *H. Richard Niebuhr*, p. 38.

61. Robert T. Handy, *A Christian America: Protestant Hopes and Historical Realities* (New York: Oxford University Press, 1971), p. 169.

62. Rauschenbusch, *Social Principles of Jesus*, in *Rauschenbusch Reader*, p. 95; *Theology for the Social Gospel*, p. 225.

63. Handy, *Christian America*, pp. 180–181.

64. Rupp, *Culture-Protestantism*, p. 55.

65. Winthrop S. Hudson, *Religion in America*, 3rd ed. (New York: Scribner, 1981), p. 316.

66. Handy, *Christian America*, p. 179; in general, pp. 174–183.

67. Clebsch, *From Sacred to Profane America*, pp. 140–141, 171–172.

68. H. R. Niebuhr, *Christ and Culture*, pp. 101, 24.

69. Ibid., pp. 106, 107, 109–110, 114.

70. Paul Ramsey, "Tradition and Reflection in Christian Life," *Perkins Journal* 35 (1982): 51.

7. Faith above History

1. H. R. Niebuhr, "Types of Christian Ethics."
2. Kliever, H. Richard Niebuhr, pp. 57–58.
3. H. R. Niebuhr, Christ and Culture, pp. 6, 117–118.
4. H. R. Niebuhr, "Types of Christian Ethics"; John A. Hutchison, The Two Cities: A Study of God and Human Politics (Garden City: Doubleday, 1957), pp. 75, 76.
5. Thomas Aquinas, Summa Theologica, II/I, Question 91, Art. 4, Basic Writings of Saint Thomas Aquinas, ed. Anton C. Pegis (New York: Random House, 1945), Vol. II, pp. 752–753.
6. H. R. Niebuhr, "Types of Christian Ethics"; Christ and Culture, p. 42.
7. Heschel, Prophets, I, p. 9.
8. John C. Bennett, Christian Ethics and Social Policy (New York: Scribner, 1946), p. 34.
9. Ibid., p. 32.
10. John C. Bennett, Christians and the State (New York: Scribner, 1958), pp. 36, 37.
11. Roland H. Bainton, Christendom: A Short History of Christianity and Its Impact on Western Civilization, Vol. I (New York: Harper Torchbooks, 1966), p. 158.
12. James P. Scull, "Roman Catholic Moral Theology (Contemporary)," in John Macquarrie, ed., Dictionary of Christian Ethics (Philadelphia: Westminster, 1967), p. 304.
13. John Macquarrie, "Just War," in Dictionary of Christian Ethics, p. 183; Bennett, Christian Ethics and Social Policy, p. 36.
14. Scull, "Roman Catholic Moral Theology (Contemporary)," p. 302. See also The Documents of Vatican II, ed. Walter M. Abbott (New York: Guild, America, Association, 1966), index under "War"; and a pronouncement of the National Conference of Catholic Bishops in the United States: The Challenge of Peace: God's Promise and Our Response (Washington: Office of Publishing Services, U.S. Catholic Conference, 1983).
15. William M. Kephart, Extraordinary Groups: The Sociology of Unconventional Life-Styles, 2d ed. (New York: St. Martin's, 1982).
16. Ibid., pp. 199-204, 213-214; "Furnishing a Glimpse of the Last Shakers," Bethlehem (Pa.) Globe Times, Jan. 27, 1978.
17. Kephart, Extraordinary Groups, pp. 204–205, 209–212, 216–217, 219–220.
18. Ibid., p. 184.
19. For analysis of the rapid decline of the Believers after the Civil War see Kephart, pp. 226–228.
20. Information garnered by A.R.E., Shaker community at Canterbury, New Hampshire, July 19, 1981.
21. Kephart, Extraordinary Groups, pp. 280, 287–289, 308.
22. Ibid., pp. 285–286.
23. Ibid., pp. 285–286, 290–291.
24. Ibid., pp. 292–293, 294–295, 280, 293–294; "Hutterites Find Peace in Sharing," Sunday Globe, Bethlehem, Pa., April 3, 1983. The Society of Brothers is a Hutterite group in southwestern Pennsylvania.
25. Kephart, Extraordinary Groups, pp. 295–297.
26. Ibid., pp. 289–290, 311.
27. Ibid., pp. 285–286, 300–301.
28. Peter Rideman, Account of Our Religion, Doctrine, and Faith, trans. Kathleen E. Hasenberg (London: Hodder and Stoughton, 1950), pp. 98–99, as cited in Kephart, Extraordinary Groups, p. 301.
29. Kephart, Extraordinary Groups, p. 300.
30. Sydney E. Ahlstrom, A Religious History of the American People, Vol. I (Garden City: Image Books, 1975), p. 296.
31. Ninian Smart, The Religious Experience of Mankind (New York: Scribner, 1969), pp. 400–407.

32. Ibid., p. 286.

33. Samson Raphael Hirsch, as cited in Leo Trepp, *Judaism: Development and Life*, 3rd ed. (Belmont, Calif.: Wadsworth, 1982), p. 8.

34. "Mysticism," *The Encyclopedia of the Jewish Religion*, ed. R.J.Z. Werblowsky and G. Wigoder (New York: Holt, Rinehart and Winston, 1965), p. 277.

35. There is no surer guide than Gershom Scholem (1897–1982), leading authority upon the Kabbalah and Jewish mysticism. Scholem's entry on "Kabbalah" in the *Encyclopaedia Judaica* exceeds 100,000 words; see Vol. X, pp. 489–654, with full bibliography. See also Scholem, *On the Kabbalah and Its Symbolism* (New York: Schocken, 1965); *Major Trends in Jewish Mysticism* (New York: Schocken, 1963); and for a fine secondary study, David Biale, *Gershom Scholem: Kabbalah and Counter-History* (Cambridge: Harvard University Press, 1979).

36. Gershom Scholem, "Kabbalah," *Encyclopaedia Judaica*, X, pp. 490, 583.

37. Ibid., pp. 490, 493, 613, 541, 552, 627-630.

38. Ibid., pp. 526, 494.

39. Ibid., pp. 618, 559.

40. "Shekhinah," *Encyclopaedia Judaica*, XIV, p. 1353; Smart, *Religious Experience of Mankind*, p. 303.

41. Scholem, "Kabbalah," pp. 579, 589; Smart, *Religious Experience of Mankind*, pp. 301–303; Trepp, *Judaism*, p. 88; "Mysticism," *Encyclopedia of Jewish Religion*, p. 279; Scholem, "Kabbalah," pp. 607, 608.

42. Scholem, "Kabbalah," p. 638.

43. Gershom Scholem, "Three Types of Jewish Piety," *Sidic* (Rome) 8 (1975): 8–12.

44. Ibid., p. 11.

45. Ibid., pp. 12–13.

46. André Schwarz-Bart's obsession takes the form of "a work of fiction" (his words): *The Last of the Just*, trans. Stephen Becker (New York: Atheneum, 1961).

47. Ibid., pp. 4–5.

48. Scholem, "Three Types of Jewish Piety," p. 13.

49. H. R. Niebuhr, *Christ and Culture*, pp. 121, 143–144.

50. Yoder, *Politics of Jesus*, p. 236.

51. As stated by Kliever, *H. Richard Niebuhr*, p. 58.

52. H. R. Niebuhr, *Christ and Culture*, pp. 145–148.

8. History and Faith in Tension

1. H. R. Niebuhr, "Types of Christian Ethics."

2. H. R. Niebuhr, *Christ and Culture*, p. 42.

3. I have adapted the ensuing points from H. R. Niebuhr's "Types of Christian Ethics" but have expanded the list and interpreted the items, primarily with aid from *Christ and Culture*.

4. H. R. Niebuhr, *Christ and Culture*, pp. 156, 150, 152–153, 149, 42, 43, 154, 155, 151, 157–159, 169; Kliever, *H. Richard Niebuhr*, p. 57.

5. June Bingham, *Courage to Change: An Introduction to the Life and Thought of Reinhold Niebuhr* (New York: Scribner, 1972), p. 32.

6. Reinhold Niebuhr, *The Nature and Destiny of Man: A Christian Interpretation*, I (New York: Scribner, 1941), chaps. 1–4.

7. Reinhold Niebuhr, *Man's Nature and His Communities: Essays on the Dynamics and Enigmas of Man's Personal and Social Existence* (New York: Scribner, 1965), pp. 77–83.

8. Ronald H. Stone, *Reinhold Niebuhr: Prophet to Politicians* (Nashville: Abingdon, 1972), pp. 49, 167.

9. Ibid., pp. 130, 132.

10. Cf. Reinhold Niebuhr, *The Nature and Destiny of Man: A Christian Interpretation*, II (New York: Scribner, 1943), chaps. 6, 7, and *passim*.

11. Cf. e.g., the critical analyses of Augustine and Luther in R. Niebuhr's *Man's Nature and His Communities*, pp. 43–46.

12. See, e.g., ibid., pp. 21 and 23, where R. Niebuhr explicitly refers to the "realism" of the volume's major essay as portraying "the double effects, good and evil, individual and social, of the unique freedom with which human beings are endowed."

13. See Stone, *Reinhold Niebuhr*, pp. 199, 166, 196.

14. J. E. Hare and Carey B. Joynt, *Ethics and International Affairs* (London: Macmillan, 1982), p. 34.

15. R. Niebuhr, *Man's Nature and His Communities*, p. 31.

16. Consult Reinhold Niebuhr, *The Self and the Dramas of History* (New York: Scribner, 1955).

17. R. Niebuhr, "Intellectual Autobiography of Reinhold Niebuhr," in Charles W. Kegley and Robert W. Bretall, eds., *Reinhold Niebuhr: His Religious, Social, and Political Thought* (New York: Pilgrim, 1984), p. 10.

18. R. Niebuhr, *Nature and Destiny of Man*, I, p. 16; *Christian Realism and Political Problems* (New York: Scribner, 1953), pp. 177–178.

19. R. Niebuhr, *Man's Nature and His Communities*, p. 27.

20. Gabriel Fackre, *The Promise of Reinhold Niebuhr* (Philadelphia: Lippincott, 1970), pp. 32–35, 37.

21. Stone, *Reinhold Niebuhr*, pp. 100, 95, 104.

22. Ibid., pp. 101–102, 97–98; Fackre, *Promise of Reinhold Niebuhr*, p. 39; R. Niebuhr, *Nature and Destiny of Man*, I, pp. 183, 192.

23. Fackre, *Promise of Reinhold Niebuhr*, p. 40.

24. Ibid., pp. 34–35.

25. R. Niebuhr, *Man's Nature and His Communities*, pp. 23–24.

26. Stone, *Reinhold Niebuhr*, pp. 163–164, 135–136; R. Niebuhr, *Man's Nature and His Communities*, p. 109.

27. Stone, *Reinhold Niebuhr*, pp. 139, 140; Reinhold Niebuhr, *The Irony of American History* (New York: Scribner, 1952), p. viii.

28. Stone, *Reinhold Niebuhr*, pp. 143, 144.

29. Ibid., p. 143.

30. R. Niebuhr, *Irony of American History*, p. 157.

31. Fackre, *Promise of Reinhold Niebuhr*, pp. 29, 39.

32. R. Niebuhr, *Man's Nature and His Communities*, p. 125.

33. Dennis P. McCann, *Christian Realism and Liberation Theology: Practical Theologies in Creative Conflict* (Maryknoll, N.Y.: Orbis Books, 1981), p. 85.

34. So Reinhold Niebuhr titles chap. 4 of his *An Interpretation of Christian Ethics* (New York: Harper & Brothers, 1935).

35. Fackre, *Promise of Reinhold Niebuhr*, pp. 45–46, 48–49, 57–58.

36. Anders Nygren, *Agape and Eros* (London: S.P.C.K., Vol. I, 1932, Vol. II, 1938); R. Niebuhr, *Nature and Destiny of Man*, II, p. 84; "Reply to Interpretation and Criticism," in Kegley and Bretall, eds., *Reinhold Niebuhr*, p. 518; Fackre, *Promise of Reinhold Niebuhr*, p. 49.

37. Stone, *Reinhold Niebuhr*, p. 231.

38. Fackre, *Promise of Reinhold Niebuhr*, p. 49; Stone, *Reinhold Niebuhr*, pp. 232, 235; John C. Bennett, "Reinhold Niebuhr's Social Ethics," in Kegley and Bretall, eds., *Reinhold Niebuhr*, p. 113.

39. R. Niebuhr, "Reply to Interpretation and Criticism," in Kegley and Bretall, eds., *Reinhold Niebuhr*, p. 526.

40. Fackre, *Promise of Reinhold Niebuhr*, p. 50.

41. R. Niebuhr, *Moral Man and Immoral Society*, preface to 1960 edition (New York: Scribner), p. ix; *Man's Nature and His Communities*, pp. 22, 55, 74-75.

42. Stone, *Reinhold Niebuhr*, pp. 164, 80; R. Niebuhr, *Interpretation of Christian Ethics*, chaps. 5, 6.

43. Reinhold Niebuhr, *The Structure of Nations and Empires: A Study of the Recurring Patterns and Problems of the Political Order in Relation to the Unique Problems of the Nuclear Age* (New York: Scribner, 1959), p. 215.

44. Fackre, *Promise of Reinhold Niebuhr*, pp. 47, 68; Stone, *Reinhold Niebuhr*, pp. 76, 251, 73.

45. R. Niebuhr, "Reply to Interpretation and Criticism," in Kegley and Bretall, eds., *Reinhold Niebuhr*, p. 518; Stone, *Reinhold Niebuhr*, pp. 77, 80; Reinhold Niebuhr, *Discerning the Signs of the Times: Sermons for Today and Tomorrow* (New York: Scribner, 1946), pp. 187, 21–38; Bingham, *Courage to Change*, p. 141; Fackre, *Promise of Reinhold Niebuhr*, pp. 47–48.

46. The lead essay in Reinhold Niebuhr's *Christianity and Power Politics* (New York: Scribner, 1940) is titled "Why the Christian Church Is Not Pacifist."

47. Fackre, *Promise of Reinhold Niebuhr*, pp. 56, 54, 52; Stone, *Reinhold Niebuhr*, pp. 73, 60, 61, 80, 103, 91.

48. Fackre, *Promise of Reinhold Niebuhr*, pp. 61, 52; Stone, *Reinhold Niebuhr*, p. 63.

49. R. Niebuhr, *Man's Nature and His Communities*, pp. 87–88.

50. Stone, *Reinhold Niebuhr*, p. 66.

51. R. Niebuhr, *Man's Nature and His Communities*, pp. 97, 43.

52. Reinhold Niebuhr, "Repeal the Neutrality Act," *Christianity and Crisis* 1 (1941) 1; Stone, *Reinhold Niebuhr*, pp. 112, 199; R. Niebuhr, *Moral Man and Immoral Society*, p. 233.

53. Stone, *Reinhold Niebuhr*, p. 233.

54. R. Niebuhr, *Man's Nature and His Communities*, pp. 76–77, 100, 104–105, 102; Fackre, *Promise of Reinhold Niebuhr*, p. 42.

55. Stone, *Reinhold Niebuhr*, p. 177.

56. Ibid., p. 176; R. Niebuhr, *Nature and Destiny of Man*, I, p. 192; II, pp. 257–258.

57. R. Niebuhr, *Nature and Destiny of Man*, II, p. 258.

58. Stone, *Reinhold Niebuhr*, p. 179.

59. Reinhold Niebuhr, "The Limits of American Power," *Christianity and Society* 17 (1952): 5.

60. Stone, *Reinhold Niebuhr*, pp. 160, 161, 163, 162; R. Niebuhr, "Reply to Interpretation and Criticism," in Kegley and Bretall, eds., *Reinhold Niebuhr*, p. 518.

61. Fackre, *Promise of Reinhold Niebuhr*, pp. 56, 57, 59; Reinhold Niebuhr, *The Children of Light and the Children of Darkness: A Vindication of Democracy and a Critique of its Traditional Defense* (New York: Scribner, 1960), pp. xv, xiii.

62. R. Niebuhr, *Nature and Destiny of Man*, I, pp. 137, 92, 140, 141, 132.

63. Ibid., pp. 141, 142, 143, 147-148.

64. R. Niebuhr, "The Peace of God," in *Discerning the Signs of the Times*, pp. 187–189, 192–194 (italics added).

65. Reinhold Niebuhr, review of Paul Tillich's *Dynamics of Faith*, in *Union Seminary Quarterly Review* 12 (1957): 112.

66. McCann, *Christian Realism and Liberation Theology*, pp. 75, 125, 76, 126, 128, 102, 104.

67. Fackre, *Promise of Reinhold Niebuhr*, p. 65.

68. R. Niebuhr, *Nature and Destiny of Man*, II, pp. 207, 156.

69. Fackre, *Promise of Reinhold Niebuhr*, p. 73.

70. Stone, *Reinhold Niebuhr*, p. 240.

71. Cf. R. Niebuhr, *Nature and Destiny of Man*, II, espec. chaps. 1–5, 9–10.

72. Stone, *Reinhold Niebuhr*, p. 166; Fackre, *Promise of Reinhold Niebuhr*, pp. 73, 68, 64, 80.

73. Fackre, *Promise of Reinhold Niebuhr*, p. 52; Stone, *Reinhold Niebuhr*, p. 232.
74. Bingham, *Courage to Change*, p. 35.
75. R. Niebuhr, *Man's Nature and His Communities*, pp. 24–25.
76. Stone, *Reinhold Niebuhr*, pp. 125–129.
77. See ibid., pp. 145-146. This difficulty is present as well in McCann, *Christian Realism and Liberation Theology*, pp. 102–103 and *passim*.
78. Bennett, "Reinhold Niebuhr's Social Ethics," in Kegley and Bretall, eds., *Reinhold Niebuhr*, p. 103.
79. Bennett, *Christian Ethics and Social Policy*, p. 77.
80. See Stone, *Reinhold Niebuhr*, pp. 145–157, and more generally chaps. 5, 6.
81. H. R. Niebuhr, *Christ and Culture*, pp. 185–186.
82. Kliever, H. *Richard Niebuhr*, p. 58.
83. H. R. Niebuhr, *Christ and Culture*, pp. 187–188.
84. Abraham J. Heschel, "A Hebrew Evaluation of Reinhold Niebuhr," in Kegley and Bretall, eds., *Reinhold Niebuhr*, p. 468. (The title assigned to this essay is wild: Heschel wrote it in English!)

9. Faith Transforming History

1. H. R. Niebuhr, "Types of Christian Ethics"; *Christ and Culture*, pp. 43, 190–195.
2. H. R. Niebuhr, *Christ and Culture*, pp. 196–205, 206–229; "Types of Christian Ethics."
3. The following exposition of Islam makes considerable reference to Yvonne Yazbeck Haddad, *Contemporary Islam and the Challenge of History* (Albany: State University of New York, 1982); and to Edward Mortimer, *Faith and Power: The Politics of Islam* (London: Faber and Faber, 1982). Haddad has studied and translated selected modern and recent major writings in Arabic, with special attention to economic, social, political, military, and intellectual factors that bear upon the Muslim understanding of the world, history, and the historical process. She depicts, basically, what she refers to as "neo-normativist" Islam, utilizing authors who defend an ideological commitment. Mortimer concentrates upon the recent and contemporary state of political Islam in six major regions of the Islamic World.
4. Mortimer, *Faith and Power*, pp. 407, 44, 35, 21, 33, 402–403, 16.
5. Ibid., pp. 288, 401, 21, 101; Haddad, *Contemporary Islam*, pp. 51, 117, 8–11, and *passim*.
6. Haddad, *Contemporary Islam*, pp. 110, 131, 21; Mortimer, *Faith and Power*, pp. 353, 122.
7. Mortimer, *Faith and Power*, pp. 39–40, 35.
8. Zefer Ishaq Ansari, "Contemporary Islam and Nationalism," *Die Welt des Islam* 7 (1961): 11, as cited in Haddad, *Contemporary Islam*, p. 41.
9. Haddad, *Contemporary Islam*, p. 79.
10. Ibid., p. 120; Mortimer, *Faith and Power*, p. 34.
11. Sayyid Qutb, as cited by ʿAbd al-Rahmān al-Ḥajjī, "Basic Principles of Islamic History," in appendix to Haddad, *Contemporary Islam*, pp. 172–173.
12. Mortimer, *Faith and Power*, p. 34.
13. Haddad, *Contemporary Islam*, p. 11.
14. Ibid., pp. 137, 235.
15. Ibid., pp. 96, xii.
16. ʿImād al-Dīn Khalīl, "The Qur'anic Interpretation of History," in appendix to Haddad, *Contemporary Islam*, pp. 200–201.
17. Haddad, *Contemporary Islam*, pp. 71, 226, 113; Anwar al-Jundī, "The Philosophy of Islamic History," in appendix to Haddad, p. 158.
18. Haddad, *Contemporary Islam*, p. 6.

19. Rāshid al-Barrāwī, "Factors That Influence History," in appendix to Haddad, *Contemporary Islam*, p. 182.
20. Haddad, *Contemporary Islam*, p. 107. Haddad is here explaining the thought of ʿImād al-Dīn Khalīl. Surahs of the Koran that explicitly affirm man's personal responsibility include 10:44; 22:10; 30:41; and 75:14–15.
21. Haddad, *Contemporary Islam*, p. 104. Haddad is here reflecting the position of Rāshid al-Barrāwī.
22. Mortimer, *Faith and Power*, p. 18.
23. Haddad, *Contemporary Islam*, pp. 139, 91, 137.
24. Ibid., pp. 60, 62, 138.
25. Ibid., p. 109.
26. Mortimer, *Faith and Power*, pp. 303–304. Twelver Shiism is the form dominant in Iran (see Mortimer, pp. 45–46 and *passim*). On the Muʿtazilites, see ibid., pp. 50–51.
27. Khomeini, as cited in Mortimer, *Faith and Power*, pp. 323, 324–325; ellipses and brackets as in source used.
28. Khomeini, as cited in ibid., p.326.
29. Said Amir Arjomand, paper entitled "Traditionalism in Twentieth Century Iran," p. 44, as cited in Mortimer, *Faith and Power*, p. 330.
30. Mortimer, *Faith and Power*, pp. 327–328.
31. See, e.g., al-Hajjī, "Basic Principles of Islamic History," in appendix to Haddad, *Contemporary Islam*, p. 170.
32. As reported in *The Christian Century* 100 (1983): 769–770.
33. *Near East Report*, 27 (1983): 148.
34. Mortimer, *Faith and Power*, p. 352; *U.S. News & World Report*, Aug. 29, 1983, p. 40.
35. Haddad, *Contemporary Islam*, p. 34.
36. Ibid., p. 34.
37. As cited by William K. Stevens, "In Pakistan, Islam Leaves Little Room for Freedom," *The New York Times*, Aug. 28, 1983.
38. Yvonne Y. Haddad, "Islam: 'The Religion of God,'" *Christianity and Crisis* 42 (1982): 358.
39. John B. Noss, *Man's Religions*, 5th ed. (New York: Macmillan, 1974), p. 543.
40. Mortimer, *Faith and Power*, pp. 337, 338.
41. *Gaudium et Spes*, n. 2, as cited in Arthur F. McGovern, *Marxism: An American Christian Perspective* (Maryknoll, N.Y.: Orbis Books, 1980), p. 110.
42. Gutiérrez, *Teología de la liberación*, p. 178; in general, chap. 10. See also Gustavo Gutiérrez, *The Power of the Poor in History: Selected Writings*, trans. Robert R. Barr (Maryknoll, N.Y.: Orbis Books, 1983), chap. 1.
43. McCann, *Christian Realism and Liberation Theology*, p. 150.
44. Gutiérrez, *Power of the Poor in History*, pp. 68, 63.
45. Juan Luis Segundo, *Liberación de la teología* (Buenos Aires: Ediciones Carlos Lohlé, 1975), pp. 101ff., 111, 194, 200–201; see also pp. 134, 138–140, 175, and espec. chap. 6.
46. Robert McAfee Brown, *Gustavo Gutiérrez* (Atlanta: John Knox, 1980), p. 26.
47. McGovern, *Marxism*, p. 178.
48. Brown, *Gutiérrez*, p. 34.
49. José Míguez Bonino, *Toward a Christian Political Ethics* (Philadelphia: Fortress, 1983), p. 39.
50. Gustavo Gutiérrez, "The Hope of Liberation," in Gerald H. Anderson and Thomas F. Stransky, eds., *Mission Trends No. 3: Third World Theologies* (New York: Paulist, 1976), p. 67; Gutiérrez, as cited in Brown, *Gutiérrez*, p. 47.
51. Line, "Truth is in Order to Goodness," pp. 162–163.
52. James M. Gustafson, interpreting the Christian ethic of H. Richard Niebuhr ("Introduction" to H. R. Niebuhr, *Responsible Self*, pp. 39–40).

53. Rubenstein, *My Brother Paul*, p. 112.

54. Gutiérrez, *Teología de la liberación*, pp. 78–79; Frederick Herzog, *Justice Church: The New Function of the Church in North American Christianity* (Maryknoll, N.Y.: Orbis Books, 1980), p. 137.

55. Segundo, *Liberación de la teología*, p. 12.

56. McGovern, *Marxism*, p. 175, interpreting Paulo Freire.

57. Ibid., pp. 176–178.

58. Brown, *Gutiérrez*, p. 52; Gutiérrez, *Teología de la liberación*, pp. 68–69; Gustavo Gutiérrez, "Terrorism, Liberation, and Sexuality," *The Witness* (April 1977), 10, as cited in Brown, *Gutiérrez*, p. 53.

59. Hordern, "Paul as a Theological Authority," p. 138.

60. Míguez Bonino, *Toward a Christian Political Ethics*, p. 31.

61. Segundo, *Liberación de la teología*, pp. 175, 133, 189, 139, 146.

62. McGovern, *Marxism*, pp. 173, 177; Brown, *Gutiérrez*, p. 15; Míguez Bonino, *Toward a Christian Political Ethics*, pp. 66ff. The final point is taken from the Medellín Conference declaration.

63. I get help here from Brown, *Gutiérrez*, pp. 56–59, 65, 68.

64. Gutiérrez, *Teología de la liberación*, p. 353.

65. At the Puebla, Mexico, conference of Latin American bishops in 1979 a long section of the declaration was devoted to a "preferential option for the poor." For Gutiérrez's assessments of Puebla, see *Power of the Poor in History*, chaps. 5, 6.

66. Gutiérrez, *Teología de la liberación*, p. 358.

67. McGovern, *Marxism*, p. 199.

68. Segundo, *Liberación de la teología*, pp. 36, 67.

69. Stendahl, *Paul Among Jews and Gentiles*, pp. 102, 106 (italics added).

70. For a delineation of the oldest historical Jesus-tradition, see Luise Schottroff und Wolfgang Stegemann, *Jesus von Nazareth—Hoffnung der Armen* (Stuttgart: Verlag W. Kohlhammer, 1978).

71. Gerald F. Moede, as reported by J. Robert Nelson, "Challenging 'Disabled Theology,' " *The Christian Century* 98 (1981): 1245.

72. Brown, *Gutiérrez*, p. 56.

73. Ibid., pp. 58–59, 65, 35; Segundo, *Liberación de la teología*, p. 95.

74. Rodney Booth, *The Winds of God: The Canadian Church Faces the '80s*, as quoted in Jean Caffey Lyles, "What to Expect from Vancouver," *Quarterly Review* 3 (1983): 17.

75. Brown, *Gutiérrez*, p. 46.

76. Gutiérrez, *Teología de la liberación*, pp. 76, 77; Brown, *Gutiérrez*, p. 33.

77. Enrique D. Dussel, "Historical and Philosophical Presuppositions for Latin American Theology," in Rosino Gibellini, ed., *Frontiers of Theology in Latin America*, trans. John Drury (Maryknoll, N.Y.: Orbis Books, 1979), p. 212.

78. Segundo, *Liberación de la teología*, p. 88.

79. Gregory Baum, "Liberation Theology and 'the Supernatural,' " *The Ecumenist* 19 (1981): 86.

80. Segundo, *Liberación de la teología*, pp. 228, 255; Brown, *Gutiérrez*, p. 17.

81. Joseph Ratzinger, *Le nouveau peuple de Dieu*, pp. 140–141, as cited in Juan Luis Segundo, *Liberation of Theology*, trans. John Drury (Maryknoll, N.Y.: Orbis Books, 1976), p. 228.

82. Segundo, *Liberación de la teología*, p. 260.

83. Brown, *Gutiérrez*, p. 17.

84. Hugo Assmann, *Theology for a Nomad Church*, trans. Paul Burns (Maryknoll, N.Y.: Orbis Books, 1976), pp. 138–139.

85. Robert McAfee Brown, Preface to Gutiérrez, *Power of the Poor in History*, p. xv.

86. Gutiérrez, *Power of the Poor in History*, p. 16.

87. McGovern, *Marxism*, pp. 3–4.

88. Ibid., p. 40.

89. Douglas Sturm, "A Liberationist on Ethics," review article of Míguez Bonino, *Toward a Christian Political Ethics*, *Christianity and Crisis* 43 (1983): 290.

90. McGovern, *Marxism*, p. 203.

91. Ibid., pp. 202, 209. The Puebla documents are contained in *Puebla and Beyond* (Maryknoll, N.Y.: Orbis Books, 1979).

92. McGovern, *Marxism*, pp. 121, 122.

93. Consult, ibid., chap. 7.

94. Bishops of the Antilles Episcopal Conference, "Justice and Peace in a New Caribbean," as cited and explained in ibid., p. 123.

95. Ibid., chap. 6.

96. Ibid., p. 183.

97. Segundo, *Liberación de la teología*, pp.. 85, 85–86 (italics in original), part of which contains words from an address by Patriarch Maximos IV Saigh before Vatican Council II, Sept. 28, 1965.

98. Brown, *Gutiérrez*, p. 70; McGovern, *Marxism*, pp. 4, 112.

99. José Míguez Bonino, *Christians and Marxists: The Mutual Challenge to Revolution* (Grand Rapids: Eerdmans, 1976), p. 115; Assmann, *Theology for a Nomad Church*, p. 142 (italics added); Gustavo Gutiérrez and Richard Shaull, *Liberation and Change*, ed. Ronald H. Stone (Atlanta: John Knox, 1977), p. 77; Segundo, *Liberación de la teología*, pp. 52, 149.

100. McGovern, *Marxism*, p. 185.

101. Baum, "Liberation Theology and 'the Supernatural,' " pp. 84, 87.

102. Assmann, *Theology for a Nomad Church*, p. 144.

103. Ibid., p. 139.

104. "Néstor Paz: Mystic, Christian, Guerrilla," selections from his "campaign journal" in Anderson and Stransky, eds., *Mission Trends No. 3*, pp 111–117.

105. Editor's introduction to "Néstor Paz," p. 111.

106. "Néstor Paz," pp. 112–114.

107. Harvey Cox, "Who Is Ernesto Cardenal?" *Christianity and Crisis* 43 (1983): 109, 126.

108. Segundo, *Liberación de la teología*, pp. 184, 179, 180–182, 178, 183.

109. Sölle, "Mysticism, Liberation and the Names of God," p. 182; Brown, *Gutiérrez*, pp. 16–17, 39–40.

110. José Míguez Bonino, "Violence: A Theological Reflection," in Anderson and Stransky, eds., *Mission Trends No. 3*, pp. 119–121, 123, 125, 126; *Toward a Christian Political Ethics*, p. 111.

111. Jacques Ellul, *Violence* (New York: Seabury, 1969), pp. 138–139.

112. Rubem Alves, as cited in Míguez Bonino, *Toward a Christian Political Ethics*, p. 90.

113. Dorothee Sölle, " 'Thou Shalt Have No Other Jeans Before Me' (Levi's Advertisement, Early Seventies): The Need For Liberation in a Consumerist Society," in Brian Mahan and L. Dale Richesin, eds., *The Challenge of Liberation Theology: A First World Response* (Maryknoll, N.Y.: Orbis Books, 1981), pp. 4–10; Herberg, *Faith Enacted as History*, p. 196.

114. "Response of Monika Hellwig to Avery Dulles," in Torres and Eagleson, eds., *Theology in the Americas*, p. 102.

115. Míguez Bonino, *Toward a Christian Political Ethics*, pp. 94ff.

116. Gutiérrez, *Liberación de la teología*, pp. 225, 319–320; Brown, *Gutiérrez*, p. 55.

117. Tracy, *Blessed Rage for Order*, pp. 244, 255, 245.

118. McCann, *Christian Realism and Liberation Theology*, pp. 230–231.

119. Felix Luna, "Liberation," in Assmann, *Theology for a Nomad Church*, p. 146.

120. Frederick Herzog, "Pre-Bicentennial U.S.A. in the Liberation Process," in Sergio Torres and John Eagleson, eds., *Theology in the Americas* (Maryknoll, N.Y.: Orbis Books, 1976), p. 143.

10. History Transforming Faith: A Prologue

1. Emil L. Fackenheim, *To Mend the World: Foundations of Future Jewish Thought* (New York: Schocken Books, 1982).

2. Tracy, *Blessed Rage for Order*, pp. 28, 32.

3. Kliever, H. *Richard Niebuhr*, pp. 58–59.

4. H. R. Niebuhr, *Christ and Culture*, p. 81.

5. Ibid., p. 93.

6. Ibid., p. 118.

7. McCann, *Christian Realism and Liberation Theology*, p. 203.

8. Agathological ethics, deontological ethics, and an ethic of responsibility are distinguished in chap. 1, pp. 8–9.

9. Gutiérrez, *Teología de la Liberación*, p. 40.

10. See, e.g., Jon Sobrino, *Christology at the Crossroads: A Latin American Approach*, trans. John Drury (Maryknoll, N.Y.: Orbis Books, 1978); cf. Clark M. Williamson, "Christ Against the Jews: A Review of Jon Sobrino's Christology," *Encounter* 40 (1979): 403–412.

11. McCann, *Christian Realism and Liberation Theology*, p. 204.

12. Kliever, H. *Richard Niebuhr*, pp. 58–59.

13. H. Richard Niebuhr, *The Meaning of Revelation* (New York: Macmillan, 1941), p. ix.

14. H. R. Niebuhr, *Christ and Culture*, p. x.

15. Kliever, H. *Richard Niebuhr*, p. 64.

16. Cf., e.g., H. Richard Niebuhr's essay, "Towards a New Otherworldliness," *Theology Today* 1 (1944): 78–87.

17. Kliever, H. *Richard Niebuhr*, p. 64.

18. H. R. Niebuhr, *Christ and Culture*, p. 196.

19. John Dillenberger and Claude Welch, *Protestant Christianity Interpreted Through Its Development* (New York: Scribner, 1954), p. 22.

20. Kliever, H. *Richard Niebuhr*, pp. 54, 39, 55.

21. H. R. Niebuhr, *Christ and Culture*, pp. 28–29; see also *Responsible Self*, appendix B, "Responsibility and Christ."

22. H. R. Niebuhr, *Radical Monotheism and Western Culture*; Kliever, H. *Richard Niebuhr*, p. 29.

23. H. R. Niebuhr, *Christ and Culture*, chap. 7; Kliever, H. *Richard Niebuhr*, p. 16.

24. Kliever, H. *Richard Niebuhr*, p. 155.

25. A. Roy Eckardt, *Your People, My People: The Meeting of Jews and Christians* (New York: Quadrangle/New York Times, 1974), p. 243; Kliever, H. *Richard Niebuhr*, p. 50; Jerry A. Irish, *The Religious Thought of H. Richard Niebuhr* (Atlanta: John Knox, 1983), p. 35; H. R. Niebuhr, *Christ and Culture*, p. 256.

26. Kliever, H. *Richard Niebuhr*, pp. 42, 77.

27. H. R. Niebuhr, *Radical Monotheism*, p. 59.

28. H. R. Niebuhr, *Christ and Culture*, p. 68.

29. See H. R. Niebuhr, *Meaning of Revelation*, pp. 59–90; also Kliever, H. *Richard Niebuhr*, pp. 93ff., 107–109.

30. Kliever, H. *Richard Niebuhr*, pp. 28–40, 44 (italics in original).

31. Ibid., pp. 15, 23.

32. James H. Cone, *A Black Theology of Liberation* (Philadelphia: Lippincott, 1970), p. 136.

33. Ibid., p. 76.
34. Eberhard Bethge, *Dietrich Bonhoeffer: Man of Vision, Man of Courage* (New York: Harper & Row, 1977), pp. 614, 375, and *passim*.

11. Historicalness: Opportunities and Perplexities

1. Tracy, *Blessed Rage for Order*, p. 130.
2. Ibid., p. 178; H. R. Niebuhr, *Christ and Culture*, pp. 246, 247–249; *Responsible Self*, pp. 71–76, 93.
3. James Russell Lowell, "The Present Crisis," Stanza 18.
4. Fackenheim, *To Mend the World*, p. 158.
5. Tracy, *Blessed Rage for Order*, p. 246.
6. Anderson, introductory comment to Herberg's essay "Historicism as Touchstone" in *Faith Enacted as History*, pp. 190–198.
7. Rubem Alves, *A Theology of Human Hope* (Washington: Corpus Books, 1969), p. 71 (italics in original); Paul Tillich, *Systematic Theology*, Vol. III (Chicago: University of Chicago Press, 1963), p. 4.
8. So writes Joanne A. Fishman, in "The Ultimate Nautical Marathon," *The New York Times Magazine*, Sept. 6, 1981, p. 45.
9. Arthur A. Cohen, *The Tremendum: A Theological Interpretation of the Holocaust* (New York: Crossroad, 1981), p. 92; Herberg, *Faith Enacted as History*, pp. 35, 32.
10. Reinhold Niebuhr, *Faith and History: A Comparison of Christian and Modern Views of History* (New York: Scribner, 1949), pp. 18, 85; *Children of Light and Children of Darkness*, p. 54.
11. Heschel, *Prophets*, I, p. 174.
12. Ibid., pp. 176, 180.
13. Line, "Truth Is in Order to Goodness," p. 170.
14. Haddad, *Contemporary Islam*, pp. 84, 139.
15. Victor Hugo, *Les Misérables*, Vol. I (New York-London: Co-Operative Publication Society, n.d.), pp. 317, 337–338.
16. I here call for help upon an early paper of mine, "Two Marginal Notes on the Prophetic View of History," *Christianity and Society* 18 (1953): 15–19.
17. Reinhold Niebuhr, Introduction to Waldo Frank, *The Jew in Our Day* (New York: Duell, Sloan and Pearce, 1944), p. 13.
18. Butterfield, *Christianity and History*, p. 60.
19. R. Niebuhr, *Faith and History*, pp. 129, 226.
20. Roger Lincoln Shinn, *Christianity and the Problem of History* (New York: Scribner, 1953), pp. 247, 250, 257, 258.
21. Butterfield, *Christianity and History*, pp. 48–55; more generally, chaps. 3–5.
22. Shinn, *Christianity and the Problem of History*, p. 252.
23. Karl Löwith, *Meaning in History* (Chicago: University of Chicago Press, 1949), p. 195.
24. Carey B. Joynt and Percy E. Corbett, *Theory and Reality in World Politics* (Pittsburgh: University of Pittsburgh Press, 1978), p. 2.
25. Herbert Butterfield, *Christianity in European History* (New York: Macmillan, 1953), p. 45; Herberg, *Faith Enacted as History*, p. 108.
26. See Anderson comments in Herberg, *Faith Enacted as History*, pp. 22, 24–25, 31.
27. R. Niebuhr, *Nature and Destiny of Man*, II, pp. 65–66.
28. Carl Michalson, "The Real Presence of the Hidden God," in Paul Ramsey, ed., *Faith and Ethics: The Theology of H. Richard Niebuhr* (New York: Harper, 1957), pp. 245, 258, 261.
29. McCann, *Christian Realism and Liberation Theology*, pp. 19–20.

30. Reinhold Niebuhr, *Does Civilization Need Religion?* (New York: Macmillan, 1927), p. 6.

31. Kliever, H. *Richard Niebuhr*, p. 47.

32. Robert McAfee Brown, *Creative Dislocation—The Movement of Grace* (Nashville: Abingdon, 1980), p. 24.

33. Ibid., p. 23 (italics added).

34. Wolfhart Pannenberg, "Freedom and the Lutheran Reformation," *Theology Today* 38 (1981): 291.

12. Which History? Whose History?

1. Dietrich Bonhoeffer, *Letters and Papers from Prison*, ed. Eberhard Bethge, trans. Reginald H. Fuller (London: SCM, 2nd ed., 1956), p. 153 (letter of June 27, 1944; italics added except for the word "historical").

2. See Dietrich Bonhoeffer, *No Rusty Swords* (London: Fontana, 1970), p. 222; also Emil L. Fackenheim, *The Jewish Return Into History: Reflections in the Age of Auschwitz and a New Jerusalem* (New York: Schocken Books, 1978), pp. 35–36, 74–75.

3. Choan-Seng Song, "From Israel to Asia—A Theological Leap," in Anderson and Stransky, eds., *Mission Trends No. 3*, p. 219.

4. Ibid., pp. 217, 214, 216.

5. Ibid., pp. 215–216, 220, 221, 222 (italics added except for the single words "is" and "does," where italics are in the original).

6. Stanley J. Samartha, "Mission and Movements of Innovation," in Anderson and Stransky, eds., *Mission Trends No. 3*, p. 236.

7. Cf. Paul M. van Buren, *A Christian Theology of the People Israel* (New York: Seabury, 1983).

8. Sloyan, *Is Christ the End of the Law?* p. 181.

9. Cook, *Jesus of Faith*, p. 13.

10. David Tracy, "Religious Values After the Holocaust: A Catholic View," in Abraham J. Peck, ed., *Jews and Christians After the Holocaust* (Philadelphia: Fortress, 1982), p. 89.

11. James Parkes, *Prelude to Dialogue: Jewish-Christian Relationships* (London: Vallentine, Mitchell, 1969), p. 193.

12. Jürgen Moltmann, "Dieu dans la révolution," in *Discussion sur 'la théologie de la révolution'* (Paris: Cerf-Mame, 1972), p. 72.

13. Kilian McDonnell, "The Determinative Doctrine of the Holy Spirit," *Theology Today* 39 (1982): 143.

14. David Tracy, "Particular Questions Within General Consensus," *Journal of Ecumenical Studies* 17 (1980): 34; Tal, "German-Jewish Social Thought," p. 328. Professor Tal is here describing what he himself calls "historism."

15. Jules Isaac, *The Teaching of Contempt: Christian Roots of Anti-Semitism*, trans. Helen Weaver (New York: Holt, Rinehart and Winston, 1964).

16. H. R. Niebuhr, *Responsible Self*, p. 67.

17. Most of the foregoing information is found in a pamphlet, *Nes Ammim 1981*, published by Nes Ammim Christian Settlement, Doar N. Asherat, Israel 25225 (some passages adapted and paraphrased); also in *News From American Friends of Nes Ammim 2* (Jan. 1984).

18. Consult, e.g., A. Roy Eckardt and Alice L. Eckardt, *Long Night's Journey Into Day: Life and Faith After the Holocaust*, rev. & enl. ed. (New York: Holocaust Library, 1987); Rolf Rendtorff and Ekkehard Stegemann, eds., *Auschwitz, Krise der christlichen Theologie* (Munich: Chr. Kaiser Verlag, 1980).

19. Tracy, "Religious Values After the Holocaust," in Peck, ed., *Jews and Christians After the Holocaust*, p. 99.

20. David Tracy, Foreword to Cohen, *The Tremendum*, pp. ix-x, xii, xiii.

21. Franklin H. Littell, "Particularism and Universalism in Religious Perspective" (unpublished lecture at Beth Tzedec Congregation, Toronto, May 11, 1972).

22. Helmut Gollwitzer, "Why Black Theology?" in Gayraud S. Wilmore and James H. Cone, eds., *Black Theology: A Documentary History 1966–1979* (Maryknoll, N.Y.: Orbis Books, 1979), pp. 154, 170.

23. Cohen, *The Tremendum*, pp. 1, 4–5, and throughout.

24. Fackenheim, *Jewish Return Into History*, p. 210.

25. The remainder of this section together with the next section of the present chapter relies upon sections of, but also expands, an essay by Alice L. Eckardt and A. Roy Eckardt, "The Holocaust and the Enigma of Uniqueness: A Philosophical Effort at Practical Clarification," *The Annals of the American Academy of Political and Social Science* 450 (1980): 165–178.

26. Yehuda Bauer, *The Holocaust in Historical Perspective* (Seattle: University of Washington Press, 1978), pp. 30–31.

27. See A. Roy Eckardt, "The Contribution of Nomothesis in the Science of Man," *American Scientist* 49 (1961): 76–87.

28. Bauer, *Holocaust in Historical Perspective*, pp. 35–36, 32.

29. Eckardt and Eckardt, *Long Night's Journey Into Day*, p. 104.

30. Ronald Reagan, as cited in *The New York Times*, Apr. 30, 1985.

31. Dalton Trumbo, *Night of the Aurochs*, ed. Robert Kirsch (New York: Viking, 1979).

32. Additional considerations are marshalled in Eckardt and Eckardt, "The Holocaust and the Enigma of Uniqueness," pp. 169–176.

33. Consult, e.g., Michael J. Cook, "Anti-Judaism in the New Testament," *Union Seminary Quarterly Review* 38 (1983): 125–137; Alan Davies, ed., *Antisemitism and the Foundations of Christianity* (New York: Paulist, 1979); and Rosemary Radford Ruether, *Faith and Fratricide: The Theological Roots of Anti-Semitism* (New York: Seabury, 1974), chap. 2.

34. John B. Cobb, *Beyond Dialogue: Toward a Mutual Transformation of Christianity and Buddhism* (Philadelphia: Fortress, 1981), pp. ix, 50.

35. Fackenheim, *To Mend the World*, pp. 22–23.

36. Consult Alice L. Eckardt, "Power and Powerlessness: The Jewish Experience," in Israel W. Charny, ed., *Towards Understanding and Prevention of Genocide*, Proceedings of International Conference on the Holocaust and Genocide, Tel Aviv, June 20–24, 1982 (Boulder, Col.: Westview Press, 1984), pp. 183–196.

37. Cone, *Black Theology of Liberation*, p. 89.

38. The materials on Jewish liberation draw upon but also recast, correct, and update an article by A. Roy Eckardt, "Toward a Secular Theology of Israel," *Religion in Life* 48 (1979): 462–473. The title of the original article unfortunately implies "a Christian theology of the people Israel."

39. *Perception* (Oct. 1978), 4.

40. Carl F. H. Henry, as quoted in *Newsweek* (June 28, 1971), 62.

41. *Eternity* (July 1967), as cited in Solomon S. Bernards, "The Arab-Israel Crisis and the American Christian Response," *The Lutheran Quarterly* (Aug. 1968), 272.

42. Philip Culbertson, "Doing Our Own Homework: Steps Toward Local Dialogue," *Christian Jewish Relations* (London) 16 (1983): 35.

43. James M. Wall, "Israel and the Evangelicals" (editorial), *The Christian Century* 94 (1977): 1083.

44. Emil Brunner, *The Divine Imperative* (New York: Macmillan, 1942), p. 291; Helmut Thielicke, *Theological Ethics*, Vol. I (Philadelphia: Fortress, 1966), pp. 276, 439–440.

45. James Parkes, *Whose Land? A History of the Peoples of Palestine* (New York: Taplinger, 1971), p. 266.

46. Cf. Parkes, *Whose Land?*, pp. 311ff.

47. In *From Time Immemorial: The Origins of the Arab-Jewish Conflict over Palestine* (New York: Harper & Row, 1984), Joan Peters explodes the false myth that foreign Jewish immigrants achieved statehood in Palestine through displacing a native Arab population.

48. As cited in *Christian Attitudes on Jews and Judaism* (London) 5 (1969): 1.

49. See Alice and Roy Eckardt, *Encounter With Israel: A Challenge to Conscience* (New York: Association, 1970), pp. 236–240, on the rightful claims of the Palestinian Arabs.

50. Cone, *Black Theology of Liberation*, pp. 59–60, 120–121; William R. Jones, *Is God a White Racist? A Preamble to Black Theology* (Garden City: Doubleday Anchor, 1973).

51. Eugene B. Borowitz, "On the New Morality," *Judaism* 15 (1966): 333.

52. Reinhold Niebuhr, "Mission and Opportunity: Religion in a Pluralistic Culture," in Louis Finkelstein, ed., *Social Responsibility in an Age of Revolution* (New York: Jewish Theological Seminary of America, 1971), p. 177.

53. H. Paul Chalfant, Robert E. Beckley, and C. Eddie Palmer, *Religion in Contemporary Society* (Palo Alto: Mayfield Pub. Co., 1981), pp. 197, 178–179.

54. Chalfant, Beckley, and Palmer, *Religion in Contemporary Society*, pp. 181–197.

55. *National Lampoon* (May 1984).

56. John A. Coleman, "Civil Religion and Liberation Theology in North America," in Torres and Eagleson, eds., *Theology in the Americas*, pp. 118, 114.

57. Ted Peters, "Pluralism as a Theological Problem," *The Christian Century* 100 (1983): 843, 845.

58. This text is appended to Robert S. Michaelsen, "The Significance of the American Indian Religious Freedom Act of 1978," *Journal of the American Academy of Religion* 52 (1984): 93–115.

59. Alice and Roy Eckardt, "The Achievements and Trials of Interfaith," *Judaism* 27 (1978): 318, 323.

60. Bernice S. Tannenbaum, *The New York Times*, Nov. 13, 1977.

61. Eckardt and Eckardt, "Achievements and Trials of Interfaith," p. 322.

62. Hartman, "On the Possibilities of Religious Pluralism," pp. 113, 114.

63. R. Niebuhr, "Mission and Opportunity," pp. 179, 187-188, 181, 180.

13. Trial of Faith, Trial of God

1. Irving Greenberg, "Cloud of Smoke, Pillar of Fire: Judaism, Christianity, and Modernity after the Holocaust," in Eva Fleischner, ed., *Auschwitz: Beginning of a New Era? Reflections on the Holocaust* (New York: Ktav, 1977), p. 29.

2. William Jay Peck, "From Cain to the Death Camps: An Essay on Bonhoeffer and Judaism," *Union Seminary Quarterly Review* 28 (1973): 162.

3. Neill Q. Hamilton, *Recovery of the Protestant Adventure* (New York: Seabury, 1981), chap. 8.

4. Ulrich E. Simon, consultation with A.R.E., London, Feb. 20, 1976.

5. Tracy, *Analogical Imagination*, pp. 282, 316.

6. Baum, Introduction to Ruether, *Faith and Fratricide*, p. 8; Gregory G. Baum, *Christian Theology After Auschwitz* (London: Council of Christians and Jews, 1976), p. 8 (italics added).

7. Wolfhart Pannenberg, *Jesus—God and Man*, trans. Lewis L. Wilkins and Duane A. Priebe (Philadelphia: Westminster, 1968), pp. 67, 255. The second English edition of *Jesus—God and Man* published in 1977 (translation from the 5th German edition) differs from the 1968 English-language edition only in the inclusion of an eleven-page afterword taking note of Pannenberg's critics. His strictures against Judaism and "the Jewish law" remain.

8. Cf. Eckardt and Eckardt, *Long Night's Journey Into Day*, p. 130.

9. Jean Daniélou, *Dialogue With Israel* (Baltimore: Helicon, 1966), p. 99.

10. Cf. Eckardt and Eckardt, *Long Night's Journey Into Day*, pp. 125–133.

11. Jones, *Is God a White Racist?*, pp. 119, 163–165; J. Deotis Roberts, *Liberation and Reconciliation: A Black Theology* (Phildelphia: Westminster, 1971), p. 146.

12. Rosemary Radford Ruether, "Christian-Jewish Dialogue: New Interpretations," *ADL Bulletin* 5 (1973): 4; *Faith and Fratricide*, pp. 248, 250, 249.

13. Jürgen Moltmann, *The Trinity and the Kingdom: The Doctrine of God*, trans. Margaret Kohl (San Francisco: Harper & Row, 1981), p. 122; Edward Schillebeeckx, *Christ: The Experience of Jesus as Lord*, trans. John Bowden (New York: Seabury, 1980), pp. 18, 802–804, 799.

14. Rosemary Ruether, "An Invitation to Jewish-Christian Dialogue: In What Sense Can We Say That Jesus Was 'The Christ'?," *The Ecumenist* 10 (1972): 22.

15. Pinchas Lapide, as cited in *Time*, May 7, 1979.

16. Peter Levinson, as cited in ibid.

17. Lapide, as cited in ibid.

18. Pinchas Lapide, *The Resurrection of Jesus: A Jewish Perspective* (Minneapolis: Augsburg, 1983).

19. See I Kings 17:22; II Kings 4:35; 13:21. Cf. also Matt. 27:52–53; John 11:1–44.

20. John T. Pawlikowski utilizes this expression in various writings.

21. Gerald O'Collins, *What Are They Saying about the Resurrection?* (New York: Paulist, 1978), pp. 58–59.

22. The substance of the foregoing conversation took place on Aug. 24, 1980 in Upper Saucon Township, Pennsylvania. Only the names are changed to protect the guilty.

23. J. (Coos) Schoneveld, "Postscript and Preface," *Immanuel* (Jerusalem) 12 (1981): 155–157.

24. J. (Coos) Schoneveld, "The Jewish 'No' to Jesus and the Christian 'Yes' to Jews," *Quarterly Review* 4 (1984): 59.

25. Robert E. Willis, "Christian Theology After Auschwitz," *Journal of Ecumenical Studies* 12 (1975): 506.

26. Elie Wiesel, *A Beggar in Jerusalem*, trans. Lily Edelman and author (New York: Avon Books, 1971), pp. 67–68.

27. Pannenberg, "Freedom and the Lutheran Reformation," p. 295.

28. Michael Brown, "On Crucifying the Jews," *Judaism* 27 (1978): 476.

29. Judith Plaskow, *Sex, Sin, and Grace: Women's Experience and the Theologies of Reinhold Niebuhr and Paul Tillich* (Washington: University Press of America, 1980), p. 166.

30. Parts of the remainder of this chapter are adapted from sections of an article by A. Roy Eckardt titled "HaShoah as Christian Revolution: Toward the Liberation of the Divine Righteousness," *Quarterly Review* 2 (1982): 52–67. That article is based upon a paper delivered at the International Conference on the Holocaust and Genocide, Tel Aviv, June 20–24, 1982.

31. Menachem Rosensaft, in Symposium on "Jewish Values in the Post-Holocaust Future," *Judaism* 16 (1967): 294.

32. Eliezer Berkovits, "The Hiding God of History," in Yisrael Gutman and Livia Rothkirchen, eds., *The Catastrophe of European Jewry: Antecedents-History-Reflections* (Jerusalem: Yad Vashem, 1976), p. 704.

33. Fackenheim, *Jewish Return into History*, pp. 281–282 (italics added in long quotation).

34. Irving Greenberg, *On the Third Era in Jewish History: Power and Politics* (New York: National Jewish Resource Center, 1980); also *The Third Great Cycle in Jewish History* (New York: National Jewish Resource Center, 1981).

35. Irving Greenberg, *The Voluntary Covenant* (New York: National Jewish Resource Center, 1982), p. 17.

36. Wiesel, *Beggar in Jerusalem*, p. 38.

37. Fackenheim, *To Mend The World*, p. 284.

38. Elie Wiesel, *The Trial of God* (as it was held on February 25, 1649, in Shamgorod), a play in three acts, trans. Marion Wiesel (New York: Random House, 1979), pp. 128, 157, 127, 133.

39. Elie Wiesel, *Souls on Fire: Portraits and Legends of Hasidic Masters*, trans. Marion Wiesel (New York: Random House, 1972), p. 107.

40. Berkovits, "Hiding God of History," p. 704.

41. Simon Wiesenthal, *The Sunflower* (New York: Schocken Books, 1976). Wiesenthal includes in his book responses by a number of persons to the moral dilemma facing him, a question that has continued to haunt him.

42. Cohen, *The Tremendum*, p. 82.

43. Consult Irving Greenberg, *Guide to Purim* (New York: National Jewish Resource Center, 1978).

44. William Novak and Moshe Waldoks, eds., *The Big Book of Jewish Humor* (New York: Harper & Row, 1981), p.17.

45. Elie Wiesel, *The Gates of the Forest*, trans. Frances Frenaye (New York: Avon Books, 1967), p. 196.

46. Wiesel, *Gates of the Forest*, p. 197.

47. Cullen Hightower, as quoted by Ira Corn, *The Globe Times* (Bethlehem, Pa.), Jan. 20, 1982.

48. Heschel, *Prophets*, I, p. 92.

49. Dietrich Bonhoeffer, *The Cost of Discipleship*, trans. R. H. Fuller and Irmgard Booth (London: SCM, 1959), pp. 34ff.

50. Tracy, *Blessed Rage for Order*, p. 184.

51. R. Niebuhr, *Self and the Dramas of History*, p. 71.

52. Paul Tillich, *The Socialist Decision*, trans. Franklin Sherman (New York: Harper & Row, 1977), p. 6.

53. Wiesel, *Gates of the Forest*, p. 223.

54. Isabel Carter Heyward, *The Redemption of God: A Theology of Mutual Relation* (Washington: University Press of America, 1982); Carol Christ, "Women's Liberation and the Liberation of God: An Essay in Story Theology," In Elizabeth Koltun, ed., *The Jewish Woman: New Perspectives* (New York: Schocken, 1976), pp. 11–17.

Epilogue: Consider the Animals

1. This epilogue is adapted from A. Roy Eckardt, "Consider the Animals," *Reflection* (Yale Divinity School) 73 (1976):13–14.

Index

Abélard, 117
Abraham, 28, 43, 45, 270, 286, 317
Absolutism, absolutization, 107, 108, 160, 192, 235–238, 247, 280, 292, 293, 294, 302, 328
Accommodationism, 115ff., 160
Acts, Book of, 39, 41, 56, 72, 79
Adam, 155
Adler, Morris, 101
Agape and *eros*, 171–172, 328
Agathological ethic, 8, 230, 258
Ahlstrom, Sydney E., 154
Akiva, Rabbi, 92
Al-Barrāwī, Rashīd, 193
Ali, 199
Alienation, 203, 217
Al-Jundī, Anwar, 193
Allah, 190, 193, 195, 198, 287
Allen, Woody, 10
Allende, Salvador, 214
Al-Sharqāwī, Mahmūd, 250–251
Alves, Rubem, 221
Aman (trust), 16
Amen (true), 16
American Indian Religious Freedom Act, 297–298
Americans for Democratic Action, 183
Amish, 152; Old Order, 151
Amnesty International, 197
Amos, 17, 20, 22, 26, 208
Anabaptists, 150, 152
Anderson, Bernhard W., 22, 26–27, 29, 247
Animals, 86, 87, 102, 114, 168, 326–328
Ann Lee, Mother, 148, 149, 150
Anthropology, 25, 92, 136, 167–170; biblical, 24–25; Christian, 128–131; and democracy, 178; Jewish, 110–111
Anti-Jewishness, antisemitism, 48, 62, 231, 266, 268, 299, 302; and God, 292–293; and *Shoah*, 281–283
Anti-Judaism, 231, 268, 302
Antispiritualization, 264
Antisupersessionism, 264
Anxiety, 169

Anti-Israelism, anti-Zionism, 285
Apocalypticism, 35, 39, 68, 77
Apodicticity, 19, 79, 82, 111, 134, 171, 318n, 319, 324
Aquinas, Thomas, 11, 143–144
Arabic, 191
Arabs, 190, 198, 274, 275
Architectonic view, 140–160, 161, 162, 166, 229
Aristotle, 144
Arjomand, Said Amir, 196
Armenians, 279
Assad, Hafez, 197
Assimilation, 148
Assmann, Hugo, 12, 211–212, 215, 217
Augustine, 29, 174, 176, 188
Auschwitz-Birkenau, 317, 323, 324
Avot, 97, 98, 102, 103, 105, 111, 157

Baba Metzia, 95, 101, 105
Bahai religion, 198
Baird, William, 47
Barth, Karl, 188
Bauer, Yehuda, 277, 278–279
Baum, Gregory, 210, 216, 304
Beatitudes, 63
Belzec, 284, 324
Ben Abuyah, Elisha, 316
Bennett, John C., 183
Berakhot, 84, 106, 114
Berkovits, Eliezer, 121, 317–318, 321, 322, 324
Berrigan, Daniel, 218
Bible, *see* Scripture
Bingham, June, 164
Birds, 351n
Bitburg, Reagan and, 279–280
Blacks, 135, 176–177; liberation of, 206; suffering of, 307
Blasphemy, 72, 90, 96
Bokser, Ben Zion, 53
Bonhoeffer, Dietrich, 12, 197, 239, 265, 266, 268, 269, 273, 324
Booth, Rodney, 210

A. ROY ECKARDT is Emeritus Professor of Religion Studies at Lehigh University; former editor-in-chief of the Journal of the American Academy of Religion; a visiting scholar at the Oxford Centre for Hebrew Studies; and author of many books, including *Jews and Christians* and *Elder and Younger Brothers*.